C

Be A Better READER

EIGHTH EDITION

NILA BANTON SMITH

GLOBE FEARON
Pearson Learning Group

The following people have contributed to the development of this product: *Art and Design:* Tricia Battipede, Robert Dobaczewski, Elizabeth Witmer; *Editorial:* Brian Hawkes, Eleanor Ripp, Jennifer M. Watts; *Manufacturing:* Michele Uhl; *Production:* Laura Benford-Sullivan, Jeffrey Engel, Pamela Gallo; *Publishing Operations:* Jennifer Van Der Heide

ISBN 0-130-23878-3

Printed in the United States of America

3 4 5 6 7 8 9 10   06 05 04 03

1-800-321-3106
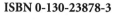
www.pearsonlearning.com

Contents

*Professional Articles include:

Students Succeed With The Premier Content-Area Reading Program

Be A Better Reader consists of eight leveled worktexts for content-area reading. This time-tested and research-based program makes it possible to provide students in middle school and high school with reading selections and skills instruction at their appropriate instructional level. Direct skill instruction before reading prepares all students for success. Four reading selections per theme-based unit cover literature, social studies, science, and mathematics. These core lessons are followed by brief skill lessons and end with a real-life skill lesson.

The Annotated Teacher's Edition for each level provides complete teaching support and additional assessment material. *The Diagnostic and Placement Guide* helps you place students in the appropriate level of *Be A Better Reader* and identifies those students who require practice in specific reading skills, while the *Progress Monitoring Package* tracks ongoing student progress.

With *Be A Better Reader*, Eighth Edition, you can:

New! • Guide students more easily with full teacher support for each lesson.

New! • Transition your students at reading levels 3 and 4 from *Caught Reading Plus* to *Be A Better Reader* with our new *Starting Out* component.

New! • Track students' mastery of key skills with the *Progress Monitoring Package*.

New! • Help your ESL/ELL students and reluctant readers gain the skills they need to read and succeed in the content areas.

New! • Extend learning opportunities with our new CD-ROM, which provides more reading selections with comprehension questions, a program scope and sequence, and valuable management tools.

New! • Engage students' interests with new reading selections comprising over 20 percent of the program.

With *Be A Better Reader*, Eighth Edition, students will:

• Learn specific reading skills with immediate application and reinforcement.

• Apply reading skills to high-interest, relevant content directly related to literature, social studies, science, and mathematics.

• Relate new reading skills to essential life skills at the end of each unit.

Ensure Success by Starting Each Lesson With Relevant Instruction.

Provides easy-to-find lessons and skills; the lesson title states the skill being taught. For a complete list of skills, see the Scope and Sequence on pages T14–T16.

Offers students a head start with **Background Information**, which tells them what the selection is about and provides them with important content, cultural background, and historical information.

Encourages student success as they read because **Skill Focus** instruction comes before they read.

Helps students organize and record their ideas using **graphic organizers**.

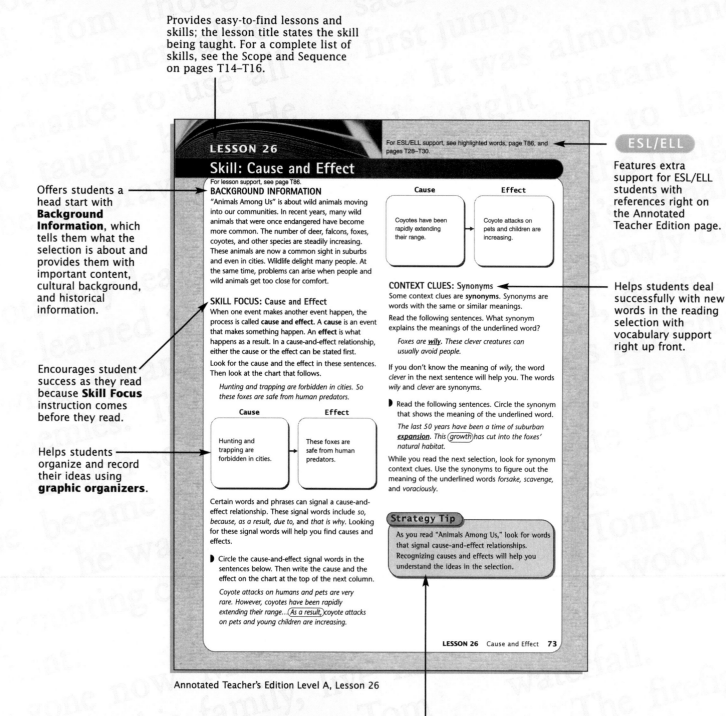

ESL/ELL

Features extra support for ESL/ELL students with references right on the Annotated Teacher Edition page.

Helps students deal successfully with new words in the reading selection with vocabulary support right up front.

Annotated Teacher's Edition Level A, Lesson 26

Aids students' understanding of the selection through the **Strategy Tip**, which tells them how to apply the lesson skill while reading.

Practice New Skills on a Reading Selection.

Engages students and introduces the lesson focus immediately with the high-interest opener.

Helps students learn new words with phonetic pronunciations.

Adds interest and aids comprehension through relevant photographs and captions.

Alerts students to new vocabulary through boldfaced words.

Challenges students to identify the main idea.

◄ READING A SCIENCE SELECTION ►

Animals Among Us

FALCONS SWOOP DOWN from New York City skyscrapers. Red foxes dig dens under porches in Washington, D.C. Black bears wander onto golf courses. Canada geese take over New Jersey soccer fields. All over the country, wild animals are moving from the countryside into our towns. Why is this happening? Let's look at some of the reasons.

Urban Falcons

Peregrine (PAIR ə grin) falcons are the fastest birds in the world. They can travel the length of a football field in a single second. Normally these birds live in rugged mountain areas. Why, then, are peregrine falcons nesting in skyscrapers? At least 12 breeding pairs and their chicks were living in New York City in 2001.

In some ways, tall city buildings are an ideal habitat for peregrine falcons. Skyscrapers offer the birds a high perch for hunting. There is also a steady supply of animals to hunt, including city birds such as sparrows, starlings, and pigeons. The city also allows peregrine falcons to escape their own **predators** (PRED ə tərz). In the wild, raccoons and owls feed on falcon eggs and chicks.

Ledges on skyscrapers provide good nesting spots and hunting perches for falcons.

74 LESSON 26 Cause and Effect

The increase in urban falcons has another cause, too. Nearly 40 years ago, the birds were in danger of dying out. That is because too many farmers were using a chemical called DDT. DDT killed insects and it also kept falcon eggs from hatching. So the U.S. government banned DDT, and scientists began raising peregrine falcons in captivity. When the scientists released these birds, many settled in and around cities.

The Foxes Go to Town

Foxes are wily. These clever creatures can usually avoid people. In addition, foxes hunt mainly at night. As a result, no one knows for sure just how many foxes there are in U.S. cities. We do know that people are seeing foxes more often, however. Golfers in Minneapolis, Minnesota, recently watched some fox cubs dash onto the green and steal a golf ball. In Toronto, Canada, officials say there are at least 40 fox dens in that city.

Why would foxes forsake the open meadows? Why would they abandon their meadows in the country for the crowded city? One reason is that there are not as many open meadows as there used to be. The last 50 years have been a time of suburban expansion. This growth has cut into the foxes' natural habitat. Many foxes have been forced to find new homes.

Moving to the city was a practical move for some foxes. Foxes are **territorial** (TAIR ə TOR ee əl) animals. Each fox marks its own area and fights off other foxes. Because most city neighborhoods have not been claimed by foxes yet, it is easy for foxes to find "open territory" there.

Also, cities make a good habitat for foxes. Empty city lots are full of moles and mice, a fox's favorite foods. Hunting and trapping are not allowed in cities, so these foxes are safe from human predators. ✗ In the city, foxes are good citizens. They go about their business silently, usually unseen. Weighing only about 12 pounds, foxes do not attack cats or dogs. They run away from young children. Foxes don't scavenge for garbage, either, unlike raccoons or dogs.

Reminds students to look for context clues—in this case, synonyms—with underscored words.

Instead of searching for a free meal, they hunt, getting rid of pests such as mice and rats.

The Bear Raiders

The voters in Cross City, Michigan, got a big surprise one recent Election Day. A 400-pound black bear kept them from leaving the building where they were voting. That same fall, more than a dozen bears entered Colorado homes. Most of the bears headed straight for the kitchen.

In autumn, bears prepare to sleep away the winter. To survive the coming winter, they eat voraciously. They hungrily gobble up wild fruits and nuts. If the summer has been very dry, there will not be enough fruits and nuts for them all.

When bears cannot find enough food in the forest, they turn to dumpsters, landfills, garbage cans, and bird feeders in cities and suburbs. As a result, people often see bears in the autumn.

If food is scarce in forests in the fall, bears might raid garbage cans to fatten up for the winter.

Bear attacks on humans are very rare. Still, these powerful animals can be dangerous to city residents. So wildlife managers in cities trap bears and release them in the wild. They may also try to scare the bears away by shooting them with stinging rubber bullets. However some bears return time after time, hoping to find an easy meal.

The Geese Mess

In the 1800s, many people hunted Canada geese for their meat. By 1900, the geese were very rare. Then in the 1960s, scientists found a group of Canada geese in Minnesota. The excited scientists took pairs of the birds to many different areas around the country.

They hoped the geese would start new flocks. The Canada geese loved their new homes. They were protected from hunters. They had plenty of grass, their favorite food. People also fed them bread. In fact, there was so much food that the geese no longer needed to migrate in winter. Because the geese had plenty of food and no predators, their numbers increased.

The goose population on golf courses, playgrounds, and parks began to skyrocket. Geese live for 20 years or more. A pair of geese can produce 100 new birds in just five years. At certain times of the year, more than 500 geese might gather in one place.

Goose droppings can make parks unsafe. They **pollute** (pə LOOT) ponds and drinking water, and cleaning up the mess is expensive. To limit the number of geese, some cities and parks now use herding dogs to keep the geese from nesting. Officials also discourage the feeding of geese. Even so, the solution to the goose problem has not been found.

Problems and Solutions

As the human population increases, people will have more encounters, or run-ins, with wild animals. Some encounters are more frightening than others. Coyote attacks on humans and pets are very rare. However, coyotes have been rapidly extending their range. They have spread from the central United States to all of the lower 48 states, Alaska, and Canada. As a result, coyote attacks on pets and young children are increasing.

In the West, people have begun building houses in remote areas where mountain lions live. People are beginning to spot the big cats in and around parks and other public places. Attacks by mountain lions are very rare. Still, getting too close to these powerful creatures could be deadly.

Can people live in peace with wildlife? Most wildlife experts urge us to try. Some towns are setting aside special paths and areas for wild animals. Others use special fences and chemical sprays to keep wildlife away.

Experts urge people to enjoy wild animals only from a distance. Approaching or feeding them can be dangerous or can cause wild animals to become pests. Experts say that it is always better to keep the "wild" in wildlife.

LESSON 26 Cause and Effect **75**

SCIENCE

Provides easy access to content-area lessons in each unit with margin tabs.

ESL/ELL

Alerts teachers to wording that may be unfamiliar to ESL/ELL students with shaded words and phrases.

Level A, Annotated Teacher's Edition

Reinforce Learning Immediately With Review Questions.

Helps students focus on the important facts and tests their literal understanding of the text with **Comprehension questions**.

Offers quick and easy reference with a skill label and answer for each question in the Annotated Teacher's Edition.

Helps students evaluate their ability to infer information not explicitly stated in the text with **Critical Thinking questions**.

Checks students' understanding of the lesson skill with **Skill Focus exercises**. In the "Skill Focus" section at the beginning of the lesson, students learned about the lesson skill. Now they complete a written activity that applies the skill to the reading selection.

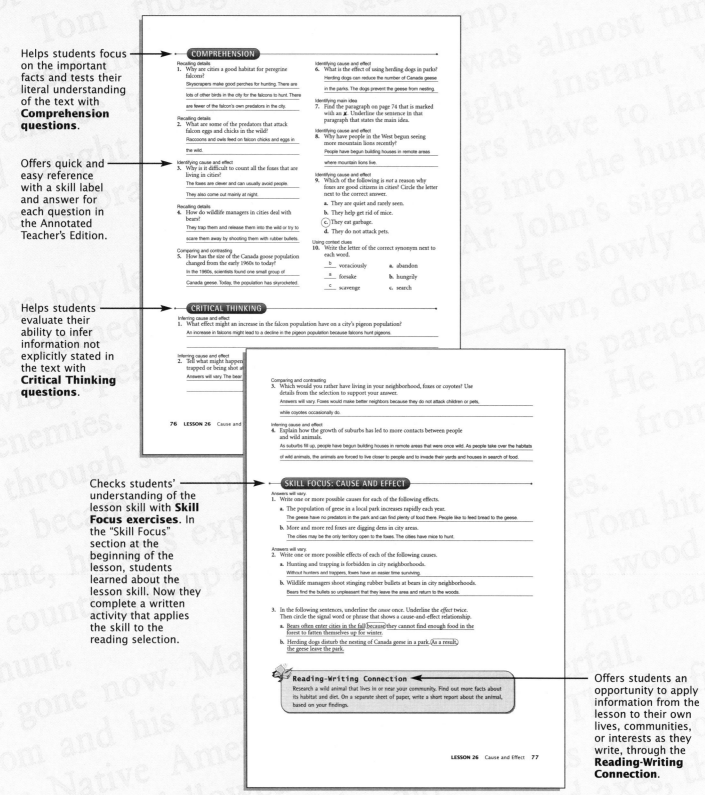

COMPREHENSION

Recalling details
1. Why are cities a good habitat for peregrine falcons?
    Skyscrapers make good perches for hunting. There are
    lots of other birds in the city for the falcons to hunt. There
    are fewer of the falcon's own predators in the city.

Recalling details
2. What are some of the predators that attack falcon eggs and chicks in the wild?
    Raccoons and owls feed on falcon chicks and eggs in
    the wild.

Identifying cause and effect
3. Why is it difficult to count all the foxes that are living in cities?
    The foxes are clever and can usually avoid people.
    They also come out mainly at night.

Recalling details
4. How do wildlife managers in cities deal with bears?
    They trap them and release them into the wild or try to
    scare them away by shooting them with rubber bullets.

Comparing and contrasting
5. How has the size of the Canada goose population changed from the early 1960s to today?
    In the 1960s, scientists found one small group of
    Canada geese. Today, the population has skyrocketed.

Identifying cause and effect
6. What is the effect of using herding dogs in parks?
    Herding dogs can reduce the number of Canada geese
    in the parks. The dogs prevent the geese from nesting.

Identifying main idea
7. Find the paragraph on page 74 that is marked with an **x**. Underline the sentence in that paragraph that states the main idea.

Identifying cause and effect
8. Why have people in the West begun seeing more mountain lions recently?
    People have begun building houses in remote areas
    where mountain lions live.

Identifying cause and effect
9. Which of the following is *not* a reason why foxes are good citizens in cities? Circle the letter next to the correct answer.
    a. They are quiet and rarely seen.
    b. They help get rid of mice.
    c. They eat garbage.
    d. They do not attack pets.

Using context clues
10. Write the letter of the correct synonym next to each word.
    b voraciously   a. abandon
    a forsake   b. hungrily
    c scavenge   c. search

CRITICAL THINKING

Inferring cause and effect
1. What effect might an increase in the falcon population have on a city's pigeon population?
    An increase in falcons might lead to a decline in the pigeon population because falcons hunt pigeons.

Inferring cause and effect
2. Tell what might happen trapped or being shot at
    Answers will vary. The bear

76 LESSON 26 Cause and

Comparing and contrasting
3. Which would you rather have living in your neighborhood, foxes or coyotes? Use details from the selection to support your answer.
    Answers will vary. Foxes would make better neighbors because they do not attack children or pets,
    while coyotes occasionally do.

Inferring cause and effect
4. Explain how the growth of suburbs has led to more contacts between people and wild animals.
    As suburbs fill up, people have begun building houses in remote areas that were once wild. As people take over the habitats
    of wild animals, the animals are forced to live closer to people and to invade their yards and houses in search of food.

SKILL FOCUS: CAUSE AND EFFECT

Answers will vary.
1. Write one or more possible causes for each of the following effects.
    a. The population of geese in a local park increases rapidly each year.
        The geese have no predators in the park and can find plenty of food there. People like to feed bread to the geese.
    b. More and more red foxes are digging dens in city areas.
        The cities may be the only territory open to the foxes. The cities have mice to hunt.

Answers will vary.
2. Write one or more possible effects of each of the following causes.
    a. Hunting and trapping is forbidden in city neighborhoods.
        Without hunters and trappers, foxes have an easier time surviving.
    b. Wildlife managers shoot stinging rubber bullets at bears in city neighborhoods.
        Bears find the bullets so unpleasant that they leave the area and return to the woods.

3. In the following sentences, underline the *cause* once. Underline the *effect* twice. Then circle the signal word or phrase that shows a cause-and-effect relationship.
    a. Bears often enter cities in the fall because they cannot find enough food in the forest to fatten themselves up for winter.
    b. Herding dogs disturb the nesting of Canada geese in a park. As a result, the geese leave the park.

Reading-Writing Connection
Research a wild animal that lives in or near your community. Find out more facts about its habitat and diet. On a separate sheet of paper, write a short report about the animal, based on your findings.

LESSON 26 Cause and Effect **77**

Offers students an opportunity to apply information from the lesson to their own lives, communities, or interests as they write, through the **Reading-Writing Connection**.

Level A, Annotated Teacher's Edition

Reinforce Skills With Brief Skills Lessons.

Gives students the opportunity to apply their new reading skills to a valuable high-interest topic—**a practical life skill**—the subject of the last lesson in each unit.

Focuses on one important skill in concise **Skill Lessons**. Students are introduced to the lesson concept and then are guided to formulate rules and generalizations.

Prepares students with techniques they can use to read and understand ads and other real-life materials.

LESSON 42
For ESL/ELL support, see page T97.

Skill: Comparing Car Ads
For lesson support, see page T97.

If you are interested in buying a new car, reading ads in newspapers and magazines should start you in the right direction. The details in ads can help you decide what kind of car will meet your needs and your budget. Then you can shop around for the best price.

Carefully read the following ads to compare the two cars.

PASHUBI: WE DESIGNED OUR CAR FOR YOU, THE DRIVER

At Pashubi, we think you are very important. So we have created the 630-X, a fully equipped luxury sports car. The 630-X surrounds the driver with more window than other sports cars. The 630-X has a steering wheel and instrument panel that can be moved up or down.

The roomy bucket seats can be easily moved and can tilt back as far as you like. The large storage area in back lifts up to become two additional seats.

There are 30 standard equipment features, including air conditioning, power windows, electrically heated outside rearview mirror, two-tone paint, and a CD player.

At $33,025, the 630-X offers more than other imported cars. You'll save on gas. You'll get an exceptional **43 EST HWY MPG, 25 EST MPG.** Use MPG for comparison. Mileage may differ depending on conditions. Highway mileage may be lower.

The 630-X. By Pashubi. It's not for everyone, but it is for you.

TILTON
The American way to get m...

You get more for your m... Take the Star, for example. ... 3,000 computer-assisted rob... any other car, which will giv... money for years to come.

The Star gives you mo... because it is sensibly priced... $20,999*. The Star gives you... with front-wheel drive. With ...

116 LESSON 42 Comparing...

A. Circle the letter in front of the phrase that best completes each sentence.

1. The Pashubi ad stresses that
   a. the gas mileage of the 630-X is comparable to that of other cars.
   b. the 630-X is designed with the driver in mind.
   c. you get more for your money when you buy the Pashubi.
   d. The 630-X is a fully equipped compact car.

2. The Tilton ad stresses that
   a. much of the Star's standard equipment is considered extra on other cars.
   b. the Star uses fewer robot welds than any other compact car.
   c. you get more for your money when you buy a Star.
   d. the Star is not easy to maintain.

3. All car ads must state the estimated miles per gallon (EST MPG) of gas that a car needs for highway (HWY) and for city driving. So a car boasting 43 EST HWY MPG, 28 EST MPG means that
   a. its estimated mileage is 43 miles per gallon for highway driving and 28 for city driving.
   b. its estimated mileage is 28 miles per gallon for highway driving and 43 for city driving.
   c. its actual mileage is 43 miles per gallon for highway driving and 28 for city driving.
   d. its actual mileage is 25 miles per gallon for highway driving and 43 for city driving.

4. Both ads advise that the gas mileage may vary from the estimates because
   a. the gas mileage the cars get probably has never been tested.
   b. the cars probably get much better mileage than the ad states.
   c. the cars may not get lower gas mileage than the ad states.
   d. the cars may get lower gas mileage than the ad states.

5. The ad states that the Star is sold for as low as $20,999, but the car pictured in the ad costs $23,698. The price of the car in the picture is probably higher because
   a. it has many of the extra features, such as two-tone paint and a luggage rack.
   b. it is not really a Star but another kind of car made by Tilton.
   c. $20,999 is the sale price.
   d. it has better mileage.

6. The standard equipment common to both the 630-X and the Star includes
   a. a leather-covered steering wheel and two-tone paint.
   b. air conditioning and a CD player.
   c. an electrically heated outside rearview mirror and power windows.
   d. a luggage rack and bucket seats.

B. Complete the chart comparing the 630-X and the Star. If no information is given for a particular item, write *NI*.

Comparing Cars		
Car Features	630-X	STAR
Price	$33,025	$20,999
Number of passengers	4	6
City gas mileage	25 EST MPG	26 EST MPG
Number of standard equipment features	30	3
Country where the car is made	No Information	US

LESSON 42 Comparing Car Ads **117**

Level A, Annotated Teacher's Edition

Provides opportunities, through **charts and graphs**, to extract information from the text, draw new conclusions, and enhance comprehension.

LESSON 28
For ESL/ELL support, see page T88.

Skill: r–Controlled Vowel Sounds
For lesson support, see page T88.

Vowels can have other sounds in addition to their long and short sounds. If the letter r comes after a vowel, the r controls the sound of the vowel. The sounds of ar, er, ir, or, and ur are called **r-controlled vowel sounds.**

A. Say the word pairs below, listening to each vowel sound. Then answer the questions that follow.

| cap | hem | sit | fog | fun |
| car | her | sir | for | fur |

1. Is the sound of the vowel in the top word of each pair long or short? ___short___

2. Does the vowel in the bottom word of each pair have a different sound? ___yes___

3. What letter follows the vowel in the bottom word of each pair? ___r___

B. Say the three words in the list that follows each number below. Listen to the vowel sound in each word. Answer each question with yes or no. Then complete the rule below.

1. bar / star / farm — Does the *a* in these words have a sound that is different from either long *a* or short *a*? ___yes___

2. herd / term / tern — Does the *e* in these words have a sound that is different from either long *e* or short *e*? ___yes___

3. shirt / bird / third — Does the *i* in these words have a sound that is different from either long *i* or short *i*? ___yes___

4. for / born / storm — Does the *o* in these words have a sound that is different from either long *o* or short *o*? ___yes___

5. burn / hurt / curve — Does the *u* in these words have a sound that is different from either long *u* or short *u*? ___yes___

RULE: When the vowel in a one-vowel word is followed by ___r___, the sound of the vowel is usually changed by the ___r___, and the sound of the vowel is neither short nor long.

C. Listen to the sound of *e, i,* and *u* in the following words. Then complete the rule below.

| jerk | term | dirt | mirth | fur | curl |
| perk | her | fir | shirk | burn | urn |

RULE: When the vowels *e, i,* and *u* are followed by ___r___, all three vowels usually have the ___same___ sound.

82 LESSON 28 r-Controlled Vowel Sounds

Level A, Annotated Teacher's Edition

Offers more learning in less time in **skills practice and reinforcement pages** without full-length reading selections. In Starting Out and Levels A, B, and C, phonic skills are reviewed.

About *Be A Better Reader* **T9**

Teaching Support Gives a Recipe for Success With Comprehensive Lesson Pages.

Highlights the skill, context clue words, ESL/ELL words, and graphic organizer.

Guides you through activating prior knowledge, identifying the objectives and previewing the text, and gives a purpose-setting question with helpful Before Reading suggestions.

Gives you step-by-step ideas for teaching each skill, including explanations and active learning suggestions.

ESL/ELL

Provides support for ESL/ELL through suggestions in ESL/ELL Strategies for each core lesson.

ESL/ELL

Supports your English Language Learners with an ESL/ELL Activity in each skill and life skill lesson.

Reinforces skills in creative ways in Extension Activities for each skill and life skill lesson.

Offers support for each skill and life skill lesson.

Helps you stay focused on the lesson purpose with During Reading reminders.

Applies the lesson content and expands on the Reading-Writing Connection with ideas offered in After Reading.

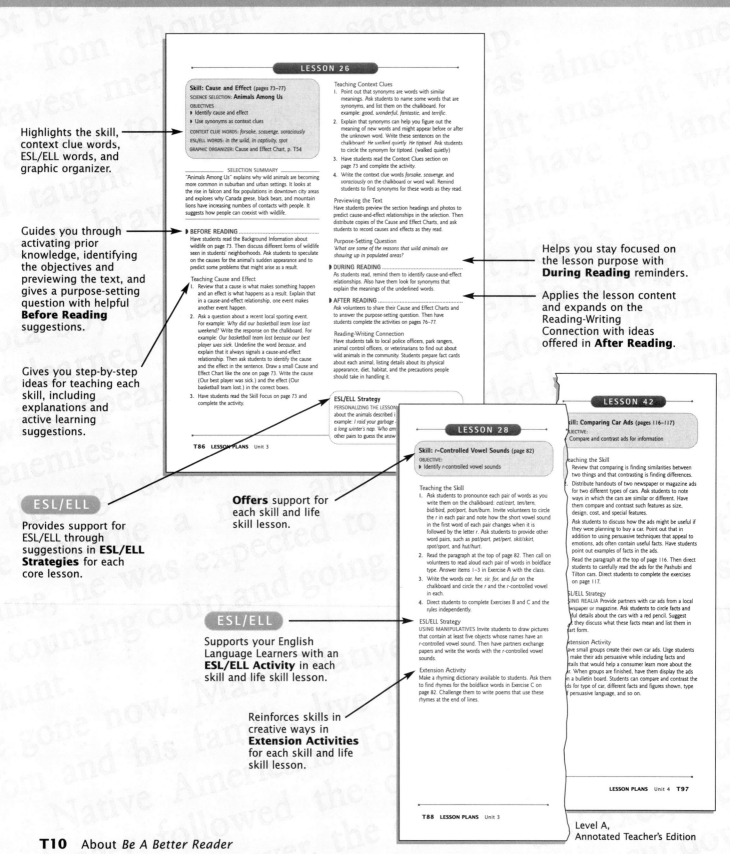

LESSON 26

Skill: Cause and Effect (pages 73–77)
SCIENCE SELECTION: **Animals Among Us**
OBJECTIVES
▶ Identify cause and effect
▶ Use synonyms as context clues
CONTEXT CLUE WORDS: *forsake, scavenge, voraciously*
ESL/ELL WORDS: *in the wild, in captivity, spot*
GRAPHIC ORGANIZER: Cause and Effect Chart, p. T54

SELECTION SUMMARY
"Animals Among Us" explains why wild animals are becoming more common in suburban and urban settings. It looks at the rise in falcon and fox populations in downtown city areas and explores why Canada geese, black bears, and mountain lions have increasing numbers of contacts with people. It suggests how people can coexist with wildlife.

▶ BEFORE READING
Have students read the Background Information about wildlife on page 73. Then discuss different forms of wildlife seen in students' neighborhoods. Ask students to speculate on the causes for the animal's sudden appearance and to predict some problems that might arise as a result.

Teaching Cause and Effect
1. Review that a cause is what makes something happen and an effect is what happens as a result. Explain that in a cause-and-effect relationship, one event makes another event happen.
2. Ask a question about a recent local sporting event. For example: *Why did our basketball team lose last weekend?* Write the response on the chalkboard. For example: *Our basketball team lost because our best player was sick.* Underline the word *because*, and explain that it always signals a cause-and-effect relationship. Then ask students to identify the cause and the effect in the sentence. Draw a small Cause and Effect Chart like the one on page 73. Write the cause (Our best player was sick.) and the effect (Our basketball team lost.) in the correct boxes.
3. Have students read the Skill Focus on page 73 and complete the activity.

Teaching Context Clues
1. Point out that synonyms are words with similar meanings. Ask students to name some words that are synonyms, and list them on the chalkboard. For example: *good, wonderful, fantastic,* and *terrific*.
2. Explain that synonyms can help you figure out the meaning of new words and might appear before or after the unknown word. Write these sentences on the chalkboard: *He walked quietly. He tiptoed.* Ask students to circle the synonym for *tiptoed*. (walked quietly)
3. Have students read the Context Clues section on page 73 and complete the activity.
4. Write the context clue words *forsake, scavenge,* and *voraciously* on the chalkboard or word wall. Remind students to find synonyms for these words as they read.

Previewing the Text
Have students preview the section headings and photos to predict cause-and-effect relationships in the selection. Then distribute copies of the Cause and Effect Charts, and ask students to record causes and effects as they read.

Purpose-Setting Question
What are some of the reasons that wild animals are showing up in populated areas?

▶ DURING READING
As students read, remind them to identify cause-and-effect relationships. Also have them look for synonyms that explain the meanings of the underlined words.

▶ AFTER READING
Ask volunteers to share their Cause and Effect Charts and to answer the purpose-setting question. Then have students complete the activities on pages 76–77.

Reading-Writing Connection
Have students talk to local police officers, park rangers, animal control officers, or veterinarians to find out about wild animals in the community. Students prepare fact cards about each animal, listing details about its physical appearance, diet, habitat, and the precautions people should take in handling it.

ESL/ELL Strategy
PERSONALIZING THE LESSON
about the animals described i
example: *I raid your garbage*
a long winter's nap. Who am
other pairs to guess the answ

T86 LESSON PLANS Unit 3

LESSON 28

Skill: r–Controlled Vowel Sounds (page 82)
OBJECTIVE:
▶ Identify r-controlled vowel sounds

Teaching the Skill
1. Ask students to pronounce each pair of words as you write them on the chalkboard: *cat/cart, ten/tern, bid/bird, pot/port, bun/burn.* Invite volunteers to circle the *r* in each pair and note how the short vowel sound in the first word of each pair changes when it is followed by the letter *r*. Ask students to provide other word pairs, such as *pat/part, pet/pert, skit/skirt, spot/sport,* and *hut/hurt.*
2. Read the paragraph at the top of page 82. Then call on volunteers to read aloud each pair of words in boldface type. Answer items 1–3 in Exercise A with the class.
3. Write the words *car, her, sir, for,* and *fur* on the chalkboard and circle the *r* and the *r*-controlled vowel in each.
4. Direct students to complete Exercises B and C and the rules independently.

ESL/ELL Strategy
USING MANIPULATIVES Invite students to draw pictures that contain at least five objects whose names have an *r*-controlled vowel sound. Then have partners exchange papers and write the words with the *r*-controlled vowel sounds.

Extension Activity
Make a rhyming dictionary available to students. Ask them to find rhymes for the boldface words in Exercise C on page 82. Challenge them to write poems that use these rhymes at the end of lines.

T88 LESSON PLANS Unit 3

LESSON 42

Skill: Comparing Car Ads (pages 116–117)
BJECTIVE:
Compare and contrast ads for information

Teaching the Skill
Review that comparing is finding similarities between two things and that contrasting is finding differences.
Distribute handouts of two newspaper or magazine ads for two different types of cars. Ask students to note ways in which the cars are similar or different. Have them compare and contrast such features as size, design, cost, and special features.
Ask students to discuss how the ads might be useful if they were planning to buy a car. Point out that in addition to using persuasive techniques that appeal to emotions, ads often contain useful facts. Have students point out examples of facts in the ads.
Read the paragraph at the top of page 116. Then direct students to carefully read the ads for the Pashubi and Tilton cars. Direct students to complete the exercises on page 117.

SL/ELL Strategy
SING REALIA Provide partners with car ads from a local wspaper or magazine. Ask students to circle facts and ful details about the cars with a red pencil. Suggest t they discuss what these facts mean and list them in hart form.

xtension Activity
ave small groups create their own car ads. Urge students make their ads persuasive while including facts and tails that would help a consumer learn more about the r. When groups are finished, have them display the ads n a bulletin board. Students can compare and contrast the ds for type of car, different facts and figures shown, type persuasive language, and so on.

LESSON PLANS Unit 4 **T97**

Level A,
Annotated Teacher's Edition

Determine Placement and Monitor Progress With Easy-to-Use Assessment Materials.

Evaluates students' mastery of skills at each level with the reproducible **Assessment Test** in the Annotated Teacher's Edition.

Prepares students for state and standardized tests with the four-choice multiple choice format.

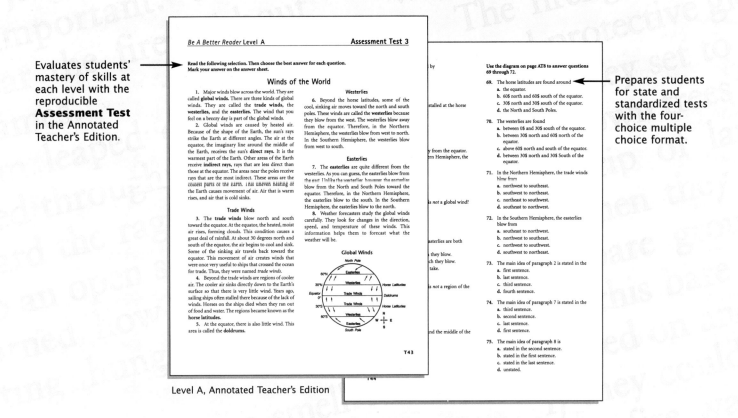

Level A, Annotated Teacher's Edition

With the *Diagnostic and Placement Guide* you can:

- Place each student confidently at the appropriate instructional level with the Placement Test.

- Verify Placement Test results quickly and identify where each student needs help, using the Diagnostic Tests and the coded Answer Key.

- Evaluate reading ability in a particular content area effectively and efficiently.

With the *Progress Monitoring Package* you can:

- Use the reproducible tests for ongoing monitoring of students' achievement.

- Help students bolster weak skills with the Reteaching the Skills section, which includes instructions for using reproducible graphic organizers.

- Track each student's progress and overall class performance with reproducible Student Performance and Class Performance Charts.

- Facilitate testing with complete instructions for administration and assessment.

Pacing Suggestions

Pacing suggestions are based on the class-period time allotments shown. Adjust the schedule, using additional teaching options, to accommodate longer time periods or block scheduling.

▶ PACING FOR A FULL-YEAR SCHEDULE (36 Weeks; 50–90 minute daily class periods)

Weeks	1–6	7–12	13–18	19–24	25–29	30–36
Unit	1	2	3	4	5	6

During each block of time, complete one unit. Provide direct instruction for the introduction page of each core lesson in the unit: literature, social studies, science, or mathematics. Then choose the combination of instructional elements below that works best for your class.

- **Reading and Practice:** For all core lessons, use the selections and question pages that follow.

- **Writing:** For all core lessons use "Reading-Writing Connections."

- **Skill Practice:** Use additional skill lessons from each unit.

- **Assessment and Reteaching:** Use "Progress Monitors" and "Reteaching the Skill" in the *Progress Monitoring Package.*

- **Independent Reading:** Use the CD-ROM of Reading Resources.

ADDITIONAL TEACHING OPTIONS

Use related programs from Pearson Learning Group/Globe Fearon.

Independent Reading: *Adapted Classics, FastBacks, Globe Reader's Collection, Freedom Fighters, Multicultural Biographies, Our Century Magazine*

Writing Skills and Practice: *Success in Writing, Writing Across the Curriculum, World of Vocabulary*

Reading-Writing Connections: *Stories Without Endings, Plays Without Endings*

▶ PACING FOR A SUMMER SCHOOL SCHEDULE
(6 Weeks; 90–120 minute daily class periods)

Each week, complete one unit. During each week, complete all four core lessons and additional skill lessons.

Weekly Schedule		
Day	Core Lessons	Skill Lesson (Remaining Lessons of Each Unit)
1	Reading Literature	Choose one or more relevant skill lessons based on students' needs.
2	Reading Social Studies	Choose one or more relevant skill lessons based on students' needs.
3	Reading Science	Choose one or more relevant skill lessons based on students' needs.
4	Reading Mathematics	Choose one or more relevant skill lessons based on students' needs.
5	Assessment: Use "Progress Monitors" and "Reteaching the Skill" in the *Progress Monitoring Package*. Use the CD-ROM of Reading Resources for independent reading. Choose from Additional Teaching Options below.	

ADDITIONAL TEACHING OPTIONS

Use related programs from Pearson Learning Group/Globe Fearon.

Independent Reading: *Adapted Classics, FastBacks, Globe Reader's Collection, Freedom Fighters, Multicultural Biographies, Our Century Magazine*

Writing Skills and Practice: *Success in Writing, Writing Across the Curriculum, World of Vocabulary*

Reading-Writing Connections: *Stories Without Endings, Plays Without Endings*

Scope and Sequence

	Starting Out	A	B	C	D	E	F	G
Word Analysis								
Compound Words	✓							
Contractions	✓							
Syllables	✓	✓	✓	✓	✓	✓	✓	
Accented Syllables		✓	✓	✓	✓	✓	✓	
Phonics								
Consonants	✓	✓						
Consonant Blends	✓	✓						
Consonant Digraphs		✓						
Long and Short Vowel Sounds	✓	✓						
Vowel Digraphs	✓							
Vowel Diphthongs	✓			✓				
Vowel-Consonant Combinations				✓				
r-controlled Vowel Sounds	✓	✓						
Schwa Sound	✓	✓	✓	✓	✓	✓	✓	
Silent Letters	✓		✓					
Hard and Soft c and g	✓		✓					
Content Area Reading								
Reading a Diagram	✓	✓	✓	✓	✓	✓	✓	✓
Reading a Flowchart						✓	✓	
Reading a Graph	✓		✓	✓	✓	✓		
Reading a Map	✓	✓	✓	✓	✓		✓	✓
Reading a Timeline			✓	✓				
Reading a Table	✓	✓						✓
Content-Area Vocabulary	✓	✓	✓	✓	✓	✓	✓	✓
Reading Math Terms and Symbols	✓	✓	✓	✓	✓	✓	✓	✓
Reading and Solving Word Problems	✓	✓	✓	✓	✓	✓	✓	✓
Using Statistics					✓	✓	✓	
Comprehension								
Cause and Effect	✓	✓	✓	✓	✓	✓	✓	✓
Drawing Conclusions	✓							
Context Clues	✓	✓	✓	✓	✓	✓	✓	✓
Fact and Opinion	✓	✓	✓	✓	✓	✓	✓	✓
Following Directions		✓	✓	✓		✓	✓	✓
Making Inferences		✓	✓	✓	✓	✓	✓	✓
Main Idea—Stated or Unstated			✓	✓	✓	✓	✓	
Main Idea and Supporting Details	✓	✓	✓	✓	✓	✓	✓	✓
Sequence of Events	✓	✓						✓
Recognizing Propaganda				✓	✓			✓

	Starting Out	A	B	C	D	E	F	G
Critical Thinking								
Analyzing								✓
Classifying		✓	✓	✓	✓		✓	
Comparing and Contrasting	✓	✓	✓	✓	✓	✓	✓	✓
Evaluating Opinions				✓				
Fallacies in Reasoning								✓
Making Generalizations	✓			✓	✓	✓	✓	
Vocabulary Development								
Analogies						✓	✓	✓
Denotation and Connotation								✓
Etymology								✓
Multiple-Meaning Words	✓	✓	✓	✓		✓	✓	✓
Nouns, Plural and Possessive	✓							
Prefixes, Suffixes, and Base Words	✓	✓	✓	✓	✓	✓	✓	✓
Synonyms and Antonyms					✓		✓	
Word Parts						✓	✓	
Understanding Word Origins			✓					
Transitional Words and Phrases								✓
Context Clues	✓	✓	✓	✓	✓	✓	✓	✓
Study Skills								
Alphabetical Order		✓	✓					
Using a Dictionary	✓	✓	✓	✓	✓	✓	✓	
Using the Library		✓	✓	✓				
Encyclopedia		✓						
Using Guide Words		✓	✓					
Outlining			✓	✓	✓	✓	✓	✓
Using Parts of a Book	✓	✓	✓	✓	✓		✓	
Using Reference Books			✓	✓				
Skimming for Information			✓					
Taking Notes				✓	✓			✓
Summarizing					✓			✓
Using a Primary Source		✓				✓	✓	✓
Improving Reading Rate				✓	✓		✓	✓

	Starting Out	A	B	C	D	E	F	G
Life Skills								
Using the Yellow Pages	✓		✓					
Comparing Car Ads		✓						
Reading a Job Application				✓				
Reading a Bank Statement					✓			
Reading a Loan Application						✓		
Reading a Résumé							✓	
Completing an Employment Application								✓
Literary Genres								
Short Story	✓	✓	✓	✓	✓	✓	✓	✓
Fable	✓							
Folk Tale			✓					
Myth				✓				
Biography			✓		✓			✓
Play		✓	✓	✓			✓	
Article	✓	✓	✓	✓	✓	✓	✓	✓
Poem					✓	✓	✓	✓
Letter						✓		
Science Fiction	✓			✓	✓		✓	
Journal				✓				
Literary Elements and Skills								
Character	✓	✓	✓	✓	✓	✓	✓	✓
Conflict and Resolution	✓	✓	✓	✓	✓	✓	✓	✓
Imagery				✓				
Plot	✓	✓	✓	✓	✓	✓	✓	✓
Setting	✓	✓	✓	✓	✓	✓		✓
Theme	✓	✓	✓	✓		✓	✓	✓
Point of View			✓	✓	✓		✓	
Mood				✓				✓
Tone						✓		✓
Satire							✓	
Figures of Speech			✓			✓		✓

PROFESSIONAL DEVELOPMENT

The *Be A Better Reader* Lesson Plan

❝WHAT THE RESEARCH SAYS❞

We know from studies that "...there are unique differences in skills used in different subject matter fields; and that while 'general reading ability' is operative in all reading to a certain extent, there is also definite need for the development of specific skills to use in the different curricular areas."

Nila Banton Smith
Reading Instruction for Today's Children

At every level and in every lesson, *Be A Better Reader* emphasizes developing background information, acquiring reading skills, comprehension, and moving beyond a text to think critically and make new connections. To achieve these goals, each lesson follows a classic three-part format: Before Reading, During Reading, and After Reading.

▶ BEFORE READING

Prereading is a time to motivate students to read the selection while equipping them with information, skills, and strategies to maximize the benefits of the reading experience.

While the Background Information section of the student text will help students access the selection, a background-building prereading discussion is ideal for generating relevant information from the students' own knowledge and experience. Often, graphic organizers can be used to elicit and record background information and relate ideas—and many of the lessons include such organizers.

The Skill Focus section is another key element of prereading. Each Skill Focus introduces a reading skill that is vital for comprehending and interpreting the reading selection. The Skill Focus provides examples drawn from the selection itself and also gives the student an opportunity to practice a given skill before beginning to read.

Because using context clues is essential for success in comprehension and vocabulary development, each prereading page of the lesson provides instruction for a particular type of context clue, such as comparisons, details, synonyms, in-text definitions, and so on. Examples of vocabulary context clues are drawn directly from the text that students are about to read. Furthermore, students are directed to use the introduced skill to identify the meaning of specific vocabulary words, thus helping them to prepare for the new vocabulary they will encounter.

The Strategy Tip that completes the prereading page of each student lesson is another valuable feature. By giving students a concrete suggestion for how to use a newly acquired skill in the text they are about to read, students get a head start in their quest for comprehension.

The lesson support on pages T65–T104 also provides valuable prereading suggestions that will further student comprehension. The purpose-setting question, for example, gives students a formal reason for reading that will help them focus on the text and identify the main points and ideas of the selection. Making predictions is another important prereading skill, and this Annotated Teacher's Edition makes specific suggestions for previewing the text by scanning the title, illustrations, diagrams, maps, photos, and text of a selection to predict what the story or article might be about.

▶ **DURING READING**

In *Be A Better Reader*, students will find timely, high-interest reading selections that will naturally engage their interest. The readability of each selection in each level of the program has been carefully controlled to help ensure successful comprehension. Illustrations, photographs, and other graphics have been chosen to complement the text, enhance meaning, and add to the overall appeal.

If students are working with graphic organizers, for example, lesson-support pages remind them to add details and information to these as they read. If visuals are prominent in a selection, students are asked to study these closely. Attention is paid to section headings that might appear in the selection and students are reminded of the underscored vocabulary words introduced in the Context Clues section for which they must figure out the meaning while reading.

▶ **AFTER READING**

After students finish reading a selection, they can complete the Comprehension, Critical Thinking, and Skill Focus questions and activities that appear at the end of each core lesson. As the name indicates, the Comprehension questions assess students' literal comprehension of the text. The answers to these questions, which can usually be stated in a few words or a sentence, are stated directly in the text. Students should realize that a close rereading of portions of the text will yield the answers for these items.

The answers to Critical Thinking questions are not stated directly in the text. Instead, students must use higher-level thinking skills, along with information in the text, to infer appropriate answers. The answers to these questions often require students to use specific reading skills, such as making inferences, comparing and contrasting, or identifying cause and effect—skills that have already been taught in the level. The students' answers to the Critical Thinking questions will vary somewhat, and suggested answers are provided in the Annotated Teacher's Edition.

The Skill Focus activities offer an opportunity to practice the specific reading skill introduced in the Skill Focus section during prereading. Since these questions are based on information in the text, they also test overall comprehension. Some students may benefit from a quick review of the lesson's Skill Focus before attempting to complete the activities.

After-reading oral activities are also important. Individually or in groups, students formally answer the purpose-setting question. They compare and discuss their predictions or any graphic organizers that they have completed. Such activities can contribute markedly to overall comprehension.

Each lesson ends with a feature called the Reading-Writing Connection. This activity, a springboard to writing about the selection, asks students to respond to new information and ideas in a thoughtful and personal way. In addition to providing beneficial writing practice, the activity aids in the long-term retention of the skills and information taught in the lesson.

"WHAT THE RESEARCH SAYS"

Comprehension is building understanding, both of a particular text and of the more global concepts around which it is built. It is an active and demanding process, especially when children are reading to learn new and difficult concepts.

Sharon Walpole
Changing Texts, Changing Thinking

Reading comprehension is a process that begins with word recognition. It does not end, however, until students have derived meaning from the ideas both stated and implied in the text and have been able to evaluate and respond to these ideas.

In *Be A Better Reader*, each lesson focuses on a specific reading skill that helps students recognize and understand a text pattern that is typical of a content area or of other reading materials that students encounter in their daily lives.

COMPREHENSION SKILLS

Comprehension questions help students process information that is stated explicitly in the text. These questions require students to recall from memory or to select from the text specific answers—in other words, to reproduce what has been stated in the text. These questions provide opportunities for students to:

1. Identify the stated main idea.
2. Identify the stated main idea and details.
3. Recall details.
4. Identify the stated cause and effect.
5. Recognize a sequence of events.
6. Recognize fact and opinion.
7. Recognize elements of a short story, such as plot, character, setting, and theme.
8. Recognize a variety of nonfiction text types or literary genres, such as plays, short stories, biographies, articles, reports, and essays.
9. Compare and contrast.

CRITICAL THINKING AND COMPREHENSION

Numerous activities and questions are included to encourage students to probe for deeper meanings that are implied but not explicitly stated in the text. These questions require students to think about the meanings that can be derived from their reading. Inferential and critical comprehension begins with literal meanings, but it advances to higher-level thinking and reasoning skills that help students to:

1. Infer unstated main idea.
2. Infer cause and effect.
3. Infer details.
4. Infer conclusions.
5. Infer comparisons and contrasts.
6. Distinguish fact from opinion.
7. Infer information about elements of a short story, such as plot, character, setting, and theme.
8. Make generalizations.
9. Evaluate validity of ideas.
10. Predict outcomes.
11. Draw conclusions.
12. Identify a point of view.

"WHAT THE RESEARCH SAYS"

Study skills are those used when there is the intent to do something with the content read, such as reading in science or social studies to gather facts, in mathematics to understand and solve a problem, or reading directions to perform a process.

Nila Banton Smith
Reading Instruction for Today's Children

Certain basic skills are called for in all subject areas in order to study and understand information. As students work with selections in literature, social studies, science, and mathematics, *Be A Better Reader* provides instruction and practice in the following study skills.

▶ PREVIEWING

Previewing a selection results in an organized "picture" or understanding of the structure of the selection. In *Be A Better Reader*, students learn to preview a selection by noting headings of sections, main ideas, and visuals.

▶ LOCATING INFORMATION

The skill of locating information includes activities that range from using a table of contents and an index to using a dictionary, an encyclopedia, and the library catalog. In *Be A Better Reader*, lessons on locational skills are self-contained and include representative examples of typical dictionary and encyclopedia entries, indexes, and tables of contents.

▶ SELECTING AND EVALUATING INFORMATION

Textbooks in the content areas contain many questions and directions that call for selection and evaluation skills. The skill of selecting and evaluating information requires students to select a piece of information and judge its worth in meeting the specifications of an activity or question. In *Be A Better Reader*, lessons on fact and opinion, primary sources, and propaganda teach students selection and evaluation skills.

▶ ORGANIZING INFORMATION

The skill of organizing information is important because of the frequency with which students must apply it when studying the material in textbooks, listening in class, writing papers, and taking tests. Organizing information calls for systematically putting together items or ideas that belong to a whole. *Be A Better Reader* includes lessons on the procedures most often used when organizing information: (1) classifying, (2) outlining, and (3) summarizing.

▶ READING VISUALS

Most content-area textbooks require students to read a variety of visuals, such as maps, timelines, diagrams, and graphs. Throughout *Be A Better Reader*, in all content areas, students are taught how to extract specific information from visuals and how to compress textual information into a brief visual presentation.

▶ FOLLOWING DIRECTIONS

Reading to follow directions is a fundamental skill needed in all content areas. In *Be A Better Reader*, students complete specific lessons in following directions. They acquire abundant experience in reading and following directions throughout each level of the program.

▶ READING SPECIAL MATERIALS

Students must be able to read special materials that they encounter outside the classroom. The last lesson in each unit of *Be A Better Reader* provides specific directions on how to read the Yellow Pages, a recipe, a floor plan, a travel brochure, an advertisement, a schedule, and so on.

▶ READING RATE

Studies indicate that most students are ready for a variety of reading rates by the end of fifth grade. Students who have acquired reading skills by only reading fiction need to learn that there are different rates at which they should read different content. In *Be A Better Reader*, emphasis is placed on adjusting the rate of reading to both the content and the purpose of the material.

"WHAT THE RESEARCH SAYS"

One way to develop comprehension abilities is to develop decoding skills. There is increasing evidence that it also helps to teach the major word chunks in English (i.e., prefixes, suffixes, base words, blends, digraphs).

Michael Pressley, University of Notre Dame
Handbook of Reading, Research, Volume III

Students need specific instruction in word recognition to ensure that they have a variety of word-attack strategies needed to read an unfamiliar word. In *Be A Better Reader*, direct instruction is provided for the following skills.

Phonetic Analysis: recognizing and identifying the sounds of consonants, consonant blends, and digraphs; recognizing and identifying vowel sounds and their variant spellings

Structural Analysis: recognizing root words, prefixes and suffixes, compound words, multisyllabic words, accent marks, and syllabication

Context Clues: determining word meaning from a particular context clue

Respellings, Footnotes, and Other Word Helps: using vocabulary aids typical of content-area textbooks

▶ VOCABULARY INSTRUCTION

Extensive reading opportunities are key to developing new vocabulary. However, in addition to independent reading, teacher-directed vocabulary instruction is needed. Teachers can assist students in developing etymological, historical, and morphological knowledge. Such instruction in word derivation is especially important as students encounter content-laden terms in science, social studies, and mathematics.

▶ WORD ANALYSIS

As students encounter more multisyllabic words, they need to learn strategies to decode these words. Structural features such as prefixes and suffixes should be studied. Then base words can be identified and studied. Students who are not reading at grade level should receive continued explicit instruction in decoding multisyllabic words and technical terminology.

▶ CONCEPT WORDS

In lessons that feature social studies, science, and mathematics selections, words that are unique to the content and whose meanings are essential to the selection are treated as concept words. These words appear in boldface type and are often followed by a phonetic respelling and a definition.

▶ ESL/ELL WORDS AND PHRASES

Be A Better Reader provides additional vocabulary support for English language learners. Idioms, expressions, and words with more than one meaning are highlighted for each literature, social studies, science, and mathematics lesson. These words and phrases can be reviewed with students before students read a selection. You may wish to have students use notebooks in which to record the words and phrases and add additional ones of their own. These word books would contain individual vocabulary entries, each with a definition as used in context and an illustration, as appropriate, for each word or phrase. The word book could serve as an ongoing vocabulary tool to be used throughout the school year.

"WHAT THE RESEARCH SAYS"

Students who have processed the text strategically using their knowledge of expository text structures will recall the text better.

D.J. Richgels, L.M. McGee, R.G. Lomax, and C. Sheard

Reading Research Quarterly

Reading research has shown that different types of text require specialized reading skills. During the preparation of *Be A Better Reader*, textbooks in literature, social studies, science, and mathematics were analyzed for text patterns, visual programs, and study aids typical of each content area. The specific skills situations that occurred most often in each content area were selected for inclusion and direct instruction.

▶ LITERATURE

The literature selections in *Be A Better Reader* were carefully selected to appeal to student interest and were written or selected at appropriate reading levels. The basic goals of the lessons with literature selections are threefold: (1) to acquaint students with a variety of literary genres; (2) to increase students' awareness of the literary elements; and (3) to provide practice in applying comprehension skills to reading literature.

Each level of *Be A Better Reader* provides a lesson that develops one of the following literary elements required in understanding and appreciating literature.

Plot

Most short stories have a plot, or sequence of events. They have a beginning, a middle, and an end, and events are arranged to build to a climax. As students read stories, they need to keep the events in order, to notice how one event leads to the next, and to be able to identify the climax, or turning point of the story.

Character

Students need to be able to identify the main character, or protagonist, in a story. They should think about what motivates characters to act as they do. They should also notice how characters develop and change by contrasting how the characters behave at the beginning of a story with how they behave at the end.

Conflict

Students should be able to recognize a story's central conflict, or problem. Most stories are built around one of three common conflicts: (1) The main character is in conflict with himself or herself. (2) The main character is in a conflict with other characters. (3) The main character is in conflict with nature, society, or some outside force over which he or she may not have any control.

Setting

Setting is the time and place of the events in a story. Awareness of setting is essential to an understanding of the characters and their conflicts.

Theme

The theme, or central message, of a story is usually the most difficult concept for students to formulate by themselves. Students need to use higher-level comprehension skills to infer the theme—the author's underlying message.

▶ SOCIAL STUDIES

Social studies texts have their own characteristic text patterns that require special reading skills. For example, social studies texts include frequent references to visuals, such as maps, graphs, and pictures. These references may require students to find information in a specific visual and then combine that information with information in the text.

Many social studies texts require students to interpret material critically. Students are expected to make inferences from facts, to distinguish fact from opinion, to analyze propaganda, to interpret primary sources, to draw conclusions and make generalizations, and to answer open-ended questions. *Be A Better Reader* provides specific instruction and practice in these skills so that students can learn to probe for deeper meanings and respond to higher-level questions.

Be A Better Reader teaches some of the following skills that aid in the comprehension of the patterns typical in social studies textbooks.

Cause and Effect

While the cause-and-effect text pattern occurs to some extent in most content areas, it occurs with the highest frequency in social studies, especially history. Every major event in history comes about as the result of some cause or set of causes, and when the event happens, its effect or effects are felt. Sometimes the effect of one event becomes the cause of another event. Thus, the student often encounters a chain of causes and effects. Students who are adept at recognizing cause-and-effect patterns will find this to be a valuable asset in studying social studies textbooks.

Sequence of Events

Another text pattern encountered in social studies presents events in specific time sequences accompanied by dates. Students should read this pattern for two purposes: (1) to grasp the chronological order of large periods or whole blocks of events; (2) to grasp times of important happenings within each period or block to associate events with dates and to think about how each event led to others.

Social studies textbooks include several kinds of visual aids designed to help students understand time relationships. These aids include charts of events and dates, chronological summaries, timelines, outline maps with dates and events, and so on. Each of these visual aids requires special reading skills.

Comparison and Contrast

A text pattern calling for the comparison of likenesses and/or the contrast of differences is common in social studies textbooks. This pattern occurs most frequently in discussions of such topics as the theories of government or policies of different leaders; physical features, products, or industries of different countries; and so on. Students who recognize a comparison and contrast chapter or section of a text can approach it with the foremost purpose of noting likenesses and differences.

Detailed Statements of Fact

Much social studies text contains many details and facts. Facts, however, are usually included within one of the characteristic text patterns already discussed. The facts in social studies textbooks are not as dense as they usually are in science textbooks, nor are they as technical. Because they are often associated with sequential events or with causes and effects, they are more easily grasped.

Combination of Patterns

A single chapter in a social studies book may contain several text patterns. For example, a chapter may contain biographical material similar to the narrative pattern, a chronology of events during a certain time period, maps and charts depicting those events, and cause-and-effect relationships. If students who start to study such a chapter have not acquired the skills necessary to recognize and process each of these text patterns and instead use the same approach in reading all of them, the resulting understandings of the concepts presented will be extremely limited.

Visuals in Social Studies

Pictures in social studies textbooks are selected to depict historical concepts and events. The ability to read pictures and the captions that accompany them allows students to gain information and implied meanings that go beyond the text. Reading pictures requires close attention to detail.

Reading maps and graphs is a highly specialized kind of reading skill. Map reading requires the recognition and interpretation of symbols for geographical features, towns and cities, boundary lines, and such features as scales of miles, color keys, and meridians. When reading graphs, students need to know how to extrapolate data and use it to make generalizations, thereby supplementing information in the text.

▶ SCIENCE

Science texts call for the use of such comprehension skills as identifying main ideas and making inferences. However, an analysis of science textbooks reveals text patterns unique to science that demand other approaches and special reading skills.

As in social studies textbooks, science texts include frequent references to such visuals as diagrams and pictures. Students need continued practice in combining text reading with visual reading in order to process all the information that is available on a science text page.

Be A Better Reader provides lessons on the following special reading skills that are needed for science textbooks.

Classification

In this pattern, living things, objects, liquids, gases, forces, and so on are first classified in a general grouping that has one or more elements in common. This group is further classified into smaller groups, each of which varies in certain respects from every other group in the general grouping. Students who recognize the classification text pattern will learn to concentrate on understanding the basis of the groupings and the chief characteristics of each one.

Explanation of a Technical Process

Another text pattern particularly characteristic of science is the explanation of a technical process. Explanation is usually accompanied by diagrams, necessitating a very careful reading of the text with continuous references to diagrams.

Cause and Effect

In this pattern, the text gives information that explains why certain things happen. In reading this type of pattern, students first read to find the causes and effects. A careful rereading is usually necessary to determine how and why the causes had such effects.

Following Directions for an Experiment

This text pattern consists of explicit directions or instructions that must be carried out exactly. The common study skill of following directions is essential in reading this science pattern, but experiments also call for the mental activities of making discriminating observations, understanding complex explanations, and drawing considered conclusions.

Detailed Statements of Fact

This pattern in science frequently involves dense facts and a definition or statement of principle. In reading this text pattern, students can make use of the reading skill of finding the main ideas and supporting details. Students first locate the most important thought or main idea in each paragraph; then they proceed to find details that reinforce the main idea—noting particularly any definitions or statements of principles.

Descriptive Problem-Solving Situations

This text pattern describes problem-solving situations by taking the reader through a series of scientific experiments conducted by one or by many people. Students should approach this pattern with the idea of finding out what each successive problem was and how it was solved.

Combination of Patterns

As in social studies textbooks, a single chapter of a science text may contain several text patterns. If students who start to study such a chapter have not acquired the skills necessary to recognize and process each of these patterns and instead use the same approach in reading all of them, then the resulting understandings of the concepts presented will be extremely limited.

Science textbooks usually contain many diagrams. Students need to learn how to go from the text to the diagrams and back to the text if they are to understand the meaning of scientific concepts. Reading diagrams requires an understanding of the purpose of diagrams, the ability to interpret color and other visual devices used to highlight parts of a diagram, and the comprehension of labels.

▶ MATHEMATICS

The reading skills needed for reading mathematics are sharply different from the skills needed in other content areas. Many students who read narrative text with relative ease have great difficulty in reading mathematics, especially word problems and abstract mathematical symbols. The mathematics selections in *Be A Better Reader* are not included for the purpose of teaching mathematics. Their function is to give students practice in reading the different types of text and symbols used in mathematics textbooks, and to apply basic reading skills to mathematics text.

One of the special characteristics of mathematics text is compactness. Every word and every symbol is important. Unlike reading in other content areas, skipping an unfamiliar word or guessing its meaning from context will impair students' progress in mathematics. Students should be aware of this difference.

Another adjustment students may have to make in reading mathematics is a change in basic left-to-right eye movement habits. Mathematics text often requires vertical or left-directed eye movements for rereading portions of the text for better understanding or for selecting certain numbers or symbols.

Reading in mathematics makes heavy demands on the comprehension skills that call for interpretation, critical reading, and creative reading. Students must weigh relationships and discover principles as a result of studying pictures and diagrams.

The inferential reading skills and the study skills of reading pictures and diagrams emphasized throughout *Be A Better Reader* should transfer to the following skills and attitudes specifically needed in working with mathematics.

Word Problems

Because problem solving is a priority in mathematics, *Be A Better Reader* includes one or two lessons on solving word problems in each level. A five-step strategy is used throughout the series. The steps in the strategy closely parallel the steps used in most mathematics textbooks. However, *Be A Better Reader* emphasizes the reading and reasoning skills necessary to solve word problems.

Explanation

Mathematical explanations are comparatively short and often contain symbols. They are usually accompanied by or are preceded by a series of exercises or questions designed to guide students in discovering the principle or process. This text pattern calls for careful reading and rereading until the process is understood.

Visuals in Mathematics

In mathematics, students must read sentences composed of word symbols and number symbols, such as equations. Recognizing and understanding symbols of various types is reading, and it should be taught as such in mathematics.

In reading equations, students have to recognize the meaning of the entire mathematical sentence, as well as the various symbols. In addition to symbols for operations, other symbols are used frequently.

Other distinctive visual elements in mathematics texts are graphs, such as bar graphs and circle graphs. While these visual aids are used in social studies and science, they almost always represent mathematical concepts.

To get the most information from a graph, students should: (1) read the title to determine exactly what is being compared; (2) read the numbers or labels to determine what the figures or labels stand for; (3) study the graph to compare the different items that are illustrated; and (4) interpret the significance of the graph as a whole.

"WHAT THE RESEARCH SAYS"

Teachers who use cross-curricular themes create active readers and writers by engaging students in authentic literacy tasks that emerge naturally from interesting and worthwhile topics and ideas.

Dr. MaryEllen Vogt
Cross-Curriculum Thematic Instruction

Good readers connect and use information and ideas from a variety of life and literary experiences. Thematic instruction fosters this process in a number of ways.

When students explore a topical theme in-depth, they tend to apply it to "real world" contexts. That is, thematic lessons from the classroom are likely to relate to and enrich various events of a student's own life. This synergy often improves the student's ability to make decisions and solve problems both inside and outside the classroom setting.

Thematic instruction is also flexible and multifaceted. Students explore a topic using different types of texts, each approaching the theme from a different perspective. Students might work individually, in small groups, or as a whole class. Each broad theme also provides a rich variety of extension activities—writing tasks, discussions, and projects.

To maximize the advantages of teaching with themes, and to tap the storehouse of information and experience that students bring to the classroom, each unit of *Be A Better Reader* is organized around a different theme. A unit theme such as "The Ocean," "Flight," or "Communications," unites the subject matter in the literature, social studies, science, and mathematics selections of the unit and develops some aspect of that theme.

To maximize the benefits of the program's thematic organization, use some of the following classroom activities as students progress through *Be A Better Reader*.

▶ THEME INTRODUCTIONS

When beginning a new unit, introduce its theme. Discuss students' associations with the theme and invite them to suggest topics that might be included in it. Have them speculate how the selections in the unit might relate to the unit theme. Let them share movies and books they know about that relate to the theme.

▶ THEME BOOKS

Provide a selection of theme-related books and magazine articles for students to peruse. When beginning a unit on "Flight," for example, provide a biography of the Wright brothers and other pioneers in flight, a short history of ballooning, a field guide to birds, magazine articles about space stations and planned flights to Mars, and books about stars and constellations. Encourage students to read some of these materials and write short book reports or critiques during the period of time you study the theme.

▶ THEME WORDS

At the beginning of a unit, provide a place for students to record theme-related vocabulary. After each reading session, ask students to record at least three new theme-related words that they have learned. When you finish a theme, review the words. Students can play a picture dictionary game. Assign different words to teams and ask them to illustrate each one. Teams challenge each other to guess the words and provide their meanings.

▶ THEME ESSAYS

At the end of a unit, have students write essays expressing their personal views of, or reactions to, some aspect of the theme. Construct essay topics based on the theme. For example, for "Challenges," you might pose the essay "What challenges do the characters in this unit successfully face?"

▶ THEME BULLETIN BOARDS

While students are working on a unit, create a theme bulletin board. The items on the bulletin board might include current-event articles, photographs, original poems, drawings, and objects that illustrate some aspect of the theme. Ask each student to write a few sentences on a notecard that explain the theme connection. Post each one on the bulletin board below the item.

"WHAT THE RESEARCH SAYS"

Larger blocks of time allow for a more flexible and productive classroom environment, along with more opportunities for using varied and interactive teaching methods.

Robert Canaday and Michael Rettig
Block Scheduling: A Catalyst for Change in High Schools. Eye on Education.

The term "block scheduling" refers to a way of organizing the school day for intermediate and high school students. Traditional scheduling generally calls for six, seven, or eight single periods of study of about 40–50 minutes each per day. With block schedules, students take fewer, but longer, classes daily. Within each block, a variety of related classroom activities take place.

In recent years, many schools have initiated block schedules with great success. Some schools use an alternating day plan, with students and teachers meeting in three to four 90- to 120-minute classes every other day. The "4 × 4" semester plan is another popular model, with students enrolling in four 90-minute courses that meet every day of the week for a semester. There is also a trimester plan, in which students take two or three 120-minute classes for 60 days, along with two or three traditional-length classes.

▶ **BENEFITS OF BLOCK SCHEDULES**

Block scheduling provides a significantly different classroom experience than traditional class periods. Some benefits of block scheduling for teacher and students are shown in the chart below.

Teacher Benefits	Student Benefits
1. can focus on more activities; more varied than straight lecture	1. increased possibilities for in-depth study
2. fewer courses to prepare each day	2. fewer classes that students must attend and prepare for each day and/or each term
3. longer blocks of time that allow and encourage the use of active teaching strategies and greater student involvement	3. fewer class changes during the school day and less of the disruption that occurs during these changes
4. more time to adapt to different learning styles	4. more time for students to learn, without lowering standards and without punishing those who need more or less time to learn

▶ **BLOCK SCHEDULING AND *BE A BETTER READER***

In block scheduling, teachers need to determine the most effective way for teaching students, considering their individual learning styles. Using selected portions of the block for formal student instruction is crucial. However, interspersed with these segments, other activities can be included that facilitate active student involvement. These include discussions, cooperative groups for projects, independent research, extra skill practice, brainstorming a writing assignment, and opportunities for advanced study. The following are suggestions for ways to use *Be A Better Reader* within the framework of a block schedule.

• Incorporate the skills presented in the literature selections of *Be A Better Reader* into instruction of other stories, novels, and plays that students are reading.

• Use the social studies, science, and mathematics articles in *Be A Better Reader* in conjunction with social studies, science, and mathematics textbooks to develop and extend key concepts.

• Use the suggestions in the Reading-Writing Connection found in the lesson plans of the Annotated Teacher's Edition to provide students with additional activities

• Use the ESL/ELL Strategy with groups of students who need additional access to lessons.

• Encourage the use of the CD-ROM for students who would enjoy additional selections about a favorite theme in *Be A Better Reader*.

• Use the *Progress Monitoring Package* to track students' ongoing progress toward mastery of key skills.

" WHAT THE RESEARCH SAYS "

Students achieve (second-language acquisition) significantly better in programs that teach language through cognitively complex content, taught through problem-solving, discovery learning in highly interactive classroom content.

Virginia P. Collier

National Clearinghouse for Bilingual Education

In order to raise the achievement level of English language learners (ELL), the new edition of *Be A Better Reader* includes strategies that have been designed to be compatible with SDAIE (Specially Designed Academic Instruction in English) and CALLA (Cognitive Academic Language Learning Approach). These approaches to teaching grade-level subject matter in English to English language learners use strategies tailor-made to help speakers of other languages access content. The goal of incorporating these strategies is to assist ELL students of intermediate fluency or higher in benefiting from instruction in complex academic content delivered through readings and accompanying instruction in specific, proven classroom strategies.

Some curriculum designers slot subjects into a continuum of challenge to English language learners based on the content area's dependency on language. The following chart represents this continuum.

Core Content and English Language Proficiency

Physical Education, Art, Music	Dependency on language alone to convey meaning is relatively low. Reliance is on modeling and demonstration. As movement strategies and artistic techniques are introduced, language proficiency becomes more important.
Mathematics	Comprehension of basics is not completely dependent on language proficiency. Through math symbols, tools (calculators and computers), real-life applications, projects, and manipulatives, content becomes more explicit. Language proficiency is more important for solving word problems.
Science	Dependence on language to convey meaning is fairly high. Nomenclature, along with concepts students may not encounter in everyday life, makes science more abstract. Use demonstration, lab partnering, hands-on experimentation, media support, science software, and videos to make comprehension more accessible.
Social Studies	Dependence on language to convey meaning is high. Many abstract and complex concepts rely heavily on language to convey meaning; primary source documents written in archaic language add to the challenge. Use simulation games, group projects, graphic organizers, and field trips.
Literature/ Reading	Dependence on language to convey meaning for vocabulary, semantics, and cultural literacy to appreciate nuances that enrich stories, poetry, and plays is almost exclusive. Beginning reading is often made easier when students bring to English the ability to read in their primary language; higher-level critical-thinking skills transfer to English, such as understanding cause and effect, main idea, and sequencing. Students learning to read in a language other than their primary language need teacher techniques and materials for those nontransferable aspects of language.

▶ STRATEGIES FOR ENGLISH LANGUAGE LEARNERS

Techniques and strategies which make abstract concepts more readily understood by English language learners include the following:

1. **Building background** to move students from the known to the new.

2. **Previewing vocabulary** to identify and teach students essential words and terms before they encounter them in the text. These are often more than the new "key terms" in a content lesson; they are often words and phrases that native English speakers at the grade level already know.

3. **Using illustrations and visuals** including photographs, drawings, artwork, posters, graphs, maps, videos, computer programs, and reproductions of documents to provide a context for learning. Students new to English literacy can focus on reading captions and labels in their textbooks, which often capture the main ideas of a lesson.

4. **Using realia** (real objects and materials) to reduce abstractions and make new concepts more explicit. Use of realia helps ELL students relate classroom teaching to real life and their own prior knowledge and experience.

5. **Using graphic organizers** including matrices, Venn diagrams, tables, charts, story maps, outlines, study guides, and webs to maximize comprehension, visually organize information into meaningful conceptual groupings, and foster a collaborative, interactive style of learning. Study guides for individual lessons, similar to computer derived handouts, can also be distributed to students to use in organizing notes as they read.

6. **Using manipulative materials/hands-on activities** including props, multimedia presentations, experiments, building models, and demonstrations to build background and context.

7. **Using nonverbal cues,** such as gestures, body language, and slowed pace of speech, to aid student comprehension.

8. **Using repetition and review** of concepts and vocabulary. Provide bilingual dictionaries.

9. **Group activities** including team projects, cooperative learning, and peer tutoring to promote interaction between class members. These strategies assure that students get adequate practice speaking the new language rather than teacher lecture as the only model of learning.

▶ **ESL/ELL STRATEGIES AND *BE A BETTER READER***

There are a number of specific strategies and approaches you can use to adapt *Be A Better Reader* to help ESL/ELL students gain access to the lesson structure.

1. Preview the *Be A Better Reader* lessons from the English language learner's point of view. Introduce the three ESL/ELL words for each selection, highlighted in the Annotated Teacher's Edition. Look for additional idioms or words with double meanings that should be clarified. Preteach the new vocabulary and idioms. Further clarify new vocabulary when it appears in the text to reinforce language acquisition while teaching content.

2. You may wish to have students create word books in which they collect words they don't know. Students can draw illustrations of idioms and then write their meanings below the pictures. Explain idiomatic expressions, simplify grammatical structures, and summarize/paraphrase material into shorter, simpler passages, where necessary.

3. Establish context and build background to personalize lessons by eliciting prior knowledge and experience. (See Background Information in the Student Edition. It is found on the first page of each selection lesson.)

4. When introducing content that is completely new or abstract, read complex material aloud to aid clarity. Talk about context clues in each selection. (See Context Clues in the Student Edition.) Have ELL students retell or summarize the text orally while you record on chart paper. This simplified text can become material that can be used as a language experience chart to teach basic English reading as well as to provide a summary of the content.

5. Use leveled questions to engage English language learners at the various levels of English proficiency in the class. In *Be A Better Reader*, the series of Comprehension questions may prove less challenging than the Critical Thinking questions.

6. Teach students key study skills and the use of textbook aids, such as visuals and graphics, which are found in *Be A Better Reader*. You can also designate one of your more fluent English students each week to be the class scribe. Course notes can then be photocopied for less proficient English language learners so they can devote complete attention to listening to and comprehending the lesson.

7. Use the ESL/ELL strategy found on the teacher support page of every *Be A Better Reader* lesson.

Elizabeth Jimenez
CEO, GEMAS Consulting
Trainer, Los Angeles County Office of Education
California Association for Bilingual Education

"WHAT THE RESEARCH SAYS"

Research has taught us that writing improves reading comprehension, and we have discovered that writing enhances learning in every academic discipline.

Dr. Marion Davies Toth
World of Language, 1990

Understanding and using the writing process allows virtually every student to write more fluently and effectively. This process consists of five steps. The following paragraphs review these steps and provide helpful suggestions for how students can benefit from them.

Step 1: Prewriting The novelist Ernest Hemingway once wrote, "My working habits are simple: long periods of thinking, short periods of writing." His remark speaks to the importance of prewriting—all the thinking and planning should occur before students begin a first draft.

During prewriting, students brainstorm, choose, and narrow a topic. They also decide how they will develop the topic, organizing their ideas and details into a logical outline or plan. Class discussions and brainstorming sessions are excellent sources of prewriting ideas. For today's students, graphic organizers, such as those provided on pages T55–T64, are an invaluable prewriting aid.

Step 2: Drafting During the drafting stage of the writing process, students rely on the prewriting work they have done as a source of ideas and details. They decide whether they have a workable subject or whether they need to go back and rethink their ideas.

The goal during drafting is to get the best ideas down on paper without worrying too much about phrasing, spelling, grammar, usage, and mechanics of writing. While drafting, students move logically from one thought to the next, using their prewriting notes as a guide but departing from them when necessary. Students need to stop frequently and read over their drafts to get ideas about how to move logically from one idea to the next. They need to be aware that there will be time later to add or delete ideas as necessary.

Step 3: Revising Revising means "seeing again," and this step of the writing process requires students to take a new look at a written draft and find ways to make it better. Many writers put away their first drafts for a while before revising. In this way, they have a fresh outlook and can more easily see what needs to be improved.

During revision, students check primarily for unity and coherence. If a piece of writing is unified, readers will not be distracted by paragraphs or sentences that stray from the main idea. If the writing has coherence, readers can take in the ideas with smooth progressions. In order to revise for unity and coherence, students may need to add some ideas and details and eliminate or rephrase others. They may also need to add transition words and phrases, such as *next, later on,* and *in the end,* so that the sentences and paragraphs flow.

Step 4: Proofreading Proofreading is the careful rereading of a revised draft to correct mistakes in spelling, grammar, usage, and mechanics. Students should be aware that proofreading will eliminate mistakes that might distract their readers or lessen the overall effectiveness of what they have written.

To proofread, students carefully read each word. They may benefit by focusing on one line at a time, using a sheet of paper to cover adjacent lines. Peer proofreading—exchanging drafts with partners—is an effective way to find errors. When students are unsure about corrections, encourage them to use a dictionary or a grammar and usage handbook. You might have students create a proofreading checklist that lists the typical errors that writers make.

Step 5: Publishing Publishing is the final step of the writing process. When a student publishes work, he or she presents it in neat, corrected final form to an audience. Oftentimes, the intended audience is the teacher. At other times, it may be classmates or other members of the school community. Studies show, however, that writings reaching new or varied authentic audiences, such as letters to an editor, are often a powerful stimulus for students to improve their writing.

Encourage students to explore new ways to publish their writing. Display work on bulletin boards and in folders in the library. Impromptu sessions in which students read aloud their work to small groups is another valuable publishing outlet. Suggest that students submit their writing to the school newspaper or literary magazine, or help them prepare writing for essay contests.

▶ THE RECURSIVE NATURE OF WRITING

Help students understand that writing is a recursive, not a lockstep, process. The five-step writing process is a valuable guide to better writing skills. All writers spend some time preparing to write, writing, revising, proofreading, and sharing their work. However, writers do not compose in exactly the same way.

Encourage students to write recursively; at any step of the writing process, students can return to an earlier step. (See page T33.) Some students might pause in revision, for example, and return to prewriting to gather more information. Other students might stop during proofreading to take more time for further revision. One of the best features of the writing process is that it allows students to use new ideas while they are creating and improving their work.

▶ THE WRITING PROCESS AND EVALUATION

Many students have difficulty suiting their writing to a purpose, clarifying a main idea, elaborating a composition with adequate details, or organizing details in logical order. Self-evaluation or peer evaluation that occurs midway through the writing process can address these and other stumbling blocks to effective communication.

After students have written their first drafts, suggest that they use a checklist, such as that shown below, to identify possible problems in their work.

- ❏ Is the subject interesting? Does it address the writing task?
- ❏ Is the main idea clearly stated?
- ❏ Is the main idea supported by adequate details?
- ❏ Are the details logically organized?

Many students find it helpful to work in pairs to evaluate each other's draft. One student can read his or her draft aloud while the other listens. In this way, both listener and writer can hear how the piece sounds and can detect areas in which revisions are needed.

▶ WRITING AND *BE A BETTER READER*

Writing is an essential part of *Be A Better Reader*. The Reading-Writing Connection activities that follow the four core lessons in every unit are a treasury of writing ideas designed to help students become better writers and more thoughtful readers. These activities deepen the students' understanding of the processes of reading by requiring them to return to the text and look more closely at its structure.

The writing tasks in *Be A Better Reader* are also springboards to self-expression. Reading aloud and discussing their writing will lead to animated classroom discussions and a general exchange of ideas that will enable students to better express their views on a wide range of topics.

Finally, the Reading-Writing Connection activities show that writing, when closely linked with reading, can become a powerful road to learning. To this end, the writing tasks often require students to activate prior knowledge, summarize and extend their understanding of the text, or offer a personal response.

Name _____   **Date** _____   **T33**

STEPS OF THE WRITING PROCESS

Check each step in the Writing Process as you complete it. Remember that you can go back to a previous step if you need to.

PREWRITING
❑ Understand the assignment.
❑ Choose a topic.
❑ Focus the topic.
❑ Gather supporting details.
❑ Organize details in an outline.

DRAFTING
❑ Write the topic sentence.
❑ Write the body.
❑ Write the conclusion.

REVISING
❑ Improve your draft.
  ▶ Answer the assignment.
  ▶ Use transitional words.
❑ Check your draft.
  ▶ Does the topic sentence contain the main idea?
  ▶ Are the supporting details organized clearly?

EDITING
❑ Find and correct errors in:
  ▶ Spelling
  ▶ Punctuation
  ▶ Capitalization
  ▶ Subject-verb agreement

PUBLISHING
❑ Share your work with others.
  ▶ Read your work to an audience.
  ▶ Display your work on a bulletin board.
  ▶ Make a class book.

"WHAT THE RESEARCH SAYS"

Testwiseness is not a substitute for knowledge of the subject matter. However, skill in taking tests can help you show what you know when it is critical to do so.

Dr. Donald L. Fields
Introductory Psychology Internet Courses at UNB

▶ TWO TYPES OF TESTS

Nonstandardized tests, often designed by teachers, measure a student's periodic progress in a particular subject. They provide information to both teacher and student as to whether the student is keeping up with the class, needs extra help, or is ahead of other students. To the extent that teacher-made tests assess the learning objectives determined at the outset of the learning period and the material taught, they are precise tools. The results of these tests are often the basis for report-card grades.

Standardized tests, by contrast, use certain measurable standards to assess student performance across an entire district, city, or state. Students take the same test according to the same rules, making it possible to measure each student's performance against that of the larger population. The group with whom a student's performance is compared is a "norm group" consisting of many students of the same age or grade.

▶ POLICIES AND PRACTICE

Students will benefit by knowing your policies for "teacher-made" tests as well as the school's policies and practices for standardized tests and the use of test scores. Early in the school year, review with students the kinds of tests they will be taking during the year and the schedule for standardized tests. Ongoing practice in taking standardized tests will also help students perform better by becoming familiar with test directions and formats.

▶ AVOIDING TEST ANXIETY

A technique for reducing test anxiety is to discuss test-taking strategies. (See page T35.) Regular reinforcement of such strategies helps students approach tests in a more relaxed manner. Also remind students to space their studying over days or weeks in order to learn the material well. Point out that cramming before a test might interfere with clear thinking. Encourage a good night's sleep before the test and an early arrival at class the next day.

▶ AFTER THE TEST

Students need to review their test results as soon as practically possible. This is especially true for teacher-made tests. A graded exam paper shows students not only where they had difficulty, but why. Take time to discuss incorrect answers with your students and find out why they answered as they did. Explore situations in which students misunderstood the wording of a question or misinterpreted what was asked. Make sure students understand any comments made on their test papers, especially in responses to essay-type answers. Have students use a checklist such as that shown below to evaluate their test performance.

❑ Did I use my time during the test well?

❑ What was asked that I didn't expect?

❑ What part of the test was most difficult for me? Why?

❑ What should I do differently in preparing for the next test?

▶ TEST-TAKING STRATEGIES

The assessment component of *Be A Better Reader* provides a wide variety of testing opportunities. Placement tests in the *Diagnostic and Placement Guide* determine the ideal level of the program at which each student should work. Four Assessment Tests included with each level of the Annotated Teacher's Edition assess students' progress during the year and evaluate how well they can apply particular skills. These tests can be used as pretests and/or posttests, depending on students' needs and your classroom management style. In addition to the program's formal tests, Comprehension, Critical Thinking, and Skill Focus questions appear at the end of each core lesson. These provide practice in such test formats as multiple-choice, fill-in, and matching. There are also a number of short and longer essay-type questions—all valuable preparation for standardized tests.

Name _____ Date _____

20 WAYS TO BOOST YOUR TEST PERFORMANCE

Check the tips that work best for you as you study for a test and take it.

As You Study

❏ 1. Make a list of the test topics you need to review.

❏ 2. Write a list of questions you think will be asked on the test. Then answer them.

❏ 3. Turn the titles of sections you are studying into questions. Look for the answers as you review.

❏ 4. Make flashcards for studying key words and phrases. Write a word or phrase on one side and the definition on the other.

❏ 5. Make an outline for the materials you need to study.

❏ 6. Look for key words in a chapter you are studying. Be sure you know what they mean. Use a dictionary to find words you do not understand.

❏ 7. Write important vocabulary words you are studying in sentences.

❏ 8. Look back at the photos, charts, and maps. Reread the captions to remember ideas about the topic.

❏ 9. List the main ideas of the subjects you are studying.

❏ 10. Be sure you know how to spell the names of people and events in the chapter. Practice writing each of them several times.

❏ 11. When you are looking for details in the text, look through the material quickly. Look for names, dates, and facts that will help you answer questions.

❏ 12. Try studying with a friend. Ask one another questions from your textbook.

Taking the Test

❏ 13. Before you begin the test, look it over. Decide how much time you can spend on each question.

❏ 14. Read the test directions carefully. Underline or circle the important words in the questions.

❏ 15. Focus on one question at a time.

❏ 16. In a multiple-choice test, cross out answers that you know are not correct.

❏ 17. In an essay test, reread what you wrote to be sure you answered the question.

❏ 18. Try to check all your answers before handing in your test paper.

❏ 19. Skip questions that you are unsure of. Then go back after you have answered the rest of the questions.

❏ 20. Keep a positive attitude. Decide to do your best and focus on the material you know.

**Read the following selection. Then choose the best answer for each question.
Mark your answers on the answer sheet.**

O Mighty Sea

1. The research submarine *Alvin* sank beneath the sunlit surface of the Caribbean Sea. On the surface, the sub had pitched and rolled. But now the sub was sinking peacefully through the fading sunlight.

2. I glanced around the sphere, the sub's interior, and then looked at Jim, the pilot. "This is like being inside a Swiss watch," I said.

3. He grinned. "You'll get used to it, Anne," he said.

4. The sphere was only 80 inches in diameter. In this very tight space, the three of us—Jim, Ted, and I—would have to work for the next six hours. Each of us had specific assignments to do. Luckily, our tasks didn't require movement within the sphere.

5. A voice startled me. It was Emory Kirshen, the surface controller onboard the ship *Jasper*.

6. "*Alvin,* this is *Jasper,*" Kirshen said. "What are your readings?"

7. Jim looked at the depth meter. "We're nearing 1,200 feet," he said, "and we're descending at 90 feet a minute."

8. As we continued our descent, the *Alvin*'s interior became darker and darker. Soon we were in total darkness. To save power, the sub's outside lights were kept off. Our only illumination came from three small lights inside the sphere.

9. Hanging over Jim's instrument panel was a small, silver medallion. I looked more closely at it. There were words engraved on the medallion: "Be kind to us, O mighty Sea."

10. I smiled to myself. The sea is neither kind nor cruel, I thought. It's only a force of nature, which is being conquered by technology.

11. I looked over at Ted. Like me, he was a geologist. He had made dives before in the *Alvin*; this was my first dive. Our mission was to bring up photographs and rock samples from the seabed.

12. I glanced at the depth meter. The sub was nearing 8,000 feet. We were within 200 feet of the bottom. Jim turned on the sub's outside lights and cameras.

13. Outside my view port, time seemed to stand still. Fish glided by in the unusual brightness. I felt relaxed in the quiet undersea world.

14. "We're 40 feet from the bottom." Jim reported to Emory. "We have visual." A moment later, we touched bottom. "*Jasper,* we've landed. We will begin sampling at Station One. We'll call back when we've finished. Over."

15. "Roger, *Alvin*. Good luck," came Emory's voice.

16. Through my view port, I could make out the seabed, a rough terrain of deep cracks and giant boulders.

17. "It's time to begin," I said to Ted. "Let's try to get a rock sample every 100 feet."

18. Jim began to operate the sub's mechanical claw. Technology had certainly made our work easier. All Jim had to do was guide the mechanical claw, and we could collect a number of rock samples without ever getting wet.

19. After about 20 minutes of work, we had picked up five rock samples. The sub's claw dropped each sample into a numbered section of a tray mounted at the front of the sub.

20. We continued cruising about 6 feet above the bottom. While Jim was busy collecting rock samples, Ted and I recorded our observations on a small tape recorder. Mounted outside the sub were two cameras that automatically took pictures of the seafloor every 10 seconds. Through his view port, Jim took more photos with a hand-held camera.

21. As we cruised along the seafloor, we spotted a broad crack across a lava flow. Jim brought the sub down into the wide fissure.

22. "Let's sample the lava while we're here," Ted said.

23. For the next 10 minutes, we collected volcanic rock samples. Then we started to rise out of the fissure. The sub shuddered to a standstill.

24. "What's wrong?" asked Ted.

25. "We've gone too far into the fissure. I think the walls are holding us in," Jim said. "I'll have to back it out."

26. Jim put the sub into reverse. It shuddered and held fast.

27. "Hang on. I'll just jockey it back and forth a bit," said Jim.

28. The sub careened forward, then pitched back. "Come on," Jim said softly. Slowly, he edged the sub forward, then back.

29. "It's getting free," Jim said. He looked at me and grinned. "It's like trying to back a large car out of a parking space for a compact."

30. The sub edged back out of the fissure. "That's it," Jim said. The *Alvin* shuddered. "Just a little more and—"

31. Suddenly, an ear-splitting roar cut through the sphere. The interior lights went out. Something hit my hand. Then it was deadly still.

32. I clicked on the emergency power switch. The sphere remained in darkness.

33. "Jim! Ted!" I called.

34. "Anne." It was Ted.

35. "Are you all right, Ted?"

36. "I'm bleeding—forehead. Where's Jim?"

37. "I don't know." I groped around in the dark. Jim was slumped over his instrument panel. I felt his pulse. "Jim's unconscious," I said, "but his pulse is all right." I found an emergency flashlight, then reached for the first-aid kit. "What happened, Ted?"

38. "I'm not sure. A boulder must have shaken loose above us and slammed into the sub."

39. As I placed a bandage on Ted's forehead, I saw that my left hand was bruised. Ted's face was streaked with blood. It was getting difficult to breathe. The boulder, or whatever had slammed into the *Alvin*, had damaged the life-support and emergency-breathing systems. We had also lost phone contact with the surface ship.

40. For a moment, fear took hold of me. What if the sub wouldn't rise? What if the ballast release had also been damaged?

41. I reached for the release lever with my uninjured hand and pulled it. Usually the sub would edge up as the steel ballast dropped from the *Alvin*. I waited. The sub remained motionless. The ballast had not dropped from the sub. I bit my lip, then pulled the lever again.

42. Suddenly, the sub lifted. We were drifting up!

43. The ascent was like a dream. I must have blacked out as the sub went up.

44. The pitching and rolling of the sub brought me to. Water slid off the view port. I could see the *Jasper* resting on the sunlit surface.

45. I turned away from the view port. Above the instrument panel, the silver medallion swayed from side to side. Sunlight struck the medallion, making it glow.

1. The main character's conflict is with
   a. himself or herself.
   b. another character.
   c. an outside force.
   d. all of the above.

2. Which sentence best describes this conflict?
   a. The main character is afraid that the sub will be unable to rise from the seafloor.
   b. The main character thinks that he or she can solve any problem.
   c. The main character tries to revive Jim.
   d. The main character cannot swim.

3. The main character faces this conflict when the sub
   a. rises.
   b. reaches the seafloor.
   c. begins its dive.
   d. is trapped.

4. How is the conflict resolved?
   a. Ted releases the ballast, and the sub rises to the surface.
   b. Anne pulls the release lever, the ballast drops, and the sub rises.
   c. Jim takes over command of the *Alvin* and manages to save the sub.
   d. The boulder falls off of the *Alvin*.

5. The first important event that leads to the climax occurs when
   a. the sub enters the fissure.
   b. the sub begins its descent.
   c. the sub reaches the seafloor.
   d. Anne sees the medallion.

6. Which event causes Anne to become involved in resolving the conflict?
   a. The *Jasper* orders the sub crew to surface.
   b. Ted and Jim are both injured.
   c. Ted is on the phone, and Jim is unconcious.
   d. The sub develops a power failure.

7. The most exciting part of the story occurs when
   a. Anne tries to release the ballast.
   b. the sub enters the fissure.
   c. Jim jockeys the sub out of the fissure.
   d. the *Jasper* begins to sink.

8. The story ends with
   a. the *Jasper* sending a rescue team.
   b. Jim regaining consciousness.
   c. the *Alvin* reaching the surface.
   d. Anne vowing to never dive again.

9. When does the story take place?
   a. in the present
   b. about 50 years ago
   c. about 100 years ago
   d. in the future

10. Where does the main action of the story take place?
    a. on the surface ship
    b. on the Caribbean Sea
    c. in the interior of a sub
    d. in a spaceship

11. What is Anne's first reaction to the setting?
    a. She thinks the sub is too small.
    b. She is confused by all the instruments.
    c. She enjoys looking out the view port.
    d. She is scared by the sea.

12. What unusual feature in this setting does Anne notice?
    a. the steel ballast
    b. the silver medallion
    c. the mechanical claw
    d. the view port

13. What is the author's main message?
    a. Geologists should only look for rocks above sea level.
    b. During undersea explorations, one must always watch for sharks.
    c. Working in a research submarine can be a rewarding experience.
    d. Despite technology, the sea is still a mysterious and dangerous force.

14. At the beginning of the story, Anne is
    a. amused by the silver medallion.
    b. upset about the silver medallion.
    c. impressed by the silver medallion.
    d. proud of her silver medallion.

15. By the end of the story, Anne has learned to
    a. get along well with others.
    b. respect the sea.
    c. handle a research submarine.
    d. read a depth meter.

16. Which of the following titles would also be appropriate for this story?
    a. "The *Alvin* Dives"
    b. "Dangers of the Caribbean Sea"
    c. "The Still Unconquered Sea"
    d. "*Jasper* Saves the Day"

17. What is the unstated main idea of paragraph 4?
    a. The sub's sphere was small.
    b. The sub had a three-person crew.
    c. Jim and Ted don't get along.
    d. The sub's working space was cramped.

18. What is the unstated main idea of paragraph 20?
    a. The sub cruised along the seafloor.
    b. As the *Alvin* cruised, the sub and crew recorded data.
    c. Cameras were an important part of the mission.
    d. Jim is a good photographer.

19. What is the unstated main idea of the last paragraph in the selection?
    a. The *Alvin* had successfully returned to the surface.
    b. The sea had spared them.
    c. Anne was happy to be alive.
    d. Silver reflects light.

20. Who is the narrator of the story?
    a. Jim
    b. Ted
    c. Anne
    d. Alvin

21. Why is first-person point of view a good way of telling this story?
    a. The narrator takes part in the story's events.
    b. The narrator reports only the facts and not his or her feelings.
    c. The narrator tells what each character thinks and feels about the event.
    d. The narrator hears about the story from someone who was there.

22. A disadvantage of this point of view is that the narrator cannot
    a. describe his or her feelings.
    b. know what really happened.
    c. make judgments about the story's events.
    d. enter the minds of the other characters.

23. Which of these events did the narrator not witness?
    a. Jim taking photos through the view port
    b. the reaction of the crew on board the *Jasper* when the *Alvin* surfaced
    c. The *Alvin* getting stuck in the fissure
    d. the mechanical claw gathering rock samples

24. Choose the correct definition of the word *port* as it is used in paragraph 13.
    a. place where boats can anchor
    b. the left side of a ship
    c. shortened form of porthole
    d. an electrical outlet

25. The word *illumination* in paragraph 8 means
    a. "light inside a sub."
    b. "to decorate with lights."
    c. "darkness."
    d. "supply of light."

26. The word *fissure* in paragraph 21 means
    a. "lava."
    b. "crack."
    c. "cliff."
    d. "seafloor."

Read the following selection. Then choose the best answer for each question.
Mark your answers on the answer sheet.

The Panama Canal

1. Until this century, there was only one way for a ship traveling east to reach the Atlantic Ocean from the Pacific Ocean. That was the long route around Cape Horn, the southernmost tip of South America. Ship crews and passengers dreaded "rounding the Horn." The currents of the Atlantic and Pacific Oceans meet at Cape Horn, causing sudden, terrible storms. In addition, thick fogs often blanket the area, and dangerous reefs lie just below the water's surface. Many ships sailing around Cape Horn have been wrecked on the reefs or have sunk in the storms.

2. Because the route around Cape Horn was long and dangerous, a shortcut—a passage between the two oceans—was needed. The best location for such a shortcut had been known for years. In 1502, Christopher Columbus was told by natives of Central America about a "narrow land between two seas." Columbus found this narrow land, the Isthmus of Panama, but he did not explore it. In 1513, the isthmus was crossed by Vasco Núñez de Balboa (bal BOH ə), a Spanish explorer. Balboa was the first European to see the Pacific Ocean from the Americas.

The First Attempt

3. Many years passed before an attempt was made to build a canal across the Isthmus of Panama. In the 1860s, France built the Suez Canal to link the Mediterranean and Red Seas. French government leaders decided to follow this achievement with another engineering feat—the building of the Panama Canal. The job was entrusted to Ferdinand de Lesseps (de LES əps). He was given responsibility for the project because his company had built the Suez Canal.

4. De Lesseps and his workers soon learned that building a canal in Panama was much more difficult than at Suez. The Suez Canal had been dug through flat, desert sands. In contrast, Panama had steep mountains, thick jungles, and wild rivers. Worse still, Panama was one of the most disease-ridden parts of the world. Workers soon began to die from yellow fever and malaria. Digging progressed slowly, interrupted by landslides that destroyed months of backbreaking work. Huge sums of money were spent on the project. Finally, in 1889, the company ran out of money, and the French had to give up the effort. They left behind tons of earth-moving equipment, miles of shallow ditches, and cemeteries where thousands of workers lay buried.

The United States Enters the Picture

5. For many years, the United States had expressed interest in building a canal across the Isthmus of Panama, but it was not until the Spanish-American War in 1898 that Americans became convinced of the need for a canal. During the war, the battleship *Oregon,* sailing in the Pacific, was ordered to join the American fleet in the Atlantic Ocean. It took the *Oregon* three months to reach the fighting in Cuba. The battleship had to sail around South America, a trip of nearly 13,000 miles (20,800 kilometers). If there had been a canal across Panama, the trip would have been about 4,500 miles (7,200 kilometers).

6. Determined to build a canal across the isthmus, the U.S. government began negotiations with Colombia to buy land for the canal. The talks broke down, however, when the Colombian government refused to accept the price offered and asked for more money. An angry President Theodore Roosevelt decided to arrange terms with Panama instead.

7. Panama was part of Colombia, but for years it had tried to become independent. On November 2, 1903, the U. S. Navy ship *Nashville* sailed into the port of Colón in Panama. The next day, Panamanians

revolted, and U.S. marines blocked the advance of Colombian troops. Panama declared its freedom from Colombia. Two weeks later, Panama and the United States signed a treaty granting the United States a 10-mile-wide canal zone across Panama.

Panama Canal

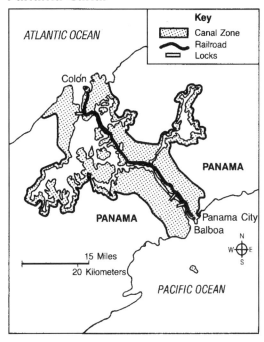

Digging the Big Ditch

8. When the French had tried to build a canal 20 years before, the causes of malaria and yellow fever were still a mystery. Now the cause of both diseases was known. Under the direction of William C. Gorgas of the U.S. Army Medical Corps, plans were carried out to destroy certain kinds of mosquitoes that caused malaria and yellow fever. Ditches were sprayed with oil. Swamps were drained. Catch basins used for drinking water were removed. Fresh water was piped through the canal zone. In just a few years, yellow fever was wiped out, and malaria was greatly reduced. Panama was no longer the "pesthole of the world."

9. The Panama Canal was a tremendous achievement, and problems in building the canal were likewise tremendous. A huge dam, one of the largest in the world, had to be built across the wild Chagres River. A deep cut 9 miles (14.4 kilometers) long had to be made through a range of mountains. Workers were plagued by hundreds of landslides; many were

killed by the slides. Because the Pacific Ocean is a higher body of water than the Atlantic Ocean, locks had to be built. These water-filled chambers with gates at either end were needed to raise and lower ships from one water level to another.

10. In charge of building the canal was Colonel George W. Goethals (goh thəlz), an army engineer. His labor force—totaling 43,400 workers—came from many parts of the world, including the United States, the West Indies, Italy, and Spain. To carry the earth and rocks away, they used 105 steam shovels, 161 locomotives, and 1,700 railroad cars. After seven years of work, the Panama Canal was completed in 1914. At a cost of thousands of lives and $400 million, the shortcut between the Atlantic and Pacific Oceans was finally achieved.

27. Choose the main idea of paragraph 2.
- **a.** Because the route around Cape Horn was long and dangerous, a shortcut—a passage between the two oceans—was needed.
- **b.** The best location for such a shortcut had been known for years.
- **c.** Balboa was the first European to see the Pacific Ocean from the Americas.
- **d.** Columbus had discovered the Americas.

28. Choose the main idea of paragraph 4.
- **a.** They left behind tons of earth-moving equipment, shallow ditches, and cemeteries where thousands of workers lay buried.
- **b.** Digging progressed slowly, interrupted by landslides that destroyed months of backbreaking work.
- **c.** Finally, the company ran out of money, and the French had to give up the effort.
- **d.** De Lesseps and his workers soon learned that building a canal in Panama was much more difficult than at Suez.

29. What is the unstated main idea of paragraph 1?
- **a.** Before this century, ships weren't reliable.
- **b.** People enjoyed sailing around Cape Horn.
- **c.** Many ships never returned from trips around South America.
- **d.** The route around Cape Horn was long and very dangerous.

30. Choose the main idea of paragraph 9.
    a. A deep cut 9 miles (14.4 kilometers) long had to be made through a range of mountains.
    b. The Panama Canal was a tremendous achievement, and the problems in building the canal were likewise tremendous.
    c. Because the Pacific Ocean is a higher body of water than the Atlantic Ocean, locks had to be built.
    d. These water-filled chambers with gates at either end were needed to raise and lower ships from one water level to another.

31. What is the unstated main idea of paragraph 3?
    a. France was a great engineering country.
    b. France built a canal across Panama.
    c. France was the first nation to attempt building the Panama Canal.
    d. France failed at building the Suez Canal.

32. What is the unstated main idea of paragraph 10?
    a. Building the Panama Canal was hard work.
    b. The dream of Columbus had come true.
    c. In both lives and dollars, the cost of building the Panama Canal was high.
    d. Colonel Goethals built the canal.

33. The main idea of paragraph 5 is that Americans became convinced of the need for a canal during the Spanish-American War. Which detail supports this main idea?
    a. The *Oregon* was ordered to reinforce the American fleet in the Atlantic Ocean.
    b. It took the *Oregon* three months to reach the fighting in Cuba.
    c. The United States had long been interested in building a canal in Panama.
    d. America won the Spanish-American War.

34. The main idea of paragraph 8 is that William Gorgas made building the canal safer. Which detail supports this main idea?
    a. Fresh water was piped through the canal zone.
    b. The causes of both malaria and yellow fever were still unknown.
    c. Panama was the "pesthole of the world."
    d. Digging the "big ditch" was hard work.

35. In Panama's revolt against Colombia, the United States played
    a. a minor role.   c. no role.
    b. an important role.   d. on Colombia's side.

36. Because certain kinds of mosquitoes were destroyed, Panama
    a. became a healthier place to live and work.
    b. was free of all mosquitoes.
    c. had fresh drinking water for all its people.
    d. lost a number of birds that relied on the mosquitoes for food.

37. The Panama Canal needs locks because
    a. there are few police officers in the area.
    b. ships need different water levels.
    c. the Colombian troops had to be blocked.
    d. the Pacific Ocean is a higher body of water than the Atlantic Ocean.

38. In contrast to the Suez Canal, the Panama Canal had to be dug
    a. with fewer people and equipment.
    b. through mountains, jungles, and rivers.
    c. through flat, desert sands.
    d. before the Spanish-American War ended.

39. Unlike the French who had worked on the canal, the Americans
    a. spent huge sums of money.
    b. could not finish the canal.
    c. used thousands of workers.
    d. knew what caused yellow fever and malaria.

40. In both the French and American efforts to build the canal, workers were
    a. plagued by landslides.
    b. without fresh, running water.
    c. subjected to cruel treatment.
    d. supervised by Colonel Goethals.

41. The French thought they would be able to build the Panama Canal because
    a. the French had built the Suez Canal.
    b. France was a rich nation.
    c. the French were determined to build the Panama Canal.
    d. Colombian people were counting on them.

42. "Panama was one of the most disease-ridden areas in the world." This statement is
   a. a fact.
   c. both of these.
   b. an opinion.
   d. none of these.

43. In contrast to the French, the Americans had a better chance of building the canal because
   a. the Americans were better builders.
   b. the Americans knew the causes of malaria and yellow fever.
   c. the French ran out of money.
   d. Colombia supported America.

44. The reason the French gave up their effort to build the canal was that
   a. too many workers died.
   b. they ran out of money.
   c. the problems were too difficult.
   d. Colombia took the land.

45. Other European countries were probably not as interested in building a canal connecting the Atlantic and Pacific Oceans as France because
   a. they had neither enough money nor workers.
   b. they were not interested in trade.
   c. they liked traveling around Cape Horn.
   d. they had no experience building canals.

46. The United States helped Panama revolt against Colombia because
   a. the United States believed in the cause.
   b. Colombia waged war on America.
   c. Colombia let Panama have full control of the Isthmus of Panama.
   d. Panama agreed to give the United States the land in exchange for their help.

47. Ditches were sprayed with oil, and swamps were drained because
   a. they were in the way of the canal.
   b. workers often stumbled into them.
   c. mosquitoes bred in them.
   d. it kept Colombian troops out of Panama.

48. Choose the correct definition of the word *catch* as it is used in paragraph 8.
   a. that which holds
   c. to grasp or seize
   b. act of catching
   d. a trick

49. Choose the correct definition of the word *plagued* as it is used in paragraph 9.
   a. excited
   c. diseased
   b. infested
   d. troubled

50. The word *entrusted* in paragraph 3 means
   a. "taken away."
   b. "not trusted."
   c. "given responsibility for."
   d. "a job assigned."

51. The word *negotiations* in paragraph 6 means
   a. "arguments."
   c. "planning."
   b. "talks."
   d. "wars."

52. The word *locks* in paragraph 9 means
   a. "closes tightly."
   b. "mechanical devices."
   c. "water-filled chambers."
   d. "parts of a firearm."

Use the map on page T41 to answer questions 53–56.

53. In which direction does the canal go across Panama?
   a. from the northwest to southeast
   b. from the northeast to southwest
   c. from the southwest to northeast
   d. from the north to the south

54. Coming into the canal from the Atlantic side, a ship passes the city of
   a. Balboa.
   c. Colón.
   b. Panama City.
   d. Panama.

55. How many locks does the canal have?
   a. 2
   c. 4
   b. 3
   d. 5

56. What is the approximate length of the Panama Canal?
   a. 30 kilometers
   c. 90 kilometers
   b. 60 kilometers
   d. 120 kilometers

Read the following selection. Then choose the best answer for each question. Mark your answers on the answer sheet.

Another Energy Source for Life

1. For many years, scientists believed that sunlight was the main source of energy for life. Now scientists know that deep in the ocean there is life that uses heat from Earth, rather than the Sun, for energy. This major discovery was made while scientists were exploring the Midocean Ridge.

The Midocean Ridge

2. The longest mountain range in the world is at the bottom of the sea. Called the Midocean Ridge, it curves around Earth like the seam of a baseball. The Midocean Ridge extends for 60,000 kilometers (37,000 miles).

3. The Midocean Ridge has been mapped by a system called sonar (SOH nar), which stands for <u>so</u>und <u>n</u>avigation <u>a</u>nd <u>r</u>anging. A sound wave, or signal, is sent from a ship. When the sound wave hits an undersea object, it is reflected back. The distance to the object is determined by how long it takes the signal to make the round trip.

4. Although scientists have been able to map the entire length of the Midocean Ridge, they have actually seen only a very small part of it. Descending in tiny submarines, scientists have seen only 64 kilometers (40 miles) of the ridge. Yet, it was along those few kilometers that scientists discovered animals unlike any they had seen before.

Warm-Water Vents

5. Earth's crust is made up of major sections, called plates. The plates move apart a few centimeters each year, forming valleys, called rifts, that run along the whole Midocean Ridge. While studying rifts in the Pacific Ocean, scientists saw fountains of black material billowing from the ocean floor like smoke coming from a chimney. These were warm-water vents.

Strange Creatures

6. Along the rifts, seawater seeps down through porous rocks, becomes heated, and comes up through the vents. The vent water registers up to 13°C (55°F) which is much warmer than the usual deep-sea chill of 2°C (35°F). Yet, heat is not the main reason that a multitude of animals gather at these hot springs. As the water rises to the ocean floor, it brings up minerals from inside Earth. The minerals set off a chemical change in bacteria that causes them to multiply rapidly. The great numbers of bacteria nourish larger forms of life. Animals gather at the vents because of the large food supply available there.

7. Many of the animals living near the vents are strange in appearance. Among the strangest are giant worms, some of them are 36 centimeters

Sonar

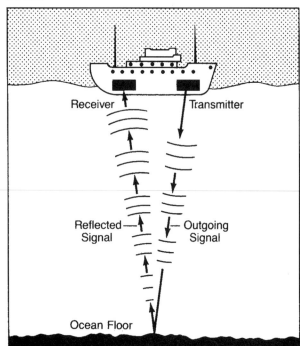

Receiver   Transmitter

Reflected Signal   Outgoing Signal

Ocean Floor

Sound waves are used to map the ocean floor and locate undersea objects.

(14 inches) long. The worm is surrounded at one end by a forest of white, tubelike projections. The worm's bright-red color is caused by a red blood pigment called hemoglobin (HEE mə GLOH bin).

8. The worm is strange in yet another way. It has no eyes, mouth, or stomach. Food and oxygen from the water are absorbed through its more than 300,000 tiny tentacles. Blood carries this nourishment throughout the worm's body.

9. Another strange animal found near the vents belongs to the jellyfish family. Using a threadlike stem, the creature fastens itself to rocks. Attached to the stem is a gas-filled bag that allows the animal to float. Around the bag are hundreds of petal-like projections that have different tasks—some capture food, others ingest it, and still others carry on reproduction.

10. Giant, smooth-shelled clams are also found living near the vents. The clams are about 30 centimeters (12 inches) long. Unlike most clams, which are gray in color, the fleshy inside of these clams is red. The color is caused by hemoglobin.

11. Crabs also live near the vents. Although they look like crabs found in shallow water, vent crabs are blind. They belong to a crustacean (krus TAY shən) family not known before. In addition, new species of barnacles (BAR nə klz), leeches, and mussels live near the vents.

12. The food chain for animals living near the vents is based on energy from inside Earth, rather than energy from the Sun. In the total darkness of the deep sea, 2.5 kilometers (1.5 miles) below the surface, another source of energy for life has been found.

57. Choose the main idea of paragraph 2.
   a. The longest mountain range in the world is at the bottom of the sea.
   b. Called the Midocean Ridge, it curves around Earth like the seam of a baseball.
   c. The Midocean Ridge extends for 60,000 kilometers.
   d. For many years, scientists believed that sunlight was the main source of energy for life.

58. Choose the main idea of paragraph 6.
   a. The great numbers of bacteria nourish larger forms of life.
   b. The minerals set off a chemical change in bacteria that causes them to multiply rapidly.
   c. Animals gather at the vents because of the large food supply available there.
   d. As the water rises to the ocean floor, it brings up minerals from inside Earth.

59. The main idea of paragraph 8 is that the worm is strange in yet another way. Which detail best supports this main idea?
   a. The worm has more than 300,000 tentacles.
   b. It has no eyes, mouth, or stomach.
   c. Blood carries nourishment throughout its body.
   d. The worm can swim.

60. Find the main idea of paragraph 10.
   a. The fleshy inside of the clam is red.
   b. The color is caused by hemoglobin.
   c. The worms are a major food source for giant clams.
   d. Giant, smooth-shelled clams are also found living near the vents.

61. When the sound wave in sonar hits an undersea object, the signal is
   a. reflected back.
   b. timed.
   c. charted on a map.
   d. absorbed into the object.

62. The giant worms are red in color because of the presence of
   a. tubelike tentacles.
   b. hot water.
   c. oxygen.
   d. hemoglobin.

63. The main reason animals gather at the vents is
   a. the higher temperature.
   b. the chemical change.
   c. the food supply.
   d. the minerals.

64. Unlike most clams, the fleshy inside of the clams found near the vents is
    a. white.
    b. red.
    c. tasty.
    d. gray.

65. In contrast to the usual temperature of deep-sea water, the temperature of vent water is
    a. lower.
    b. higher.
    c. about the same.
    d. unknown.

66. The clams in paragraph 10 could be classified as unusual clams because they
    a. are surrounded by white, tubelike projections.
    b. have no eyes, mouth, or stomach.
    c. have red, fleshy insides.
    d. descended in tiny submarines.

67. The vent crab is a new species of
    a. crustacean.
    b. barnacle.
    c. hemoglobin.
    d. vertebrate.

68. What do vent crabs and shallow-water crabs have in common?
    a. They both live in shallow water.
    b. Their meat is a bright red.
    c. They both live in cold water.
    d. They look alike.

69. In what way are crabs found near vents different from shallow-water crabs?
    a. These crabs are blind.
    b. These crabs have extra claws.
    c. These crabs are about a foot long.
    d. These crabs have no mouth or stomach.

70. In their undersea explorations, scientists
    a. purposely looked for another source of energy for life.
    b. accidentally discovered another source of energy for life.
    c. confidently expected to find another source of energy for life.
    d. failed at finding another source of energy for life.

71. In further explorations of the Midocean Ridge, scientists are likely to find
    a. more undersea animals.
    b. more ships.
    c. more sources of energy for life.
    d. more undersea volcanoes.

72. Choose the correct definition of the word *registers* as it is used in paragraph 6.
    a. keeps a record of
    b. makes an impression
    c. shows on a scale
    d. enrolls

73. Choose the correct definition of the word *multiply* as it is used in paragraph 6.
    a. grow in number
    b. spread
    c. perform multiplication
    d. in many ways

74. What is the meaning of the word *wave* in paragraph 3?
    a. crest of water
    b. section
    c. rifts
    d. signal

75. What is the meaning of the word *multitude* in paragraph 6?
    a. small number
    b. large number
    c. average number
    d. none

Use the diagram on page T44 to answer questions 76–79.

76. The two basic parts of a ship's sonar unit are the
    a. reflected signal and outgoing signal.
    b. ship and ocean floor.
    c. transmitter and receiver.
    d. sound waves and plates.

77. The outgoing signal is sent by the
    a. plane.   c. transmitter.
    b. receiver.   d. ocean floor.

78. The outgoing signal is reflected off the
    a. transmitter.   c. receiver.
    b. ocean floor.   d. ship.

79. The reflected signal is picked up by the
    a. sound waves.   c. ocean floor.
    b. transmitter.   d. receiver.

Questions 80–83 are word problems. Use the space below for your calculations.

80. The battleship *Oregon* had to sail around South America, taking 104 days to complete the trip. If there had been a canal across Panama, the trip would have been about 7,200 kilometers. Assume that the *Oregon* could travel 200 kilometers a day. How much time would the ship have saved if it had gone through the canal?
    a. 14 days
    b. 36 days
    c. 68 days
    d. Not enough information is given to solve the problem.

81. At point A, a ship sends out a sonar signal showing that the ocean depth is 9,186 meters. At point B, the signal takes 8 seconds to return. The signal travels at 1,531 meters per second. How much deeper is the ocean floor at point B than at point A?
    a. 3,062 meters
    b. 7,346 meters
    c. 12,248 meters
    d. Not enough information is given to solve the problem.

82. The average temperature of the water near the surface of the Atlantic Ocean is 27°C. The following two temperature readings are taken: 23°C and 30.5°C. Which is closer to the average?
    a. 23°C
    b. 30.5°C
    c. They are equally close to the average.
    d. Not enough information is given to solve the problem.

83. The average depth of the Atlantic Ocean is 3,926 meters, and the lowest depth is 9,219 meters. The lowest depth in the Pacific Ocean is 11,033 meters. Which ocean has a greater range between its average depth and its lowest depth?
    a. Atlantic Ocean
    b. Pacific Ocean
    c. The range of depths are equal.
    d. Not enough information is given to solve the problem.

Use the following dictionary entry to answer questions 84–88.

---

fa·vor (fā′vər) *n.* **1** a helpful and kind action [I did my sick friend the *favor* of shopping for her.] **2** liking or approval [The waiter tried to win our *favor*.] **3** a small gift or souvenir [Every guest at the party received a pen as a *favor*]. ◆*v.* **1** to like or approve of [We *favor* any plan for lower taxes] **2** to help or aid [The dark night *favored* his escape.] **3** to prefer or help in an unfair way [The umpire seemed to favor the other team.] **4** to look like [The baby *favors* her mother.] **5** to use gently so as to keep from hurting [he *favors* his injured leg.] **—in favor of, 1** supporting or approving. **2** to the advantage of. **— in one's favor,** to one's advantage.

---

84. How many noun meanings of the entry word are given?
    a. 5
    b. 2
    c. 8
    d. 3

85. How many verb meanings of the entry word are given?
    a. 3
    b. 5
    c. 2
    d. 8

86. Which of the following is the respelling of the entry word?
    a. fā′ vər
    b. —in favor of
    c. [I did my sick friend the *favor* of shopping for her.]
    d. a helpful and kind action

87. Which of the following is a verb meaning of the entry word?
    a. We *favor* any plan for lower taxes.
    b. supporting or approving
    c. a helpful and kind action
    d. to help or aid

88. The second idiom given in the entry is
    a. —liking or approval.
    b. —to the advantage of.
    c. —in one's favor.
    d. —in favor of.

Use the following index from a science book to answer questions 89–94.

Comets, 79–80
Compounds, 125–126, 131–132
Conservation
    air, 483
    fossil fuels, 477
    land, 468–470
    minerals, 473–474
    water, 480–481, 490
Continental drift
    fossils as proof of, 427, 453
    ocean-floor spreading, 404–407, 454
    plate movements, 410–411
    theory, 400–404, 405
Continents, 28–29, 185–186, 199–206
    formation of, 404, 450–452
    margins, shelves, 244–245, 249
Copper
    sources, 141, 333, 470, 471
    uses, 141–142, 470, 472
Core, of Earth, 29, 192–193

---

89. On what page(s) would you find information on water conservation?
    a. 483
    b. 480–481, 490
    c. 404–407, 454
    d. 404, 450–452

90. On how many separate pages of the book would you find information on the sources of copper?
    a. 4
    b. 141–471
    c. 2
    d. 472

91. How many subtopics are listed under the topic *Continents*?
    a. 5
    b. 4
    c. 2
    d. 28–29, 185–186, 199–206

92. If the book had information about constellations, after which topic would it be listed?
    a. Compounds
    b. Continental drift
    c. Conservation
    d. Stars

93. If the book had information about computers, before which topic would it be listed?
    a. Compounds
    b. Comets
    c. Uses
    d. Conservation

94. How many pages does the book have on the uses of copper?
    a. 4
    b. 6
    c. 8
    d. 141

95. What prefix would you add to change the meaning of *freezing* to "below freezing"?
    a. *non-*
    b. *semi-*
    c. *un-*
    d. *sub-*

96. What suffix would you add to change the meaning of *danger* to "having danger"?
    a. *-ly*
    b. *-ous*
    c. *-ity*
    d. *-ness*

97. Choose the correct way to divide the word *member* into syllables.
    a. mem ber
    b. memb er
    c. me mber
    d. me mb er

98. Choose the correct way to divide the word *margin* into syllables.
    a. mar gin
    b. marg in
    c. ma rgin
    d. m arg in

99. Which of the following shows the accent mark correctly placed?
    a. hon est ly´
    b. hon est´ ly
    c. hon´ est ly
    d. hon´ est ly´

100. Which word shows the schwa sound correctly circled?
    a. l(e)gal
    b. l(e)m on
    c. h(i)n der
    d. fo c(u)s

Assessment Tests for Level C are designed to measure students' level of achievement in each of the important comprehension and study skills that receive emphasis in all levels of *Be A Better Reader*. The tests may be used in conjunction with the tests provided in the *Diagnostic and Placement Guide* as pretests and/or posttests, depending on students' needs and your particular classroom management style. Combined with an overview of students' performance on each lesson, the tests should enable you to refine your assessment of students' performance and determine students' readiness to advance to the next level. The four tests in Level C can be administered separately or at one time, depending on the time available. Because directions are provided for each test, students should be able to take the tests independently. The skill for each test item is identified in the Answer Key below. Following the skill is the number of the lesson or lessons in Level C where that skill is treated as a Skill Focus. To simplify the scoring process, you can use the Answer Key to make a scoring mask, which when placed over the answer sheet, reveals only those items that are correct. The total score is equal to the number of correct items. Criterion scores are not specified in this book, but you can refer to the Scoring Rubric in the *Diagnostic and Placement Guide* for more information on grading.

Test 1

1. c Identifying conflict and resolution (41)
2. a Identifying conflict and resolution (41)
3. d Identifying conflict and resolution (41)
4. b Identifying conflict and resolution (41)
5. a Identifying plot (1)
6. d Identifying plot (1)
7. a Identifying plot (1)
8. c Identifying plot (1)
9. a Identifying setting (33)
10. c Identifying setting (33)
11. a Identifying setting (33)
12. b Identifying setting (33)
13. d Inferring theme (11)
14. a Inferring theme (11)
15. b Inferring theme (11)
16. c Inferring theme (11)
17. d Inferring the unstated main idea (8, 18)
18. b Inferring the unstated main idea (8, 18)
19. b Inferring the unstated main idea (8, 18)
20. c Identifying point of view (48)
21. a Identifying point of view (48)
22. d Identifying point of view (48)
23. b Identifying point of view (48)
24. c Recognizing multiple meanings of words (45)
25. d Using detail context clues (2, 12, 34)
26. b Using synonym context clues (3, 22)

Test 2

27. a Identifying the main idea (8, 18, 27)
28. d Identifying the main idea (8, 18, 27)
29. d Inferring the unstated main idea (8, 18)
30. b Identifying the main idea (8, 18, 27)
31. c Inferring the unstated main idea (8, 18)
32. c Inferring the unstated main idea (8, 18)
33. b Identifying the main idea and supporting details (27)
34. a Identifying the main idea and supporting details (27)
35. b Making inferences (28, 50)
36. a Identifying cause and effect (12, 22, 35)
37. d Identifying cause and effect (12, 22, 35)
38. b Comparing and contrasting (2)
39. d Comparing and contrasting (2)
40. a Comparing and contrasting (2)
41. a Making inferences (28, 50)
42. a Distinguishing fact from opinion (37)
43. b Making inferences (28, 50)
44. b Identifying cause and effect (12, 22, 35)
45. d Making inferences (28, 50)
46. d Making inferences (28, 50)
47. c Making inferences (28, 50)
48. a Recognizing multiple meanings of words (45)
49. d Recognizing multiple meanings of words (45)
50. c Using detail context clues (2, 12, 34)

51.	b	Using synonym context clues (3, 22)
52.	c	Using detail context clues (2, 12, 34)
53.	a	Reading a map (34)
54.	c	Reading a map (34)
55.	b	Reading a map (34)
56.	b	Reading a map (34)

Test 3

57.	a	Identifying the main idea (8, 18, 27)
58.	c	Identifying the main idea (8, 18, 27)
59.	b	Identifying the main idea and supporting details (27)
60.	d	Identifying the main idea and supporting details (27)
61.	a	Identifying cause and effect (12, 22, 35)
62.	d	Identifying cause and effect (12, 22, 35)
63.	c	Identifying cause and effect (12, 22, 35)
64.	b	Comparing and contrasting (2)
65.	b	Comparing and contrasting (2)
66.	c	Classifying (3)
67.	a	Classifying (3)
68.	d	Classifying (3)
69.	a	Classifying (3)
70.	b	Making inferences (28, 50)
71.	a	Making inferences (28, 50)
72.	c	Recognizing multiple meanings of words (45)
73.	a	Recognizing multiple meanings of words (45)
74.	d	Using appositive context clues (13, 42)

75.	b	Using detail context clues (2, 12, 34)
76.	c	Reading text with diagrams (13)
77.	c	Reading text with diagrams (13)
78.	b	Reading text with diagrams (13)
79.	d	Reading text with diagrams (13)
80.	b	Solving word problems (23)
81.	a	Solving word problems (23)
82.	b	Solving word problems (23)
83.	d	Solving word problems (23)

Test 4

84.	d	Using a dictionary (9)
85.	b	Using a dictionary (9)
86.	a	Using a dictionary (9)
87.	d	Using a dictionary (9)
88.	c	Using a dictionary (9)
89.	b	Using an index (46)
90.	a	Using an index (46)
91.	c	Using an index (46)
92.	c	Using an index (46)
93.	d	Using an index (46)
94.	a	Using an index (46)
95.	d	Adding prefixes to words (17)
96.	b	Adding suffixes to words (29)
97.	a	Dividing words into syllables (24)
98.	a	Dividing words into syllables (24)
99.	c	Locating the accented syllable (25)
100.	d	Locating the schwa sound (26)

STUDENT ANSWER SHEET

	Test 1		Test 2		Test 3		Test 4
	a b c d		a b c d		a b c d		a b c d

Test 1

1. ◯ ◯ ◯ ◯
2. ◯ ◯ ◯ ◯
3. ◯ ◯ ◯ ◯
4. ◯ ◯ ◯ ◯
5. ◯ ◯ ◯ ◯
6. ◯ ◯ ◯ ◯
7. ◯ ◯ ◯ ◯
8. ◯ ◯ ◯ ◯
9. ◯ ◯ ◯ ◯
10. ◯ ◯ ◯ ◯
11. ◯ ◯ ◯ ◯
12. ◯ ◯ ◯ ◯
13. ◯ ◯ ◯ ◯
14. ◯ ◯ ◯ ◯
15. ◯ ◯ ◯ ◯
16. ◯ ◯ ◯ ◯
17. ◯ ◯ ◯ ◯
18. ◯ ◯ ◯ ◯
19. ◯ ◯ ◯ ◯
20. ◯ ◯ ◯ ◯
21. ◯ ◯ ◯ ◯
22. ◯ ◯ ◯ ◯
23. ◯ ◯ ◯ ◯
24. ◯ ◯ ◯ ◯
25. ◯ ◯ ◯ ◯
26. ◯ ◯ ◯ ◯

Test 2

27. ◯ ◯ ◯ ◯
28. ◯ ◯ ◯ ◯
29. ◯ ◯ ◯ ◯
30. ◯ ◯ ◯ ◯
31. ◯ ◯ ◯ ◯
32. ◯ ◯ ◯ ◯
33. ◯ ◯ ◯ ◯
34. ◯ ◯ ◯ ◯
35. ◯ ◯ ◯ ◯
36. ◯ ◯ ◯ ◯
37. ◯ ◯ ◯ ◯
38. ◯ ◯ ◯ ◯
39. ◯ ◯ ◯ ◯
40. ◯ ◯ ◯ ◯
41. ◯ ◯ ◯ ◯
42. ◯ ◯ ◯ ◯
43. ◯ ◯ ◯ ◯
44. ◯ ◯ ◯ ◯
45. ◯ ◯ ◯ ◯
46. ◯ ◯ ◯ ◯
47. ◯ ◯ ◯ ◯
48. ◯ ◯ ◯ ◯
49. ◯ ◯ ◯ ◯
50. ◯ ◯ ◯ ◯
51. ◯ ◯ ◯ ◯
52. ◯ ◯ ◯ ◯
53. ◯ ◯ ◯ ◯
54. ◯ ◯ ◯ ◯
55. ◯ ◯ ◯ ◯
56. ◯ ◯ ◯ ◯

Test 3

57. ◯ ◯ ◯ ◯
58. ◯ ◯ ◯ ◯
59. ◯ ◯ ◯ ◯
60. ◯ ◯ ◯ ◯
61. ◯ ◯ ◯ ◯
62. ◯ ◯ ◯ ◯
63. ◯ ◯ ◯ ◯
64. ◯ ◯ ◯ ◯
65. ◯ ◯ ◯ ◯
66. ◯ ◯ ◯ ◯
67. ◯ ◯ ◯ ◯
68. ◯ ◯ ◯ ◯
69. ◯ ◯ ◯ ◯
70. ◯ ◯ ◯ ◯
71. ◯ ◯ ◯ ◯
72. ◯ ◯ ◯ ◯
73. ◯ ◯ ◯ ◯
74. ◯ ◯ ◯ ◯
75. ◯ ◯ ◯ ◯
76. ◯ ◯ ◯ ◯
77. ◯ ◯ ◯ ◯
78. ◯ ◯ ◯ ◯
79. ◯ ◯ ◯ ◯
80. ◯ ◯ ◯ ◯
81. ◯ ◯ ◯ ◯
82. ◯ ◯ ◯ ◯
83. ◯ ◯ ◯ ◯

Test 4

84. ◯ ◯ ◯ ◯
85. ◯ ◯ ◯ ◯
86. ◯ ◯ ◯ ◯
87. ◯ ◯ ◯ ◯
88. ◯ ◯ ◯ ◯
89. ◯ ◯ ◯ ◯
90. ◯ ◯ ◯ ◯
91. ◯ ◯ ◯ ◯
92. ◯ ◯ ◯ ◯
93. ◯ ◯ ◯ ◯
94. ◯ ◯ ◯ ◯
95. ◯ ◯ ◯ ◯
96. ◯ ◯ ◯ ◯
97. ◯ ◯ ◯ ◯
98. ◯ ◯ ◯ ◯
99. ◯ ◯ ◯ ◯
100. ◯ ◯ ◯ ◯

	Test 1	Test 2	Test 3	Test 4		
Number Possible	26	30	27	17	Total	100
Number Incorrect					Total	
Score					Total	

CLASS RECORD-KEEPING CHART

Test Item	Skill	Name									
1–4	Identifying conflict and resolution										
5–8	Identifying plot										
9–12	Identifying setting										
13–16	Inferring theme										
17–19, 29, 31–32	Inferring the unstated main idea										
20–23	Identifying point of view										
24, 48–49, 72–73	Recognizing multiple meanings of words										
25–26, 50–52, 74–75	Using context clues										
27–28, 30, 57–58	Identifying the main idea										
33–34, 59–60	Identifying the main idea and supporting details										
36–37, 61–63	Identifying the cause and effect										
38–40, 64–65	Comparing and contrasting										
42	Distinguishing fact from opinion										
41, 43, 45–47, 70–71	Making inferences										
53–56	Reading a map										
66–69	Classifying										
76–79	Reading text with diagrams										
80–83	Solving word problems										
84–88	Using a dictionary										
88–94	Using an index										
95–100	Recognizing prefixes, suffixes, syllables, accented syllables, and schwa sound										
	Total Incorrect										
	Score (subtract total incorrect from 100)										

"WHAT THE RESEARCH SAYS"

To prepare children conceptually for ideas to be encountered in reading, help them link what they know to what they will learn. An organizer provides a frame of reference for comprehending text precisely for this reason—to help readers making connections between their prior knowledge and new material.

Vacca, Vacca, and Gove
Reading and Learning to Read

Research in reading since the early 1980s has led to some major inroads in helping readers comprehend more effectively. This research shows that building on a learner's schema, or prior knowledge, together with scaffolding, or support mechanisms, enables readers to make the necessary connections that improve comprehension. The graphic organizer, used in tandem with a reader's background knowledge, provides the necessary support that allows learners to bridge gaps in their understanding.

According to David Hyerle (*Visual Tools for Constructing Knowledge*, 1996) graphic organizers foster a collaborative, interactive style of learning. Hyerle introduces the term *visual tools*, which he feels broadens the concept of the term *organizer* beyond the sole purpose of helping students organize information. Indeed, visual tools can be used for brainstorming and facilitating dialogue, open-ended thinking, mediation, metacognition, theory development, and self-assessment. The real value of introducing graphic organizers or visual tools is to provide students with a lifetime set of skills that they can use independently to become problem solvers and learn to read, write, and think with greater facility and meaning.

Be A Better Reader incorporates the strategic use of graphic organizers into the selection lessons in every level of the program. Once students begin internalizing these organizers, they can learn to use them as their own visual tools when encountering similar reading and thinking problem-solving situations.

Graphic organizers used in *Be A Better Reader*:
- *Cause and Effect Chart*
- *Character Traits Map*
- *Classification Chart*
- *Comparison and Contrast Chart*
- *Conflict and Resolution Chart*
- *Details About Setting Map*
- *Drawing Conclusions Map*
- *Fact and Opinion Chart*
- *Flowchart*
- *Generalization Chart*
- *Idea Web*
- *Inference Chart*
- *KWL Chart*
- *Main Idea and Supporting Details Map*
- *Outline*
- *Plot Diagram*
- *Prediction Chart*
- *Pros and Cons Chart*
- *Story Map*
- *Sequence Chart*
- *Steps in a Process Map*
- *Venn Diagram*
- *Who, What, Where, When, Why Chart*

This comprehensive set of organizers, used throughout *Be A Better Reader*, provides scaffolding activities to support the improvement of all students' literacy development. They are particularly useful for struggling readers and English language learners who will learn to use organizers to guide them on the way toward independent reading, learning, and problem solving.

John Edwin Cowen, Ed.D.
Peter Sammartino School of Education
Fairleigh Dickinson University

Name _____ Date _____

PREDICTION CHART

Page	What I Predict	What Happens

GRAPHIC ORGANIZERS T55

COMPARISON AND CONTRAST CHART

Things Being Compared	How They Are Alike	How They Are Different

Name _____   Date _____

CLASSIFICATION CHART

Name of Group	Feature 1	Feature 2	Feature 3	Feature 4

Name _____   Date _____

IDEA WEB

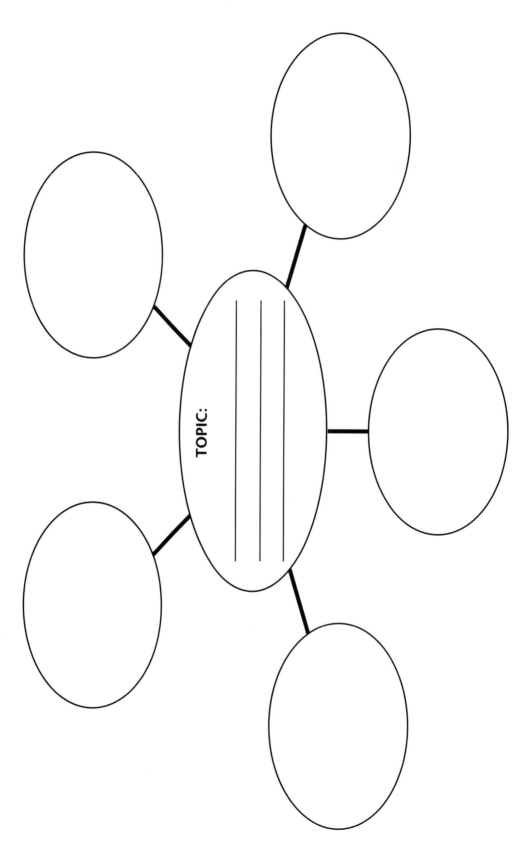

TOPIC:

Name _____   Date _____

CAUSE AND EFFECT CHARTS

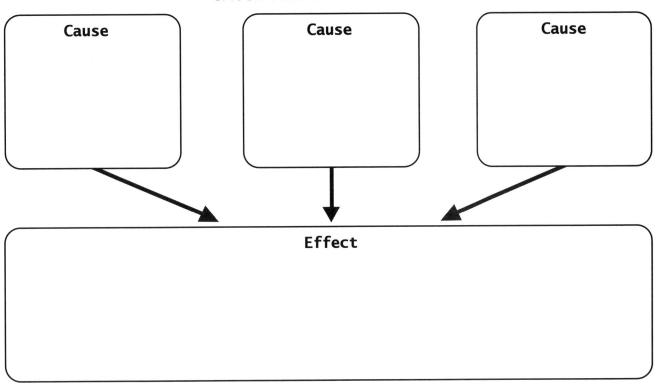

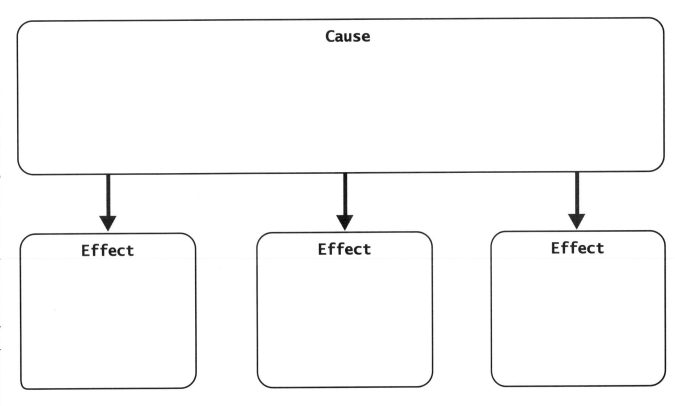

Name _____   Date _____

KWL CHART

K What I Know	W What I Want to Know	L What I Learned

Name _____ Date _____

INFERENCE CHART

Details in the Selection	What I Already Know	Inference
+	**=**	

SEQUENCE CHART

1.

2.

3.

4.

5.

Name _____ Date _____

DETAILS ABOUT SETTING MAP

Topic: _____

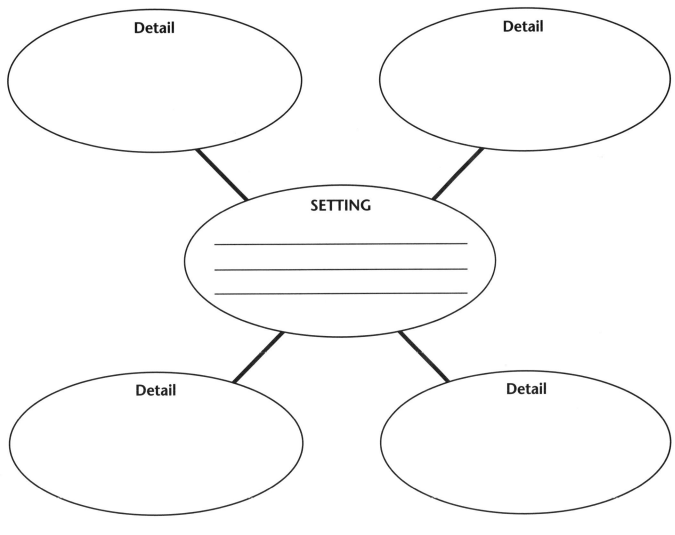

GENERALIZATION CHART

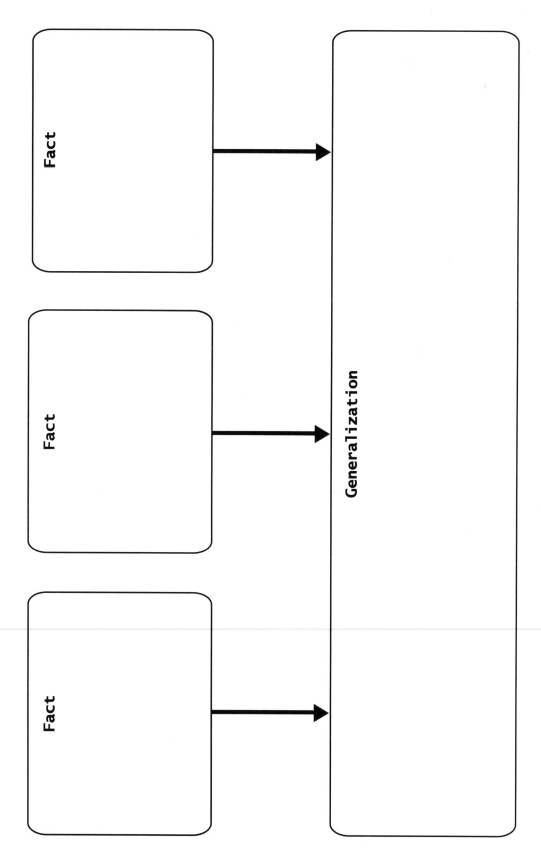

Fact

Fact

Fact

Generalization

UNIT 1 ADVENTURES IN FLIGHT

LESSON 1

Skill: Plot (pages 6–10)

LITERATURE SELECTION: **The Flight of Daedalus**

OBJECTIVES:
- Identify plot
- Use footnotes as context clues

CONTEXT CLUE WORDS: *Minotaur, Sicily, Apollo*

ESL/ELL WORDS: *fist of iron, give himself up, born to it*

GRAPHIC ORGANIZER: Prediction Chart, p. T55

SELECTION SUMMARY

In the Greek myth "The Flight of Daedalus," Daedalus, a master inventor, plans an ingenious escape from Crete, where King Minos holds him prisoner. He fashions wings from wax and feathers, and with his son, Icarus, he flies away from the island. Daedalus warns Icarus about the danger of flying too close to the sun, but the boy, excited by the experience of flying, soars higher and higher. Eventually his wings melt, and he falls into the ocean and drowns. The grief-stricken Daedalus flies on to Sicily and then gives up flying forever.

▶ BEFORE READING

Have students read the Background Information about myths on page 6. Ask volunteers to briefly tell some myths they know, such as the stories of Hercules or King Midas.

Teaching Plot

1. Remind students that a story's plot is the series of events that happen in a story. These events include the beginning, rising action, climax, falling action, and conclusion. Write these events on the chalkboard in Plot Diagram format as shown on page 6.

2. Invite a volunteer to retell the plot of an exciting movie. Stop the student periodically, and ask other volunteers to point out which part of the plot on the diagram the story plot has reached. List students' ideas on the diagram.

3. Have students read the Skill Focus on page 6 and complete the activity.

Teaching Context Clues

1. Remind students that a footnote is an explanation of a name or special word that appears in a selection. Write the following sentence on the chalkboard. *In Greek*

myths, Zeus[1] *is the god who is most powerful.* Ask students what the small numeral[1] next to the word *Zeus* indicates. (There is a footnote that tells who *Zeus* is.) Then ask where the footnote about Zeus would be found? (at the bottom of the page)

2. With students, work on creating a footnote for Zeus. Use a dictionary if necessary. ([1]Zeus: Husband of Hera; the leader of the gods in Greek mythology)

3. Have students read the Context Clues section on page 6 and complete the activity.

4. Write the context clue words *Minotaur, Sicily,* and *Apollo* on the chalkboard or word wall. Remind students to look for footnotes in the selection that tell the meanings of these words.

Previewing the Text

Have students preview the title and the illustrations to predict what might happen in the story. Then distribute copies of the Prediction Chart, and ask students to predict what might happen to Daedalus in the story.

Purpose-Setting Question

What happens to Daedalus's son, Icarus, in this myth, and what lesson does the fate of Icarus teach us?

▶ DURING READING

As students read, remind them to focus on the myth's plot. Also remind students to read the footnotes to find out the meanings of the underlined words.

▶ AFTER READING

Have students discuss their Prediction Charts. Then ask students to answer the purpose-setting question and to complete the activities on pages 9–10.

Reading-Writing Connection

Before students write their paragraphs about pride, have them list examples of actions that a proud person might take. On the chalkboard, classify volunteers' examples in two columns: *Good* and *Dangerous.*

ESL/ELL Strategy

ROLE-PLAYING Have partners role-play Daedalus and Icarus as they prepare to fly away. Afterward, have students discuss how the characters they portrayed were probably feeling.

Skill: Comparing and Contrasting (pages 11–15)

SOCIAL STUDIES SELECTION: **Flying to Fame**

OBJECTIVES:
▸ Compare and contrast information
▸ Use details as context clues

CONTEXT CLUE WORDS: *spectator, endeavor, vastness*

ESL/ELL WORDS: *left on the bench, record-breaking, broke barriers*

GRAPHIC ORGANIZER: Comparison and Contrast Chart, p. T56

SELECTION SUMMARY

"Flying to Fame" compares and contrasts the lives and accomplishments of two pioneering aviators, Amelia Earhart and Sally Ride. In 1932, Earhart became the first woman to fly solo across the Atlantic Ocean. In 1983, astronaut Sally Ride became America's first woman in space, when she was chosen to fly as part of the team aboard the space shuttle *Challenger.*

▸ **BEFORE READING** ....

Have students read the Background Information about flight on page 11. Invite volunteers to share the achievements of famous pilots and astronauts they have heard of, such as Charles Lindbergh, the Wright Brothers, and Alan Shepard.

Teaching Comparing and Contrasting

1. Remind students that *comparing* means finding out how two things are alike, and *contrasting* means noticing how they are different. Explain that social studies books often compare and contrast the qualities and achievements of important people in history. In that way, readers can learn the qualities that leaders share, as well as what makes each person unique.

2. Encourage students to identify similarities and differences between two political leaders or two athletes they know about. On the chalkboard, list ways in which the two people are alike under the heading *Compare* and their differences under the heading *Contrast.*

3. Have students read the Skill Focus on page 11 and complete the Contrast Chart.

Teaching Context Clues

1. Review that details are small pieces of information that help explain the meanings of new or unusual words.

2. Write the following sentence on the chalkboard. *The old airplane was a biplane.* Ask volunteers to explain what a biplane is. Then ask: *What details could we add to the sentence to help readers who don't know this word?* Then rewrite the sentence, adding students' details. (For example: The old airplane was a biplane with two sets of connected wings, one above the other.)

3. Have students read the Context Clues section on page 11 and complete the activity.

4. Write the context clue words *spectator, endeavor,* and *vastness* on the chalkboard or word wall. Remind students to look for details in the selection to help them figure out the meanings of these words.

Previewing the Text

Have students read the title and section headings and look at the photographs with their captions. Then distribute copies of the Comparison and Contrast Chart. Ask students to list similarities and differences between the two aviation pioneers as they read.

Purpose-Setting Question

In what ways were Amelia Earhart and Sally Ride similar?

▸ **DURING READING** ....

As students read, remind them to compare and contrast Earhart and Ride. Also ask them to look for details to help them figure out the meanings of the underlined words.

▸ **AFTER READING** ....

Suggest that students use their Comparison and Contrast Charts to help them answer the purpose-setting question and to complete the activities on pages 14–15.

Reading-Writing Connection

Before students write about the aviation pioneer they admire more, have the class discuss what character traits the two women share. (bravery, determination, and competitiveness) Then have students decide which of these character traits they most admire and which woman better demonstrated the trait.

ESL/ELL Strategy

USING MANIPULATIVES Have partners design a plaque to honor Earhart or Ride. The award should include a visual image and a few sentences to represent the woman's achievements.

Skill: Classifying (pages 16–20)

SCIENCE SELECTION: **On the Wings of a Bird**

OBJECTIVES:
▶ Classify information
▶ Use synonyms as context clues

CONTEXT CLUE WORDS: *analogous, pliant, vulnerable*
ESL/ELL WORDS: *lift, anchored, cruise along*
GRAPHIC ORGANIZER: Classification Chart, p. T57

SELECTION SUMMARY

"On the Wings of a Bird" explains how birds fly and how scientists classify birds according to their wing size, wing shape, and habitat. It also compares and contrasts a bird's wing and a human arm. The article then discusses the relationship between wing size and flapping rate, and the relationship between wing shape and flight speed. It ends with a description of various take-off and landing strategies.

▶ BEFORE READING

Have students read the Background Information on page 16 about birds and flight. Ask volunteers to describe birds they have seen and what they noticed about how the birds lifted off the ground, flew, and landed.

Teaching Classifying

1. Remind students that classifying is a way to organize information by grouping similar things together. Explain that classifying is very important in science. For example, in order to understand the vast variety of life on Earth, scientists classify plants and animals into groups.

2. Write the following list of animals on the chalkboard, and ask students to divide them into two groups: *robin, bee, butterfly, blue jay, owl, mosquito*. Have students explain what similarities and differences they used to classify the animals into two groups: *birds* (robin, blue jay, owl) and *insects* (bee, butterfly, mosquito).

3. Have students read the Skill Focus on page 16 and complete the chart.

Teaching Context Clues

1. Review that authors often include synonyms, or words with similar meanings, in the same or a nearby sentence to help readers figure out the meanings of unfamiliar words.

2. Write the following sentence on the chalkboard. *The eagle was rising into the sky, gradually ascending until it was just a tiny dot.* Ask students what word in the sentence is a clue to the meaning of *ascending*. (rising) Explain that *rising* and *ascending* are synonyms.

3. Have students read the Context Clues section on page 16 and complete the activity.

4. Write the context clue words *analogous, pliant,* and *vulnerable* on the chalkboard or word wall. Remind students to look for synonym context clues to help them figure out the meanings of these words.

Previewing the Text

Have students preview the title, section headings, diagram, and photographs to predict what kinds of information they will learn about birds. Then distribute copies of the Classification Chart. As they read, ask students to list on the chart the three groups of birds described in the article and the features of the birds in each group.

Purpose-Setting Question

How do wing shape and wing size affect the way different kinds of birds fly?

▶ DURING READING

As students read, remind them to add details to their Classification Charts. Also ask them to look for synonyms to help them figure out the meanings of the underlined words.

▶ AFTER READING

Ask students to use the information on their charts to answer the purpose-setting question and to complete the activities on pages 19–20.

Reading-Writing Connection

Before students write their descriptions of a familiar bird, suggest that they look up information about the bird on the Internet or in a field guide to birds.

ESL/ELL Strategy

USING RESOURCES Have pairs of students do research on a bird of their choice, using the Internet or a reference book. Then ask them to draw a labeled diagram of the bird. Have them list the names of the bird's body parts, such as *crown, beak, tail, breast, primaries,* and *secondaries*.

Skill: Reading Mathematical Terms (pages 21–24)

MATHEMATICS SELECTION: **Reading Mathematical Terms and Symbols**

OBJECTIVES:
▶ Read mathematical terms and symbols
▶ Use math word clues

ESL/ELL WORDS: *dimensions, figure, symbol*

GRAPHIC ORGANIZER: Idea Web, p. T58

_____ SELECTION SUMMARY _____

"Reading Mathematical Terms and Symbols" introduces students to some of the terms that they will need to understand when they study geometry. In particular, the lesson explores the concepts of *point, line, plane, intersect, perpendicular,* and *parallel,* explaining the mathematical meanings of these terms. Students practice applying these terms in a variety of mathematical contexts.

▶ **BEFORE READING** ....

Read aloud the Background Information about geometry on page 21. Have volunteers name some geometric shapes, draw them on the chalkboard, and identify everyday objects that have these shapes.

Teaching Mathematical Terms

1. Review that some words have familiar meanings in everyday life and special meanings in math. Explain that knowing mathematical terms is important for success in math. Write the words *point, line, plane, intersect, perpendicular,* and *parallel* on the chalkboard. Ask students to suggest where they might hear or use these words in everyday life. On the chalkboard, write the meanings that students suggest for each word. Have volunteers use the words in sentences.

2. Have students read the Skill Focus on page 21 to find the mathematical definitions of the words. Ask volunteers to write the math meaning of each word on the chalkboard next to its everyday meaning. Suggest that students use the words in sentences that show their math meanings.

3. Have students read the Skill Focus on page 21 and fill in the chart.

Teaching Word Clues

1. Review the terms *point, line, plane, intersect, perpendicular,* and *parallel* listed on the chalkboard.

2. Have volunteers find examples of each term inside the classroom. (For example, the rows of desks are parallel, the walls are perpendicular to the floor, and so on.)

3. Have students read the Word Clues section on page 21.

Previewing the Text

Have students preview the selection, studying the diagrams that illustrate the mathematical terms. Distribute copies of the Idea Web to students, and as they read ask them to write information in the ovals about the terms. Decide together what the topic of the Idea Web should be.

Purpose-Setting Question

What are the mathematical meanings of point, line, plane, intersect, perpendicular, *and* parallel?

▶ **DURING READING** ....

As students read, remind them to carefully study the boldface terms and the symbols to learn their mathematical meanings.

▶ **AFTER READING** ....

Ask volunteers to use their Idea Webs to answer the purpose-setting question. Then have students complete the activities on pages 23–24.

Reading-Writing Connection

Before students write about an item that includes perpendicular lines, point out a few examples in the classroom. Then challenge pairs of students to list as many examples of perpendicular lines as they can and share their lists.

ESL/ELL Strategy

USING MANIPULATIVES Ask students to draw illustrations of everyday places and things that illustrate the concepts *parallel, intersect,* and *perpendicular.* For example, they might draw a city scene with streets and buildings and label the parts that show these mathematical concepts. Then have pairs discuss each other's illustrations.

LESSON 5

Skill: Vowel Diphthongs (page 25)

OBJECTIVE:
▶ Identify vowel diphthongs: *oi, oy, ow, ou*

Teaching the Skill

1. Say the words *soy, soil, moist,* and *toy.* Ask students what vowel sound they hear in each word. (oi) Then write the four words on the chalkboard. Ask students to identify the letters that stand for the vowel sound in each word. Underline the *oy* or *oi* in each word. Review that when this vowel sound appears at the beginning or in the middle of a word, it is usually spelled *oi.* When this same sound is found at the end of a word, it is spelled *oy.*

2. Explain that *oy* and *oi* stand for the same vowel sound. They are called vowel diphthongs. Ask volunteers to name other words that include the vowel diphthongs *oy* and *oi,* and list them on the chalkboard. (possible responses: joy, oil)

3. Proceed similarly with the vowel diphthongs *ou* and *ow.* Say the words *brown, mouse, crowd,* and *sound.* Have students identify the vowel sound they hear in each word. (ou) Then write these words on the chalkboard, and have students identify the letters that stand for the vowel sound in each word. Ask volunteers to name other words that include the vowel diphthongs *ou* and *ow.* (possible responses: round, crown)

4. Have a volunteer read aloud the opening paragraph on page 25. Then, have students complete Exercise A independently. Repeat with the second paragraph of explanatory text and Exercise B.

ESL/ELL Strategy

USING MANIPULATIVES Ask groups of students to cut out pictures of objects whose names include the sound represented by the vowel diphthongs *oi* and *oy* or by the vowel diphthongs *ou* and *ow.* Have students say the name of each object.

Extension Activity

Challenge students to write original sentences like those in Exercises A and B. Each sentence should have a blank that can be filled in with a word containing one of the vowel diphthongs in the lesson. Have students exchange papers and complete each other's sentences, identifying the vowel diphthong in each word they fill in.

LESSON 6

Skill: Vowel-Consonant Combinations (page 26)

OBJECTIVE:
▶ Identify vowel-consonant combinations: *aw, al, au*

Teaching the Skill

1. Say the words *hawk, false,* and *caught.* Ask students what vowel sound they hear in each word. (ô) Write the three words on the chalkboard. Ask students to identify the letters in each word that stand for the vowel sound they hear. (aw, al, au)

2. Underline the vowel-consonant combinations *aw* and *al* and the vowel pair *au.* Explain that all three of these letter combinations can stand for the same vowel sound.

3. Invite volunteers to name other familiar words that include this vowel sound. Draw three columns on the chalkboard with the headings *aw, al,* and *au.* Ask volunteers to say their example words and write them in the appropriate columns. (saw, draw; salt, halt; cause, sauce)

4. Have students read the opening paragraph on page 26. Then have students complete the exercise independently.

ESL/ELL Strategy

USING VISUALS Ask small groups of students to draw scenes that contain at least five objects whose names are spelled with the letter combinations *aw, al,* or *au.* Challenge them to include as many objects as possible. Then have students exchange papers and say the names of the *aw, al,* or *au* objects in the picture.

Extension Activity

Have partners write stories using words with the letter combinations *aw, al,* and *au.* Instead of actually writing these letters, have them leave a blank in the words that contain the letters. After students complete their stories, have them exchange papers and fill in the letters *aw, al,* or *au* where appropriate.

LESSON 7

Skill: Syllables (page 27)

OBJECTIVES:
- Divide compound words into syllables
- Divide words with double consonants into syllables

Teaching the Skill

1. Remind students that a syllable is each part of a word in which they can hear a vowel sound. Point out that there are rules they can use that will help them divide words into syllables.

2. Explain that one rule exists for compound words. Review that compound words are words formed from two smaller words, and explain that each smaller word contains at least one syllable. Write these compound words on the chalkboard as you say them aloud: *baseball, homework,* and *flashlight.* Have volunteers identify the two smaller words that make up each compound word and draw a slash in each compound word to show how to divide it into syllables. (base/ball, home/work, flash/light)

3. Have a volunteer read aloud Rule 1. Then have students complete Exercise A independently.

4. Say aloud the words *happen, mitten,* and *sunny* as you write them on the chalkboard. Ask volunteers to identify the double consonants in each word and then draw a slash to show how to divide it into syllables. (hap/pen, mit/ten, sun/ny) With the class, conclude that the rule for syllabicating words with double consonants is to divide them between these consonants.

5. Ask a volunteer to read aloud Rule 2. Then have students complete Exercise B.

ESL/ELL Strategy

USING MANIPULATIVES Ask students to draw pictures that show five objects named by compound words or words with double consonants. Then have them exchange their pictures with a partner, guess the pictured words, write the words, and divide them into syllables.

Extension Activity

Have students write a short paragraph about a topic that interests them, using as many words as possible from Exercises A and B. Then have them exchange papers, identify the compound words and words with double consonants, and divide these words into syllables.

LESSON 8

Skill: Main Idea—Stated or Unstated (pages 28–29)

OBJECTIVE:
- Identify the stated or unstated main idea of a paragraph

Teaching the Skill

1. Elicit that the main idea is the most important idea in a paragraph. Review that sometimes a paragraph includes a sentence that states the main idea. In other paragraphs, the main idea is not stated. In these paragraphs, students must infer, or figure out, the main idea by asking themselves what the paragraph is all about.

2. Distribute the following paragraph on a handout. Ask students to think about all the details in the paragraph to figure out what main idea the writer is expressing about the moon.

   The Moon has no air and no wind. There is no water there either. On the Moon, the sky is black, even during the day. The Moon's surface—dust and rocks—is too hot to touch by day. By night, the Moon is colder than any place on Earth.

3. Together determine if the main idea is stated. (no) Ask students to offer the unstated main idea of the paragraph. (The Moon is a bleak place unsuited for human life.) Ask students to name the details in the paragraph that helped them figure out this main idea. (no air, no wind, no water, dark, severely hot or cold)

4. Have students read the introductory paragraphs and then complete the exercises on page 29.

ESL/ELL Strategy

ORGANIZING INFORMATION Have students think of a sentence that states a main idea about a career that they would like to pursue. For example: *A career in law enforcement is an opportunity to help others.* Have students write their main idea on a sheet of paper, and then under their main idea, list three or more detail sentences to support it.

Extension Activity

Ask small groups to skim through chapters in a science or social studies textbook for three examples of paragraphs that do not have stated main ideas. Have them write a main idea sentence for each one.

LESSON 9

Skill: Using a Dictionary (pages 30–31)

OBJECTIVE:
▶ Understand and use dictionary guide words, respellings, parts of speech labels, definitions, and idioms

Teaching the Skill

1. Review that using a dictionary is the best way to check the spelling and pronunciation of a word and to find out a word's meanings. Ask volunteers to describe situations in which they might look up a word in a dictionary.

2. On the chalkboard, write the word *harangue,* or any other word that is probably unfamiliar to students. Ask students with dictionaries to find the dictionary entry for the word and tell the class the page on which it was found.

3. Have them share the word's pronunciation and meaning and describe the steps they used to find the entry. Elicit that dictionary entries are arranged in alphabetical order and that each page of a dictionary has guide words in boldface type that identify the first word and the last word on that page. Ask students how they knew how far to go in the *h* section to find the entry for *harangue.* Point out that when words begin with the same first letter, they are arranged according to the alphabetical order of their second letters, third letters, and so on.

4. Write on the chalkboard the respelling and part of speech label for *harangue,* and explain them. Show an idiom by having a volunteer look up the word *hot,* and point out the idiom *hot under the collar.*

5. Have students read pages 30–31 and complete the exercises.

ESL/ELL Strategy

USING RESOURCES Assign each student five words from Exercise A. Have students look up their five assigned words in a dictionary and then orally share each word's pronunciation and meanings in a small group.

Extension Activity

Have pairs of students make up guide-word exercises like the one in Exercise B. Using the actual guide words from a dictionary, have them list, in random order, words that appear on that page, before that page, and after that page. Then have them exchange papers and complete each other's exercises.

LESSON 10

Skill: Reading Help-Wanted Ads (pages 32–33)

OBJECTIVE:
▶ Read help-wanted ads

Teaching the Skill

1. Review that help-wanted ads in the classified section of a newspaper are listings of jobs that employers hope to fill. Bring in copies of a local newspaper, and have students find the classified section.

2. Have students find and read aloud examples of these help-wanted ads. Ask questions about the ads to check if students understand how to interpret the abbreviations and how to follow the directions to apply for each job.

3. Have students turn to the ads on page 32, and ask volunteers to read them aloud and summarize them in their own words. Remind students that an abbreviation is a shortened form of a word. Elicit examples, such as *St.* for *street* and *P.O.* for *post office.* Discuss why employers might use abbreviations in ads. (in order to save money; newspapers charge by the number of words in the ads)

4. Direct students to read the text on page 32 and complete the exercises on page 33 independently, using the ads on page 32.

ESL/ELL Strategy

USING REALIA Have pairs of students read the help-wanted ads of their local newspapers and make a list of at least six abbreviations they find, writing the meaning of each one. Then have pairs compare their lists.

Extension Activity

Have students write ads for jobs or careers they would like to have someday. Remind them to make the ads brief and to use abbreviations. Students can compile their ads into a class help-wanted section.

LESSON 11

Skill: Theme (pages 34–38)

LITERATURE SELECTION: **A Simple Arrangement**

OBJECTIVES:
▶ Infer a story's theme
▶ Use antonyms as context clues

CONTEXT CLUE WORDS: *adept, proportion, serene*

ESL/ELL WORDS: *spray, stab of envy, confetti*

GRAPHIC ORGANIZER: Prediction Chart, p. T55

SELECTION SUMMARY

In "A Simple Arrangement," Tomi, a Japanese-American girl, is reluctantly spending a year with her grandparents in Japan. Once she is there, she has difficulty mastering Japanese customs and traditions, especially when compared with her model Japanese cousin, Keiko. One day, after several frustrating events, Tomi unexpectedly finds serenity in her grandfather's traditional garden. Realizing that she has been trying too hard, Tomi relaxes and begins to focus on the task at hand. She soon finds success by finishing a traditional Japanese flower arrangement.

▶ BEFORE READING

Have students read the Background Information about Japanese customs on page 34. Find Japan on a map of the world. Ask volunteers to share what they know about life in Japan and how it contrasts with life in the United States.

Teaching Theme

1. Review that a story's theme is the meaning or message about life that the author wants to share with the readers. Sometimes the author states the theme directly, but usually readers have to figure out the theme for themselves by examining the story's events and what the characters say, think, and do.

2. Retell a fable or a fairy tale such as "The Elephant and the Mouse" or "The Tortoise and the Hare." Then ask students what message or lesson the tale teaches about life. (Even the smallest, weakest person can be helpful to others. Or, slow and steady wins the race.)

3. Have students read the Skill Focus on page 34 and complete the chart.

Teaching Context Clues

1. Review that antonyms are words with opposite meanings. Explain that writers often include antonyms in their writing to help readers figure out the meanings of unfamiliar words in the same or nearby sentences.

2. Write the following sentences on the chalkboard. *I wasn't frazzled. I was totally relaxed.* Then ask what word is the opposite of *frazzled.* (relaxed)

3. Have students read the Context Clues section on page 34 and complete the activity.

4. Write the words *adept, proportion,* and *serene* on the chalkboard or word wall. Remind students to look for antonyms to figure out the meanings of these words.

Previewing the Text

Have students preview the title and illustration. Then distribute copies of the Prediction Chart, and ask students to write their predictions about what might happen in the story.

Purpose-Setting Question

What important lessons does Tomi learn from her experiences in Japan?

▶ DURING READING

Remind students to consider what theme or message about life the story conveys and to look for antonyms to figure out the meanings of the underlined words.

▶ AFTER READING

Encourage students to share their Prediction Charts. Then ask students to answer the purpose-setting question and to complete the activities on pages 37–38.

Reading-Writing Connection

Before students write about a difficult new situation, suggest that they use an Idea Web (p. T58) to list specific details about the situation and how they felt about it.

ESL/ELL Strategy

PERSONALIZING THE LESSON Encourage pairs of students to share personal narratives of important events from their lives. Then have students state in a sentence what lesson they learned from each experience.

Skill: Cause and Effect (pages 39–44)

SOCIAL STUDIES SELECTION: **Worlds Under Our Feet**

OBJECTIVES:

▶ Identify chains of causes and effects

▶ Use details as context clues

CONTEXT CLUE WORDS: *demolished, integral, inhabitants*

ESL/ELL WORDS: *unearthed, burying the past, cover the stories*

GRAPHIC ORGANIZER: Cause and Effect Charts, p. T59

SELECTION SUMMARY

"Worlds Under Our Feet" describes the work of archaeologists who excavate sites in cities. In 1978, archaeologists unearthed a major Aztec temple in Mexico City. When construction workers unearth lost sites, conflicts can arise between archaeologists and builders. The article defines "virtual archaeology" as a combination of traditional archaeology and cutting-edge computer graphics. A summary of the benefits of studying the past is given.

▶ BEFORE READING

Have students read the Background Information about archaeologists on page 39. Ask volunteers to share what they know about archaeology. If any students know about an accidental discovery of a historical site, invite them to share what they recall about the event.

Teaching Cause and Effect

1. Remind students that a cause is an event that makes something happen. An effect is what happens as a result of the cause. Point out that sometimes a chain of causes and effects occurs when an effect of one cause becomes the cause of another effect.

2. On the chalkboard, write *I overslept.* Then draw an arrow, and ask a volunteer to write the first effect of oversleeping. (For example, I was late for school.) Then draw a second arrow and ask: *What happened as a result of being late for school?* Have another volunteer write the second effect in the chain, and then draw another arrow. Continue in this way until the chain is complete.

3. Have students read the Skill Focus on page 39 and complete the Cause and Effect Chart.

Teaching Context Clues

1. Point out that details can act as context clues to figure out the meanings of new words.

2. Write the following sentences on the chalkboard. *Usually archaeologists and builders compromise. Each side benefits, but each must make sacrifices.* Ask a volunteer to underline the details in the sentences that help them figure out the meaning of the word *compromise.* (Each side benefits, but each must make sacrifices.)

3. Have students read the Context Clues section on page 39 and complete the activity.

4. Write the context clue words *demolished, integral,* and *inhabitants* on the chalkboard or word wall. Remind students to look for details as they read to help them figure out the meanings of these words.

Previewing the Text

Have students preview the selection's title, section headings, and photographs to predict what kinds of causes and effects they will read about. Then distribute copies of the Cause and Effect Chart, and ask students to take notes on chains of causes and effects as they read. Modify the chart, as necessary.

Purpose-Setting Question

In what ways do cities provide archaeologists with opportunities and challenges?

▶ DURING READING

As students read, remind them to look for causes and effects. Also ask them to look for details to help them figure out the meanings of the underlined words.

▶ AFTER READING

Allow time for students to share their Cause and Effect Charts. Then ask students to answer the purpose-setting question and to complete the activities on pages 43–44.

Reading-Writing Connection

Before students begin to write their diary entries about a typical day on an archaeological dig, have them brainstorm about and take notes on the dig's location, challenges, and findings.

ESL/ELL Strategy

USING RESOURCES On a globe or world map, have students locate Mexico City, Mexico; Athens, Greece; Miami, Florida; Cleveland, Ohio; New York City, New York; and London, England. Have them orally describe the locations of these places.

Skill: Reading a Diagram (pages 45–49)

SCIENCE SELECTION: **The Nervous System**

OBJECTIVES:

▸ Read text with diagrams

▸ Use appositive phrases as context clues

CONTEXT CLUE WORDS: *hemispheres, involuntary, internal*

ESL/ELL WORDS: *organs, switchboard, groove*

GRAPHIC ORGANIZER: KWL Chart, p. T60

_____ SELECTION SUMMARY _____

"The Nervous System" describes the internal communications network that enables the human body to function and react to the environment. The text describes the neuron, the basic unit of the nervous system, and how bundles of neurons form nerves that work together to perform specific jobs in the body. The article describes the basic parts of the nervous system and the functions of each, including the main parts of the brain.

▸ **BEFORE READING** ....

Have students read the Background Information about the nervous system on page 45. Ask volunteers to share what they know about the parts and functions of the human nervous system.

Teaching Reading a Diagram

1. Remind students that a diagram is a drawing that shows the structure of something or the relationship between different parts of a system. Bring in and show students assembly instructions or user's guides to appliances that have diagrams. Explain how you have used these diagrams to assemble or repair objects. Point out that to effectively use diagrams, it is important to read the captions and labels. When diagrams appear in context, it helps to read the paragraphs before the diagram first, then study the diagram, and then read the paragraphs after the diagram.

2. Have students describe situations in which they have needed to read diagrams. These might include assembling a new game, appliance, or tool; repairing an automobile or other vehicle; or creating a craft item. Have volunteers explain how reading diagrams made these tasks easier.

3. Ask students to read the Skill Focus on page 45, study the diagram of the neuron, and answer the questions.

Teaching Context Clues

1. Remind students that an appositive phrase is a group of words that is placed after another word to explain its meaning. It is set off with commas or dashes and often starts with *or*.

2. Write the following sentence on the chalkboard. *Ramon studies biology.* Ask students to define biology. Then ask what appositive phrase could be added to the sentence to help readers learn the meaning of biology. (the science of living things) Write on the chalkboard *Ramon studies biology, or the science of living things.*

3. Have students read the Context Clues section on page 45 and complete the activity.

4. Write the context clue words *hemispheres, involuntary,* and *internal* on the chalkboard or word wall. Remind students to look for appositive phrases that help explain the meanings of these words as they read.

Previewing the Text

Have students preview the section headings, diagrams, and boldfaced words. Then distribute copies of the KWL Chart, and ask students to fill them in as they read.

Purpose-Setting Question

What are the main parts of the human nervous system and what do they do?

▸ **DURING READING** ....

As students read, remind them to study the diagrams along with the text. Also remind students to look for appositive phrases that explain the meanings of the underlined words.

▸ **AFTER READING** ....

Ask volunteers to share facts they listed in the third column of the KWL Charts. Suggest that students use their KWL Charts to answer the purpose-setting question and to complete the activities on pages 48–49.

Reading-Writing Connection

After students have explained which part of the nervous system they would like to know more about, have groups decide on one topic and research it as a team.

ESL/ELL Strategy

USING MANIPULATIVES Have partners make a model of either a neuron or the human brain, based on the diagrams in the selection. Have them label and present their models.

Skill: Reading Decimals (pages 50–53)

MATHEMATICS SELECTION: **How to Read Decimals**

OBJECTIVES:

▶ Read decimals

▶ Use the suffix -th as a word clue

ESL/ELL WORDS: *dimes, financial world, digits*

GRAPHIC ORGANIZER: KWL Chart, p. T60

_____ SELECTION SUMMARY _____

"How to Read Decimals" teaches students how to read and understand numbers with decimal points by introducing the concept of place value. The article also provides practice in reading numbers with decimal points.

▶ **BEFORE READING** ....

Have students read the Background Information about decimals on page 50. Invite volunteers to describe every-day situations in which they see numbers with decimal points. (buying a cafeteria lunch, using a stopwatch in gym class)

Teaching Decimals

1. Remind students that a decimal point is a period separating a number into two parts. Then write $1\frac{1}{10}$ on the chalkboard, and ask students if they know another way to write it. (1.1) Tell students that the number 1.1 is a decimal and that the period in the number is a decimal point.

2. Ask students to read the number 1.1. (one and one tenth) Then ask a volunteer to write and read a decimal that means $1\frac{2}{10}$ (1.2; one and two tenths)

3. Repeat Steps 1 and 2, asking students how to write $1\frac{25}{100}$ as a decimal (1.25) and then to read the decimal (one and twenty-five hundredths).

4. Direct students to read the Skill Focus on page 50 and complete the chart.

Teaching Word Clues

1. Review that a suffix is a word part added to the end of a base word to change its meaning. For number words, -th is a common suffix.

2. Write the following phrases on the chalkboard: ten pies, one tenth of a pie. Underline the words *ten* and *tenth*. Elicit that the suffix -th changes the value of a

number word from more than one whole to less than one whole.

3. Ask students how the amounts named by *ten* and *one tenth* differ. If students have difficulty answering, draw ten small circles on the chalkboard, and label the group *ten pies*. Then draw one circle, divide it into ten parts, and shade one of the parts. Label the shaded section *one tenth of a pie.*

4. Have students read the Word Clues section on page 50 and complete the activity.

Previewing the Text

Have students preview the selection, studying the place-value charts. Then distribute copies of the KWL Chart, and ask students to fill them in as they read.

Purpose-Setting Question

Why is it important to be able to read numbers with decimals?

▶ **DURING READING** ....

As students read, remind them to use the place-value chart on page 51 to help them understand the value of each decimal they encounter. Also remind them to look for words that have the suffix -th and to make sure they understand the meanings and pronunciations of these words.

▶ **AFTER READING** ....

Allow time for students to share the information on their KWL Charts. Then direct students to answer the purpose-setting question and to complete the activities on pages 52–53.

Reading-Writing Connection

Before students write their paragraphs about how decimals and fractions are used in everyday life, have them meet in small groups to brainstorm a list of examples. Encourage them to think about measurements they have made, items they have bought, prices they have paid, and sports statistics they have seen.

ESL/ELL Strategy

USING VISUALS Suggest that students draw a large circle on a sheet of paper. Then ask them to shade in 0.5 of the circle. Have students figure out what fraction of the circle is filled in. ($\frac{1}{2}$) Then ask students to work with partners to shade in other decimal amounts on circles, noting the amount filled in as a decimal and a fraction.

Skill: Vowel-Consonant Combinations (page 54)

OBJECTIVE:

▶ Identify sounds represented by vowel-consonant combinations: *air, ear, are*

Teaching the Skill

1. Read aloud the following sentence. *A bear knocked over a chair in the town square.* Ask a volunteer to identify the three words in the sentence that have the same vowel sound. (bear, chair, square) Write these three words on the chalkboard, and have students identify which letters in each word stand for the sound they have in common. Underline *ear, air,* and *are,* and explain that they are vowel-consonant combinations.

2. On the chalkboard, form three columns labeled *air, ear,* and *are.* Then call on volunteers to name other words with the "air" sound and one of these spellings. Have them write their words on the chalkboard in the correct column. (possible responses: pear, tear, wear; fair, hair, stair; care, dare, fare)

3. Conclude that the words have the same vowel sound, but the letters for that sound are different in each word.

4. Next write the following sentence on the chalkboard. *I heard that the bear caused a lot of fear.* Ask a volunteer to read the sentence aloud. Encourage students to suggest other words that are spelled with *ear* and have the same sound as *fear.* (near, beard, shears) Then ask for other words spelled with *ear* that have the same sound as *heard.* (learn, earth, early) Point out the three words with the *ear* spelling pattern and the different sounds they stand for.

5. Ask students to read the explanatory text and complete the exercises on page 54.

ESL/ELL Strategy

USING MANIPULATIVES Have students draw illustrations that show words spelled with the vowel-consonant combinations *air* and *ear.* Have partners exchange pictures, write the word that names each picture, and circle the letters that stand for the vowel sound.

Extension Activity

Several words with the *air* sound can be spelled differently, depending on their meaning. Have students make a glossary that explains the differences in meaning between the following pairs of words: *bear/bare, hair/hare, fair/fare, pear/pair,* and *stair/stare.*

Skill: Syllables (page 55)

OBJECTIVES:

▶ Divide words with prefixes or suffixes into syllables

▶ Divide words with two consonants between two sounded vowels into syllables

Teaching the Skill

1. Remind students that a syllable is a part of a word in which they can hear a vowel sound. Review that a prefix is a word part added to the beginning of a word to change the word's meaning and that a suffix is a word part added to the end of a word to change its meaning.

2. Write the following words with prefixes on the chalkboard, and have volunteers circle each prefix and underline each base word: *preheat, rework, defrost,* and *undo.* Point out that each prefix and each base word is a syllable.

3. Repeat Step 2 with students to identify the suffixes and base words of *lowly, spiteful, movement,* and *farmer.*

4. Now say the following words: *winter, napkin, plastic.* Ask students how many vowel sounds they hear in each word (2) and how many syllables each word has (2). Write the words on the chalkboard and underline the vowels in each word. Then ask how many consonants come between the vowels in each word. (2) Explain that when two consonants come between two sounded vowels, a word is divided between the two consonants. Have volunteers divide each word into syllables. (win/ter, nap/kin, plas/tic)

5. Have students turn to page 55 and read the rules. Then direct them to complete Exercises A and B independently.

ESL/ELL Strategy

USING MANIPULATIVES Have partners write five words from Exercise A and five words from Exercise B on ten separate index cards. Have students cut each card into two parts to show where each word should be divided. Partners then shuffle the cards and put them back together again. Then have students pronounce the words.

Extension Activity

Ask students to list the prefixes and suffixes that are used in the words in Exercise A on page 55. Challenge them to write three other words that contain each prefix or suffix.

LESSON 17

Skill: Prefixes (page 56)

OBJECTIVE:
▸ Understand prefixes: *bi-, de-, mid-, non-, semi-, sub-, tri-, uni-,* and *re-*

Teaching the Skill

1. Review that a prefix is a word part added to the beginning of a base word to change its meaning. As examples, write the words *semicircle* and *defrost* on the chalkboard. Ask volunteers to circle the prefix in each word. (semi-, de-)

2. Ask what *semi-* means (half) and what *de-* means (away from, undo). Then have students figure out the meanings of *semicircle* and *defrost.* (half a circle; to undo the frost, or thaw)

3. Write the following list of prefixes on the chalkboard and discuss their meanings: *bi-, de-, mid-, non-, semi-, sub-, tri-, uni-,* and *re-*. Then give students the following list of base words: *night, fiction, turn, cycle, code,* and *marine.* Ask volunteers to add one of the prefixes to each word and tell the new word's meaning. (possible responses: midnight, return, bicycle, tricycle, recycle, unicycle, decode, nonfiction, submarine)

4. Direct students to complete the excercises on page 56.

ESL/ELL Strategy

USING MANIPULATIVES Ask pairs of students to write each prefix in Lesson 17 on a separate index card. Have them place the cards in a bag. Then have them take turns drawing out a card, saying the prefix, and then suggesting a base word to which the prefix could be added. Have students use the words they form in oral sentences.

Extension Activity

Ask groups of students to use a dictionary to find and write ten other familiar words beginning with the prefixes taught in this lesson.

LESSON 18

Skill: Main Idea—Stated or Unstated (page 57)

OBJECTIVE:
▸ Identify the stated or unstated main idea of a paragraph

Teaching the Skill

1. Remind students that the main idea is the most important idea in a paragraph. Review that supporting details in a paragraph tell more about the main idea. Also review that in some paragraphs the main idea is stated directly. In other paragraphs the main idea is not stated. It must be inferred, or figured out, from the supporting details.

2. Write the following paragraph on the chalkboard or distribute copies to students.

   The ancient Greeks were performing dramas more than 2,500 years ago. In India, there were playwrights at work at least 2,000 years ago. In China, plays were performed 1,400 years ago.

3. Ask students to think about all of the details in the paragraph and then decide which sentence tells its main idea. Help students determine that the main idea is not stated and that it must be inferred. Elicit that all of the details tell about how old drama is in different countries. Ask volunteers to state a possible main-idea sentence. (In many countries around the world, drama is a very old art form.)

4. Have students read the explanatory paragraphs on page 57 and complete the exercises.

ESL/ELL Strategy

ORGANIZING INFORMATION Have students create a list of the main ideas and supporting details of each paragraph in the selection about Nō and Kabuki plays.

Extension Activity

Have students work in small groups to list details about a recent performance or sporting event at your school. Then ask them to write a main-idea sentence that summarizes their details.

Skill: Following First-Aid Directions
(pages 58–59)

OBJECTIVE:
▶ Follow directions for a first-aid technique

Teaching the Skill

1. Review that when following directions, it's important to perform the steps in the correct order. Ask students to describe some special skills or abilities that they have learned in recent years. For example, swimming the butterfly stroke, performing a dance, or dressing a cut. Point out that they had to follow oral or written directions in order to learn these skills. Write a volunteer's directions on the chalkboard as a model.

2. Ask students if they are familiar with any first-aid procedures to follow in emergency situations. Explain that choking is one such emergency. Choking occurs when food or another foriegn body completely blocks a person's air passage, making it impossible for the person to breathe or speak. Then have students read the first two paragraphs on page 58.

3. Call on students to read aloud the steps of "First Aid for the Choking Victim." You might want to call on volunteers who are familiar with first aid to demonstrate the steps.

4. Have students complete the exercises on pages 58–59.

ESL/ELL Strategy

NOTE-TAKING Have partners take turns reading aloud the steps of "First Aid for the Choking Victim." Have them stop after each step and take notes to make sure they understand the meaning of each word in that step. If they are unsure of a word's meaning, they can write it down and then look up the word in a dictionary.

Extension Activity

Ask partners to research and write directions for a different emergency situation such as using escape routes for fires, using a fire extinguisher, or calling the police after a robbery. Have them number the steps of the directions and describe the actions as clearly as possible. Students can also make illustrations for their directions.

LESSON 20

Skill: Mood (pages 60–65)

LITERATURE SELECTION: **The Dolphin Disaster**

OBJECTIVES:

▶ Identify mood

▶ Use comparisons as context clues

CONTEXT CLUE WORDS: *aspired, cove, ebbing*

ESL/ELL WORDS: *wheeled, crank, matter of moments*

GRAPHIC ORGANIZER: Prediction Chart, p. T55

___SELECTION SUMMARY___

In "The Dolphin Disaster," the residents of a small, seaside town help some dolphins that are in danger of being stranded on a beach in a nearby cove. Spooner Hemming and his sister, Audrey, organize people in their town to form a line in the shallow waters of the cove. Most of the dolphins are directed to deeper water and are saved.

▶ **BEFORE READING** ....

Have students read the Background Information about dolphins on page 60. Ask volunteers to share what they already know about dolphins.

Teaching Mood

1. Remind students that "mood" is the atmosphere, or feeling, an author creates in a story using only words. Ask volunteers to name some different moods that people they know have experienced recently. (happiness, anger, peace, pessimism, excitement, and so on) Explain that a story, too, has an overall mood, or feeling and that authors use vivid sensory details for sights, sounds, and smells, to convey emotion as they describe a story's setting and characters.

2. Write the word *scary* on the chalkboard. Ask students to provide sensory words and phrases that would create this mood. List them on the chalkboard. (distorted shadows, creaking doors, the smells of leaking gas or smoke) Try the same technique for a peaceful mood.

3. Have students read the Skill Focus on page 60 and complete the chart.

Teaching Context Clues

1. Explain that reading selections often contain sentences with comparisons that can help them visualize the

meanings of unfamiliar words. Comparisons often begin with the word *like* or *as*.

2. Write the following sentence on the chalkboard. *Like children at a playground, the dolphins frolicked in the water.* Then ask: *What do you think the word* frolicked *means?* (played) *What comparison in the sentence helps you understand the word's meaning?* (like children at a playground)

3. Have students read the Context Clues section on page 60 and complete the activity.

4. Write the words *aspired, cove,* and *ebbing* on the chalkboard or word wall. Remind students to look for comparisons to help them figure out the meanings of these words.

Previewing the Text

Have students study the title and the illustrations. Then distribute copies of the Prediction Chart, and ask students to make predictions about what might happen.

Purpose-Setting Question

How do Spooner and Audrey help the dolphins avoid getting stranded?

▶ **DURING READING** ....

As students read, remind them to think about the story's mood. Also have students look for comparisons that are clues to the meanings of the underlined words.

▶ **AFTER READING** ....

Allow time for students to share the predictions they recorded and revised on their Prediction Charts. Then ask students to answer the purpose-setting question and to complete the activities on pages 63–65.

Reading-Writing Connection

Before students write about cooperating with others to complete an important project, have the class brainstorm and create a list of different kinds of situations in which people need to work together to achieve a goal.

ESL/ELL Strategy

ORGANIZING INFORMATION Distribute copies of the Comparison and Contrast Chart (p. T56) to partners to use in comparing and contrasting two different settings, such as an old, abandoned house and a school cafeteria. Then have students summarize the overall mood that each setting might create.

Skill: Recognizing Propaganda (pages 66–71)

SOCIAL STUDIES SELECTION: Remember the *Maine*

OBJECTIVES:

▶ Recognize propaganda techniques

▶ Use footnotes as context clues

CONTEXT CLUE WORDS: *detention camps, man-of-war, tenders*

ESL/ELL WORDS: *hot news topic, screaming headlines, picked up*

GRAPHIC ORGANIZER: Inference Chart, p. T61

_____ SELECTION SUMMARY _____

"Remember the *Maine*" describes how the mysterious sinking of the U.S. battleship *Maine* in Havana in 1898 led to the Spanish-American War. Newspaper propaganda, or yellow journalism, created anti-Spanish sentiment in the American public and in Congress. This eventually led to a declaration of war against Spain.

▶ BEFORE READING

Have students read the Background Information about the battleship *Maine* on page 66. Ask volunteers to suggest other events from history and current events that have led to conflicts between and within nations. (1941 Pearl Harbor attack—Japan and United States; 1939 Poland Invasion—Germany and Great Britain)

Teaching Recognizing Propaganda

1. Remind students that propaganda is the spreading of information with the intention of persuading people by using emotions rather than facts.

2. Bring in a magazine ad paid for by a corporation or a direct-mail solicitation from a political group or nonprofit organization that could be considered propaganda. Ask what this group wants us to believe or do and what words and images are being used to persuade us.

3. Review the difference between facts and opinions. A fact is a statement that can be proved or checked. An opinion is a judgment that cannot be proven. Point out that propaganda often presents opinions as if they were facts or uses facts that are misleading.

4. Have students read the Skill Focus on page 66 and complete the chart.

Teaching Context Clues

1. Review that a footnote is a brief explanation of a phrase in text, that is numbered and found at the bottom of the page. Footnotes help explain unknown words where there are no other context clues.

2. Write the following sentence on the chalkboard. *Before 1860, many Americans urged the annexation[1] of Cuba.* Discuss what the small raised numeral [1] next to *annexation* means. (A footnote at the bottom of the page tells more about this word.) Then on the chalkboard, write this footnote: [1]*Annexation: the taking over of an area by another country.* Ask a volunteer to explain what the word *annexation* means. (the taking over of an area by another country)

3. Have students read the Context Clues section on page 66 and complete the activity.

4. Write the context clue words *detention camps, man-of-war,* and *tenders* on the chalkboard or word wall. Remind students to use footnotes to find the meanings of these words as they read.

Previewing the Text

Have students preview the section headings and the newspaper on page 68 to predict what this article will be about. Then distribute copies of the Inference Chart, and ask students to fill it in as they read.

Purpose-Setting Question

How did propaganda help start the Spanish-American War?

▶ DURING READING

As students read, remind them to look for both the propaganda and the facts about the sinking of the *Maine*. Also remind them to read the footnotes to find the meanings of the underlined words.

▶ AFTER READING

Allow time for students to share their Inference Charts and to answer the purpose-setting question. Then have students complete the activities on pages 69–71.

Reading-Writing Connection

To help students find a photograph and write a headline for it, bring in tabloid newspapers, and have students discuss particular headlines, photographs, and errors of fact that are used to sway people's emotions.

ESL/ELL Strategy

ROLE-PLAYING Have groups of students play the roles of politicians who are opposed to going to war with Spain.

Skill: Cause and Effect (pages 72–76)

SCIENCE SELECTION: **The Amazing Sea Journeys**

OBJECTIVES:
▸ Identify causes and effects
▸ Use synonyms as context clues

CONTEXT CLUE WORDS: *collectively, feat, susceptible*

ESL/ELL WORDS: *mouth of a river, suited, schools*

GRAPHIC ORGANIZER: Cause and Effect Charts, p. T59

SELECTION SUMMARY

"The Amazing Sea Journeys" describes the annual migration patterns of four sea animals—eels, salmon, gray whales, and loggerhead turtles. The article explores the possible causes and effects of these mysterious migration patterns.

▸ BEFORE READING

Have students read the Background Information about animal migration on page 72. Ask volunteers to name some familiar animals that migrate with the change of seasons. Discuss possible reasons for these annual migrations.

Teaching Cause and Effect

1. Remind students that a cause is a condition or event that makes something happen. An effect is what happens as a result of a cause. Explain that sometimes several causes can lead to one effect or many effects can have one cause.

2. Write the following effect on the chalkboard. *The population of the city declined.* Ask volunteers to suggest three possible causes for this effect. (A major factory closed, and people could not find jobs; young people left to get an education and never moved back; air pollution caused people to look for more pleasant places to live.) On the chalkboard, show the multiple effects of the single cause in a Cause and Effect Chart such as the one on page 72.

3. Direct students to read the Skill Focus on page 72 and complete the chart.

Teaching Context Clues

1. Review that synonyms are words with the same or similar meanings. Point out that synonyms in the same or a nearby sentence can help readers uncover the meaning of a new word.

2. Write the following sentence on the chalkboard. *Some animal migrations are very hazardous, while others are not dangerous at all.* Ask students how you can tell from this sentence what the word *hazardous* means. (The word *dangerous* has the same meaning as hazardous.)

3. Have students read the Context Clues section on page 72 and complete the activity.

4. Write the context clue words *collectively, feat,* and *susceptible* on the chalkboard or word wall. Remind students to look for synonyms to help them figure out the meanings of these words.

Previewing the Text

Have students preview the selection's title, photo, and section headings. Then distribute the Cause and Effect Charts, and ask students to fill them in as they read.

Purpose-Setting Question

In what ways are the migrations of the four sea animals amazing?

▸ DURING READING

As students read, remind them to look for examples of causes and effects. Also remind students to look for synonyms to help them figure out the meanings of the underlined words.

▸ AFTER READING

Allow time for students to share their Cause and Effect Charts. Then ask students to answer the purpose-setting question and to complete the activities on pages 75–76.

Reading-Writing Connection

Before students write about another sea animal that migrates, have them search the Internet to find Web sites with useful information on this topic. One excellent site can be found at *www.learner.org/jnorth.*

ESL/ELL Strategy

USING RESOURCES Have partners use a world map to trace the migratory paths of gray whales and loggerhead sea turtles, using the locations mentioned in the article. Then have partners share their findings with other pairs of students.

Skill: Word Problems (pages 77–80)

MATHEMATICS SELECTION: **Word Problems That Have Unnecessary Information**

OBJECTIVES:
▸ Solve word problems with unnecessary information
▸ Use math key words

ESL/ELL WORDS: *dove, arithmetic operations, extracted*

GRAPHIC ORGANIZER: Sequence Chart, p. T62

_____ SELECTION SUMMARY _____

"Word Problems That Have Unnecessary Information" presents a five-step strategy for solving math word problems that require two operations. These steps are read the problem, decide how to find the answer, estimate the answer, carry out the plan, and reread the problem. The selection also shows how to distinguish facts that are necessary and unnecessary to solve a problem.

▸ **BEFORE READING** ....

Have students read the Background Information about math word problems on page 77. Ask volunteers to describe situations in which they have had to solve math problems in order to complete a project or make a decision.

Teaching Word Problems

1. Review that the sentences in a word problem contain information to solve it but sometimes also contain unnecessary information. Describe a real-life situation that requires the solving of a math word problem. Add a piece of unnecessary information. For example: *My friend drives 17 miles each way to work. She works 5 days a week. Her car gets 20 miles per gallon of gas. How many miles does she drive each week back and forth to work?*

2. Use the problem above to model the process of identifying unnecessary information. First ask: *What question do we need to answer to solve this problem?* (How many miles does the friend drive back and forth to work each week?) *To answer this question, do we need to know how far she drives each day?* (yes) *Do we need to know how may days a week she works?* (yes) *Do we need to know how many miles her car can go on a gallon of gas?* (No, the problem does not ask about gas, only about distance.) Together, figure out the total distance your friend travels. (17 × 2 = 34; 34 × 5 = 170 miles)

3. Have students read the Skill Focus on page 77 and complete the activity.

Teaching Word Clues

1. Point out that understanding key words makes solving word problems easier.

2. Read aloud or write the following simple problem on the chalkboard. *Ryan earned $20. Sam earned $30. How much did the two boys earn all together?* ($50) Ask volunteers to solve the problem. Then ask how they knew to add. (The words *all together* are a signal to add.) Ask if students know any other math words that are signals to add. (and, total, in all) Ask if they know any math words that are signals to subtract. (how much less, left, difference)

3. Have students read the Word Clues section on page 77 and complete the activity.

Previewing the Text

Have students read the selection's title and the section headings. Then distribute copies of the Sequence Chart. Students list in order the steps for solving word problems.

Purpose-Setting Question

How can you tell when information in a math word problem is unnecessary?

▸ **DURING READING** ....

As students read, remind them to look for unnecessary information in solving word problems and for key words that will help them decide which operation to use.

▸ **AFTER READING** ....

Allow time for students to share their Sequence Charts. Then ask students to answer the purpose-setting question and to complete the activities on pages 79–80.

Reading-Writing Connection

To help students prepare to write about situations that require solving word problems, suggest that groups brainstorm topics such as sports, hobbies, and travel plans.

ESL/ELL Strategy

USING MANIPULATIVES Have pairs of students write each of the five steps for solving math word problems on a separate index card. Suggest that they read the problem to each other and then tell how they will follow each step of the problem-solving sequence.

Skill: Syllables (pages 81–82)

OBJECTIVES:
▶ Divide words with one consonant between two sounded vowels into syllables
▶ Divide words with blends or digraphs into syllables

Teaching the Skill

1. Remind students that dividing words into syllables will help them pronounce and read new words. Tell them that in this lesson they will learn three new rules for dividing words.

2. Write the words *pupil, unit, habit,* and *value* on the chalkboard. Have a volunteer draw a line between the syllables. (pu/pil, u/nit, hab/it, val/ue) Discuss which words have a long vowel sound in the first syllable (pupil, unit) and which have a short vowel sound (habit, value). Have students write two rules for dividing words with one consonant between two sounded vowels. (When the first vowel is long, divide before the consonant. When the first vowel is short, divide after the consonant.)

3. Write the words *extreme* and *vibrate* on the chalkboard. Have a volunteer draw a line between the syllables. (ex/treme, vi/brate) Have students determine a rule for dividing words with consonant blends. (Treat the blend as if it were one letter and follow the other rules.)

4. Write *table, turtle,* and *candle* on the chalkboard. Have volunteers draw a line between the syllables. (ta/ble, tur/tle, can/dle) With students, come up with a rule for dividing this kind of word into syllables. (When words end in -*le*, the -*le* and the consonant before it make up a syllable.)

5. Have students read the explanatory text and complete the activities on pages 81–82.

ESL/ELL Strategy

USING MANIPULATIVES Have partners write five words from each exercise on an index card. Then ask them to shuffle the cards and take turns picking a card and dividing the word into syllables.

Extension Activity

Have students read a paragraph from a book of their choice. Then on a separate sheet of paper, ask them to list as many words as they can that they could divide into syllables, using the three guides they have learned in this lesson.

Skill: Accented Syllables (page 83)

OBJECTIVES:
▶ Locate the primary accented syllable in a word of two syllables
▶ Locate the secondary accented syllable in a word of four or more syllables

Teaching the Skill

1. Point out that the accented syllable is the one that gets the most stress in a word. Ask students the following questions, accenting the syllables in capital letters. *Do you listen to MU sic or mu SIC? Do children play with BAL loons or bal LOONS?* Help students to see which syllable in each word is accented, or stressed.

2. Write the words *mu´ sic* and *bal loon´* on the chalkboard, pointing out the accent mark used to indicate the accented syllable in each word.

3. Ask volunteers to name some familiar two-syllable words. Have them say each word and tell which syllable they stress when they say it. Then have them write their words on the chalkboard, using an accent mark to show the accented syllables.

4. Write the word *cat´ er pil´ lar* on the chalkboard. Point out the primary and secondary accents in the word. Ask: *Which accent mark is printed in darker type?* (primary accent) Explain that the primary accent falls on the syllable that is stressed most. The secondary accent falls on the other stressed part of the word. Ask students for other examples of words of four or more syllables and tell on which syllables the primary and secondary accents fall.

5. Have students read the explanatory text and complete the exercises on page 83.

ESL/ELL Strategy

USING REALIA Ask students to cut out five magazine pictures and label the objects they see in each picture. Then have them divide each word in their labels into syllables and place an accent mark on the stressed syllable or syllables in each word. Afterward, have students look up each word in a dictionary to check their work.

Extension Activity

Have students make a list of all the students in your class. Then have them divide each name into syllables and mark the accented syllable or syllables in each name.

Skill: Schwa Sound (page 84)

OBJECTIVE:
▶ Locate the schwa sound in words

Teaching the Skill

1. Review that the schwa sound is like the sound of "uh." Its symbol is an upside down e (ə) in dictionary spellings. Write the word *animal* on the chalkboard, and ask what sound the letter *i* stands for in this word. (the "uh" sound) Then write the word *zebra,* and ask if this word has the "uh" sound, too. (yes) Ask what letter the "uh" sound stands for in this word. (the letter *a*) Then write the word *lion,* and ask the same questions. (yes; the letter *o*)

2. Conclude that the soft "uh" sound they hear in *animal, zebra,* and *lion* is the schwa sound and that in different words, the schwa sound is represented by different vowels: *a, e, i, o,* or *u.* Dictionary respellings use the ə symbol to represent the sound.

3. Help students determine in which syllable the schwa sound is found. Write *speller, damsel,* and *noble* on the chalkboard. Ask a volunteer to place the accent mark in each word, and underline the syllable that contains the schwa sound in each word. (spell´ er, dam´ sel, no´ ble) Help students to conclude that the schwa is always found in the unaccented syllable of a word.

4. Have students complete the exercises on page 84.

ESL/ELL Strategy

USING REALIA Have partners read aloud a short article in a newspaper or magazine. Ask them to circle each letter that stands for the schwa sound they hear.

Extension Activity

Have students write a paragraph on a topic of their choice. Then have students locate the schwa sounds and circle the letters each one stands for.

Skill: Main Idea and Supporting Details (pages 85–86)

OBJECTIVE:
▶ Identify the main idea and supporting details of a paragraph

Teaching the Skill

1. Review that the most important part of a paragraph is the main idea and that the supporting details in the paragraph give more information about the main idea. Tell students that a paragraph is like a table. The most important part of a table—the top—is supported by legs.

2. Distribute the following paragraph on a handout. Help students to determine its main idea and supporting details.

   The American colonists were prepared for the battles of Lexington and Concord. They had formed an army of farmers called minutemen, who were ready to fight on a minute's notice. The colonists had also collected gunpowder in preparation for a battle. Colonists such as Paul Revere were also secretly watching the British army to keep track of its movements.

3. Together, determine that the first sentence is the main idea. All the other sentences support it.

4. Have students read the explanatory text and paragraphs on page 85 and complete the exercise on page 86.

ESL/ELL Strategy

ORGANIZING INFORMATION Give pairs of students a main-idea sentence such as the following: *Playing on a sports team has many benefits.* Then direct them to write three or more details that support the main idea.

Extension Activity

Ask students to read passages about the American Revolution in a social studies text, encyclopedia, or nonfiction library book. Direct them to find paragraphs with a stated main idea and supporting details. Then have students note the main idea and supporting details of one paragraph.

LESSON 28

Skill: Making Inferences (pages 87–88)

OBJECTIVE:
▸ Make inferences

Teaching the Skill

1. Review that to infer is to figure out information that the author does not state directly. Explain that authors expect readers to combine details in the text with what they know from their own experience to make inferences.

2. Read the following dialogue.

   "Haven't found it yet?" Rob asked, as Nan sifted through the sand.

   "No," replied Nan sadly, hoping to see the glint of gold among the pebbles, sticks, and bits of shells. Her finger looked so bare without it.

   "You'll find it soon," said Rob. "I'll help you look after I go for a short swim."

3. Help students make an inference about where Nan and Rob are and what Nan has lost. (at the beach; her ring) Have volunteers note the details in the dialogue that helped them make these inferences. (sand, swim; glint of gold, her finger) Also have them list what they already know about beaches and rings that helped them make the inferences. (It is easy to lose small things in the sand.)

4. Have students turn to page 87 and read the instructional text at the top of the page. Then distribute copies of the Inference Chart (p. T61), and ask students to complete it as they read the passage about Phillis Wheatley.

5. Have students complete page 88 independently.

ESL/ELL Strategy

ORGANIZING INFORMATION Hand out copies of the Inference Chart (p. T61). Have students work in pairs. Ask one student to tell about a personal experience he or she had recently. Ask the other student to record details about the experience and then to make at least one inference based on the details. Next have students reverse roles and repeat the process.

Extension Activity

Divide students into groups and ask them to read a short story and discuss it. Then have students use an Inference Chart (p. T61) to make several inferences based on details in the story.

LESSON 29

Skill: Suffixes (page 89)

OBJECTIVE:
▸ Add suffixes

Teaching the Skill

1. Remind students that a suffix is a word part added to the end of a word to change its meaning.

2. Write the following sentence on the chalkboard. *My friend and I value our friendship.* Have a volunteer underline the two similar words in the sentence and explain how the words differ in spelling and meaning. (Underline *friend* and *friendship*. A *friend* is a person attached to another by feelings of affection, and *friendship* is the state of being a friend.) Then circle the word part *-ship,* and explain that it is a suffix.

3. Write the suffixes *-ity, -let, -ly, -or, -ous, -ship, -ure,* and *-ward* on the chalkboard. Brainstorm words that use each suffix. (sincerity, piglet, yearly, actor, joyous, membership, pleasure, outward) Have volunteers write each example word on the chalkboard and circle its suffix.

4. Have students read the introductory paragraph and the list of suffixes and their meanings. Then have students complete the exercises on page 89.

ESL/ELL Strategy

USING MANIPULATIVES Have pairs of students write each of the following base words on a separate self-stick note: *partner, sister, fail, drop, sail, thunder, up, prosper.* Then have them write each of the suffixes on page 89 on a separate self-stick note. Have students combine each base word with a suffix to form a new word. Have them use each new word orally in a sentence.

Extension Activity

Have students read magazine and newspaper articles, circling words that include the suffixes listed on page 89. Then have them make a two-column chart in which they list the base word and the suffix for each word they found.

Skill: Using a Library Catalog (pages 90–91)

OBJECTIVE:
▶ Use a library catalog

Teaching the Skill

1. Review that a library catalog helps to locate a book in a library quickly and easily. Have students describe the procedure they normally follow to find a book in a library. Ask them whether their method is different if they know the title or author of a specific book or only the subject of the book they want.

2. If your school has an Internet connection, you might want to log on to the catalog of a local library and show students how to locate books in the library. Point out that this is a time-saving way to find out whether the library owns the book you need and whether the book is currently available at the library.

3. Have students read the explanatory text on page 90 and then direct students to look at the sample screen from a computerized library catalog. Help them use the information shown on the screen to complete Exercise A on page 91. Discuss the words *publisher* and *subjects*. Point out the abbreviations for *copyright* and *illustrated*.

4. Have students complete Exercises B and C independently.

ESL/ELL Strategy

USING RESOURCES Have pairs of students think of a topic that interests them and then use a library catalog to locate three books on that topic. Ask students to make a list of the books they identify, including each book's title, author, and call number.

Extension Activity

Have students think about a nonfiction book that they might like to write someday. Ask them to create a library-catalog entry that would appear on a computer screen when someone searched for their book. Students should model their entries on the samples shown on pages 90 and 91.

Skill: Outlining (pages 92-93)

OBJECTIVE:
▶ Make an outline

Teaching the Skill

1. Explain that an outline shows the order and relationship of the main ideas and important details in a piece of writing. Point out that writers often plan their writing by making an outline. Additionally, outlining is a good way to take notes about an article or a chapter of a textbook.

2. Ask volunteers to recall what they know about outlines. Have them describe situations in which they have made outlines to study for a test or to write a report.

3. Ask students to help you write the frame of an outline on the chalkboard, using the Roman numerals I and II, the letters A and B indented below each Roman numeral, and the Arabic numbers 1 and 2 indented below each capital letter.

4. As a class, select a topic, such as *Why Our School Should Offer More Extracurricular Activities*. Use your outline to organize ideas. Together, fill in the outline with the main ideas next to the Roman numerals, the major supporting details next to the letters, and the minor supporting details next to the Arabic numbers. Conclude that your outline now contains an organized plan for explaining why the school should offer more extracurricular activities.

5. Have students read the explanatory text and complete the exercise on pages 92–93.

ESL/ELL Strategy

SUMMARIZING Ask partners to use their completed outlines on page 93 to orally summarize what they have learned about cargo ships, without looking at the actual paragraphs of the selection.

Extension Activity

Encourage students to read a chapter in their social studies or science textbook that they will have to study this week. Using the outline form, have them list the main ideas and major and minor details in the chapter. Suggest that students use their outline as a study tool for that chapter.

Skill: Reading Drug Labels (pages 94–95)
OBJECTIVE:
▸ Read a drug label

Teaching the Skill

1. Bring in empty packages from over-the-counter medications such as cough syrup or allergy pills. Have students study the labels and list the types of information they find. (the purpose of the medicine, how much to take, how often to take it, warnings about possible side effects and dangers)

2. Have students discuss why it is important to read medicine labels carefully and to use these products as the labels direct. Point out that taking too much of a drug could cause damage to the body or make a person sick. Taking too little, on the other hand, might make the drug less effective.

3. Have students turn to page 94 and study the two sample drug labels on the page. Ask students why they might take Formula D (for a cough due to a cold) and why they might take Dramadon (for seasickness). Discuss the meanings of terms, such as *prevention of,* and *motion sickness,* as well as abbreviations, such as *FL OZ* and *mil.*

4. Have students read the explanatory text and complete the exercises on page 95.

ESL/ELL Strategy

NOTE-TAKING Have pairs of students make a list of medicine-related words that they see in the labels on page 94. These might include *dose, administer, relieves, drowsiness, nausea, vomiting, tablet,* and *asthma.* Have students discuss and write the definitions of these terms.

Extension Activity

Have pairs of students role-play a customer and a pharmacist in a drugstore. The customer should ask for advice about a medicine to take for a cough or for seasickness. The pharmacist should recommend one of the products shown on page 94 and answer the customer's questions about how much to take and any warnings he or she needs to know about before taking the drug.

LESSON 33

Skill: Setting (pages 96–101)

LITERATURE SELECTION: **Triumph and Tragedy**

OBJECTIVES:
▶ Identify and analyze setting
▶ Use word groupings as context clues

CONTEXT CLUE WORDS: *sheer, grappling, catastrophe*

ESL/ELL WORDS AND PHRASES: *Golden Age, face, would-be companion*

GRAPHIC ORGANIZER: Details About Setting Map, p. T63

SELECTION SUMMARY

"Triumph and Tragedy" tells the true story of Edward Whymper, a young Englishman who was the first person to climb the Matterhorn. Whymper's 1865 expedition focused on the importance of inventing safer climbing equipment.

▶ BEFORE READING

Have students read the Background Information about mountain climbing on page 96. Ask volunteers to share what they know about this challenging sport.

Teaching Setting

1. Remind students that all stories have a setting—a time and place in which the events take place. Invite a student to describe the setting of a favorite story or movie. Draw a Details About Setting Map on the chalkboard using a volunteer's example.

2. Explain that some settings create conflict or suspense in a story. Have students name books or movies with settings that challenge or endanger the main characters. For example, students might recall works set in a desert in which the setting was hot, dry, and desolate. Ask students what kinds of conflicts could arise from a desert setting. (Characters could become lost, overheated, or thirsty.)

3. Have students read the Skill Focus on page 96 and complete the chart.

Teaching Context Clues

1. Explain that an unknown word can sometimes be understood when it is grouped with other words in the same category.

2. Write the following sentence on the chalkboard. *To practice our climbing skills, we scrambled up rocky cliffs, crags, and mountain peaks.* Ask students to guess what crags are. Discuss how the words *rocky cliffs* and *mountain peaks* help you guess the meaning of the word *crags*. To confirm their guess, have students look up the word *crag* in a dictionary. (steep, rugged rock or cliff)

3. Have students read the Context Clues section on page 96 and complete the activity.

4. Write the context clue words *sheer, grappling,* and *catastrophe* on the chalkboard or word wall. Remind students to look for word groupings in the selection to help them figure out the meanings of these words.

Previewing the Text

Have students study the story's title and illustrations. Then distribute copies of the Details About Setting Map, and ask students to record details on it as they read.

Purpose-Setting Question

How did Edward Whymper experience triumph and tragedy on the same day?

▶ DURING READING

As students read, remind them to look for details of the setting that made it difficult for Whymper to reach his goal. Suggest that students look for word groupings to help them figure out the meanings of the underlined words.

▶ AFTER READING

Allow time for students to share their Details About Setting Maps. Then ask them to answer the purpose-setting question and to complete the activities on pages 99–101.

Reading-Writing Connection

Before students describe equipment needed for a dangerous sport, have them use an Idea Web (p. T58) to analyze the dangers of the sport, the need for safety equipment, and precautions athletes can use to avoid injuries.

ESL/ELL Strategy

ROLE–PLAYING Have partners role-play an interview between Whymper and a newspaper reporter covering the dangers and challenges of his Matterhorn climb.

Skill: Reading a Map (pages 102–107)

SOCIAL STUDIES SELECTION: **The Great Mountain Ranges of the World**

OBJECTIVES:
▶ Read a relief map
▶ Use details as context clues

CONTEXT CLUE WORDS: *avalanche, moderate, eke*

ESL/ELL WORDS: *crown, foothills, roof of the world*

GRAPHIC ORGANIZER: Classification Chart, p. T57

SELECTION SUMMARY

"The Great Mountain Ranges of the World" describes eight of the world's major mountain ranges: the Rocky Mountains, the Appalachian Mountains, the Alaskan Mountains, the Andes Mountains, the Atlas Mountains, the Alps, the Ural Mountains, and the Himalayas. It describes the location, elevation, and historical facts about the ranges.

▶ BEFORE READING

Have students read the Background Information about mountains and mountain life on page 102. Ask volunteers to share what they know about mountains, based on their own experiences or information they have read. Use a world physical map to help students locate each of the mountain ranges discussed in the selection.

Teaching Reading a Map

1. Remind students that a relief map is a map that shows the differences in height of various parts of Earth's surface. Ask students to look through their social studies textbook, an encyclopedia, or other reference book to find examples of relief maps. Call students' attention to the vertical-elevation scales that appear in these maps. Ask students to identify what colors or symbols the maps use to indicate elevation.

2. With students, draw a fictitious relief map on the chalkboard. Use different colors of chalk to portray differences in elevation. Invite a volunteer to the chalkboard to help explain the different elevation levels and the vertical-elevation scale.

3. Have students read the Skill Focus on page 102 and answer the question based on the relief map.

Teaching Context Clues

1. Discuss that details in a sentence can help readers understand a new word. Write the following sentence on the chalkboard. *Glaciers slid down the mountain.* Ask volunteers to explain what glaciers are. Discuss what details could be added to this sentence to help readers who don't know what glaciers are.

2. Use students' contributions to rewrite the sentence, adding details such as those in the following sentence. *The huge glaciers slid slowly down the mountain, filling the valley with fields of ice and snow.*

3. Have students read the Context Clues section on page 102 and complete the activity.

4. Write the context clue words *avalanche, moderate,* and *eke* on the chalkboard or word wall. Remind students to look for details to help them figure out the meaning of the words.

Previewing the Text

Have students preview the title, the section headings, the relief map, and the elevation illustration. Then distribute copies of the Classification Chart. Ask students to list on the chart the name and features of each mountain range and to classify the mountains according to their elevation.

Purpose-Setting Question

What are the eight major mountain ranges of the world?

▶ DURING READING

As students read, remind them to use the elevation illustration and relief map to help classify the mountain ranges and to look for details to figure out the meanings of the underlined words.

▶ AFTER READING

Allow time for students to share their Classification Charts. Then ask them to answer the purpose-setting question and to complete the activities on pages 106–107.

Reading-Writing Connection

Before students describe and explain the effects of a nearby mountain range, have them study a relief map of the United States to identify the highest mountains in your region.

ESL/ELL Strategy

USING RESOURCES Have partners use a relief map of the world to create an itinerary. Have them plan a trip to visit all of the mountain ranges mentioned in the selection.

Skill: Cause and Effect (pages 108–112)

SCIENCE SELECTION: **The Theory of Plate Tectonics**

OBJECTIVES:
▶ Identify causes and effects
▶ Use antonyms as context clues

CONTEXT CLUE WORDS: *rifts, advocated, gradually*

ESL/ELL WORDS: *plates, debatable, landmass*

GRAPHIC ORGANIZER: Cause and Effect Charts, p. T59

SELECTION SUMMARY

"The Theory of Plate Tectonics" summarizes the scientific theory that says that Earth's crust is made up of seven plates that float on hot liquid rock and gas. The gradual movement of these plates explains a number of natural occurrences, including earthquakes and volcanoes. The theory of plate tectonics supports an earlier theory called continental drift, which suggests that all the continents were once one giant landmass.

▶ BEFORE READING

Have students read the Background Information about plate tectonics on page 108. Have volunteers share what they know about the causes of earthquakes and volcanoes.

Teaching Cause and Effect

1. Remind students that a cause is an event that makes something happen. An effect is what happens as a result of the cause. Explain that one cause can often lead to several effects and several causes can lead to one effect.

2. Write the following effects on the chalkboard in a Cause and Effect Chart like the one on page 108. *A forest fire destroys 10,000 acres. Crops wither and die. A water-conservation emergency is in effect.* Ask students what might be one cause of these three effects. (There is little rainfall.)

3. Have students read the Skill Focus on page 108 and complete the activity.

Teaching Context Clues

1. Review that antonyms are words with opposite meanings. Point out that antonyms in the same or a nearby sentence can help readers uncover the meaning of a new word.

2. Write the following sentence on the chalkboard.

The layer of the earth below tectonic plates is molten, not solid. Ask students if they can guess the meaning of *molten* from reading the sentence. (liquid) Then ask what antonym clue to the word's meaning appears in the sentence. (not solid)

3. Have students read the Context Clues section on page 108 and complete the activity.

4. Write the context clue words *rifts, advocated,* and *gradually* on the chalkboard or word wall. Remind students to look for antonyms to help them figure out the meanings of these words.

Previewing the Text

Have students preview the selection, studying the title, section headings, maps, and diagrams. Then distribute copies of the Cause and Effect Charts. As they read, have students write examples of single causes that have multiple effects and single effects that are the result of more than one cause.

Purpose-Setting Question

What are some effects of the movement of Earth's tectonic plates?

▶ DURING READING

As students read, remind them to look for single causes that have multiple effects. Also remind them to look for antonym context clues to help them figure out the meanings of the underlined words.

▶ AFTER READING

Suggest that students use their Cause and Effect Charts to help them answer the purpose-setting question and to complete the activities on pages 111–112.

Reading-Writing Connection

Before students write an explanation of the causes and effects of a particular geographic feature in their state, have them research the feature by obtaining brochures from a local state park or by visiting the Web site of your state's department of travel and tourism.

ESL/ELL Strategy

USING MANIPULATIVES Suggest that partners use sheets of paper, cardboard, or clay to demonstrate their understanding of the theory of plate tectonics. Ask students to use the boldface words in the selection to explain the movements they demonstrate.

Skill: Reading Percents (pages 113–116)

MATHEMATICS SELECTION: **How to Read Percents**

OBJECTIVES:
- Read percents
- Use math word clues

ESL/ELL WORDS: *digits, value, sign*

GRAPHIC ORGANIZER: KWL Chart, p. T60

SELECTION SUMMARY

"How to Read Percents" introduces the concept of percent, defining it as a certain number compared to 100. The selection also teaches students how to convert percents to decimals and then decimals to percents. Next they learn to change a percent to a fraction and then a fraction to a percent.

▶ BEFORE READING

Have students read the Background Information about percents on page 113. Ask volunteers to describe some other real-life situations in which they have heard or used the word *percent*.

Teaching Reading Percents

1. Review that the word *percent* refers to a certain number compared to 100. Explain that the whole amount of anything is expressed as 100 percent. A number such as "a 10 percent chance" means 10 chances out of a 100. Explain that decimals, fractions, and percents can all be used to express the same amounts.

2. *Ask: Is it more likely to rain if the chances of rain are 0.5, $\frac{1}{2}$, or 50%?* (The chance is the same.) Write the decimal, fraction, and percent on the chalkboard. To help students see that these amounts are equal, draw a circle under each amount, and ask a volunteer to shade in the circle to represent each amount. Then ask students what they notice about the shaded sections in the three circles. (They are the same.) Summarize by pointing out that percents can be written as fractions and decimals and that decimals and fractions can be changed to percents.

3. Have students read the Skill Focus on page 113 and complete the grids.

Teaching Word Clues

1. Write the word *percent* on the chalkboard, and explain that it comes from the Latin root *centum*. *Centum* means "one hundred" or "each hundred."

2. Write the root *centum*, and ask volunteers to name other English words that contain the same root and explain their meanings. (century, 100 years; cent, one hundredth of a dollar; centennial, a hundredth anniversary)

3. Have students read the Word Clues section on page 113.

Previewing the Text

Have students preview the title, section headings, and sample math problems. Then distribute copies of the KWL Chart. In the first column of the chart, ask students to write what they already know about percents. In the second column, have them write what they would like to learn. Students should fill in the third column of the chart with facts as they read.

Purpose-Setting Question

How do you change a percent to a decimal or a fraction?

▶ DURING READING

As students read, remind them to notice how numbers can be converted between percents, fractions, and decimals.

▶ AFTER READING

Allow time for students to share their KWL Charts. Then have students answer the purpose-setting question and complete the activities on pages 115–116.

Reading-Writing Connection

Before students describe three places where they have seen numbers written as percents, suggest they work in small groups to brainstorm a list of situations in which they have seen or heard percents.

ESL/ELL Strategy

SUMMARIZING Have partners read the four rules at the top of page 115, one at a time. Ask them to work together to paraphrase each rule and then, on a separate sheet of paper, give an example to illustrate it.

Skill: Evaluating Opinions (pages 117–118)

OBJECTIVE:
▶ Evaluate opinions

Teaching the Skill

1. Review that an opinion is a statement that tells how someone feels, and a fact is a statement that can be checked or proven. Express to the class one opinion you have about your community or school. For example: The computers at our school are badly in need of upgrading.

2. Explain that it is possible to determine whether an opinion is valid by providing facts. Ask volunteers to suggest some facts that might support your opinion to determine if it is a valid opinion. (The computer software is outdated.) Write the word *facts* on the chalkboard, followed by the facts students provide. For each fact, ask: *How could we check if your statement is true?*

3. Finally, have students evaluate your opinion by asking: *Do you think my opinion is valid? Could we think of enough facts to support it?*

4. Have students turn to page 117 and read the instructional paragraph. Ask students if they can think of any words that people often use to express their opinions. (possible words: best, worst, beautiful, ugly, easy, difficult)

5. Direct students to read the article on pages 117 and 118 and complete the exercise.

ESL/ELL Strategy

PERSONALIZING THE LESSON Have students write an opinion about their favorite TV show, sports team, or musical group. Ask them to list three or more facts to support their opinion and show it to be valid.

Extension Activity

Have the class identify an issue on which different students have different opinions, such as *Cities are a dangerous place to live.* Ask the students on one side of the issue to list facts that support their opinion. Ask the other group of students to list facts that support their opinion. Then have students debate the issue in class.

Skill: Improving Reading Rate (pages 119–121)

OBJECTIVE:
▶ Use strategies to improve reading rate

Teaching the Skill

1. Remind students that having a rapid reading rate helps them to read more in a short period of time. Ask: *Can you read an adventure novel at a faster rate than a science textbook? Why or why not?* Have volunteers share information about the rates at which they read different types of materials. Ask for explanations of these differences. (A novel tends to use language that is easier to understand than a science textbook.)

2. Have students read the top of page 119. Then ask a volunteer to read aloud the four bad reading habits listed in the middle of the page. Have students answer the questions about their reading habits independently. Then ask volunteers to suggest why these habits might cause people to read more slowly.

3. Ask students to practice reading the short passage on the bottom of page 119. Stress that being able to take in groups of words in one glance will increase their reading speed.

4. Have students mark their starting time on the line before beginning to read "Friends or Enemies" on page 120.

5. Suggest that students answer the questions on page 119 before calculating their reading rates. Stress that understanding what you read is just as important as increasing your reading rate. Help students calculate their reading rate.

ESL/ELL Strategy

NOTE-TAKING Have groups of students work together to create a list called How to Improve Your Reading Rate. Ask them to list five or more suggestions. Students can use the suggestions in the lesson or base their list on their own experiences.

Extension Activity

Encourage students to calculate their reading rates for three different types of reading material, such as a magazine article, a chapter from a novel, and a textbook chapter.

LESSON 39

Skill: Taking Notes (pages 122–123)

OBJECTIVE:
▶ Take notes

Teaching the Skill

1. Remind students that taking notes will help them remember the information as they read. Then slowly read aloud a few paragraphs from a newspaper or magazine article. Ask students to take notes as you read.

2. Call on volunteers to read aloud their notes. Ask how they decided what to write and what to leave out. Conclude that the best notes are those that summarize the main parts.

3. Have students read the explanatory paragraphs on page 122. Then have a volunteer read aloud the four suggestions to help students take notes.

4. Direct students to read "Explorations to the New World" on page 122 and to take notes on the passage on page 123. Students can complete the chart on the bottom of the page.

ESL/ELL Strategy

SUMMARIZING Have pairs of students use their notes and the chart on page 123 to orally summarize the selection. Ask them to do so without looking back at the selection itself. Afterward, have students evaluate their notes, deciding whether they recorded the main ideas and details they needed to summarize the selection.

Extension Activity

Bring in and distribute copies of a science or social studies article. Have students read the article and take notes. When they have finished, have pairs of students compare and contrast their notes. Stress that while their main ideas should be the same, the wording and selection of details are likely to differ.

LESSON 40

Skill: Reading a Road Map (pages 124–125)

OBJECTIVE:
▶ Read a road map

Teaching the Skill

1. Review that a road map shows how to get from one place to another by car and how far it is between places. Bring in road maps of your state or region, and pass them around for students to study. Ask students to note the types of information they see on the maps. List some of these on the chalkboard. (the symbols that identify highways, towns, and campgrounds; the key that explains the symbols; the scale of miles; the compass rose.)

2. Encourage volunteers to recall times when they have used road maps during car trips. In particular, have them explain how route numbers, names of cities and towns, the scale of miles, and the key can all be very helpful when making a trip to an unfamiliar location.

3. Have students read the introductory paragraph on page 124. Then ask students to study the sample road map on the page. Have volunteers point to the map's scale of miles and its key. Point out that the key is divided into three sections—Highway Markers, Road Classification, and Special Features. Then have students read the paragraph below the map.

4. Have students complete the exercises on pages 124–125 independently.

ESL/ELL Strategy

USING REALIA Using a road map of their state or region, have pairs of students plan at least two trips that they could take by car. For each trip, have them list their destination, the highways they would take, and the total mileage. Students might also list points of interest they would pass along the way.

Extension Activity

Give partners a road map. One student writes a set of directions to reach a city or town, without naming it. For example: *Starting in Gatlinburg, I drive north on Routes 321 and 441 to Sevierville. I then turn east and drive five miles on Route 411. Where am I?* The partner then uses the map to locate the locations described in the directions and to determine the final destination.

LESSON 41

Skill: Conflict and Resolution (pages 126–131)

LITERATURE SELECTION: **The Campaign for Kate**

OBJECTIVES:

▶ Identify conflict and resolution

▶ Use a dictionary to find word meanings

CONTEXT CLUE WORDS: *clamber, priority, fatigue*

ESL/ELL WORDS: *bright and early, hit the showers, I'm beat*

GRAPHIC ORGANIZER: Prediction Chart, p. T55

SELECTION SUMMARY

The play, "The Campaign for Kate," is about two swim team members, Kate Fenton and Maria Cortez. The girls' coach believes that Kate has the talent to make the Olympic team. Kate, however, is unsure whether she is willing to make the sacrifices necessary to prepare for the Olympics. Maria, who lacks Kate's natural talent but is devoted to swimming, urges Kate to train harder. For a while, Kate stops practicing and starts spending time on her campaign for school office, but in the end she decides to rededicate herself to swimming.

▶ BEFORE READING

Have students read the Background Information about Olympic training on page 126. Ask volunteers to share what they know about Olympic athletes and how they prepare for the international games.

Teaching Conflict and Resolution

1. Remind students that a conflict is a struggle or problem that a story's character faces. A resolution is how the character deals with, or resolves, the conflict.

2. List the following three types of conflicts on the chalkboard and discuss examples of each: conflict with self, conflict with another character, and conflict with an outside source. Have volunteers describe examples of conflicts from books they have read recently. Ask students what kind of conflict each was and how it was resolved by the end of the book.

3. Have students read the Skill Focus on page 126 and complete the chart.

Teaching Context Clues

1. Remind students to look for context clues to help them figure out a new word's meaning. Then ask students what to do if there are not enough context clues to show a word's meaning. (Look up the word in the dictionary.)

2. Have a volunteer look up the word *optimism* in a dictionary, and read the definition. (to take the most hopeful or cheerful view of matters) Ask how he or she found the word. Review the importance of guide words, alphabetical order, and multiple meanings.

3. Have students read the Context Clues section on page 126 and complete the activity.

4. Write the context clue words *clamber, priority,* and *fatigue* on the chalkboard or word wall. Remind students to look up these words in a dictionary as they read.

Previewing the Text

Have students preview the play, studying its title, illustrations, and structure (scenes, boldface type for names of actors, and italic type for the setting and stage directions). Then distribute copies of the Prediction Chart. As they read, ask students to record what they predict the play will be about.

Purpose-Setting Question

What is the campaign that Kate decides to dedicate herself to?

▶ DURING READING

As students read, remind them to think about the conflicts Kate faces. Also remind them to look up the meanings of the underlined words in a dictionary.

▶ AFTER READING

Ask volunteers to share their Prediction Charts. Then ask students to answer the purpose-setting question and to complete the activities on pages 129–131.

Reading-Writing Connection

Before students describe a conflict and resolution they or someone they know has experienced suggest that they use a Sequence Chart (p. T62) to organize their details.

ESL/ELL Strategy

ROLE-PLAYING Have groups of students read aloud the dialogue among Kate, Maria, and Mr. Meacham in the play. Ask them to use their voices to express the conflicts.

Skill: Reading a Timeline (pages 132–137)

SOCIAL STUDIES SELECTION: **Swifter, Higher, Stronger**

OBJECTIVES:
▶ Read a timeline
▶ Use appositive phrases as context clues

CONTEXT CLUE WORDS: *sound, pentathlon, decathlon*

ESL/ELL WORDS: *motto, hand-to-hand, height of its power*

GRAPHIC ORGANIZER: KWL Chart, p. T60

—————— SELECTION SUMMARY ——————

"Swifter, Higher, Stronger" traces the history of the Olympic Games, beginning with an account of the first Olympic athletes of ancient Greece, whose motto was "swifter, higher, stronger." These early games, held for about 1,200 years, came to an end in A.D. 390. The Olympics were finally reborn in 1896, largely through the efforts of Baron de Coubertin of France, who hoped the games would foster world peace. The text and timeline of the article note major developments that have occurred in the games over the last century.

▶ **BEFORE READING** ....

Have students read the Background Information about the Olympic Games on page 132. On a map of the world, have students locate some of the countries in which the Olympic Games took place, such as Germany, Spain, Japan, Mexico, and South Korea. Ask students to share what they know about these countries.

Teaching Reading a Timeline

1. Remind students that a timeline is a chart that lists events in chronological order, or the time order in which they occurred.

2. Call on students to identify memorable class events that have occurred during the school year—field trips, school plays, sporting events, and so on. On the chalkboard, draw a horizontal timeline, and divide it into the months of the school year thus far. Encourage volunteers to come to the chalkboard and write each event in its proper place on the timeline.

3. Ask students to read the Skill Focus on page 132. Then have them study the short timeline and answer the questions.

Teaching Context Clues

1. Review that an appositive phrase explains the meaning of a word in the same or nearby sentence. It often starts with the word *or* and is set off by commas or dashes.

2. Write this sentence on the chalkboard. *My favorite winter Olympic event is the luge, or sled race.* Ask a volunteer to underline the appositive phrase (or sled race) and explain the meaning of *luge* (Luge is a sled race.).

3. Have students read the Context Clues section on page 132 and complete the activity.

4. Write the context clue words *sound, pentathlon,* and *decathlon* on the chalkboard or word wall. Remind students to look for appositive phrases that explain the meanings of these words.

Previewing the Text

Have students preview the selection's title, section headings, and timeline. Then distribute copies of the KWL Chart. Have students fill in what they know about the information they previewed and what they want to learn about it. As students read, ask them to list what they learn.

Purpose-Setting Question

In *what ways were the ancient Olympic Games different from the modern ones?*

▶ **DURING READING** ....

As students read, remind them to look at the dates and events on the timeline on pages 133–134. Also ask them to look for appositive phrases that explain the meanings of the underlined words.

▶ **AFTER READING** ....

Have students answer the purpose-setting question. Then have them use their Sequence Charts to help them complete the activities on pages 135–137.

Reading-Writing Connection

Before students write paragraphs describing their favorite Olympic sport and explaining why they like it, have them use the Idea Web (p. T58) to organize details about the sport.

ESL/ELL Strategy

ORGANIZING INFORMATION Have partners take turns describing important events in the history of the Olympics from ancient times to the present. Ask students to identify and describe the important events in Olympic history.

Skill: Following Directions (pages 138–142)

SCIENCE SELECTION: **Work and Machines**

OBJECTIVES:

▸ Follow directions

▸ Use diagrams as context clues

CONTEXT CLUE WORDS: *fulcrum, effort arm, resistance arm*

ESL/ELL WORDS: *equation, function, arm*

GRAPHIC ORGANIZER: Sequence Chart, p. T62

_____ SELECTION SUMMARY _____

"Work and Machines" explains the scientific meaning of work, the forces involved in doing work, and an explanation of how levers and pulleys make work easier. Students can use equations to calculate the mechanical advantage of each simple machine. An experiment demonstrates the mechanical advantage of using a fixed pulley to lift an object.

▸ **BEFORE READING** ....

Have students read the Background Information about simple machines on page 138. Then ask volunteers to identify everyday examples of each type of simple machine, such as a crowbar, window blinds, a ramp, an axe head, a car jack, and a doorknob.

Teaching Following Directions

1. Ask students to describe recent situations in which they had to follow directions to program a VCR, repair a bicycle, or do a craft project. Discuss whether the directions they had were adequate. Then have volunteers list features that make directions easier to follow. (short, numbered steps; definitions of terms; labeled diagrams; simple, easy-to-follow language)

2. On the chalkboard, write the five parts to the directions for a science experiment: *Problem, Aim, Materials, Procedure,* and *Observations or Conclusions.* With students, describe each step. Then ask a volunteer to explain why it is so important to follow directions in a science experiment. (Otherwise, the experiment will not work and could become dangerous.)

3. Have students read the Skill Focus on page 138 and complete the activity.

Teaching Context Clues

1. Review that a diagram is a drawing that helps explain a thing by showing all the parts, how it is put together, and how it works. Review the importance of reading the title, the caption, and the labels.

2. Ask a student to explain the process of completing a hobby such as model-car building. Have the volunteer draw a diagram of a model car on the chalkboard. Ask the student to repeat his or her original explanation, this time while pointing to parts of the diagram. Discuss how the diagram helped to understand the process being explained.

3. Have students read the Context Clues section on page 138 and complete the activity.

4. Write *fulcrum, effort arm,* and *resistance arm* on the chalkboard or word wall. Remind students to use the diagrams to help them figure out the meanings of these words.

Previewing the Text

Have students preview the title, the section headings, the diagrams, and the experiment. Then distribute copies of the Sequence Chart. Have students use their Sequence Charts to take notes on the steps to follow in the experiment.

Purpose-Setting Question

How do simple machines make work easier?

▸ **DURING READING** ....

As students read, remind them to record the steps of the experiment on their Sequence Charts. Also remind them to use the diagrams in the selection to help them figure out the meanings of the underlined words.

▸ **AFTER READING** ....

Have students share their Sequence Charts. Then ask students to answer the purpose-setting question and to complete the activities on pages 141–142.

Reading-Writing Connection

Before students describe an example of a pulley or lever and explain how it works, have the class brainstorm a list of examples of these simple machines. For example, window blinds use pulleys, and tools such as shovels are levers.

ESL/ELL Strategy

USING MANIPULATIVES Have partners use small objects in the classroom to demonstrate to each other how a lever works. For example, they could use a pencil or a ruler as a lever and an eraser for a fulcrum. Have students use terms in the selection as they explain how the lever works.

Skill: Reading a Graph (pages 143–146)

MATHEMATICS SELECTION: **Costs of World War II**

OBJECTIVES:

▸ Read circle graphs

▸ Use math word clues

ESL/ELL WORDS: *peak, in uniform, armed forces*

GRAPHIC ORGANIZER: KWL Chart, p. T60

_____ SELECTION SUMMARY _____

"Costs of World War II" teaches students to interpret circle graphs as they read about the costs—in both money and lives lost—of fighting World War II. The text explains that each sector of a circle graph represents a percentage of the total amount represented by the circle. The selection also explains how to convert the percentages shown on a circle graph to the amounts they represent.

▸ BEFORE READING ....

Have students read the Background Information about World War II on page 143. Ask students if they know anyone who served in World War II or who has told them about life in the 1940s. Ask them to recall any memories of this period that their friends or relatives have shared with them.

Teaching Reading a Graph

1. Review that graphs show a great deal of numerical information in an easy-to-use visual format. Display newspapers or news magazines that include circle graphs. Have volunteers read the titles of the graphs and summarize the information shown in them.

2. On the chalkboard, write the title *Teenagers' Favorite Sports*. Then draw a circle. Explain that the circle represents all, or 100%, of teenagers who were polled about their favorite sports. Point out that in a poll of 100 teenagers, 50 said that football was their favorite sport, 25 named basketball, and another 25 named baseball. Ask how they would divide this circle to show the 50 students who chose football. (in half because 50 is half of 100) Divide the circle in half, and label one half *Football, 50%*. Next ask a volunteer to divide the other half of the circle on the chalkboard and to show the percentages of teenagers who chose basketball and baseball. Have the volunteer label these sectors. (Basketball, 25%; Baseball, 25%) Conclude that a circle graph shows parts of a whole.

3. Ask students to read the Skill Focus on page 143 and complete the activity.

Teaching Word Clues

1. Have students read the Word Clues section on page 143.

2. Point to the circle graph you made on the chalkboard. Tell students that the numbers on which you based the graph are called the *data*. The three sections of the graph are called its *sectors*. The words and numbers next to each sector are called the graph's *labels*.

3. Write these words on the chalkboard for reference as students read the selection.

Previewing the Text

Have students preview the circle graphs. Then hand out copies of the KWL Chart. Have students fill in what they know about circle graphs and what they want to learn about them. As students read, ask them to list what they learn.

Purpose-Setting Question

How does a circle graph show information?

▸ DURING READING ....

As students read, have them study the circle graphs. Also have them look for the math words *data, sectors,* and *labels* and notice how they are used in the selection.

▸ AFTER READING ....

Allow time for students to share the information on their KWL Charts. Then ask students to answer the purpose-setting question and to complete the activities on pages 145–146.

Reading-Writing Connection

Before students take their polls and make their circle graphs, have them look through recent editions of newspapers and magazines to identify issues about which their classmates might have a variety of opinions.

ESL/ELL Strategy

USING MANIPULATIVES Have pairs of students make their own circle graphs. They could graph the number of boys and girls in the total class.

Skill: Multiple-Meaning Words (page 147)

OBJECTIVE:
▶ Recognize words with multiple meanings

Teaching the Skill

1. Remind students that many words have more than one meaning. Some words have an everyday meaning and also a special meaning in subjects such as literature, social studies, math, science, or music.

2. Write the following sentences on the chalkboard. Ask students to think about the meaning of the word *sound* in each sentence. *The house was so quiet I couldn't hear a <u>sound</u>. The whales entered the <u>sound</u> from the sea.* Students will be familiar with the meaning of the word as it is used in the first sentence. Ask if they know the social studies meaning of the word *sound* used in the second sentence. (a passage of water connecting two larger bodies of water)

3. Write the following words on the chalkboard: *mouth, cape, pole.* Ask volunteers to give an everyday meaning and a social studies meaning for each word. (social studies meanings: *mouth,* the part of a river that empties into an ocean or other body of water; *cape,* a point of land that extends into the water; *pole,* the northernmost or southernmost spot on Earth)

4. Have students read the sentences and the list of words at the top of page 147. Then have students complete the exercise independently.

ESL/ELL Strategy

USING MANIPULATIVES Have students draw pictures or cartoons that illustrate the two meanings of four of the words in the lesson. Below each picture, have students write a caption, using the word in its correct meaning. Students then discuss their cartoons in small groups.

Extension Activity

Have students use a dictionary to find two additional meanings for six of the words in the list on page 147. Ask them to make a glossary that gives all four meanings they have learned for each word.

Skill: Using an Index (pages 148–149)

OBJECTIVE:
▶ Use an index

Teaching the Skill

1. Explain that an index is the quickest way to find information in a nonfiction or reference book and that it is found at the back of the book. Review that an index lists all the important subjects included in the book.

2. Have students locate the index in one of their textbooks. Ask them what they notice about the index. Elicit that the index lists in alphabetical order the topics covered in the book. It also lists the page numbers where those topics are mentioned.

3. Choose a list of topics that have entries in various parts of the textbook's index. Ask students to find these entries in the index. Also have them identify the pages on which these topics are discussed in the textbook. They should then turn to the page or pages indicated to identify where on those pages the topic word appears.

4. Have students turn to page 148 and read the instructional paragraphs. Then have them study the sample index on page 149. Ask them to guess in what type of book they might find this index. (a general science textbook) Then have them complete the exercise independently.

ESL/ELL Strategy

USING REALIA Have pairs of students write five additional questions based on the entries in the index on page 149. Then have the pairs exchange their questions with other pairs and answer each other's questions.

Extension Activity

Give students a subject, such as World War II, to research, using nonfiction library books. Assign specific topics related to World War II, such as Pearl Harbor, D-Day, Omaha Beach, and Iwo Jima, to different students. Ask them to check the indexes of books about World War II and to list the pages of the books on which they can find their assigned topic.

Skill: Comparing Travel Packages (pages 150–151)

OBJECTIVE:

▶ Understand and compare travel packages

Teaching the Skill

1. Review that travel packages are arrangements made to cover vacation plans. Bring in some travel-package brochures for students to examine. You might find some at a local travel agent's office or on the Internet. Pass around the brochures, and have students comment on what they like most or least about each travel package.

2. Ask students what features a person might compare when trying to decide between two different travel packages. (the price of each, what kind of hotels are offered, whether free meals or other benefits are offered, sightseeing possibilities, whether there are activities that will appeal to different members of a family)

3. Have students turn to page 150 and study the two travel packages. Review common terms found in travel packages. Explain that a *reservation* is an accommodation arranged in advance, and *occupancy* is how many people will be staying in the room.

4. Then have students complete the exercises on pages 150–151.

ESL/ELL Strategy

USING VISUALS Have partners use the travel information on page 150 to discuss whether they would prefer to spend their vacation at the Gulf Inn Resort in Galveston or the Colonial Motel in Williamsburg.

Extension Activity

Have students create a travel-package brochure to attract vacationers to a site in their own state or region. Suggest that they provide information for each of the categories listed on the Comparison and Contrast Chart in Exercise B.

LESSON 48

Skill: Point of View (pages 152–157)

LITERATURE SELECTION: **The Principal Problem**

OBJECTIVES:
▶ Identify point of view
▶ Use a dictionary to find word meanings

CONTEXT CLUE WORDS: *coincidence, aerobics, malfunctioned*

ESL/ELL WORDS: *on the other hand, to say the least, hide and seek*

GRAPHIC ORGANIZER: Prediction Chart, p. T55

_____ SELECTION SUMMARY _____

"The Principal Problem," told through the first-person diary entries of a student, describes what happens after the arrival of a junior high school's new principal—a Delta computer nicknamed Dellie. At first students like the new principal, because Dellie does whatever they want, but then chaos reigns.

▶ **BEFORE READING** ....
Have students read the Background Information about computers on page 152. Ask students to share some of the complaints they have heard people make about computers and discuss whether any of these complaints are valid.

Teaching Point of View

1. Review that point of view is the eye through which a story is written. Explain that every story has a narrator, or storyteller, and that different types of narrators tell a story differently. Point out that most stories are written from a first-person or third-person point of view.

2. Ask a volunteer to narrate an event that happened to him or her recently, such as missing the bus or winning an award. Point out to the class that the narrator was a character in the story and used first-person pronouns such as *I, me,* and *my* to narrate events. Explain that this story was told in *first-person point of view.*

3. Ask another volunteer to retell the same story, describing what happened to the person who first told the story. Explain that this narrator uses third-person pronouns such as *he* and *she, his,* and *her* to tell what happened. This story was told in *third-person point of view.*

4. Have students read the Skill Focus on page 152 and complete the activity.

Teaching Context Clues

1. Write the following sentence on the chalkboard. *That computer is obsolete.* Ask students if there are any context clues in the sentence that help figure out the word's meaning (no) and how we can find out what *obsolete* means (look up the word in a dictionary).

2. Have a volunteer look up the word and tell the class its meaning. (old-fashioned or out-of-date)

3. Have students read the Context Clues section on page 152 and complete the activity.

4. Write the context clue words *coincidence, aerobics,* and *malfunctioned* on the chalkboard or word wall. Remind students to use a dictionary to look up the meanings of these words.

Previewing the Text
Have students preview the selection's title, illustration, and story format. Distribute copies of the Prediction Chart, and ask students to predict what might happen in the story.

Purpose-Setting Question
What "principal problem" do the students at Gloria Willis Junior High have?

▶ **DURING READING** ....
As students read, remind them to think about who is telling the story and how this point of view affects their understanding of story events. Also remind them to look up the meanings of the underlined words in a dictionary.

▶ **AFTER READING** ....
Have students discuss their Prediction Charts. Then ask students to answer the purpose-setting question and to complete the activities on pages 155–157.

Reading-Writing Connection
Before students write about how they would feel if their teachers were replaced by computers, have them discuss if a computer could be a good teacher.

ESL/ELL Strategy

PERSONALIZING THE LESSON Have students write three diary entries that tell about events in their lives over the course of several days, using first-person pronouns.

Skill: Making Generalizations (pages 158–163)

SOCIAL STUDIES SELECTION: **From the Abacus to the Personal Computer**

OBJECTIVES:

▶ Make generalizations

▶ Use a glossary

CONTEXT CLUE WORDS: *computer, data, binary, CD-ROM*

ESL/ELL WORDS: *speedometer, carryout, gobbled up*

GRAPHIC ORGANIZER: Generalization Chart, p. T64

SELECTION SUMMARY

"From the Abacus to the Personal Computer" provides a historical overview of inventions that have made calculations easier. Beginning with the abacus, developed some 2,500 years ago in China, the article traces such developments as the invention of Pascal's *Machine Arithmetique* in 1642, Babbage's attempt to construct a digital computer in 1833, and early tabulating machines used by the U.S. Census Bureau, beginning in the 1880s.

▶ BEFORE READING

Have students read the Background Information about computers on page 158. Ask volunteers to share what they know about the history of computers or some recent developments in computer technology.

Teaching Making Generalizations

1. Review that a generalization is a broad statement that applies to many examples or events. We can make a generalization by thinking about related facts and what they have in common.

2. Write these sentences side by side in individual boxes on the chalkboard. *Emily likes to play tennis. Emily likes to swim. Emily likes to play softball. Emily likes to play soccer.* Then ask students what general statement they could make about Emily, based on these facts. (Emily enjoys many sports.) Write this generalization in a box below the other four and draw lines from them to this box.

3. Have students read the Skill Focus on page 158 and complete the chart.

Teaching Context Clues

1. Review that a glossary is an alphabetical collection of terms and their meanings that is found at the back of a textbook. Have students turn to the back of their social studies or science textbook and find its glossary. Point out that a glossary contains definitions of all the specialized vocabulary used in the book. Using a glossary is a quick, easy way to find out the meanings of new and unusual words in a textbook.

2. Explain that some historical and scientific articles also include glossaries. Have students look at the glossary on pages 161–162. Ask a volunteer to read the definition of the word *modem*.

3. Have students read the Context Clues section on page 158 and complete the activity.

4. Write the words *computer, data, binary,* and *CD-ROM* on the chalkboard or word wall. Ask students to look up these words in the selection's glossary.

Previewing the Text

Have students preview the selection's title, section headings, and photographs. Then distribute copies of the Generalization Chart. Ask students to list facts about the development of computers and then use them to make generalizations.

Purpose-Setting Question

What were the major historical inventions that led to the development of modern computers?

▶ DURING READING

As students read, remind them to record details and make generalizations. Encourage them to use the glossary at the end of the article to look up the meanings of the underlined words.

▶ AFTER READING

Allow time for students to share their Generalization Charts. Then ask students to answer the purpose-setting question and to complete the activities on pages 162–163.

Reading-Writing Connection

Before students write an explanation of how computers can make learning more interesting, have the class brainstorm a list of ways in which they have used computers to do research to learn about new subjects.

ESL/ELL Strategy

PERSONALIZING THE LESSON Have pairs of students discuss the availability of computers and Internet service in your school and your local library. Ask them to list several facts on this subject and make a valid generalization.

Skill: Making Inferences (pages 164–168)

SCIENCE SELECTION: **What Is a Computer?**

OBJECTIVES:

▶ Make inferences

▶ Use diagrams as context clues

CONTEXT CLUE WORDS: *arithmetic unit, input equipment, output equipment*

ESL/ELL WORDS: *rolled into one, ring up, the outside world*

GRAPHIC ORGANIZER: Inference Chart, p. T61

SELECTION SUMMARY

"What Is a Computer?" explains what computers can and cannot do. It also contrasts digital and analog computers, recognizing the most important uses of each. The article describes the three basic components of computer hardware—the central processing unit, the input equipment, and the output equipment—and it offers a brief explanation of computer codes.

▶ BEFORE READING

Have students read the Background Information about "What Is a Computer" on page 164. Ask volunteers to share what they know about how computers work and how computers help us in our daily lives.

Teaching Making Inferences

1. Review that making inferences requires students to combine the details in a selection with what they already know to help them figure out unstated information.

2. Distribute the following paragraph on a handout. *Jack got a really bad virus last week. It left him feeling terrible. The virus destroyed half of his files before he noticed it.* Ask students what kind of a virus Jack had. (a computer virus) Then ask how they were able to infer this fact, even though the sentences did not state it directly. (The sentences state that the virus destroyed half his files, and we know that computer viruses damage computer files.) Point out that students used details from the story plus what they already knew.

3. Have students read the Skill Focus on page 164 and complete the activity.

Teaching Context Clues

1. Review that diagrams act like context clues in that they give information about an object's parts, how it is put together, and how it works.

2. Provide computer manuals with diagrams, such as those used in a school computer lab. Have volunteers read the labels and captions on the diagrams. Then ask if students can figure out clues to any new words by looking at the diagrams and reading their labels and captions.

3. Have students read the Context Clues section on page 164 and complete the activity.

4. Write the context clue words *arithmetic unit, input equipment,* and *output equipment* on the chalkboard or word wall. Remind students to use the diagrams in the article to help them figure out what these words mean.

Previewing the Text

Have students preview the selection's title, section headings, and diagrams. Point out that the paragraphs are numbered for easy reference. Then distribute copies of the Inference Chart. Ask students to list details from the selection on their charts and to use what they already know about computers to make inferences.

Purpose-Setting Question

What are the three basic components of a digital computer, and what does each component do?

▶ DURING READING

As students read, remind them to list details and make inferences. Also remind them to use the diagrams to figure out the meanings of the underlined words.

▶ AFTER READING

Allow time for students to share their Inference Charts. Then ask students to answer the purpose-setting question and to complete the activities on pages 167–168.

Reading-Writing Connection

Before students write their explanations about what happens inside a computer, suggest that they work in small groups to create a diagram of the process they will explain. This will help them organize their ideas.

ESL/ELL Strategy

ROLE-PLAYING Have partners role-play a salesperson and a customer at a computer store. The customer asks the salesperson questions about the computers for sale. The salesperson answers them. Both players use concept words from the article in their questions and answers.

Skill: Understanding Computer Language
(pages 169–171)

MATHEMATICS SELECTION: **Computer Language**

OBJECTIVES:
▶ Understand computer language
▶ Use computer language as word clues

ESL/ELL WORDS: *monitor, delivered, mechanisms*

GRAPHIC ORGANIZER: Sequence Chart, p. T62

SELECTION SUMMARY

"Computer Language" explains how computer programmers communicate with computers by using computer languages. It then presents detailed information about one of these languages, BASIC. The article explains how the lines of a program must be written for a computer to understand it. The text includes a few short examples of a BASIC program, as well as information about how a computer translates the numbers and letters of a computer language into binary code.

▶ **BEFORE READING**

Have students read the Background Information about computer programming on page 169. Invite volunteers to share what they already know about computer programming with the class.

Teaching Understanding Computer Language

1. Explain that in order for a computer to perform, it must be programmed, or given instructions by a computer programmer. Although different sets of instructions, or languages, are used to program computers, all computers process information the same way.

2. To demonstrate a simple program in BASIC, type the following set of instructions on the classroom computer, if possible.

   10 PRINT "I LOVE MY COMPUTER"

   20 END

   Explain that each line or command of a program is numbered so that the computer follows the commands in order. Show students the printed output: I LOVE MY COMPUTER. Then ask volunteers to try more examples of a simple BASIC program.

3. Have students read the Skill Focus on page 169 and complete the activity.

Teaching Word Clues

1. Have students turn to the Word Clues section on page 169. List the computer words *RUN, LET,* and *END* on the chalkboard. Review what these three words mean in everyday language. (to go by moving the legs rapidly; to give or allow; the limit or to stop) Point out that they have special meanings in computer language, but knowing the everyday definition will help to understand them better.

2. As students read, ask them to note details in the text that help explain the meanings of these computer-related words.

Previewing the Text

Have students preview the use of words in capital letters. Ask students to make predictions about what they will learn, based on the selection's title and the lines of computer code. Then hand out copies of the Sequence Chart. Ask students to record the steps to follow when writing a program in the BASIC language.

Purpose-Setting Question

What are computer languages, and why are they necessary?

▶ **DURING READING**

As students read, have them add information about computer language to their Sequence Charts. Also have them look for the computer-related words in boldface.

▶ **AFTER READING**

Have students share their Sequence Charts and answer the purpose-setting question. Then have them complete the activities on page 171.

Reading-Writing Connection

Before students write their four-line computer program, ask students who are familiar with computers to answer any questions that other students may have.

ESL/ELL Strategy

ORGANIZING INFORMATION Have pairs of students make a Comparison and Contrast Chart (p. T56), showing how BASIC is both similar to and different from a foreign language.

LESSON 52

Skill: Using Reference Books (pages 172–173)

OBJECTIVE:
▶ Compare reference books

Teaching the Skill

1. Remind students that reference books can provide all kinds of information on nearly any subject. Pass around a dictionary, an atlas, an almanac, and a volume from a set of encyclopedias.

2. On the chalkboard, label four columns: *dictionary, encyclopedia, atlas,* and *almanac.* Ask volunteers to list details about each reference book that distinguishes it from the others. For example, students might note the general categories of information in each book (words, topics, maps, and annual records respectively), how it is organized (alphabetized, part of the world), and when it might be most useful (simple definition, more detail, map of location, most updated info).

3. Have students read page 172. Ask volunteers to contrast the information in the sample dictionary entry *gibbon* with the information in the sample encyclopedia entry.

4. After students have read about the atlas, point out that it is a one-volume reference that may contain different kinds of maps, including political maps, population maps, relief maps, and product maps.

5. Have students complete the exercise on page 173 independently.

ESL/ELL Strategy

USING RESOURCES Have partners write four simple questions, each one that can be answered by checking a dictionary, an encyclopedia, an atlas, or an almanac. Have partners exchange their questions with other pairs, decide which reference book would be the best place to look for the answer to each question, and then to use that book to find the answer.

Extension Activity

Have students locate online encyclopedias and dictionaries. Ask them to create Comparison and Contrast Charts (p. T56) showing similarities and differences between the electronic versions and the book versions of the references.

LESSON 53

Skill: Reading a Job Application (pages 174–175)

OBJECTIVE:
▶ Read a job application

Teaching the Skill

1. Review that a job application is a written form that asks for information about someone's work experience, education, and interests. Bring in a few blank job applications, and pass them around for students to examine.

2. Ask students who have applied for part-time or summer jobs to share their experiences with job applications. Stress that employers are impressed by an application that is neatly and completely filled out.

3. Ask students to read the explanatory text and to study the sample job application on page 174. Discuss what kinds of information the applicant is asked to provide on the application. (name, address, phone number, Social Security number, education and employment record, hobbies, references, the kind of job wanted, the start date, and whether looking for a full-time job or a part-time job) Go over difficult terms, such as *employment record, positions,* and *references.*

4. Have students complete the exercises on page 175.

ESL/ELL Strategy

USING MANIPULATIVES To prepare students to fill out an actual job application, have them list on three separate index cards the following: the names and addresses of schools they have attended with the years they attended; part-time jobs they have held; and the names, addresses, and phone numbers of two references.

Extension Activity

Ask students to write a résumé of their work experience, education, and interests. Provide a few sample résumés for students to use as models. Explain that having a résumé on hand will help them fill out job applications, since the information listed on a résumé closely parallels the information required on a job application.

C

Be A Better
READER

EIGHTH EDITION

NILA BANTON SMITH

GLOBE FEARON
Pearson Learning Group

Pronunciation Key

Symbol	Key Word	Respelling	Symbol	Key Word	Respelling
a	act	(akt)	u	book	(buk)
ah	star	(stahr)		put	(put)
ai	dare	(dair)	uh	cup	(kuhp)
aw	also	(AWL soh)			
ay	flavor	(FLAY vər)	ə	a *as in*	
				along	(ə LAWNG)
e	end	(end)		e *as in*	
ee	eat	(eet)		moment	(MOH mənt)
er	learn	(lern)		i *as in*	
	sir	(ser)		modify	(MAHD ə fy)
	fur	(fer)		o *as in*	
				protect	(prə TEKT)
i	hit	(hit)		u *as in*	
eye	idea	(eye DEE ə)		circus	(SER kəs)
y	like	(lyk)	ch	chill	(chil)
ir	deer	(dir)	g	go	(goh)
	fear	(fir)	j	joke	(johk)
				bridge	(brij)
oh	open	(OH pen)	k	kite	(kyt)
oi	foil	(foil)		cart	(kahrt)
	boy	(boi)	ng	bring	(bring)
or	horn	(horn)	s	sum	(suhm)
ou	out	(out)		cent	(sent)
	flower	(FLOU ər)	sh	sharp	(shahrp)
oo	hoot	(hoot)	th	thin	(thin)
	rule	(rool)	*th*	then	(*then*)
			z	zebra	(ZEE brə)
yoo	few	(fyoo)		pose	(pohz)
	use	(yooz)	zh	treasure	(TREZH ər)

The following people have contributed to the development of this product: ***Art and Design:*** Tricia Battipede, Robert Dobaczewski, Elizabeth Witmer; ***Editorial:*** Brian Hawkes, Eleanor Ripp, Jennifer M. Watts; ***Manufacturing:*** Michele Uhl; ***Production:*** Laura Benford-Sullivan, Jeffrey Engel; ***Publishing Operations:*** Jennifer Van Der Heide

Acknowledgments: The dictionary definitions in this book are from Webster's New World™ Dictionary, Basic School Edition. Copyright © 1989 by Hungry Minds, Inc. All rights reserved. Reproduced here by permission of the publisher. "Gibbon" excerpted from THE WORLD BOOK ENCYCLOPEDIA © 2002 World Book, Inc. (Volume 8, page 185). Used by permission. A & W Publishers for the almanac entry. Reprinted by permission of A & W Publishers, Inc., from INFORMATION PLEASE ALMANAC 1982. Copyright © 1981 by Simon & Schuster, a Viacom Company.

NOTE: Every effort has been made to locate the copyright owner of material reprinted in this book. Omissions brought to our attention will be corrected in subsequent printings.

Photos: p. 12: Bettmann/CORBIS; p. 13: Bettmann/CORBIS; p. 18: Frank Lane Picture Agency/CORBIS; p. 18: Stuart Westmorland/CORBIS; p. 28: NASA/Roger Ressmeyer/CORBIS; p. 40: Nick Wheeler/CORBIS; p. 41: Hulton-Deutsch Collection/CORBIS; p. 74: Pearson Learning; p. 97: Bettmann/CORBIS; p. 119: Seth Resnick/PictureQuest; p. 139: Pearson Learning; p. 159: Bettmann/CORBIS; p. 159: Bettmann/CORBIS; p. 160: Hulton-Deutsch Collection/CORBIS; p. 161: Bettmann/CORBIS; p. 161: PhotoDisc; p. 161: Antonio

Globe Fearon
Pearson Learning Group

ISBN 0-130-23860-0

Printed in the United States of America

3 4 5 6 7 8 9 10   06 05 04 03

1-800-321-3106
www.pearsonlearning.com

Contents

Contents
continued

How to Use *Be A Better Reader*

For more than thirty years, **Be A Better Reader** has helped students improve their reading skills. **Be A Better Reader** teaches the comprehension and study skills that you need to read and enjoy all types of materials—from library books to the different textbooks that you will encounter in school.

To get the most from **Be A Better Reader**, you should know how the lessons are organized. As you read the following explanations, it will be helpful to look at some of the lessons.

In each of the first four lessons of a unit, you will apply an important skill to a reading selection in literature, social studies, science, or mathematics. Each of these lessons includes the following nine sections.

▶ BACKGROUND INFORMATION

This section gives you interesting information about the selection you are about to read. It will help you understand the ideas that you need in order to learn new skills.

▶ SKILL FOCUS

This section teaches you a specific skill. You should read the Skill Focus carefully, paying special attention to words that are printed in boldface type. The Skill Focus tells you about a skill that you will use when you read the selection.

▶ CONTEXT CLUES OR WORD CLUES

This section teaches you how to recognize and use different types of context and word clues. These clues will help you with the meanings of the underlined words in the selection.

▶ STRATEGY TIP

This section gives you suggestions about what to look for as you read. The suggestions will help you understand the selection.

▶ SELECTIONS

There are four kinds of selections in **Be A Better Reader**. A selection in a literature lesson is similar to a selection in a literature anthology, library book, newspaper, or magazine. A social studies selection is like a chapter in a social studies textbook or an encyclopedia. It often includes maps or tables. A science selection, like a science textbook, includes special words and sometimes diagrams. A mathematics selection will help you acquire skill in reading mathematics textbooks.

▶ COMPREHENSION QUESTIONS

Answers to the questions in this section can be found in the selection itself. You will sometimes have to reread parts of the selection to complete this activity.

▶ CRITICAL THINKING ACTIVITY

The critical thinking activity includes questions whose answers are not directly stated in the selection. For these questions, you must combine the information in the selection with what you already know in order to infer the answers.

▶ SKILL FOCUS ACTIVITY

In this activity, you will use the skill that you learned in the Skill Focus section at the beginning of the lesson to answer questions about the selection. If you have difficulty completing this activity, reread the Skill Focus section.

▶ READING–WRITING CONNECTION

In this writing activity, you will have a chance to use the information in the selection you read, by writing about it. Here is your chance to share your ideas about the selection.

Additional Lessons

The remaining lessons in each unit give you practice with such skills as using a dictionary, an encyclopedia, and other reference materials; using phonics and syllabication in recognizing new words; locating and organizing information; and adjusting your reading rate. Other reading skills that are necessary in everyday life, such as reading a bus schedule, are also covered.

Each time you learn a new skill in **Be A Better Reader**, look for opportunities to use the skill in your other reading at school and at home. Your reading ability will improve the more you practice reading!

unit one

For ESL/ELL support, see highlighted words, page T65, and pages T28–T30.

Adventures in Flight

For theme support, see page T26.

LESSON 1

Skill: Plot

For lesson support, see page T65.

BACKGROUND INFORMATION

"The Flight of Daedalus" is a Greek myth that is more than 5,000 years old. Like most myths, it was handed down by word of mouth for many generations before it was written down. Myths focus on important conflicts in human life. "The Flight of Daedalus" focuses on people's desire to fly and on the effect of pride on human life.

SKILL FOCUS: Plot

A story's **plot** is the series of events that happen in the story. Most plots have five parts, which are shown in the following diagram.

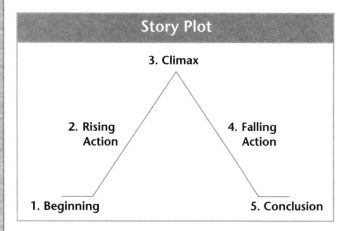

Story Plot

3. Climax

2. Rising Action

4. Falling Action

1. Beginning

5. Conclusion

1. **Beginning** The beginning of the plot introduces the main characters and the setting.

2. **Rising Action** The plot begins to build as a conflict develops. The main character struggles to achieve a goal or to solve a problem.

3. **Climax** The plot events build to a climax, or high point. This is the most exciting part of the story and often marks a turning point.

4. **Falling Action** The events after the climax show how the characters resolve, or deal with, the conflict in the story.

5. **Conclusion** A final event ends the story.

▶ Choose an exciting short story or novel you have read recently. Think about the parts of its plot. Make a large copy of the Story Plot Diagram on a separate sheet of paper. Then fill in events from the story under the correct labels. Diagrams will vary.

CONTEXT CLUES: Footnotes

Footnotes are explanations of names and other special words that appear in a selection. When you read an unfamiliar name of a person, place, or thing, look for a footnote to help you figure it out. Words with footnotes have a small raised number next to them. The footnotes themselves appear at the bottom of a page. Notice the footnote in the sentence below.

With a fist of iron, he ruled the kingdom of Crete.[1]

Notice the raised number after the word *Crete*. The number is a signal to look at the bottom of the page for a footnote with the same number. The footnote will give a definition or an explanation of the term. Here is the footnote that explains *Crete*.

[1] *Crete (KREET): an island southeast of Greece.*

▶ Read the following sentence and the footnote. Then underline the details in the footnote that tell you the meaning of *Labyrinth*.

The most famous structure that Daedalus built for Minos was the Labyrinth.[2]

[2] *Labyrinth (LAB ə rinth): <u>a building on ancient Crete with many winding passages and blind alleys; a maze.</u>*

As you read the myth, use footnote clues to find the meanings of *Minotaur*, *Sicily*, and *Apollo*.

> **Strategy Tip**
>
> As you read "The Flight of Daedalus," use the diagram and the explanations on this page to help you understand the story's plot.

THE FLIGHT OF DAEDALUS

Long, long ago lived a proud and terrible king. His name was Minos (MEYE nohs). With a fist of iron, he ruled the kingdom of Crete.[1]

Daedalus (DED ə ləs), another proud man, also lived on the island of Crete. He was a sculptor and a builder. He may have been the finest builder of his time. Daedalus built many fine buildings for King Minos.

The most famous structure that Daedalus built for Minos was the Labyrinth.[2] It was designed as a prison and a trap. No one could find a way out of its passageways without knowing the design. Minos was very pleased with the Labyrinth. He imprisoned his enemies there. The Labyrinth was also home to the dreaded Minotaur.[3]

One day Minos became very angry with Daedalus. The builder had given away the secret of the Labyrinth. In anger, Minos imprisoned Daedalus in the Labyrinth. Within a short time, however, Daedalus managed to escape.

The sculptor found his son, Icarus (IK ə rəs), and planned to flee from Crete. However, Minos was determined to recapture Daedalus. The king's soldiers searched all the ships before they left the island.

Minos knew that Daedalus and Icarus were hiding in the countryside, but he didn't care. He was sure that Daedalus and Icarus could not escape from Crete. So Minos decided to let Daedalus wander free for a while. "Soon the master builder will realize that he is trapped here. He will have to admit that he is in my power and will give himself up. Then I will give him many difficult tasks to perform."

Daedalus tried many times to find a way to escape from the island. He stood on the rocky hills of Crete and stared out to sea. Above him, the sea gulls and other sea birds wheeled and dipped in the sky. Below, the sun glistened on the water in the

harbor and on the helmets of Minos's soldiers. Daedalus could see the trap that Minos had set.

"I cannot let Minos defeat me," he thought. "I must escape with my son. There must be a way off the island."

At times, Daedalus feared that he and his son would be captives on Crete forever. However, his quick mind kept searching for a way out. As he pondered, he watched the many birds that soared high in the blue sky. Suddenly, Daedalus was struck by a thought. "Minos may rule the land and sea, but he cannot control the air!" Daedalus said, as he watched feathers drop from the wings of the sea gulls.

He quickly sent his son in search of stray sea gull feathers. Icarus found tiny, soft feathers. He picked up long, strong feathers. He gathered black plumes and white ones. He found blue feathers and brown feathers. Soon Icarus had made a great mound of feathers of all kinds.

Then Daedalus set to work. He built a large wooden frame shaped like a bird's wing. He fastened feathers to it. Some he sewed on; others he stuck on with wax. Finally he used wax to mold all the feathers into shape. Once he had finished this frame, he made another one and covered it with feathers, too. Now he had two huge wings, like those of a giant bird.

Daedalus fastened the wings to his shoulders. Would they work? He flapped the wings and tried to fly. After some minutes, the wings lifted him from the ground.

He could fly! However, Daedalus soon learned that there was more to flying than flapping his

---

[1] Crete (KREET): an island southeast of Greece.
[2] Labyrinth (LAB ə rinth): a building on ancient Crete with many winding passages and blind alleys; a maze.
[3] Minotaur (MIN ə tor): a monster with a bull's head and a man's body; the monster ate human victims.

LITERATURE

"Don't fly too close to the water," he would say. "The fog will weigh you down. Also don't fly close to the sun. Its warmth will melt the wax on your wings."

Icarus listened impatiently to his father's warnings. He thought, "I can take care of myself!"

One fair morning, Daedalus said, "The wind is just right today. We shall fly to Sicily."[4]

Strapping on their wings, Daedalus and Icarus walked to the top of a rocky hill. Daedalus flapped his huge wings, rose in the air, and flew out over the sea. Icarus lifted himself with his wings and followed. Minos could never catch them now!

Daedalus headed out over the ocean, beating the air strongly and surely. Icarus swooped and turned as he followed his father. Flying free in the air, Icarus knew the joy of being a bird. He looked down at the white-capped waves. How wonderful to be soaring above them! Then he looked at the clouds above. How exciting it would be to fly above them!

Icarus forgot his father's warnings. Beating his wings faster and faster, he rose up and up. As he flew higher, the sun flickered and gleamed on his feathers. On and on he flew, higher and higher. The sun grew brighter.

The air became very warm, but Icarus flew on. As he flew, it became more and more difficult

wings. He had to learn to swoop, to soar on the winds, to turn, and to gather speed.

Working as fast as he could, Daedalus then made wings for Icarus. Icarus watched gleefully as his father sewed and glued the feathers in place. Icarus could scarcely wait to put on the wonderful wings.

At last, the wings were finished. Daedalus fastened them to his son's shoulders. Icarus looked very handsome. The beautiful wings covered his entire body. His golden hair shone in the sunlight, and his eyes sparkled with excitement.

Icarus quickly learned to fly. He seemed to have been born to it. His father, knowing how daring Icarus could be, warned him often to be careful.

[4] Sicily (SIS əl ee): an island in southern Italy.

to climb higher. His wings drooped. Feathers began to fall like snowflakes. The sun's heat was melting the wax! Furiously, Icarus beat his wings, but they could no longer support him. As he fell toward the glittering ocean far below, Icarus cried out to his father.

Daedalus heard the cry and turned. He caught only a glimpse of his son as Icarus plunged into the white-capped waves. Nothing remained except a few feathers floating on the surface.

In deep grief, Daedalus flew on to Sicily. He went to the temple of the sun god <u>Apollo</u>.[5] There he hung up his wings as an offering to the god.

Daedalus had beaten his enemy, Minos, but at the terrible cost of the life of his son. Perhaps the gods were punishing Daedalus for daring to do something that humans were not meant to do: fly with the wings of a bird.

[5] Apollo (ə POL oh): a Greek god; the son of Zeus, king of the gods.

COMPREHENSION

Recalling details
1. Identify the three story characters.

   a. _____Minos_____, king of Crete

   b. _____Daedalus_____, a master builder

   c. _____Icarus_____, his son

Recalling details
2. What did the builder make for the king that pleased the king very much?

   Daedalus made the Labyrinth.

Identifying cause and effect
3. Explain why Daedalus was imprisoned.

   He gave away the secret of the Labyrinth, which made

   Minos very angry.

Recalling details
4. Explain how Daedalus attached feathers to the wings he made.

   He used wax to attach some feathers to the wooden

   frames.

Identifying cause and effect
5. What caused the feathers to drop from Icarus's wings?

   When Icarus flew too close to the sun, the heat melted

   the wax and the feathers fell off.

Using context clues
6. Complete each statement with the correct word.

   Minotaur   Sicily   Apollo

   a. In Greek mythology, _____Apollo_____ is the god of light and the sun.

   b. The temple of Apollo is located in _____Sicily_____, an island in southern Italy.

   c. In Greek mythology, the _____Minotaur_____ is a terrible monster that ate people.

CRITICAL THINKING

Making inferences
1. Discuss why it was a foolish idea for Minos to try to imprison Daedalus in the Labyrinth.

   Daedalus built the maze, so he knew the way out. He was able to escape easily.

Making inferences
2. Tell why Icarus ignored his father's warnings about flying too close to the sun.

   He was proud and daring. He was so excited about flying that he forgot to be careful.

Inferring comparisons and contrasts
3. Why didn't Daedalus, like Icarus, forget himself and fly too close to the sun?

   Daedalus was older and wiser. He concentrated on reaching safety.

4. Explain how each character's pride leads to his downfall, or defeat, in the story.

Minos's pride makes him careless about letting Daedalus wander freely. Daedalus's pride in his skills as a builder and in

beating Minos costs him his son. Icarus's pride in his ability to fly costs him his life.

5. Do you think that Daedalus will ever fly again? Use an event from the story to support your answer.

Answers will vary. No. At the end of the story, Daedalus is so sad over the death of his son that he hangs up his wings as an

offering to Apollo.

SKILL FOCUS: PLOT

The following list describes some of the events in the myth of Daedalus. On the diagram below, write the letter or letters of each event next to the correct part of the plot. It may help if you first decide which event is the climax.

a. Daedalus escapes from the Labyrinth.

b. Daedalus sees Icarus fall into the sea.

c. Daedalus builds two pairs of wings so that he and Icarus can escape from Crete.

d. Daedalus hangs up his wings as an offering to the sun god Apollo.

e. Using their wings, Daedalus and Icarus head for Sicily.

f. Icarus, ignoring Daedalus's warnings, flies too close to the sun.

g. Alone, Daedalus flies to Sicily.

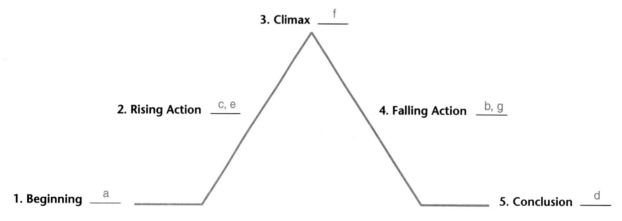

3. Climax _f_

2. Rising Action _c, e_

4. Falling Action _b, g_

1. Beginning _a_

5. Conclusion _d_

Reading-Writing Connection

On a separate sheet of paper, write one paragraph describing pride as a good quality and another paragraph describing pride as dangerous. Use examples from everyday life to support your main ideas.

LESSON 2

For ESL/ELL support, see highlighted words, page T66, and pages T28–T30.

Skill: Comparing and Contrasting

For lesson support, see page T66.

BACKGROUND INFORMATION

In "Flying to Fame," you will read about two women pioneers in the history of flight. Many men and women have contributed to the amazing progress in flight. One woman was Amelia Earhart, a record-setting pilot of the 1930s. Another is Sally Ride, the first American woman in space.

SKILL FOCUS: Comparing and Contrasting

Comparing and contrasting are important ways to understand information. **Comparing** is finding out how two or more things are alike. **Contrasting** is noticing how they are different.

Writers can show comparison and contrast in different ways. One way is to first tell all about one person or thing and then tell all about the other one.

Read the following two paragraphs. Think about how you might compare and contrast the pilots.

Cal Rodgers, a little-known pioneer of flight, was the first person to fly across the United States. Taking off from New York in 1911, he landed 69 times before finally reaching California. In all, the 3,220-mile flight took 50 days.

Another little-known pioneer was Harriet Quimby. In 1912, Quimby flew across the English Channel. The first American woman pilot, she crossed the 22-mile stretch of water between England and France in about 30 minutes.

Compare the two paragraphs. Notice the similarities between the two pilots. Both were pioneers, and neither one was famous. Notice the differences. Rodgers was a man; Quimby was a woman. Rodgers flew a long flight over land in the United States. Quimby flew a short flight over water in Europe.

▶ Use details from the two paragraphs to complete the Contrast Chart below.

CONTEXT CLUES: Details

When you read a word that you do not know, look for context clues to help you understand it. Context clues are words near the new word that make its meaning clearer. Often these clues are **details**, or small pieces of information that help you understand what the word means.

Read the sentence below.

*Sally Ride **donned** her space suit and her helmet with the ease that you slip on a coat and hat.*

If you don't know the meaning of *donned*, the phrase *with the ease that you slip on a coat and hat* can help you. The details in the phrase help you see that *donned* means "put on."

▶ Circle the details that help you figure out the meaning of the word *gender*.

*These two women were also pioneers for their **gender**. They have proven that (women, as well as men,) have the courage and determination to make history.*

As you read the selection, use details to help you understand the meanings of the underlined words *spectator*, *endeavor*, and *vastness*.

Strategy Tip

As you read "Flying to Fame," look for ways in which Amelia Earhart and Sally Ride are alike and different.

Contrast Chart		
Cal Rodgers	**Topic**	**Harriet Quimby**
flew across U.S.	Achievement	flew across English Channel
1911	Date	1912
3,220 mi./50 days	Length of Flight	22 mi./30 min.

Flying to Fame

AMELIA EARHART AND SALLY RIDE are **pioneers** (PEYE ə NIRZ) in the history of flight. They are two of the brave people who dared to venture into the unknown and prepare the way for later accomplishments in flight. These two women are also pioneers for their **gender** (JEN dər). They have proven that women, as well as men, have the courage and determination to make history.

✗ In 1932, a young woman named Amelia Earhart set off on a dangerous flight. She pulled on her leather flying gear, adjusted her goggles, and climbed into her propeller plane. Alone, she took off from Newfoundland, Canada, to cross the Atlantic Ocean. The world cheered when Earhart landed safely in Ireland. Amelia Earhart had become the first woman to fly solo across the Atlantic.

✗ Half a century later, on June 18, 1983, another woman set out to make history. Sally Ride donned her space suit and her helmet with the ease that you slip on a coat and hat. She climbed aboard the *Challenger* space shuttle with three other astronauts and blasted off into outer space. Sally Ride became the first American woman in space.

In 1932, Amelia Earhart became the first woman to fly solo across the Atlantic.

Amelia Earhart

Amelia Earhart was born on July 24, 1897, in Atchison, Kansas. While growing up, she liked to experiment with daring stunts. Once, Earhart jumped off her father's barn, using an umbrella for a parachute. Another time, she built a roller coaster on the roof of her father's tool shed. Even as a child, she was daring and full of ideas.

At the age of 19, Amelia Earhart discovered flying. She was working as a nurse's aide in a Canadian military hospital. One of her friends was a pilot in the Royal Flying Corps. She spent her free time at a nearby airfield, watching him fly. However, being only a spectator made her feel like a young athlete left on the bench to watch.

In her early twenties, Earhart began her thrilling and dangerous career as a pilot. The engines of early airplanes were not much bigger than a modern motorcycle engine. In her first two months of flying, Earhart made two crash landings. She was a natural pilot, however. She worked hard to save enough money to buy her own plane in 1922.

When Amelia Earhart took to the air, flying was still a risky new endeavor. It was a difficult task that required skill, courage, and the determination to keep trying to succeed. Earhart pushed herself and the world's flying records to the limit. She set her first record by flying at 14,000 feet (4,200 meters), breaking the women's **altitude** (AL tə tood) record.

✔ In 1927, Charles Lindbergh made the first solo flight across the Atlantic Ocean. In 1932, Amelia Earhart became the first woman to fly solo across the Atlantic. Her flight brought her international fame. It also inspired her to set one new record after another.

✔✔ In 1935, Earhart became the first person to fly nonstop alone from Honolulu, Hawaii, to the U.S. mainland. Later she became the first person to fly nonstop from Los Angeles to Mexico City and from Mexico City to Newark, New Jersey.

Amelia Earhart's daring flights made her a hero to Americans. She was admired and cheered wherever she went. Her accomplishments seemed especially remarkable at the time because of her gender. Earhart, herself, deeply believed in gender equality. She believed that women "must earn true respect and equal rights from men by accepting responsibility."

Amelia Earhart's greatest challenge came on May 17, 1937. She had decided to attempt another record-breaking flight. She was ready to make a 27,000-mile (43,200-kilometer) trip around the world. She asked Fred Noonan, an experienced **navigator** (NAV ə GAY tər), to fly with her and plan the route they should take. Taking off from Oakland, California, they flew to Florida. Then they went on to South America, across the Atlantic to Africa, and on to Asia. Finally they arrived on the island of New Guinea (GIN ee). From there, they faced the most dangerous part of their journey. They would have to fly 2,556 miles (4,090 kilometers) across the Pacific Ocean and then land on tiny Howland Island. On July 2, Earhart and Noonan took off across the Pacific. Somewhere between New Guinea and Howland Island, the plane disappeared. Amelia Earhart and Fred Noonan were never heard from again.

Sally Ride

Even as a young girl, Sally Ride enjoyed challenges. She competed successfully with neighborhood boys in baseball and football. Once she threw a ball so hard that it broke a friend's nose. At the age of 12, Ride began to play tennis. She was soon winning tournaments. Sally Ride learned early to work hard at everything she did.

✚ As a young woman, Ride never planned a career in flying. In college, she continued to play tennis. She also studied hard. She spent nine years earning degrees in English, science, and physics.

"Then one day in 1977," Ride said, "I read an announcement in the paper that NASA was accepting applications. And all of a sudden, I realized that I wanted to do it. There was no question in my mind." Ride wrote to the National Aeronautics and Space Administration (NASA). She expressed her interest in becoming an astronaut. They accepted her immediately, along with five other women.

By the time Sally Ride joined NASA in 1978, astronauts had already walked on the moon. Training and scientific know-how were most important for space-age pilots. Ride joined a team of astronauts training for space flights. She worked closely with NASA scientists and other crew members.

After her training, Sally Ride was chosen by NASA to be the first woman to go up in the *Challenger* space shuttle. Ride was one of two mission specialists aboard the shuttle. Her job was to test a robot arm that put satellites into orbit. Ride's training for the mission was demanding. She had to practice many new skills. Ride and the other astronauts spent hours every day in conditions like those they would face in outer space. There they would have no weight because gravity would not exist.

As one of the first women astronauts, Sally Ride broke barriers for her gender. Treated with respect by fellow crew members, Ride was simply another good astronaut. She had confidence in NASA and in her own abilities and training.

Amelia Earhart took off across the huge, lonely Pacific Ocean to achieve a dream. Sally Ride faced an even greater vastness as she blasted off into the endless stretch of emptiness known as outer space. Amelia Earhart and Sally Ride will both be remembered as brave women and as pioneers in the history of flight.

Sally Ride was the first American woman in space.

Recalling details
1. Identify the first flight record that Amelia Earhart set.

   She broke the women's altitude record.
   _____

Recalling details
2. How did Sally Ride break barriers for women?

   She was the first American woman in space. She was

   treated with respect by her fellow crew members.

Identifying the main idea
3. On page 12, reread the two paragraphs that have an ✗ next to them. Underline the sentence that states the main idea in each paragraph.

Using context clues
4. Decide if each statement is true or false. Write T or F on the lines provided.

   ___F___ a. A spectator plays in a football game.

   ___T___ b. Learning to ride a bicycle can be a difficult endeavor for some children.

   ___T___ c. A lot of furniture is needed to fill the vastness of a large living room.

CRITICAL THINKING

Making inferences
1. Explain why Earhart asked Noonan to accompany her on her flight around the world.

   She needed the help of an experienced navigator.
   _____

Inferring cause and effect
2. What effect did Ride's space flight have on future astronaut teams?

   Because of her successful efforts, there are now more women astronauts.
   _____

Inferring details
3. On page 13, reread the paragraph with a ✚ next to it. Which of the following statements can you infer from the paragraph?

   a. Sally Ride hated to fly.

   b. Sally Ride is very intelligent.

   c. Sally Ride was a bad student.

   d. Sally Ride was often timid about facing new experiences.

Inferring the unstated main idea
4. On page 12, reread the paragraph with a ✔ next to it. Write a sentence that describes its main idea.

   Answers will vary. Earhart matched Lindbergh's flight and set many new records.
   _____

Inferring the unstated main idea
5. On page 12, reread the paragraph with ✔ ✔ next to it. Write a sentence that describes its main idea.

   Answers will vary. Earhart set three nonstop distance records.
   _____

A. Use the following chart to outline similarities between Amelia Earhart and Sally Ride. In the middle of the chart are general topics. Reread the selection for information on how the women's lives are similar. For each topic, write one sentence about each woman. The first one is done for you.

Comparison Chart		
Amelia Earhart	**Topic**	**Sally Ride**
Earhart was active and daring as a child.	Childhood	Ride was active and competitive as a child.
Earhart was the first woman to try many dangerous flights.	Breaking barriers for women	Ride was one of the first woman astronauts.
Earhart set many flight records during her life.	Record setting	Ride was the first American woman in space.
Earhart risked her life many times and finally lost it during a dangerous flight.	Taking risks	Ride's space flight involved many dangers.

B. Use the following chart to outline differences between Amelia Earhart and Sally Ride. In the middle of the chart are general topics. Reread the selection to find out how the women's lives are different on these topics. Then write one sentence about each.

Contrast Chart		
Amelia Earhart	**Topic**	**Sally Ride**
At 19, Earhart knew she wanted to fly.	Beginning of flying career	Ride did not fly until she joined NASA after college.
Earhart flew propeller planes over record distances all over the world.	Destination and type of aircraft	Ride flew in a shuttle in outer space.
Earhart did most of her flying solo.	Teamwork	Ride worked on a team with other astronauts.

Reading-Writing Connection

Which of the two women do you admire more: Amelia Earhart or Sally Ride? On a separate sheet of paper, write a paragraph explaining your reasons.

LESSON 3

For ESL/ELL support, see highlighted words, page T67, and pages T28–T30.

Skill: Classifying

For lesson support, see page T67.

BACKGROUND INFORMATION

"On the Wings of a Bird" describes how birds fly. Some birds can cruise at speeds of 20 to 50 miles (32 to 80 kilometers) per hour, and some can go twice that fast. When they migrate, some birds fly for 1,000 miles (1,600 kilometers) without stopping. The design of a bird's body makes it a perfect flying machine. Scientists classify birds according to the size and shape of their wings and where they live.

SKILL FOCUS: Classifying

Classifying is a way to organize information by grouping similar things together. You may not realize it, but you classify people and things every day.

When scientists classify plants and animals, they break large groups into smaller ones. The members of each smaller group are similar in some way. Sea gulls and terns, for example, are two kinds of sea birds that are similar in many ways. Both have long wings, and both are powerful fliers. Both are found in beach areas. Scientists classify these two kinds of birds in the same group.

Flamingos and ibises are two other kinds of birds that live along the shore. However, they are not classified in the same group as sea gulls and terns. Scientists have classified flamingos and ibises in their own group. Can you figure out why?

When reading about different groups of animals, ask yourself these questions.

- How are the animals in the same group similar?

- How are the animals in one group different from the animals in another group?

▷ Complete the chart below. Use what you already know or look up information about sea gulls and flamingos to list ways they are different.

CONTEXT CLUES: Synonyms

Sometimes a context clue will be a **synonym** in the same or next sentence. Synonyms are words with similar meanings.

What synonym in the sentences below can help you figure out the meaning of the word *fused*?

> The finger bones are **_fused_**, so the bird cannot move them. Yet the bird's thumb is not joined to the fingers—the bird can open and close it.

If you don't know the meaning of *fused*, the synonym *joined* can help you. *Fused* and *joined* are synonyms. A bird's finger bones are joined together.

▷ Read the following sentences from the selection. Circle a synonym for the underlined word.

> The longest flight feathers, called primaries, are (attached) to the bird's hand section.... Another group of flight feathers, called secondaries, are **_affixed_** to the bird's lower-arm bones.

In the next selection, use synonym context clues to figure out the meanings of the underlined words *analogous*, *pliant*, and *vulnerable*.

Strategy Tip

When reading "On the Wings of a Bird," notice how the birds classified in one group are alike and how they are different from the birds in the other groups.

Sea Gulls and Flamingos		
Bird	**Where It Lives**	**What It Looks Like**
Sea gull	all kinds of climate	white or gray; long wings
Flamingo	warm tropical climate	pinkish; longer legs and neck than sea gull

On the Wings of a Bird

PEOPLE HAVE ALWAYS DREAMED of flying through the air like birds. In the past, people believed that birds used their wings like oars to "row" through the air. Today we know that birds actually fly in a way that is similar to how airplanes with propellers fly.

How Birds and Airplanes Fly

An airplane wing has a special shape, called an **airfoil**. This shape keeps the plane up in the air. The bottom of an airfoil is flat, while the top is curved. Air flowing past an airfoil breaks up and then meets again behind the wing. The air on top of the curved wing has to go faster to get over the curve. This fast-moving air pulls away from the wing. At the same time, the slow-moving air on the bottom of the wing pushes up. This pulling on top and pushing on the bottom is called lift, which is what keeps an airplane in the air. Meanwhile, propellers give the airplane a forward movement, called **thrust.**

If you look carefully at a bird, you will see that its inner wing, close to its body, also has an airfoil shape. This is the part of the wing that keeps bird in the air during flight.

To move forward, the bird uses the feathers at the end of its wing like propellers. Of course, a bird's feathers do not rotate like propellers. However, they do change position each time a bird flaps its wings. On the downstroke, the wing moves down and forward until the feathers are even with the bird's beak. Then the feathers quickly twist around and face front. Air flows over them, giving the bird the same forward pull that a propeller gives a plane.

To steer, a bird tips its wings from side to side. For balance, the bird raises or lowers its tail feathers, or moves them sideways.

How Wings Compare With Arms

Although you could not fly by flapping your arms, your arm bones are <u>analogous</u> (ə NAL ə gəs) to the bones in a bird's wing. How are the two structures similar? A bird's wing is made up of three sections, just as our arms are made up of an upper arm, a lower arm, and a hand. (See Figures 1 and 2.)

A bird's "hand" section is longer and narrower, compared with the rest of its arm, than a human hand is, compared to the rest of our arm. A bird's hand also has fewer bones—just two fingers and a thumb. These finger bones are fused, so the bird cannot move them. Yet the bird's thumb is not joined to the fingers—the bird can open and close it.

Many of the bones in a bird's wings are hollow. Hollow bones are an **adaptation** (ad ap TAY shən), a change that has occurred in the bird's body over time to help it survive. These hollow bones help birds fly more easily. Although they are hollow, the bones are strong and <u>pliant</u>, making the wings flexible in flight.

Long flight feathers are anchored to the bones of a bird's wing. The longest flight feathers, called *primaries*, are attached to the bird's hand section.

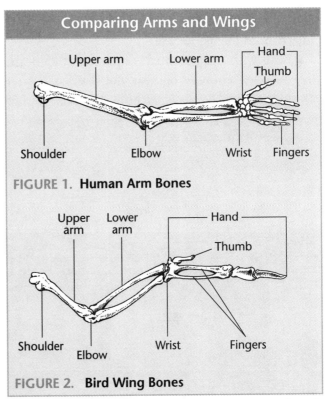

Comparing Arms and Wings

FIGURE 1. **Human Arm Bones**

FIGURE 2. **Bird Wing Bones**

A bird's "hand" is long and narrow, with two fused finger bones and a flexible thumb.

Birds usually have ten primaries on each wing, which twist around and face front to give the bird its forward movement.

Another group of flight feathers, called *secondaries*, are shorter and affixed to the bird's lower-arm bones. There are usually more secondaries than primaries. A third group of flight feathers, the *tertiaries* (TER shee AIR eez), are located on the upper-arm section of the wing.

Classifying the Wings of Birds

Scientists classify birds according to the size and shape of the birds' wings and where the birds live. By studying the shape and size of a bird's wing, you can tell a great deal about how it lives.

Short, rounded wings are clues that a bird lives in woods, shrubs, or underbrush. Songbirds that perch on branches have short, rounded wings. These birds include sparrows, cardinals, and robins. With short, rounded wings, they can dart through trees and bushes without hurting themselves.

Ground-feeding birds have short, stubby wings. These ground-feeders include quail and woodcocks. Their short wings allow them to turn sharply in tight places. They can make quick escapes by flapping hard and fast for short distances. However, they cannot fly fast for long.

Birds with long, pointed wings are fast fliers and live in open country or near the sea. They often sweep through the sky, snatching insects in midair.

Land birds in this group include swallows, swifts, and falcons. Shore birds in this group include sandpipers and plovers.

Birds that glide and soar belong to a group with big wings. This group, which includes eagles, hawks, and vultures, soar over land areas. They all have very wide wings, with deep slots in the wing tips. These slots prevent the birds from stalling as they circle slowly overhead. Other birds in this group, such as gulls and albatrosses, soar over the sea. They have very long, narrow wings with sharp tips.

Wing Size and Rate of Flapping

The size of a bird's wings determines how fast the bird must flap, or beat, them. Large wings have more lifting power than small ones, so large birds can flap their wings more slowly and still stay in the air. A vulture, for example, beats its wings only about once per second. Each stroke of its huge wings drives the vulture forward with great force.

Medium-sized birds, such as ducks and crows, must flap their wings two or three times per second to stay in the air. Small birds with stubby wings have to work even harder. A sparrow beats its wings 14 times per second, and a chickadee flaps about 25 times per second. The smallest bird, a hummingbird, beats its tiny wings about 70 times per second. The wings move so fast that they make a humming sound, which gives the bird its name.

Birds that live in woods, shrubs, and underbrush have short, rounded wings.

Birds that glide and soar have long, wide wings.

Wing Shape and Flight Speed

Different factors can affect a bird's speed while in the air. A sparrow heading home to its nest may cruise along at about 15 to 20 miles (24 to 32 kilometers) per hour. If an enemy suddenly starts to chase the sparrow, though, it may speed up to 35 miles (56 kilometers) per hour. Wind is a factor, too. If a bird is flying with the wind, it gets an extra push from behind. Flying against the wind slows it down.

The most important factor that determines flight speed, however, is the shape of a bird's wings. Songbirds with short, rounded wings cannot fly very fast. Their average speeds are about 15 to 25 miles (24 to 40 kilometers) per hour. Birds with long, pointed wings can usually fly about 40 to 50 miles (64 to 80 kilometers) per hour. Birds with big wings can fly 60 miles (96 kilometers) per hour or faster.

The fastest birds of all are falcons and swifts. Although their wings are not as big as those of eagles, the wings of falcons sweep back like those on a jet. With this arrangement of wings, a peregrine falcon can approach speeds of 100 miles (160 kilometers) per hour.

Taking Off and Landing

Take-offs and landings are the most difficult parts of a bird's flight. If a bird does not get off to a fast start, its wings will not lift it into the air. That is why birds flap their wings harder than usual when they are taking off. Birds always take off into the wind to get some help.

✔ Birds with long legs, such as herons and cranes, push off from the ground to get themselves into the air. The webbed feet of ducks and geese help them to run across the surface of the water until they gain enough flight speed. Many shore birds reach take-off speed by running across the sand while flapping their wings hard. Large birds, such as eagles, perch atop cliffs and high trees. To take off from these high places, they can simply leap into the air.

During landing, a bird is most <u>vulnerable</u>. Coming in too slowly is unsafe, because a bird might suddenly lose its lift and crash to the ground. Coming in too rapidly is also dangerous because a bird can easily damage its delicate wings and body by hitting a branch or other landing site too hard.

When a bird closes in on a landing target, it slows down in stages. First it spreads and lowers its tail. Then it lowers its legs and pushes them forward. Finally it "puts on the brakes" by cupping each wing like a parachute and fanning it back and forth.

Small songbirds usually land on branches. When they do, their legs bend at the joints, acting like shock absorbers. Larger birds that land on open ground slow down by running to a stop. Ducks and geese, which land on water, have the easiest of landings. They simply push their webbed feet forward and skid to a splashing stop.

Every creature on Earth adapts to fit a specific environment and a specific way of life. The adaptations of different kinds of birds have allowed them to make themselves at home in many different environments. Since ancient times, the beauty and grace of birds in flight have provided inspiration to people all over the world.

SCIENCE

COMPREHENSION

Recalling details
1. Describe the shape of an airfoil.

An airfoil is a shape with a flat bottom and a curved top.

Identifying main idea
2. How does the size of a bird's wings affect the rate at which it beats its wings?

The larger the wings, the less often the bird needs to

beat them to stay in the air.

Recalling details
3. Where do birds with short, rounded wings often live?

They live in forests, shrubs, or underbrush.

Using context clues
4. Draw a line to match each word with its synonym.

similar   a. vulnerable

flexible   b. analogous

unsafe   c. pliant

Inferring cause and effect

1. Explain why having hollow bones helps a bird to fly.

   Hollow bones make a bird's body lighter. Having a lighter body makes it easier for the bird to take off and stay in the air.

Drawing conclusions

2. Scientists studying a bird noted that it usually beat its wings 2.5 times per second. Draw a conclusion about this bird's size.

   This bird is probably medium-sized, perhaps as big as a crow or a duck.

Making inferences

3. A thrush is a songbird about 8 inches long. About how fast might it normally fly?

   It probably flies about 15 to 25 miles per hour.

Inferring main idea

4. Look at the paragraph with a ✔ next to it. Write a sentence that states the main idea of the paragraph.

   Answers will vary. Depending on their size, shape, and habitat, birds take off in different ways.

Making inferences

5. A loon usually runs across the surface of a lake to gain enough speed to take off. Describe what type of feet a loon probably has.

   A loon has webbed feet.

SKILL FOCUS: CLASSIFYING

Complete the chart below, using details from the selection about each type of wings.

Types of Wings				
Wing Shape	**Names of Birds**	**Habitat**	**Type of Flight**	**Speed**
Short, rounded	sparrows, robins, cardinals, quails	woods, underbrush	short, with twists and turns	15–25 mph
Long, pointed	swallows, sandpipers, plovers	open land or along the shore	fast, sweeping	40–50 mph
Big, wide	vultures, eagles, hawks	open land	soaring and gliding	60 mph or more

Reading-Writing Connection

On a separate sheet of paper, write a paragraph about a bird that you often see in your neighborhood. Describe the bird in as much detail as you can. Write about the bird's wings, its habitat, and how it flies. If you wish, draw an illustration of the bird.

LESSON 4

For ESL/ELL support, see highlighted words, page T68, and pages T28–T30.

Skill: Reading Mathematical Terms

For lesson support, see page T68.

BACKGROUND INFORMATION

"Reading Mathematical Terms and Symbols" explains some math terms that will help you when you study geometry. In geometry, you will learn about familiar shapes, such as squares, triangles, and circles. The most basic concepts in geometry, however, are the point, the line, and the plane. This selection will help you understand these basic mathematical terms.

SKILL FOCUS: Reading Mathematical Terms

Some words have a familiar meaning in everyday life and a special meaning in math. Knowing mathematical terms is important for success in math. In ordinary speech, for example, the word *point* can mean "the main idea" or "a certain time." A *line* is a group of people waiting to buy or do something. A *plane* is a flying mode of transportation.

In mathematics, the words *point*, *line*, and *plane* have special meanings.

- A **point** is a position that has no dimensions. It cannot be seen.

- A **line** is many points placed next to each other. It goes on forever in one dimension.

- A **plane** has length and width but no height. It goes on forever in two dimensions.

Other words such as *intersect, perpendicular,* and *parallel* have special math meanings, too.

- When two lines or planes cross, they **intersect**. Two streets, for example, can cross each other, or intersect.

- When lines or planes intersect and form square corners, they are **perpendicular**. The walls of most rooms, for example, are perpendicular to the floor.

- Lines or planes that do not intersect are **parallel** when they travel in the same direction forever and are always the same distance apart. For example, two airplanes can fly parallel to each other at the same distance apart.

▶ Think about the meanings of the words *point*, *line*, and *plane*. Then fill in the chart below with their everyday meaning and math meaning.

Answers will vary.

Meanings of Words		
Word	**Everyday Meaning**	**Math Meaning**
point	main idea; tip	position that has no dimensions
line	group of people waiting to buy or do something	many points next to each other; goes on forever
plane	flying mode of transportation	has length and width; goes on forever in two dimensions

WORD CLUES

As you read the next selection, look for these important words: *point, line, plane, intersect, perpendicular,* and *parallel*. The diagrams in the selection will help you understand their mathematical meanings. Also pay close attention to the symbols that stand for mathematical terms. These symbols are shortened ways of writing math words.

Strategy Tip

When reading, "Reading Mathematical Terms and Symbols," be sure that you understand each idea before you go on to the next one. In math, it is very important to fully understand every idea in order to understand the one that follows it.

Reading Mathematical Terms and Symbols

To study geometry, you must understand three important terms. They are *point, line,* and *plane*. A **point** has no dimensions. It cannot be seen. It has no size. A point is shown by a dot and named with a capital letter. This is the symbol for point *A*.

●A

A **line** is many, many points placed next to each other. It is endless in length but has no width. When a line is drawn, it looks as if it has a beginning and an end. However, the arrows on the line show that it goes on forever. A line can be named with a small letter. This is line *s*.

A line can also be named using two points. A capital letter is used to name each of the two points on the line. The two points can be placed anywhere on the line. This is line *AB*. The symbol for line *AB* is $\overleftrightarrow{AB}$.

Like a line, a **plane** goes on and on. It never ends. A plane has length and width but no height. A plane is named with a capital letter. Following this paragraph is plane *M*. The four-sided figure shows that it is a plane. Each side of a plane goes on forever. When you see this figure, you should remember that the sides do not mean that the plane

ends. The capital letter that names the plane is in the lower-right corner of the figure.

✔ When two lines cross, they **intersect**. Two lines intersect at a point. This is line *x* and line *y* intersecting at point *O*.

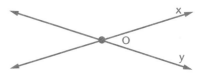

Two lines can intersect and form square corners. The lines are **perpendicular** to each other. Line *l* is perpendicular to line *m*. The symbol for showing that line *l* is perpendicular to line *m* is *l*⊥*m*.

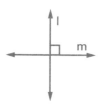

Sometimes two lines never intersect. The distance between them is always the same. When two lines never intersect, they are said to be **parallel** to each other. Line *a* is parallel to line *b*. The symbol to show that line *a* is parallel to line *b* is *a*‖*b*.

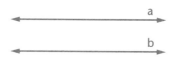

A line can also intersect a plane. A line and a plane intersect at a point. This diagram shows line *RS* intersecting plane *P* at point *L*. The dotted line shows the part of the line that is behind the plane.

Two planes can also intersect. When planes intersect, they always intersect in a line. This diagram shows plane *S* and plane *T* intersecting along line *CD*.

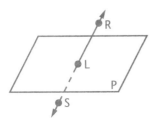

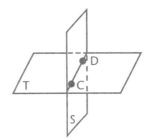

COMPREHENSION

Recalling details
1. Which mathematical term describes something with no dimensions? ____point____

Recalling details
2. Which mathematical term describes something with length but no width? ____line____

Recalling details
3. Which mathematical term describes something with length and width but no height? ____plane____

Recalling details
4. When two lines cross, they ____intersect____.

Recalling details
5. Two lines that never intersect are ____parallel____ to each other.

Recalling details
6. Two lines that intersect and form square corners are ____perpendicular____ to each other.

Identifying the main idea
7. Reread the paragraph with a check mark next to it. Draw a line under the sentence that states the main idea.

CRITICAL THINKING

Making inferences
1. Could two lines intersect each other at two points? Why or why not?

   No. After the lines intersect, they continue forever in different directions.

Making inferences
2. Could two planes intersect in a point? Why or why not?

   No. Planes have both length and width. The place where they intersect will have one dimension. A point has no

   dimensions.

Making inferences
3. Write the words *plane, point,* and *line* in order from the one that takes the least space to the one that takes the most space.

   ____point____   ____line____   ____plane____

MATHEMATICS

A. Write the name or symbol for each figure.

1.

line *AB* or $\overleftrightarrow{AB}$

2. •C

point *C*

3.

plane *X*

4.

line *d*

5.

g‖*h*

6.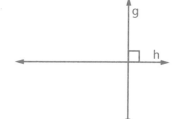

t⊥*s*

B. Draw a diagram for each name or symbol.

1. point *X*   •X

2. $\overleftrightarrow{CD}$

3. line *m*

4. plane *D*

5. *f*‖*g*

6. *g*⊥*h*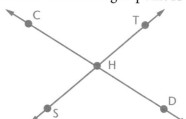

7. line *CD* and line *ST* intersecting at point *H*

8. line *XY* intersecting plane *M* at point *C*

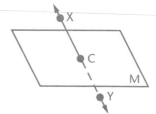

Reading-Writing Connection

On a separate sheet of paper, write a paragraph describing something around you that includes perpendicular lines. Give as many details as possible.

Skill: Vowel Diphthongs

For lesson support, see page T69.

> Say the words *oil* and *boy* to yourself. Listen to their vowel sound. The letters *oi* and *oy* stand for the same vowel sound. When this vowel sound appears at the beginning or in the middle of a word, it is usually spelled *oi*. When this same sound is at the end of a word, it is spelled *oy*. This sound is called a **vowel diphthong.**

A. Read the sentences below. Choose a word from the list to complete each sentence. Write the word on the line. Then circle the letters in each word that stand for the vowel diphthong.

coin	annoy	broil
enjoy	coil	noise

1. Some children __annoy__ their parents by breaking their toys.

2. This vine will __coil__ around the tree.

3. Cars in heavy traffic often make __noise__ by honking their horns.

4. Mr. Larsen is planning to __broil__ the hamburgers over charcoal.

5. Joe and Ann __enjoy__ going to hockey games.

6. Numismatics, or __coin__ collecting, is a popular hobby.

> Say the words *out* and *cow* to yourself. Listen to their vowel sound. The letters *ou* and *ow* stand for the same vowel sound. This sound is also called a vowel diphthong.

B. Read the sentences below. Choose a word from the list to complete each sentence. Write the word on the line. Then circle the letters in each word that stand for the diphthong.

town	cloud	crowd	shout
pouch	blouse	plow	brow

1. The cowhands rode off in a __cloud__ of dust.

2. Heather wore her blue __blouse__ with her gray skirt.

3. A __town__ is larger than a village but smaller than a city.

4. In earlier times, an ox was used to pull a __plow__.

5. The female kangaroo carries her young in her __pouch__.

6. A large __crowd__ gathered at the scene of the fire.

7. Neil wiped the sweat from his __brow__.

8. Kerry tried to __shout__ to the other players on her team.

Skill: Vowel-Consonant Combinations

For lesson support, see page T69.

The **vowel-consonant combinations** *aw* and *al* and the vowels *au* stand for the same sound you hear in the words *claw*, *bald*, and *auto*. The vowel sound in all three words is the same, but the letters that stand for the sound are different.

Read the sentences below. Choose a word from the list to complete each sentence. Write the word on the line. Then circle the letters in each word that stand for the same sound you hear in the words *claw*, *bald*, and *auto*.

hawk	thaw	because	caught	fault	salt	ball
yawn	crawl	sauce	dawn	false	paw	gnaw
taught	pause	bald	haul	straw	halt	law

1. Tired people often __yawn__.

2. Last year Ms. White __taught__ geometry.

3. It is not healthy for people to put too much __salt__ on their food.

4. Carol __caught__ four fish within a short time.

5. An answer that is not true is __false__.

6. The sun rises at __dawn__.

7. Mr. Barlaz poured __sauce__ over the spaghetti.

8. Most babies __crawl__ before they learn to walk.

9. It is Robert's __fault__ that we are late for dinner.

10. Althea left the party early __because__ she was tired.

11. The hot sun made the ice start to __thaw__.

12. My cat hurt its __paw__ while running on the gravel driveway.

13. Ruth was told to __pause__ before reading the story.

14. My grandfather is __bald__.

15. This __hawk__ has a very sharp beak.

16. Ming's new truck can __haul__ our glass to the recycling plant.

17. My large __straw__ hat will protect my face from sunburn.

18. The horse will __halt__ if you pull on the reins.

19. The players kicked the __ball__.

20. After dinner, our dog would __gnaw__ on the bones that we gave him.

21. To drive when you are too young is against the __law__.

Skill: Syllables

For lesson support, see page T70.

> One way to help you pronounce long words is to divide the words into **syllables**. Then pronounce each syllable until you can say the whole word. There are several different rules for deciding how a word should be divided into syllables.

RULE 1: Compound Words

One of the easiest rules to use in dividing words is the one that is used with a compound word. Because a compound word is made up of two words, it must have at least two syllables. Always divide a compound word into syllables by separating it between the two smaller words first. If one or even both of the smaller words in a compound word have more than one syllable, it may be necessary to use another rule. However, you can pronounce most compound words if you divide them into two words.

sailboat   sail boat

A. Read each of the following compound words. Divide the word into two syllables by writing each of the two smaller words separately on the line next to the compound word.

1.	weekday	week day	7.	bathtub	bath tub
2.	seaweed	sea weed	8.	baseball	base ball
3.	flashlight	flash light	9.	windshield	wind shield
4.	driftwood	drift wood	10.	drumstick	drum stick
5.	grassland	grass land	11.	highchair	high chair
6.	withdraw	with draw	12.	background	back ground

RULE 2: Words With Double Consonants

Another rule is for words with double consonants. Divide the word into two syllables between the two same consonants and read each syllable.

tennis   ten nis

B. Divide the following two-syllable words into syllables. Write each syllable separately on the line next to the word.

1.	raccoon	rac coon	8.	rabbit	rab bit
2.	penny	pen ny	9.	tunnel	tun nel
3.	lesson	les son	10.	splatter	splat ter
4.	slipper	slip per	11.	muffin	muf fin
5.	lettuce	let tuce	12.	gossip	gos sip
6.	kitten	kit ten	13.	hammer	ham mer
7.	sudden	sud den	14.	traffic	traf fic

Skill: Main Idea—Stated or Unstated

For lesson support, see page T70.

> When you read a textbook or reference book, the **main idea** of each paragraph will often be stated in a sentence. The rest of the paragraph will contain the supporting details that give additional information about the main idea.
>
> Sometimes the main idea of a paragraph is not stated in one of the sentences. The information given in the paragraph will help you to **infer**, or figure out, the main idea yourself. To do this, you need to ask yourself what the paragraph is about. Then think of a sentence that summarizes this idea.

Read the following selection from beginning to end to become familiar with the content. Then reread each paragraph. Think about whether the main idea in each paragraph is stated or unstated.

Shooting for the Moon

1. Dr. Mae Jemison leads an adventure-filled life, but one of her most exciting days was September 12, 1992. "I had this big smile on my face," said Jemison. "I was so excited. This is what I had wanted to do for a very long time." Jemison was aboard shuttle mission STS-47 Spacelab, a cooperative mission to outer space between the United States and Japan.

2. Space travel is exciting, but in some ways it only emphasizes what a small planet Earth is. "The first thing I saw was Chicago. I looked out the window and there it was," she said about seeing her hometown from the shuttle. "I looked over at one point, and there was Somalia."

3. Dr. Jemison believes that space technology benefits everyone, especially people in the so-called developing nations. *Developing nations* is a term that means all the countries without major industries. In the space age, she says, old-fashioned telephone lines and electrical generators are no longer necessary. She thinks that the space age will enable the developing nations to skip over the industrial age.

4. When she was in medical school, Jemison studied social medicine in Cuba. Later she practiced medicine with rural Kenyan villagers and Cambodians who had escaped Communist rule in Thailand. She also worked as a Peace Corps medical officer in Sierra Leone and Liberia.

5. Jemison insists, however, that she does not do what she does just for the good of other people. "I don't believe in [doing good just to be unselfish]," she said. "I've gotten much more out of what I have done than the people I was supposed to be helping." Jemison was in a camp in Thailand for refugees, people who had left their countries to escape war and find freedom. "I learned more about medicine there than I could have in a lifetime somewhere else," she said.

6. Only a handful of women have gone up in space, and Jemison was the first African American woman to do so. "When I'm asked about the

Dr. Mae Jemison is performing a pre-flight switch check in the space shuttle *Atlantis*.

relevance to black people of what I do, I take that as an [insult]. It presupposes that black people have never been involved in exploring the heavens, but this is not so. Ancient African empires—Mali, Songhay, Egypt—had scientists and astronomers.

7. "The fact is that space and its resources belong to all of us, not to any one group," Jemison emphasizes. "We need more African Americans and Latinos in the field. If we're not there from the beginning, helping to determine what happens to these resources, we'll have no say in how they are to be used."

8. Jemison chose some very special objects to take with her in the shuttle: "an Alvin Ailey American Dance Theater poster, an Alpha Kappa Alpha banner, a flag that had flown over the Organization of African Unity, and [important writings] from Chicago's DuSable Museum of African American History and the Chicago public school system." She explained, "I wanted everyone to know that space belongs to all of us. There is science in dance and art in science."

9. When poet Nikki Giovanni interviewed Jemison in 1993 after her shuttle mission, she asked Jemison what her ideal space trip would be. Jemison replied, "Me in a clear bubble floating through the galaxy… shooting for the moon." When asked whom she would take with her, she said, "Sneeze, my cat. I think I'd like to have Sneeze. He came with me from Africa, so he's used to flying. Then if some aliens came by and invited me to another galaxy—well, look for me on a television mystery. I'm gone."

A. For each paragraph in the selection, if the main idea is stated, write *stated* on the line. If the main idea is unstated, choose a main idea from the sentences below and write the letter on the line. You will not use all the listed main ideas.

a. Jemison's cat, Sneeze, came with her from Africa, so he's used to flying.

b. Dr. Jemison has done much to help people all over the world.

c. Black people have always been involved in studying the mysteries of the universe.

d. Jemison worked as a Peace Corps officer in Sierra Leone and Liberia.

e. Old-fashioned telephone lines and electrical generators are no longer necessary in the developing world.

f. On September 12, 1992, Jemison reached her goal of going up in a space shuttle.

g. Jemison has a clear picture of her ideal space trip.

Paragraph 1:	f	**Paragraph 6:**	c
Paragraph 2:	stated	**Paragraph 7:**	stated
Paragraph 3:	stated	**Paragraph 8:**	stated
Paragraph 4:	b	**Paragraph 9:**	g
Paragraph 5:	stated		

B. Now go back to each paragraph that has a stated main idea. Underline the sentence that states the main idea.

Skill: Using a Dictionary

For lesson support, see page T71.

For ESL/ELL support, see page T71.

In a dictionary, you may find pages of words that all begin with the same first three letters. To find a word on these pages, you will need to look at the fourth letter of the word. When words begin with the same three letters, they are arranged in **alphabetical order** according to the fourth letter of the words. For example, the word *collar* is listed before the word *color* because *l* comes before *o* in the alphabet.

A. On the numbered lines, write each set of words below in alphabetical order according to the first four letters in each word. Cross out each word in the list after you write it.

beam	1.	beach	stole	1.	stock
beagle	2.	bead	stove	2.	stodgy
bear	3.	beagle	stomach	3.	stoke
beauty	4.	beak	stoop	4.	stole
beat	5.	beam	store	5.	stomach
beach	6.	bean	stodgy	6.	stone
beaver	7.	bear	stop	7.	stoop
bean	8.	beat	stoke	8.	stop
bead	9.	beauty	stone	9.	store
beak	10.	beaver	stock	10.	stove

At the top of each dictionary page are two words in boldface type. These words are called **guide words**. Guide words help you quickly and easily find the entry words, the words for which the dictionary gives definitions. They tell you the first and the last entry word on the page. All the other entry words on the page come between these two words in alphabetical order.

B. Below is a pair of guide words that might appear on a dictionary page. Following them is a list of entry words. If the entry word would be on the same page as the guide words, write *yes* next to the word. If the entry word would appear on an earlier page, write *before*. If the entry word would appear on a later page, write *after*.

parboil / parson

1.	parrot	yes	**7.**	pastry	after
2.	part	after	**8.**	pardon	yes
3.	parcel	yes	**9.**	paragraph	before
4.	pass	after	**10.**	parlor	yes
5.	parasol	before	**11.**	Paris	yes
6.	parent	yes	**12.**	parade	before

In a dictionary, an entry word, plus all the information about it, is called an **entry**. The entry word always appears in boldface type. If the entry word has more than one syllable, it is divided into syllables to show where the word can be divided at the end of a line of writing. The entry word is followed by a **respelling** of the word in parentheses. The respelling shows you how to say the word. The **part-of-speech label** follows the respelling. The labels are usually abbreviated as follows: *adj.* for adjective, *adv.* for adverb, *conj.* for conjunction, *interj.* for interjection, *n.* for noun, *prep.* for preposition, *pron.* for pronoun, and *v.* for verb.

The **meanings** of an entry word are arranged according to parts of speech. For example, if an entry has noun meanings, all the noun meanings are grouped together and numbered following the *n.* label. Any meanings the word may have for any other part of speech are numbered and placed after the abbreviated part-of-speech label. Many words that appear in dictionary entries are synonyms for the entry word.

At the end of some entries are idioms. An **idiom** is a group of words that has a meaning different from the meaning that the individual words have by themselves.

C. Use the following dictionary entry to answer the questions below.

> **name** (nām) *n.* **1** a word or words by which a person, animal, thing, or place is known: title [Grace, Lopez, Wyoming, and poodle are *names.*] **2** a word or words used instead of the real name, sometimes in order to insult [They were mean and called him *names,* such as "liar" and "cheat."] **3** reputation [Guard your good *name.*] ◆*v.* **named, nam′ing 1** to give a name to [He *named* the child after her mother.] **2** to tell the name or names of [Can you *name* all the presidents?] **3** to refer to; mention [to *name* an example]. **4** to choose for a certain position; appoint [She was *named* president of the company.] **5** to fix or set, as a date for a meeting, a price, etc. —**in the name of, 1** for the sake of [in the *name* of good sense]. **2** by the authority of [Open in the *name* of the law!] —**to one's name,** belonging to one.

1. What is the entry word? _____ name _____

2. Write the respelling. _____ nām _____

3. How many noun meanings follow the part-of-speech label *n*? _____ 3 _____

4. How many verb meanings follow the part-of-speech label *v*? _____ 5 _____

5. Write the first verb meaning. _____ to give a name to _____

6. Write the second idiom. _____ to one's name _____

7. Write the two synonyms given for the entry word as a noun. _____ title, reputation _____

8. Write the idiom that has the same meaning as the underlined words in the following sentence.

   I ordered the equipment <u>by the authority of</u> my supervisor. _____ in the name of _____

Skill: Reading Help-Wanted Ads

For lesson support, see page T71.

Help-wanted ads are found in the classified section of the newspaper. The classified section lists advertisements for all kinds of things arranged by subject. In the help-wanted listings, ads for the same kinds of jobs are listed together. Each ad begins with a job title or a descriptive heading that identifies the job. Ads are listed in alphabetical order by job title or key word. Sometimes a job agency places ads. A job agency provides the service of hiring employees for companies.

Most help-wanted ads give the job seeker a variety of information. In addition to the job title, a help-wanted ad may describe the skills needed for the job. It may also state that previous experience, or former work in the same type of job, is required. An ad tells how to apply for the job. Other information, such as salary, or pay, may be included.

Because help-wanted ads must give a lot of information in a small amount of space, abbreviations, or shortened forms of words, are used. For example, *exp.* is the abbreviation for the

word *experience*. Sometimes the abbreviations contain the first few letters of the word; sometimes the abbreviations use only consonants. If you use context clues, you can usually figure out the abbreviations.

Sometimes an ad may state that the company requires a résumé. A résumé is a sheet of written information about yourself and your work experience that you make available to a company. If the company wants to meet you after reading your résumé, someone at the company will contact you for an interview.

Examine the help-wanted ads below.

BANKING

ASST MANAGER

San Jose-based bank seeks exp. asst manager for new branch location. Responsible for developing and managing relationships with clients. Spanish-speaking prefd. We offer a competitive benefits pkg. Fax résumé with cover letter and sal. rqrmnts to Union Bank, 555-7938.

BANKING

Head Teller. Prestigious bank looking for head teller. Must have 5 yrs bank exp. Must be good with numbers and people. Responsible for staff training and development. Competitive salary. Great oppty for the right person. Apply online at www.Hartbank.com.

BANKING

Lending officer. Financial company has immed. opening for individual with lending exp. Needs strong oral and written communication skills. Call Mr. Temprano at 555-0901, Wkdys, 10–4.

BANKING

Secy—Executive Offices
Must type 60 wpm and have computer and spreadsheet skills; P/T Mon–Thurs 8A.M.–11A.M. For appt., call Jonathan Chong at 555-8188.

BANKING

TELLER TRAINEE

Entry-level positions at major area bank. Must be H.S. grad. No exp. necessary. Responsible for handling cash and general office duties. Interviews 9–5, Sept 7, 8, 9 at 736 N. Bayview Ave., Rm. 400. Ask for Don Sullivan.

BANKING

Teller. Local credit union seeks F/T teller for dwntwn branch. Recent grad OK. Must work Sats. $12/hr. $250 hiring bonus. Fax résumé to Travis Price, 555-3231.

BANKING
Jobs! Jobs! Jobs!
Tellers   to $20,000
College Grad Trainees to $30,000
Loan Officers   to $40,000
Branch Managers   to $60,000
Accountants   to $80,000
Banking Unlimited Agency will find the right job for you. 30 E. Orange Street, Suite 1000; 555-7690

A. Read the abbreviations from the help-wanted ads on page 32. On the lines, write the words the abbreviations stand for. If necessary, use context clues from the ads.

1. grad   _____graduate_____
2. P/T   _____part time_____
3. immed.   _____immediate_____
4. prefd   _____preferred_____
5. Sats   _____Saturdays_____

6. yrs   _____years_____
7. secy   _____secretary_____
8. sal   _____salary_____
9. oppty   _____opportunity_____
10. rqrmnts   _____requirements_____

B. Use the information in the ads to answer the questions.

1. Where would you go to apply for a job as a teller trainee? _____736 N. Bayview Ave., Rm. 400_____

2. For which position could you apply online? _____head teller_____

3. Which job might be appropriate for someone who wants to work just a few hours a day? _____secretary_____

4. According to the Banking Unlimited Agency, how much might a trainee earn? _____$30,000_____

5. Which job ad asks for someone with good skills at speaking and writing? _____lending officer_____

6. Which bank wants a Spanish-speaking assistant manager for one of its branches? _____Union Bank_____

7. How much experience would you need to apply for the job as head teller at Hart Bank? _____five years_____

8. Which two ads suggest faxing a résumé to show interest in a job? _____assistant manager at Union Bank and teller at a local credit union_____

9. How would you learn more about the jobs that the Banking Unlimited Agency offers?
   _____Call the agency at 555-7690, or visit their office at 30 E. Orange Street, Suite 1000._____

10. What is the highest-paying job that the Banking Unlimited Agency lists? _____accountant_____

11. How is the local credit union trying to attract applicants? _____The credit union is offering a $250 bonus to people who take the job._____

12. Jonelle just graduated from high school and has no job experience. She needs a job, but doesn't want to work on weekends. What job might be best for her? _____teller trainee at the major area bank_____

13. Why do you think the Hart Bank wants a head teller who is "good with numbers and people"?
    _____The head teller is probably responsible for counting cash and keeping financial records; he or she also needs good interpersonal skills to manage other employees and deal with customers._____

14. The head teller position offers a "competitive salary." What is a competitive salary?
    _____A competitive salary is an income that is as high or higher than people in similar jobs in other banks earn._____

unit two

For ESL/ELL support, see highlighted words, page T72, and pages T28–T30.

A Look at the Past and Present

For theme support, see page T26.

LESSON 11

Skill: Theme

For lesson support, see page T72.

BACKGROUND INFORMATION

When a young Japanese-American girl in "A Simple Arrangement" spends a year with her grandparents in Japan, she struggles to adapt to Japanese customs. Before 1945, Japanese families were bound by strict customs. Now these rules have relaxed somewhat. However, family relationships and customs are still much more formal in Japan than in the United States.

SKILL FOCUS: Theme

Theme is the meaning or message of a story. It is an important idea about life that the author wants to share with readers.

Sometimes an author states the theme of a story directly. Usually, however, you will have to figure out the theme for yourself. To do that, pay attention to what the characters do and say. In addition, a story's title can be a clue to its theme.

The following questions will help you infer the theme of a story.

- What does the story's title mean?
- What do the main characters discover about themselves in the story?
- What do the characters learn about life?
- What message is the author giving to readers?

▌ Many stories and movies have similar themes, or messages about life. In the next column is a chart with two common themes. Next to each one, write the name of a story you know that conveys that message.

Common Themes	
Theme	**Story or Movie**
People must often over-come many difficulties to achieve an important goal.	Answers will vary.
People often do not realize how valuable life is until a tragedy strikes.	Answers will vary.

CONTEXT CLUES: Antonyms

Some context clues are **antonyms**, or words with opposite meanings.

In the sentence below, look for the antonym that helps you figure out the meaning of *outspoken*.

*Keiko was shy, not **outspoken** like Tomi.*

If you don't know the meaning of *outspoken*, the word *shy* can help. *Shy* and *outspoken* are antonyms, so *outspoken* means "not shy."

▌ Read the following sentences. Circle the antonym that helps you figure out the meaning of the underlined word.

*Manners are much more (casual) in America, Tomi thought. In Japan, everyone's behavior seems so **formal**.*

Use antonym context clues to find the meanings of the underlined words *adept*, *proportion*, and *serene* in the following selection.

> **Strategy Tip**
>
> As you read, use the questions on this page to help you figure out the story's theme.

A Simple Arrangement

"I give up!" Tomi cried. She threw the spray of yellow flowers to the floor.

Her cousin Keiko blinked her eyes in amazement. Keiko was shy, not outspoken like Tomi. Tomi had never learned to keep her feelings to herself as Japanese girls are taught to do. Keiko did not know what to say.

"I'm sorry that I shouted," Tomi said. She bent down to pick up the flowers. "It's just that I'll never learn to arrange flowers."

"Yes, you will," Keiko said gently. "It is the Japanese way."

"That's just it!" Tomi burst out again. "I'm not Japanese. I'm American. I was born in California, and I lived there all my life until now. My parents may be Japanese, and I may look Japanese, but that just makes it harder. Everyone expects me to do things the Japanese way, but I can't!"

All the anger Tomi had felt these last few months came rushing out. She hadn't wanted to come to Japan in the first place. When her grandparents had invited her to spend a year in Japan, however, Tomi's father said that it was a fine idea. Once Father made up his mind, it was no use arguing. The word of a Japanese father is not questioned—even in America!

Once she was in Japan, Tomi had honestly tried to be the sort of girl her grandparents wanted her to be. She had worked very hard at doing well in school and at becoming adept in flower arranging. However, her hands seemed clumsy working with flowers. She felt that she did everything wrong.

"I think you are very lucky to be both Japanese and American," Keiko said. "You have two homes and two languages. That is something special."

"You're the one who's lucky," said Tomi. "You belong here. I don't."

Tomi cut three flowers from the spray and put them in the bowl as she had seen Mr. Tanaka, her teacher, do many times. She had cut the stems in the Japanese way so that they were three different lengths. The flower with the short stem represented Earth. The tall flower stood for heaven. The medium length flower stood for human beings, who link heaven and Earth.

Once heaven, human beings, and Earth were in harmony, the flower arrangement succeeded. An arrangement was supposed to have proportion. However, Tomi's flowers looked unbalanced. The design was all wrong. It was supposed to be so simple to achieve a pleasing arrangement of flowers. Why couldn't she learn how to do it? Would Tomi ever be able to please her grandparents?

Tomi sighed. "I hoped I could make a pretty flower arrangement for the party tonight," she said sadly. "It would make Grandmother so happy."

Keiko's eyes danced at the thought of the celebration. "Are you going to wear the kimono that Grandmother and Grandfather gave you when you arrived here?" she asked. "It is so beautiful."

"I know it is," Tomi said, "but I wouldn't feel right wearing it." The long, flowing kimonos that many Japanese women wear on special occasions looked lovely on them. Kimonos were really much prettier than Western clothes, Tomi thought. Yet she would make a fool of herself in a kimono. Kimonos are narrow, so you have to take short steps with your knees close together. Otherwise the kimono will flap open. Tomi was sure she would forget about walking properly. She would look clumsy and silly. It was better not to even try.

"It's time for me to go home and help my family get ready for tonight," Keiko said. She got to her feet and crossed the room in quick, graceful steps.

Tomi felt a stab of envy as she watched her cousin. Keiko would wear a kimono to the family gathering tonight. Keiko would know the right things to do and say, too. Manners are much more casual in America, Tomi thought. In Japan, everyone's behavior seems so formal. It is so important to do everything just right. Tomi always seemed to do everything wrong.

After Keiko had gone, Tomi felt tears in her eyes. She thought about her family back in California. More than anything, she wanted to feel like part of a family again. She would never be accepted here, not when she couldn't even arrange a few flowers!

Tomi picked up the flowers again. The words of Mr. Tanaka came back to her: "Arranging flowers is a simple thing, but it cannot be done unless your heart is <u>serene</u>."

"That must be my problem," Tomi said to herself. "My heart is anything but serene. I feel tense and anxious. My heart is not at peace."

Just then, Grandmother came into the room. Her arms were filled with packages of food for the party.

"I smell rice burning!" Grandmother said.

Oh, dear! Tomi suddenly remembered that she had put rice on the stove to cook. She had hoped to please Grandmother by making the evening rice, but she had forgotten it. The water must have boiled away. The rice would be black and burned. Couldn't she do anything right?

Tomi fled from the house. Once she was in the garden, she let the tears fall. She sank into the soft moss and put her face in her hands. She had never felt so lost and alone.

It was very quiet. Her sobbing slowed, and she wiped her eyes. She looked around the garden. How beautiful it was! A pine branch was reflected in the little pond. The cherry tree was a huge ball of white blossoms.

It was a tiny garden, yet every inch of it was a delight. Her grandfather had planned it that way, she knew. It was very Japanese to draw from each thing its special beauty. The Japanese found joy in the smallest things. Things as simple as the moon rising or a bird singing were treated as treasures.

Tomi had been in the garden many times, but she had always been too busy to notice how carefully planned yet simple it was. Few other Americans would have noticed it either, she thought. Americans moved too fast. They didn't have time to watch a flower bud.

Perhaps she had been trying to move too fast, Tomi thought. She had been in such a great hurry to learn everything right away. If she moved a bit more slowly, perhaps she would find the beauty in simple things. The Japanese knew there was comfort in beauty. I'm lucky to be Japanese, Tomi thought. Lucky to be here. Lucky just to be alive!

Tomi hugged that warm feeling to her as she went back inside. Her heart was full of joy as she slipped off her shoes at the door.

"Where is the pot I burned, Grandmother?" she asked. "I want to scrub it clean."

"I've done it for you," said Grandmother.

Tomi waited for her to say more about the burned rice. Tomi had acted like an American again, wasting food! However, her grandmother just went on with the preparations for dinner. She knows I can't help being what I am, Tomi thought. I am American, too.

Relieved, she picked up the yellow flowers again. This time her hands moved easily as she placed the stems in the bowl. She arranged the flowers slowly and with love for their beauty.

She stepped back to see the results. It was a very simple arrangement. There were just three stems. Yet it looked natural, almost as if the spray grew right out of the bowl. It was beautiful and right and Japanese.

That night, Tomi put on the silk kimono that her grandparents had given her. It was as blue as the

sky and had peach blossoms scattered across it. The long, flowing sleeves fell almost to the floor.

That evening, Tomi's steps were not always as tiny as they should have been. Most of the time, though, she remembered how to walk, and she knew she looked fine. Like Keiko, Tomi helped make the passing moments of the evening beautiful.

Grandmother said nothing about the flowers, and Grandfather didn't mention the kimono, but Tomi saw the glow of pride in their eyes. She felt their love reach out and wrap her like a cloak.

In the garden, the wind blew among the cherry trees, scattering the white flowers like confetti against the moon. Tomi watched each petal fall through the air of the peaceful Japanese evening.

COMPREHENSION

Identifying cause and effect
1. Why does Tomi go to Japan?

   Her grandparents have invited her to spend a year

   living with them.

Recalling details
2. Explain why Keiko says Tomi is lucky.

   Tomi has two homes, two languages, and belongs to

   two cultures.

Recalling details
3. Why does Tomi think that Keiko is lucky?

   Keiko fits in perfectly, and Tomi doesn't. Tomi feels as if

   she doesn't belong.

Recalling details
4. What do the shortest, tallest, and medium-sized flowers in a Japanese arrangement represent?

   The shortest represents Earth. The tallest represents

   heaven. The medium-sized one represents human beings.

Identifying cause and effect
5. Why does Tomi run to the garden and cry?

   She is angry with herself for burning the rice and does

   not want to face her grandmother after another failure.

Recalling details
6. Explain why Tomi doesn't want to wear a kimono.

   She is afraid of making a fool of herself by not

   walking properly.

Using context clues
7. Draw a line to match each word with its meaning.

   proportion   a. skilled

   adept   b. calm and peaceful

   serene   c. balance of parts

CRITICAL THINKING

Drawing conclusions
1. If Keiko visited the United States, what customs and traits might she have to get used to?

   Answers will vary. She would have to get used to the fast pace of life, to casual manners, to people who freely express their

   emotions, and to the freedom and independence that women enjoy.

Making inferences
2. Describe how Tomi is changing as a result of her time in Japan.

   Answers will vary. She is beginning to slow down and appreciate the beauty of small things.

   She is becoming more serene.

Making inferences
3. Describe the grandparents' attitude toward Tomi at the end of the story.

   They feel pride, love, and acceptance of their granddaughter. They are pleased that Tomi is learning about her

   Japanese heritage.

4. Mr. Tanaka told Tomi that flower arranging is done with different lengths of stems and a serene heart. Part of this statement is a fact, and part is opinion. Which is which?

The part about the stems is fact. The part about the serene heart is opinion.

5. Do you think Tomi is likely to keep some Japanese customs when she is back in the United States?

Answers will vary. Tomi might wear the kimono for special occasions and try flower arranging again. However, she will

probably never learn to hide her feelings, especially when she is back home among other Americans.

SKILL FOCUS: THEME

1. Think about the title of the story. To what kind of arrangement does it refer?

It refers to Tomi's efforts to create a simple flower arrangement, following the formal rules of traditional

Japanese flower arranging. It also refers to Tomi's arrangement living in Japan with her grandparents.

2. Explain why Tomi has difficulty with the simple arrangement.

Answers will vary. She moves too quickly and is too impatient. She is too nervous and trying too

hard to please her grandparents. She does not appreciate the beauty of small things done well.

3. What other Japanese customs are difficult for Tomi?

She has trouble hiding her feelings. She has trouble walking gracefully in a kimono. She has trouble with

Japan's formal manners. She has trouble learning to move more slowly and to be more patient.

4. Why is Tomi's visit to her grandparents' garden a turning point for her?

She begins to appreciate the simple beauty in the Japanese way. She becomes more serene.

5. Discuss the author's message or theme.

Answers will vary. It is important to look for the beauty in every moment. The customs and traditions of other countries,

while different, are not necessarily better or worse than those of one's own country. With special effort, one can appreciate

and belong to two cultures at the same time.

Reading-Writing Connection

On a separate sheet of paper, write a paragraph describing a time when you felt that you could not find a way to fit in or adapt to a new situation.

Skill: Cause and Effect

For ESL/ELL support, see highlighted words, page T73, and pages T28–T30.

For lesson support, see page T73.

BACKGROUND INFORMATION

"Worlds Under Our Feet" tells about archaeologists (ARK ee AHL ə jəsts) working in cities. Archaeologists are scientists who study the people, customs, and life of the past. To learn more, they excavate (EKS kə vayt), or dig, at sites where people once lived. As they carefully dig through layers of soil, they find clues about how people lived in the past. These clues might include pieces of broken pottery, tools, statues, walls, temples, and even entire cities.

SKILL FOCUS: Cause and Effect

When one event causes another event to happen, the process is called cause and effect. A **cause** is an event that makes something happen. An **effect** is what happens as a result of the cause.

One effect can be the cause of another effect. That effect can then cause something else to happen. In this way, a chain of causes and effects occurs.

The following paragraph explains a chain of causes and effects.

> Archaeological digs in cities have another benefit, too. When archaeologists go to work in cities, local newspapers and TV stations cover the stories. As a result, people in the area come out to see the sites. This causes people to become more interested in archaeology and history. The end result is that the general public acquires a higher level of knowledge about the city and its past.

The first cause is archaeologists digging in cities. The effect is that newspaper and TV reporters cover the event. The effect of the media coverage is to encourage people to come out and see the site. This causes people to learn more about their city's history.

▶ Complete the cause-and-effect chain at the bottom of the page. Use details from the paragraph. The first parts of the chain have been done for you.

CONTEXT CLUES: Details

The **details** in sentences are often context clues. Such details can help you figure out the meaning of a new word. In the sentences below, look for details that explain the meaning of the underlined word.

> *Inside the temple, archaeologists found more than 600 <u>artifacts</u>. These included life-sized statues, as well as hundreds of smaller Aztec objects.*

If you don't know the meaning of *artifacts*, the details *life-sized statues* and *smaller Aztec objects* will help. These details suggest that artifacts are objects preserved from the past.

▶ Read the following sentence. Circle the details that help you figure out the meaning of the underlined word.

> They <u>surveyed</u> the site, making maps showing where they would dig.

In the following selection, use details to figure out the meanings of the underlined words *demolished, integral,* and *inhabitants.*

Strategy Tip

As you read "Worlds Under Our Feet," look for cause-and-effect relationships. Recognizing causes and effects will help you understand the ideas in the selection. Keep in mind that the effect can cause something else to happen.

Cause	Effect/Cause	Effect/Cause	Effect/Cause	Effect
Archaeologists dig in cities.	Newspapers and TV cover the dig.	People come out to see the dig.	People get more interested in archaeology and history.	People have a greater knowledge of the city's history.

WORLDS UNDER OUR FEET

The Lost Temple of the Aztecs

In early 1978, workers laying cables in the center of Mexico City had a big surprise. Suddenly their equipment struck a huge stone. This was no ordinary stone. It was perfectly round and covered with ancient carvings!

Work at the site stopped. **Archaeologists** came to investigate. They soon realized that the stone stood for the legendary Aztec moon goddess. According to historical records, this fabulous stone had been kept at the Great Temple of the Aztecs. This temple was once the most sacred place in the Aztec world. Would an excavation of the site reveal the temple?

Mexican archaeologists planned carefully before digging. They surveyed the site, making maps showing where they would dig. They also determined the techniques they would use.

We often think of archaeologists digging in deserts and jungles. Yet today more archaeological sites are in crowded cities. Construction workers often find these sites by accident.

Excavating a site in a busy, modern city is expensive and difficult. In Mexico City, for example, archaeologists had to make sure their digging would not damage surrounding buildings. People who lived and worked in the area had to be protected. The site itself had to be secure. Water was another problem. Mexico City was built on the site of a lake. Ground water was close to the surface and could flood the site.

The Great Temple of the Aztecs was gradually unearthed. The topmost level had been demolished by the Spanish conquerors. Although that part of the building had been destroyed, five lower levels remained intact.

First built in 1325, the temple had been rebuilt several times. Inside the temple, archaeologists found more than 600 **artifacts** (ART ə fakts). These included life-sized statues, as well as hundreds of smaller Aztec objects. Today visitors from all over the world can see and marvel at the ancient Aztec temple and the artifacts that were buried with it.

In 1978, electrical workers in Mexico City accidentally discovered the site of this ancient temple.

Other Archeological Discoveries

The Aztec temple in Mexico City was an extraordinary discovery. Yet less dramatic sites are found every year. In recent years, workers burying cables in Barcelona, Spain, found a stone wall and tower that had surrounded the city in the 1400s. Construction workers in New York City uncovered an African American graveyard from the 1700s. In Athens, Greece, work on a new subway line yielded ancient statues and buildings. Discoveries like these present archaeologists with special opportunities and difficult decisions.

Just how do temples, walls, cemeteries, and even entire cities get buried underground? Over the years, the ground level gradually rises, burying the past beneath it. Layers of decaying plants pile up. Soil, eroded from rocks and hills, is deposited. Pieces of demolished buildings and even garbage raise the ground level.

Century after century, this material piles up in horizontal layers, covering entire buildings. This process is called **stratification** (STRAT ə fə KAY shən). Studying the layers deposited over the centuries is one way that archaeologists date artifacts from the past.

Uncovering Colonial America

For archaeologists, every new site is a chance to learn about the past. In cities, construction sites often present the best digging opportunities. In 2000, for example, a four-block park behind Independence Hall in Philadelphia was dug up to build a new museum.

Dozens of houses built in the 1700s and 1800s had once stood on the site. They had been bulldozed years ago to build the park, called Independence Mall. Now while digging up the mall, workers exposed the foundations, yards, and wells of houses that were hundreds of years old.

Archaeologists were excited. A bit of colonial America had suddenly been unsealed. They were eager to learn as much as they could. Over the next few months, they uncovered nearly a million artifacts from the 1600s and 1700s.

Most of the artifacts were of little material value—scraps of newspaper, kitchen tools, bottles, lamps, and shoes. However, the artifacts were of great historical value because they revealed the **diversity** (də VER sə tee) of the colonial population.

Among the artifacts were Native American beads and tools, as well as the remains of a log cabin where free African Americans or Native Americans had lived. Americans from many different ethnic backgrounds and income levels had apparently been living peacefully in the same small neighborhood at the same time that the Constitution was being written just a few blocks away.

Archaeological digs in cities have another benefit, too. When archaeologists go to work in cities, local newspapers and TV stations cover the stories. As a result, people in the area come out to see the sites. This causes people to become more interested in archaeology and history. The end result is that the general public acquires a higher level of knowledge about the city and its past.

Archaeology or Development?

In the United States, government officials support the work of archaeologists. Because construction work can destroy valuable artifacts, Congress passed a law that requires builders to allow archaeologists to study construction sites before the work begins.

Inspired by the success of this federal law, many states and cities passed similar laws to protect their local heritage. As a result of these new laws, an increasing number of artifacts from our nation's past are being preserved.

At a new construction site, archaeologists first take samples from a few small sections of the ground. Usually they find nothing at all. In some cases, however, the laws protecting these sites have proven their value.

At one site in Ohio, for example, a company planned to build a new industrial park. When

New laws require builders to allow archaeologists to study a construction site before building begins.

archaeologists took samples at the site, they found artifacts from a Native American community that may have existed there more than 10,000 years ago.

Sometimes discoveries are made after construction gets underway. In these cases, conflicts can develop between archaeologists and builders. Archaeologists work slowly and carefully. They see the earth as a gold mine of clues about the past. Often they want to preserve their discoveries.

Builders, however, have different goals. For them, time is money, and they have tight schedules to meet. If an archaeological site is preserved, builders may have to give up their plans to develop the site. For them, preserving the past may mean a loss of money and opportunity.

Usually the archaeologists and the builders compromise. Each side benefits, but each must make sacrifices. Because most sites cannot be preserved, archaeologists may study them intensely for a short period of time. In order to have a permanent record of their work, they take photographs and measurements of everything they find. The site itself will soon disappear beneath a building. However, archaeologists have preserved evidence that can be studied for clues to the past.

Cooperation in Athens

A good example of cooperation between archaeologists and builders occurred in Greece in 1994. The city of Athens was about to extend its subway system. Athens, the birthplace of democracy, was the center of culture in ancient Greece. The digging of new subway tunnels was bound to uncover archaeological sites.

The construction companies in charge of the new subway made an important decision: Archaeology would be an <u>integral</u> part of the project. They would allow archaeologists to have full access to the sites. Construction companies even provided money for these studies.

By studying ancient writings, archaeologists identified the sites where ruins might be found. Ancient shrines, gardens, and schools were all discovered at the sites of some of the new subway stations. The construction companies planned the construction so that archaeologists would have more time at these sites. One of the most important

sites was a school where **Aristotle** (AR is tot əl), a Greek philosopher, once taught.

Once they were fully studied, the excavations at Athens were covered up. However, the new Athens subway became a mini-museum. Displays of artifacts appear in several stations. One of the stations was designed around the remains of ancient buildings found there.

Saving the Sites

Archaeologists, citizens, and politicians often work together to save important sites. In 1991, for example, construction workers digging near City Hall in New York City found a cemetery. In the 1700s, this ground had become the final resting place of thousands of African Americans.

When the graveyard was unearthed, many African Americans regarded it as an important part of their cultural heritage. As a result, they wanted the site to be preserved. Archaeologists wanted to preserve the site, too, because it was the earliest and largest colonial cemetery ever found.

These two groups pressured local and national government officials to give the burial site the care and recognition it deserved. As a result, bones and artifacts from the site were sent to a university for study. The site was declared a landmark by both New York City and the U.S. government.

There will be a memorial to mark the place where the bones will be reburied. There will also be a museum at the site to interpret the historic and scientific importance of the findings.

Another controversial site was uncovered in Miami in 1999. In the heart of Miami's business district, a high-rise building was under construction. While digging the foundation, workers found a perfectly round, 40-foot-wide circle of carved stones and post holes.

Archaeologists agreed that the long-vanished Tequesta Indians had built the circle about 2,000 years ago. The Indians had probably used the circle as a calendar. Almost nothing is known about Miami's earliest <u>inhabitants</u>. For this reason, archaeologists saw the site as a rare opportunity to find out how people in the area lived thousands of years ago. The builder, however, was determined to finish the construction project.

In order to save the site, archaeologists and Native Americans wrote letters and made speeches. As a result, many schoolchildren and other citizens became involved in the crusade to save the site. Thanks to the efforts of concerned citizens, county officials seized the site and stopped construction.

Virtual Archaeology

In many cities, the cost of preserving ancient sites is too high. Also modern buildings may be blocking part of the site. Yet these problems disappear with a technique called "time slicing."

Two thousand years ago, the Romans invaded Great Britain. One of the large cities they built there was called Viroconium. It now lies buried under a town called Wroxeter. Today archaeologists are uncovering the ancient Roman city. They are doing so, however, without moving a shovelful of soil!

Using a portable radar machine, archaeologists send electrical pulses into the ground. When these pulses hit something in the ground, they bounce back to a receiver. The receiver registers the "echoes" and sends them to a computer. These "echoes" reveal the size and shape of buried structures. Using this data, the computer makes a three-dimensional image of the underground site.

At Viroconium, archaeologists are time-slicing a 140-acre site. One of the computer's first images shows a stone church. Nearly 100-feet long, it may be the oldest-known church in England. The computer has also mapped ancient Roman buildings. When the project is complete, you will be able to tour the entire underground site by popping a CD-ROM into your computer.

For many people, virtual archaeology may not seem as satisfying as real dirt and stone. Still it is a practical, money-saving tool. Archaeologists can use this new tool to "uncover" sites that would otherwise remain a mystery.

Past and Future

Today many archaeological sites and objects are threatened as never before. Why should we protect and preserve them? Why should we study the past?

For most people, the past is a source of interest and wonder. The past can teach us many practical lessons we can apply to our lives today. We can take pride in what the people before us have accomplished. The past is something that belongs to everyone. In that way, the past unites us all.

COMPREHENSION

Recalling details
1. What clue led archaeologists to discover the Great Temple of the Aztecs in Mexico City?

Workers laying cables there came upon a huge stone

that stood for the Aztec moon goddess. Historical

records said that the stone had been kept in the temple.

Identifying main idea
2. Explain how federal and state laws help archaeologists.

Federal and state laws require that archaeologists be

allowed to study sites before building begins.

Identifying main idea
3. Explain why the 40-foot stone circle found in Miami was an important discovery.

The stone was probably a calendar built more than

2,000 years ago by the earliest inhabitants of Florida,

the Tequesta Indians, about whom little is known.

Comparing and contrasting
4. How do the views of builders and archaeologists usually differ regarding archaeological sites in cities?

Archaeologists like to explore the site slowly and

carefully. Builders prefer to complete their projects

quickly.

Using contest clues
5. Answer each question. Write *yes* or *no* on the line.

___yes___ a. Does material from demolished buildings add to stratification?

___yes___ b. Is studying historical texts an integral part of archaeology?

___no___ c. Do the earliest inhabitants of an area always leave behind written records?

LESSON 12 Cause and Effect **43**

Making inferences

1. Discuss how stratification helps archaeologists to date artifacts from the past.

   As a result of stratification, the oldest artifacts lie in the deepest layers of soil. Layers closer to the surface contain objects

   deposited more recently.

Drawing conclusions

2. Explain why it is important for builders and archaeologists to cooperate closely.

   Answers will vary. The archaeologists' need to uncover new information must be balanced with the builders' need to

   complete a project. By cooperating and compromising, both can accomplish more.

Drawing conclusions

3. What can average citizens do to help preserve archaeological finds in their towns?

   Answers will vary. They can write letters to government officials, urging them to pass laws to protect and preserve sites.

   They can write letters to the editor of newspapers or make speeches.

SKILL FOCUS: CAUSE AND AFFECT

Read the following paragraph. Then fill in the cause-and-effect chain to show the series of events that lead to the final effect. The first cause is provided for you.

> In the United States, government officials support the work of archaeologists. Because construction work can destroy many valuable artifacts, Congress passed a law that requires builders to allow archaeologists to study construction sites before the work begins. The success of this law inspired many states and cities, and they passed similar laws to protect their local heritage. As a result of all these new laws, an increasing number of artifacts from the nation's past are being preserved.

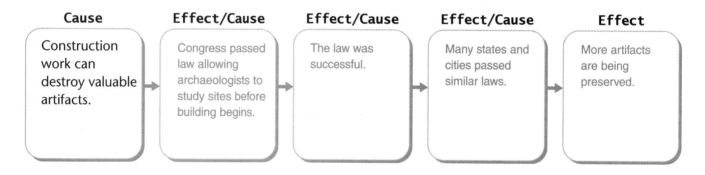

Cause	Effect/Cause	Effect/Cause	Effect/Cause	Effect
Construction work can destroy valuable artifacts.	Congress passed law allowing archaeologists to study sites before building begins.	The law was successful.	Many states and cities passed similar laws.	More artifacts are being preserved.

Reading-Writing Connection

Suppose that you were on one of the archaeological digs described in the selection. On a separate sheet of paper, write a diary entry that tells what you might have seen and done on a typical day. Explain why you think your work is important.

For ESL/ELL support, see highlighted words, page T74, and pages T26–T28.

Skill: Reading a Diagram

For lesson support, see page T74.

BACKGROUND INFORMATION

In "The Nervous System," you will read about the human nervous system. Made up of billions of nerve cells, the nervous system carries messages that allow the body to function and to respond to the outside world. Our thoughts, emotions, and movements are all products of our nervous system. The selection begins with the smallest unit of the nervous system, the neuron, and progresses to the largest unit, the central nervous system.

SKILL FOCUS: Reading a Diagram

Diagrams can help you understand the words and ideas in a science selection. A diagram is a drawing that shows the structure of something or the relationships between different parts of a system. When interpreting a diagram, read the paragraphs near the diagram first. Then study the diagram.

Sometimes a paragraph in the text will refer you to a diagram. It might say, for example, "See Figure 2." Usually that is the best time to pause in your reading and study the diagram.

To understand a diagram, read its title, caption, and labels. The title tells you what the diagram shows. The caption explains the diagram in more detail. Labels name the parts of the diagram.

Often you will want to go back and reread the paragraphs that refer to a diagram. Using the text and the diagram together is the best way to get a full understanding of a science topic.

The following steps will help you understand the diagrams in your reading.

1. Read the paragraphs that come just before and just after the diagram. Then study the diagram.

2. Look back at the diagram from time to time as you continue to read.

3. Use the diagram and the text together to sum up what you have read.

▶ Study the diagram of a neuron, or nerve cell at the top of the next column. Then answer the questions that follow.

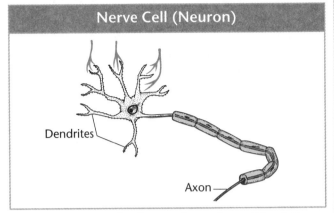

Nerve Cell (Neuron)

Dendrites

Axon

How many axons lead away from the cell body?

one

How many dendrites are shown as part of this neuron? _____ seven

CONTEXT CLUES: Appositive Phrases

An **appositive phrase** is a group of words that explains the meaning of a new word. Usually the appositive phrase appears right after the new word and is set off with commas or dashes. In the sentence below, find the appositive phrase that helps you figure out the meaning of *conscious*.

*The cerebrum controls all **conscious** activity, or those activities that you are aware of.*

If you don't know the meaning of *conscious*, the appositive phrase *those activities that you are aware of* gives you the meaning.

▶ Read the following sentence. Circle the appositive phrase that shows the meaning of *spinal cord*.

*This part of the brain connects directly to the **spinal cord**, a long bundle of nerves that extends down through the backbone.*

Use appositive phrases to find the meanings of the underlined words *hemispheres*, *involuntary*, and *internal* in the following selection.

> **Strategy Tip**
>
> As you read, use the steps on this page to understand the diagrams.

The Nervous System

THE NERVOUS SYSTEM is the body's communication system. It carries messages about the outside world and about the body itself. It carries messages that allow muscles to move. It also keeps the body's organs functioning.

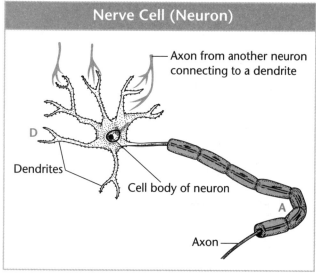

FIGURE 1. **The neuron is the basic unit of the nervous system.**

Neurons

The basic unit of the nervous system is the **neuron** (NUR ahn), or nerve cell. A neuron has three parts. It has a cell body and two kinds of threads that extend from it. The long thread is the **axon** (AK sahn), and the short threads are the **dendrites** (DEN drytz). See Figure 1.

Some neurons have more than one dendrite, but most neurons have only one axon. The dendrites carry messages to the cell body. The axon carries messages away from the cell body. The axon of one neuron connects to a dendrite of another neuron. When a message travels through the nervous system, it is sent by the axon of each neuron. The dendrite of the next neuron receives the message from the axon and passes it on.

Nerves are bundles of neuron fibers, or threads. Different kinds of nerves do different jobs in the nervous system. **Sensory** (SEN sər ee) **nerves** carry messages to the brain and the spinal cord. Motor nerves carry messages from the central nervous system to the body's muscles. Connecting nerves connect sensory and motor nerves. See Figure 2.

Parts of the Nervous System

The nervous system has two basic parts. The **central nervous system** is made up of the brain and the spinal cord. The **peripheral** (pə RIF ər əl) **nervous system** is made up of the nerves that branch

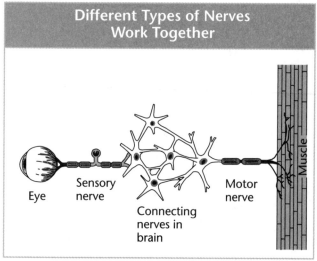

FIGURE 2. **Different kinds of nerves do different jobs in the body.**

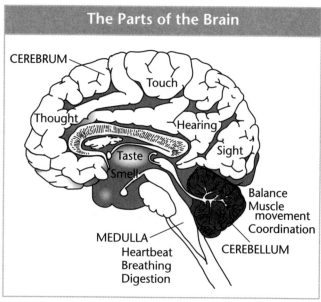

FIGURE 3. **The brain is the center of the nervous system. It has three main parts.**

out from the brain and the spinal cord. The **autonomic** (aw toh NOM ik) **nervous system** is a part of the peripheral nervous system. It is made up of the nerves that regulate the internal organs of the body.

Central Nervous System The brain is like the switchboard of a telephone system. Most of the "calls" from the outside world travel through the nerves to the brain. The brain takes in the information from the nerves and sends out orders through the nerves. Although the brain is the main control center, the spinal cord also plays a major role in receiving and sending messages to the sensory and motor nerves.

The brain itself is divided into three main parts: the **cerebrum** (sə REE brəm), the **cerebellum** (ser ə BEL əm), and the **medulla** (mi DUL ə). See Figure 3. The cerebrum is the largest part of the brain. It is divided into two hemispheres, or halves, by a deep groove. The left hemisphere controls the right side of the body. It is thought to affect the use of language, mathematics, and logical thinking. The right hemisphere controls the left side of the body. Scientists think it affects musical and artistic ability and emotions.

Information from the five senses comes to the cerebrum. It is the thinking part of the brain, where memory is stored. The cerebrum controls all conscious activity, or those activities that you are aware of.

The cerebellum is located underneath the cerebrum. It controls balance and movement of the muscles. The cerebellum also regulates how groups of muscles work together. For example, it coordinates the movements between the hands and the eyes that allow a person to catch a ball. That is, it makes the hands and eyes work well together. The cerebellum affects involuntary activity, the kind of activity that you are not conscious of.

The medulla is the part of the brain that regulates the body's internal organs—the organs inside the body. It controls such vital activities as breathing, the beating of the heart, and the digestion of food. It also controls sneezing, coughing, hiccupping, vomiting, and swallowing.

This part of the brain connects directly to the spinal cord, a long bundle of nerves that extends down through the backbone. All messages to and from the brain go through the spinal cord.

Peripheral Nervous System The peripheral nervous system is made up of the nerves that connect the central nervous system to the rest of the body. *Periphery* (pə RIF ər ee) means "outer edge." The peripheral nervous system reaches the outer parts of the body, including the hands and feet. See Figure 4.

Nerves of the peripheral nervous system work closely with the central nervous system. The optic nerve, for example, connects the back wall of the eye to the brain. When a person sees something, the eyes receive the image. The image is then sent to the brain by the optic nerve. The brain then "tells" the person what he or she is seeing.

Not all messages are carried to the brain. The nerves can bypass the brain for faster reactions. When a person touches something hot, for example, he or she doesn't first think "hot" before moving. The person moves almost instantly, without thinking. This is called a reflex action. In a reflex action, the command to move is sent from the spinal cord instead of the brain.

The autonomic nervous system controls the beating of the heart, the digestion of food, and

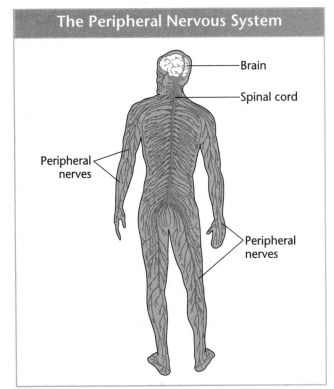

FIGURE 4. The peripheral nervous system branches out from the brain and the spinal cord and reaches the outer parts of the body.

breathing. *Autonomous* (aw TAHN ə məs) means "independent." The autonomic nervous system works independently of a person's thoughts. The heart beats, food is digested, and breathing continues automatically. The medulla is the control center for the autonomic nervous system. Messages that begin in the medulla keep the body's internal organs functioning.

The **sympathetic** (sim pə THET ik) and the **parasympathetic** (pair ə sim pə THET ik) **systems** are the two parts of the autonomic nervous system. The sympathetic system works to speed up the heart and send more blood to the muscles during times of physical activity, anger, or stress. The parasympathetic system works to slow down the heartbeat and send blood back to the digestive system during times of rest. In these ways, the body always gets the power and the rest that it needs.

COMPREHENSION

Recalling details
1. Describe a neuron.

   A neuron is a nerve cell, the basic unit of the nervous

   system.

Recalling details
2. Explain the purpose of dendrites.

   They receive messages from other neurons and pass

   them on to the neuron's cell body.

Recalling details
3. Tell how the axon is different from dendrites.

   The axon carries messages away from the cell body.

Recalling details
4. What activities do scientists believe are affected by the left side of the brain?

   They believe it affects language, mathematics, and

   logical thinking.

Recalling details
5. Explain the purpose of the autonomic nervous system.

   It controls the internal organs of the body.

Using context clues
6. Complete each sentence by filling in the correct word.

   hemispheres   involuntary   internal

   a. The engine and the transmission are among the ___internal___ parts of a car.

   b. A globe can be divided into two halves, or ___hemispheres___.

   c. When the pupil of the eye enlarges in bright sunlight, it is a(n) ___involuntary___ action.

CRITICAL THINKING

Circle the letter of the statement that best completes each sentence or answers each question.

Making inferences
1. A reflex action is faster than an action that involves thought because the nerve message that causes it

   (a.) travels a shorter distance.   c. is hotter.

   b. occurs when a person is angry.   d. is stronger.

Inferring cause and effect
2. Which of the following would cause a reflex action?

   a. solving a math problem   c. deciding what to order in a restaurant

   b. seeing a good friend   (d.) stepping on a sharp rock

3. If a person saw a charging lion, which part of the autonomic nervous system would react?

    a. peripheral system   **c.** parasympathetic system

    (b.) sympathetic system   **d.** central nervous system

4. When a person awakens from a nap feeling refreshed, it is because the parasympathetic nervous system has

    a. stopped the body's functions.   **(c.)** slowed down the body's functions.

    b. speeded up the body's functions.   **d.** reversed the body's functions.

5. If the heart did not have nerves,

    a. it would expand.   **c.** it would not be part of the central nervous system.

    (b.) it could not receive the message to beat.   **d.** it would beat too fast.

6. If a person is left-handed, which hemisphere of the cerebrum controls the activity of writing?

    a. left   **(b.)** right   **c.** both   **d.** neither

SKILL FOCUS: READING A DIAGRAM

1. Look at Figure 1. Put a ✔ on the cell body. Put a *D* next to a dendrite and an *A* next to the axon.

2. Look at Figure 2. In your own words, explain how the nervous system might work if a person sees danger and runs from it.

    The eyes see the danger. The message is carried by the sensory nerves to the connecting nerves in the brain. The

    connecting nerves carry the message to the motor nerves, which send the message to the leg muscles, and the person

    runs.

3. Look at Figure 3. Name the three parts of the brain and the function of each part.

    The cerebrum controls all conscious activity, thinking, and memory and also receives information from the five senses. The

    cerebellum controls involuntary activity, such as balance, muscle movement, and coordination. The medulla regulates the

    internal organs. It controls breathing, the beating of the heart, and the digestion of food.

4. In your own words, explain what is shown in Figure 4.

    Answers will vary. The peripheral nervous system connects the central nervous system to the rest of the body. It extends all

    the way to the hands and feet.

Reading-Writing Connection

On a separate sheet of paper, write a paragraph explaining which part of the human nervous system you would like to know more about. Give reasons for your choice.

For ESL/ELL support, see highlighted words, page T75, and pages T28–T30.

For lesson support, see page T75.

BACKGROUND INFORMATION

"How to Read Decimals" explains decimals and how to read the names of the values shown to the right of a decimal point. You may not use the word *decimals* very often, but decimals are definitely part of your life. On any given day, for example, your family might buy 10.3 gallons of gas and then drive 3.4 miles to the store. There you might buy 3.5 pounds of apples and 1.87 pounds of hamburger. When you get to the cash register, the price of your purchases is shown in decimals, too—$12.74. Understanding decimals is a big help in everyday life.

SKILL FOCUS: Reading Decimals

Some numbers are written with periods called **decimal points**. A decimal point separates a number into two parts. The digits to the left of the decimal point are whole numbers. The digits to the right of the decimal point are parts of a whole. For example, the number 126.73 has a decimal point. The decimal point shows that 126 is a whole number. Since 73 is to the right of the decimal point, it represents only part of a whole number. The number 33.4 also has a decimal point. It shows you that 33 is a whole number and that 4 represents only part of a whole.

When reading a decimal, say the word *and* in place of the decimal point. The number 126.73, for example, is read as *one hundred twenty-six and seventy-three hundredths*. The number 33.4 is read as *thirty-three and four tenths*.

▶ Look at each decimal in the first column of the chart below. In the second column, write the words that show how to say each number.

WORD CLUES

A **suffix** is a word part added to the end of a base word to change its meaning. For number words, *-th* is a common suffix. When the suffix *-th* is added to a number word such as *ten*, *hundred*, or *thousand*, the value of the number word is decreased. A math word with the suffix *-th* has a value of less than a whole number. The suffix *-th* can be used with any place value to the right of the decimal point. The suffix *-th* makes a very big difference. A *hundred* kilometers, for example, is very different from a *hundredth* of a kilometer. If you run 100 kilometers, you have run 10,000 times farther than a hundredth of a kilometer!

▶ Add the suffix *-th* to each of these number words. Write the new words on the lines.

ten	tenth
hundred	hundredth
thousand	thousandth

Strategy Tip

When reading "How to Read Decimals," remember the names of the place values to the right of the decimal point. These numbers represent values of less than 1.

Saying Decimals	
Decimal	**How to Say It**
8.9	eight and nine tenths
33.65	thirty-three and sixty-five hundredths
12.1	twelve and one tenth
147.98	one hundred forty-seven and ninety-eight hundredths

How to Read Decimals

A period that appears in a number is called a **decimal point**. The places to the left of a decimal point show whole numbers—numbers with values of 1 or more.

```
ten thousands
  thousands
    hundreds
      tens
        ones

6   1  ,  2   8   4  .  3   9   5   7
```

The whole number in the example above is sixty-one thousand, two hundred eighty-four.

Places to the right of a decimal point are called **decimal places**. They show values of less than 1. The suffix *-th* is used in naming each decimal place. The places to the right of the decimal point are tenths, hundredths, thousandths, and ten-thousandths.

```
ten thousands
  thousands
    hundreds
      tens
        ones   tenths
                 hundredths
                   thousandths
                     ten-thousandths

6   1  ,  2   8   4  .  3   9   5   7
```

The tenths place is the first place to the right of the decimal point. A number in the tenths place is $\frac{1}{10}$ as large as the same number in the ones place. Think about a dollar bill. It takes 10 dimes to make a dollar. A dime is one tenth of a dollar. One tenth can be written as the decimal 0.1 or as the fraction $\frac{1}{10}$. A dime is 0.1 or $\frac{1}{10}$ of a dollar.

The hundredths place is the second place to the right of the decimal point. A number in the hundredths place is $\frac{1}{100}$ as large as the same number in the ones place. It takes 100 pennies to make a dollar. A penny is one-hundredth of a dollar. One-hundredth can be written as the decimal 0.01 or as the fraction $\frac{1}{100}$. A penny is 0.01 or $\frac{1}{100}$ of a dollar.

The thousandths place is the third place to the right of the decimal point. A number in the thousandths place is $\frac{1}{1,000}$ as large as the same number in the ones place. This is a very small part of a dollar, and no coin is made for that value. One-thousandth of a dollar is called a *mil*. Mils are used in the financial world. It takes 1,000 mils to make a dollar. One-thousandth can be written as the decimal 0.001 or as the fraction $\frac{1}{1,000}$. A mil is 0.001 or $\frac{1}{1,000}$ of a dollar.

The ten-thousandths place is the fourth place to the right of the decimal point. A number in the ten-thousandths place is $\frac{1}{10,000}$ as large as the same number in the ones place. One ten-thousandth can be written as the decimal 0.0001 or as the fraction $\frac{1}{10,000}$.

A number with digits only in the decimal places can be written in two ways.

0.7 or .7

These two numbers have the same value. You read this number as though it were a whole number: *seven*. Then you add the name of the place value: *tenths*. The number is read like this: *seven tenths*.

ones	tenths	hundredths	thousandths	ten-thousandths	
0 •	7				seven tenths
0 •	0	4			four hundredths
0 •	6	1			sixty-one hundredths
0 •	0	0	2		two thousandths
0 •	8	3	5		eight hundred thirty-five thousandths
0 •	0	3	4	2	three hundred forty-two ten-thousandths
0 •	9	0	3	1	nine thousand thirty-one ten-thousandths

A number that includes digits on both sides of the decimal point is read in two groups.

9,295.17

First read the digits to the left of the decimal point as a whole number: *nine thousand two hundred ninety-five*. The decimal point stands for the word *and*. Then read the decimal value as though it were a whole number: *seventeen*. Then add the name of the place value of the last digit: *hundredths*. The number is read like this: *nine thousand two hundred ninety-five and seventeen hundredths*.

The number can also be written as a whole number and a fraction. The decimal number is written as a fraction. The whole number remains the same. Because 7, the last digit in the decimal, is in the hundredths place, the denominator of the fraction is 100. It is read the same as the decimal number.

$$9,295 \frac{17}{100}$$

Read the following number.

$$263.783$$

Read the digits to the left of the decimal point first. Say the word *and* when you reach the decimal

point. Then read the digits to the right of the decimal point. Because the last digit is in the thousandths place, add the word *thousandths*. The number is read like this: *two hundred sixty-three and seven hundred eighty-three thousandths*. The number is written as a whole number and a fraction as below.

$$263 \frac{783}{1,000}$$

Look at the following number.

$$49.5036$$

It is read like this: *forty-nine and five thousand thirty-six ten-thousandths*.

Remember that a decimal point separates whole numbers from numbers that are less than one whole. The numbers to the right of a decimal point are always less than 1.

COMPREHENSION

Recalling details
1. Write the place values on the lines for each digit in this number.

ten thousands   thousands   hundreds   tens   ones   tenths   hundreths   thousandths   ten-thousandths

1   2   ,   3   4   5   .   6   7   8   9

Recalling details
2. When you hear *and* in a number being read, it stands for a ___decimal point___.

Recalling details
3. If a dollar bill is one, what part of a dollar is a dime? A penny? A mil? Write each amount as a fraction and as a decimal.

one dime   = $\frac{1}{10}$ or   0.1   of a dollar.

one penny = $\frac{1}{100}$ or   0.01   of a dollar.

one mil   = $\frac{1}{1,000}$ or   0.001   of a dollar.

CRITICAL THINKING

Making inferences
1. Tell about the places in your daily life where you see decimals and fractions used.

Answers will vary. Decimals appear at the gas pump

and on food labels. Fractions appear in recipes.

Inferring cause and effect
2. These numbers all have the same digits. Explain why the numbers have different values.

0.015   .0015   .0105

The digits are in different places to the right of the

decimal point.

Making inferences
3. Circle the smallest value in each row.

a.	.7	.04	.71	(.001)
b.	.04	.102	.5	(.05)
c.	.317	(.0146)	.09	.4

Making inferences
4. Circle the largest value in each row.

a.	.08	.095	(.2)	.18
b.	.27	(.41)	.0896	.38
c.	.1	.09	.075	(.275)

A. Write each number in the correct columns. Add the decimal points where they belong.

	ten thousands	thousands	hundreds	tens	ones	tenths	hundredths	thousandths	ten-thousandths
54 and 9 tenths				5	4	.9			
6,702 and 8 tenths		6,	7	0	2	.8			
7 hundredths						.0	7		
1 and 38 hundredths					1	.3	8		
7 thousandths						.0	0	7	
91 thousandths						.0	9	1	
643 thousandths						.6	4	3	
56 and 2 thousandths				5	6	.0	0	2	
312 and 54 thousandths			3	1	2	.0	5	4	
6 ten-thousandths						.0	0	0	6
923 ten-thousandths						.0	9	2	3
1,246 ten-thousandths						.1	2	4	6
172 and 73 ten-thousandths			1	7	2	.0	0	7	3
4,317 and 6,431 ten-thousandths		4,	3	1	7	.6	4	3	1
80,008 and 8 ten-thousandths	8	0,	0	0	8	.0	0	0	8

B. Write the fraction for each decimal.

0.2 $\frac{2}{10}$ 0.0091 $\frac{91}{10,000}$ 884.18 $884\frac{18}{100}$

0.65 $\frac{65}{100}$ 6.9 $6\frac{9}{10}$ 329.861 $329\frac{861}{1,000}$

0.634 $\frac{634}{1,000}$ 45.05 $45\frac{5}{100}$ 25.0106 $25\frac{106}{10,000}$

0.4372 $\frac{4372}{10,000}$ 2,379.025 $2,379\frac{25}{1,000}$ 7,563.4007 $7,563\frac{4,007}{10,000}$

C. Draw lines to match the decimals, the fractions, and the correct way to read each number. The first one has been done for you.

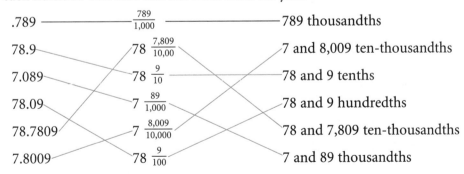

.789 —— $\frac{789}{1,000}$ —— 789 thousandths

78.9 $78\frac{7,809}{10,00}$ 7 and 8,009 ten-thousandths

7.089 $78\frac{9}{10}$ 78 and 9 tenths

78.09 $7\frac{89}{1,000}$ 78 and 9 hundredths

78.7809 $7\frac{8,009}{10,000}$ 78 and 7,809 ten-thousandths

7.8009 $78\frac{9}{100}$ 7 and 89 thousandths

Reading-Writing Connection

On a separate sheet of paper, write two paragraphs describing a real-life situation in which knowing about decimals and fractions can help you.

Skill: Vowel-Consonant Combinations

For lesson support, see page T76.

> The **vowel-consonant combinations** *air*, *ear*, and *are* can stand for the same sound. The words *hair*, *bear*, and *square* have the same vowel sound, but the letters that stand for the sound are different in each word.

A. Choose a word from the list to complete each sentence below. Then circle the letters in each word that stand for the same sound you hear in *hair*, *bear*, and *square*.

share	prepare	pears	stare
wear	stairs	chair	fair

1. Theo's favorite fruit is _____pears_____.

2. Clarkstown School is having a book _____fair_____ next week.

3. Jorge helped his father _____prepare_____ dinner by making the salad.

4. If you _____stare_____ at the sun, you could damage your eyes.

5. My sister and I _____share_____ clothes.

6. It is considered proper to push your _____chair_____ in before you leave the table.

7. Sarah likes to _____wear_____ heavy sweaters in the winter.

8. You have to walk up two flights of _____stairs_____ to get to my apartment.

> The vowel-consonant combination *ear* can stand for different sounds. The words *bear*, *earth*, and *beard* have the same vowel letters followed by *r*, but the vowel sound the letters stand for is different in each word.

B. Choose a word from the list to complete each sentence below.

clear	search	fear	early
heard	tear	learn	near

1. When Warren lost his key, we had to _____search_____ to find it.

2. Have you _____heard_____ the news about Governor Harris?

3. We got up _____early_____ every morning when we camped last summer.

4. Elena will _____learn_____ how to drive a car next year.

5. Please be careful not to _____tear_____ your dress.

6. Many people _____fear_____ certain kinds of animals.

7. The sky is always bright blue on a _____clear_____ day.

8. Jamal wanted to sit _____near_____ his best friend, Mohammed.

Skill: Syllables

For lesson support, see page T76.

RULE 3: Words With a Prefix or Suffix

A prefix always has at least one sounded vowel. This means that a prefix always contains at least one syllable. You can divide a word that has a prefix between the prefix and the base word.

misspell   mis spell

Most suffixes have at least one sounded vowel. This means that a suffix usually contains at least one syllable. You can divide a word that has a suffix between the base word and the suffix.

quickly   quick ly

A. Divide each of the words below into two syllables between the prefix or suffix and the base word. Write each syllable separately on the line next to the word.

1. backward   back ward
2. worthless   worth less
3. mistrust   mis trust
4. impure   im pure
5. fearful   fear ful
6. biplane   bi plane
7. rainy   rain y
8. midday   mid day

9. statement   state ment
10. preheat   pre heat
11. painter   paint er
12. nonsense   non sense
13. nearness   near ness
14. redo   re do
15. mistreat   mis treat
16. yearly   year ly

RULE 4: Words With Two Consonants Between Two Sounded Vowels

A word that has two consonants between two sounded vowels is usually divided into syllables between the two consonants.

winter   win ter

B. Divide each of the words below into two syllables. Write each syllable separately on the line next to the word.

1. signal   sig nal
2. blanket   blan ket
3. master   mas ter
4. admit   ad mit
5. plastic   plas tic
6. sandal   san dal
7. helmet   hel met

8. window   win dow
9. escape   es cape
10. dentist   den tist
11. walnut   wal nut
12. napkin   nap kin
13. magnet   mag net
14. perfume   per fume

Skill: Prefixes

For lesson support, see page T77.

A **prefix** is a word part that is added to the beginning of a word to change its meaning. Nine prefixes and their meanings are given below.

Prefix	Meaning	Prefix	Meaning
bi-	having two, or happening every two	sub-	under or below
de-	away from or undo	tri-	having three, or happening every three
mid-	middle	uni-	having only one
non-	not	re-	again
semi-	half or partly		

A. Read each word below and the meaning that follows it. Write the correct prefix next to each word.

1. ___mid___day   middle of the day

2. ___bi___monthly   once every two months

3. ___de___frost   to become unfrozen

4. ___sub___freezing   below freezing

5. ___semi___sweet   partly sweet

6. ___de___rail   to go off the rails

7. ___tri___angle   a shape with three angles

8. ___semi___circle   half a circle

9. ___uni___cycle   one-wheeled vehicle

10. ___non___sense   not making sense

11. ___re___play   play again

B. Use one of the words above to complete each sentence below.

1. It is so cold outside that it must be ___subfreezing___.

2. Another word for twelve o'clock noon is ___midday___.

3. We sat in a ___semicircle___ around the fire.

4. Mr. Barker had to ___defrost___ his freezer.

5. A ___unicycle___ is difficult to ride because it has only one wheel.

6. I read the letter, but it sounded like ___nonsense___ to me.

7. A broken track caused the train to ___derail___.

8. Our craft club meets ___bimonthly___.

9. Because they tied their last game, the two teams had to ___replay___ it.

10. In geometry class, we learned how to calculate the angles of a ___triangle___.

Skill: Main Idea—Stated or Unstated

For lesson support, see page T77.

When you read a textbook or reference book for information, the **main idea** of each paragraph will often be stated in a sentence. The rest of the paragraph will contain the supporting details that give additional information about the main idea.

Sometimes the main idea of a paragraph is not stated in one of the sentences. The information in the paragraph will help you to **infer**, or figure out, the main idea. To do this, think of a sentence that summarizes the supporting details of the paragraph.

Read the selection below. Decide if the main idea in each paragraph is stated or unstated.

Nō and Kabuki Plays

1. Plays are an important form of entertainment in most countries. Two kinds of drama unique to Japan are Nō and Kabuki. Music is used in both types of drama. Originally, men performed both men's and women's parts in Nō and Kabuki plays. These are the only similarities between the two types of Japanese drama.

2. Kabuki costumes are fancy, bright, and heavy. On the other hand, Nō costumes are quite simple. Kabuki stages are huge and elaborate. Nō stages are only 18 feet (5.4 meters) square. The only scenery used on a Nō stage is a background wall with a tree painted on it. The audience must use a lot of imagination.

3. Nō plays started in the fourteenth century to entertain the upper classes. All parts of a Nō play must follow a certain set of rules. A Nō actor may look as if he is sleepwalking. The action of the play is slow. Certain actions stand for certain things. For example, a few steps forward mean the end of a journey. An important part of a Nō play is the chorus that chants much of the story.

4. Kabuki plays were developed in the seventeenth century for the common people. Theater was the main amusement of the merchants of that time. Kabuki plays reflect the merchants' happy moods. The players wear thick makeup and exaggerate their movements and facial expressions to communicate feelings.

5. Music is important to Kabuki plays. Kabuki actors sing, dance, and speak their lines to music in the background. Musicians play instruments, such as flutes, drums, and gongs. They also use the samisen, a three-stringed instrument shaped somewhat like a banjo. Another common instrument has two small blocks of wood that are banged on the floor.

A. For each paragraph of the selection, if the main idea is stated, write the word *stated* on the line. If the main idea is unstated, choose a main idea from the sentences given below and write the letter on the line.

   a. Because Kabuki plays are more exciting, they are more popular than Nō plays.
   b. A Nō play is noted for its rules and for the controlled movements of the players.
   c. Kabuki plays reflect the fun and showiness preferred by seventeenth-century Japanese merchants.
   d. One difference between Nō and Kabuki plays is that Nō is simpler.
   e. Kabuki actors exaggerate their movements to show emotions.

Paragraph 1: _____stated_____   **Paragraph 3:** _____b_____   **Paragraph 5:** _____stated_____

Paragraph 2: _____d_____   **Paragraph 4:** _____c_____

B. Go back to each paragraph that has a stated main idea. Underline the sentence that states the main idea.

Skill: Following First-Aid Directions

For lesson support, see page T78.

Choking occurs when food or another foreign body completely blocks a person's air passage, making it impossible for the person to breathe or speak. A person choking on food could die in as little as four minutes. A **first-aid technique** called **abdominal thrusts** can be used to rescue a choking person. This procedure forces the object blocking the breathing passage out through the mouth.

If a choking victim can speak or cough, he or she should try to cough up the object. If the person cannot cough up the object, call an ambulance. If a victim cannot speak or cough, he or she is not getting air, and abdominal thrusts should be used. Choking victims who cannot speak should signal for help by clutching their throat.

First Aid for the Choking Victim
Abdominal Thrusts

WHAT TO LOOK FOR IN THE VICTIM
1. Cannot speak or breathe
2. Skin turns blue
3. Collapses

Universal sign for choking

WITH THE VICTIM STANDING OR SITTING

1. Stand behind the victim or behind the victim's chair if he or she is sitting. Wrap your arms around the victim's waist.

2. Place the thumb side of your fist against the victim's abdomen, above the navel and below the rib cage.

3. Grab your fist with the other hand and give quick inward and upward thrusts into the abdomen. Repeat these thrusts until the object is forced out or the victim becomes unconscious.

4. If the victim is sitting, stand behind the victim's chair and perform the procedure the same way.
5. After the object is dislodged, the victim should see a doctor for follow-up care.

WHEN THE VICTIM IS UNCONSCIOUS

1. Call 911.
2. Sweep two fingers inside the victim's mouth to try to remove the object. If this does not remove the object, follow steps 3–7.
3. Straddle both of the victim's legs.
4. Place the heel of one hand on the middle of the abdomen just above the navel. Place the other hand on top. Point the fingers of both hands toward the victim's head.
5. Give quick thrusts toward the head and into the abdomen.
6. After giving five thrusts, lift the victim's lower jaw and tongue with your fingers and thumb. Slide one finger down inside the victim's cheek and try to hook the object out. Repeat thrusts if object blocking the air passage has not been freed.
7. After the object is dislodged, the victim should see a doctor for follow-up care.

NOTE: If you are alone and start to choke, press your abdomen onto a firm object, such as a counter, desk, or table.

A. Look at the steps below and on the next page for performing abdominal thrusts when the victim is standing or sitting. They are not in the correct order. Write *1* in front of the step you would follow first, *2* in front of the next step, and so on.

_____3_____ Place the thumb side of your fist against the victim's abdomen, above the navel and below the rib cage.

_____1_____ Stand behind the victim or behind the victim's chair if he or she is sitting.

_____5_____ Repeat these thrusts until the object is forced out or the victim
becomes unconscious.

_____2_____ Wrap your arms around the victim's waist.

_____4_____ Grab your fist with the other hand and give quick inward and
upward thrusts into the abdomen.

**B. Read the statements about abdominal thrusts below. On the line, write *T* if the
statement is true or *F* if the statement is false.**

_____F_____ 1. A victim is a person who gives first aid.

_____T_____ 2. When food completely blocks the air passage, it is impossible for a person to
breathe or speak.

_____F_____ 3. Abdominal thrusts require that the choking victim be slapped on the back
four times.

_____F_____ 4. Abdominal thrusts can be done with the victim standing, sitting, or lying on
his or her stomach.

_____T_____ 5. Someone choking can perform abdominal thrusts on himself or herself if no
help is around.

_____T_____ 6. If a choking victim cannot speak or breathe, he or she is not getting any air.

_____T_____ 7. You could save a person's life using abdominal thrusts.

_____F_____ 8. Abdominal thrusts force food down a choking person's throat into the stomach.

_____T_____ 9. The rescuer faces the victim who is lying down.

_____T_____ 10. A rescuer may need to repeat abdominal thrusts several times to free the object
blocking the air passage.

C. Write the answer to each question. Use complete sentences.

1. For what kind of emergency are abdominal thrusts used? They are used on someone who is choking.

2. Why do you think it is important for everybody to know how to perform
abdominal thrusts? It is important because abdominal thrusts could save the life of a person who is choking.

3. Why are choking victims unable to speak or breathe? Their air passage is blocked by the food that they are
choking on.

4. What do rescuers do with their hands for standing or sitting victims? They make a fist.

5. What do rescuers do with their hands for victims lying down? They place one hand on top of the other.

6. How should you let someone know that you are choking? You should clutch your throat with your hands.

unit three

For ESL/ELL support, see highlighted words, page T79, and pages T28–T30.

The Sea Around Us

For theme support, see page T26.

Skill: Mood

For lesson support, see page T79.

BACKGROUND INFORMATION

In "The Dolphin Disaster," you will read about a group of dolphins that become trapped and need to be rescued. Although dolphins live in the sea, they are air-breathing, warm-blooded mammals in the same family as whales. To find their way in the ocean, dolphins send out sound waves and listen for echoes. In this way, they find out about objects in their path without using their eyes.

SKILL FOCUS: Mood

Mood is the atmosphere, or feeling, an author creates in a story. Some moods might be happy, scary, sad, or suspenseful. A writer creates mood by using vivid details that appeal to readers' senses and other words that convey emotion. Often the story's setting also helps to create a mood.

Read the passage below. Notice the words and phrases that build a mood of suspense.

The abandoned beach house, isolated on the lonely dune, seemed too quiet as Chris entered. As he passed down a dark hallway, a door creaked open at the back of the house. A sudden chill ruffled the hair on the back of his neck.

The setting above, an abandoned and isolated beach house, helps to create a suspenseful mood.

▶ Read the passage below. Then fill in the chart to identify the mood of the passage.

Sunlight danced on the warm, emerald waters of Pleasant Bay. Happy children stretched out on the golden sand or played in the gentle surf. Sea gulls soared overhead in a clear, blue sky.

Identifying Mood	
Setting	Pleasant Bay
Details that convey emotion	danced; warm, emerald waters; happy children; golden sand; gentle surf; clear, blue sky
Overall mood	Answers will vary: happy, cheerful, contented

CONTEXT CLUES: Comparisons

Comparisons in a sentence can help you figure out the meanings of new words. The words *like* and *as* usually signal a comparison.

In the following sentence, look for the comparison that explains the meaning of *winch*.

*He ran the nylon rope over the **winch**, which looked like a spool with a crank at the side.*

The author compares the winch to a spool with a crank on the side. If you don't know what a *winch* is, the comparison helps you visualize its appearance.

▶ Read the following sentence. Circle the comparison that helps you figure out the meaning of the underlined word.

*Beaching the boat, he **sprinted** up the low cliff* (like a runner racing for the finish line.)

As you read the selection, use comparison context clues to figure out the meanings of the underlined words *aspired*, *cove*, and *ebbing*.

> **Strategy Tip**
>
> As you read "The Dolphin Disaster," look for vivid details that convey emotion. Use these details to decide the story's overall mood.

The Dolphin Disaster

Skreek! A single sea gull wheeled across the low, gray sky. The fog was closing in on Port Hegen like a dirty cotton curtain. Most of the lobster boats were still outside the harbor. Ralph Hemming was busy setting his lobster traps when he spotted the first of the dolphins.

"Must be two hundred, maybe three hundred dolphins out there," he said, using the radio that linked his boat to shore. "Odd. Haven't seen them this close to shore in years."

Annie Sloan's voice came over the radio. "We had some up at the cape last year. A story in the newspaper said that over a dozen died. They got trapped in shallow water."

The radio crackled as another voice came in. "Hey, Ralph. Do you have Spooner with you?"

Hemming swung his rumbling boat toward a bright red float that marked one of his sunken traps. He pressed the microphone button. "He's on the wharf mending some of our traps."

"Too bad," said the other voice. "Spooner might have an idea why they're headed so close to the shallows. He knows all about these things."

Other voices on the radio agreed. Meanwhile Ralph Hemming was busy hooking up his trap line, a rope tied to the trap. He ran the nylon rope over the winch, which looked like a spool with a crank at the side. By turning the crank, the winch would pull the heavy, wooden trap up from the bottom, 100 feet below.

Ralph thought about his son, Spooner. For a 16-year-old, Spooner knew the sea well. He was always reading about the sea and its creatures. In some ways, he knew more about the ocean than some adults who had spent their lives on the water. One thing was sure, though. Spooner wouldn't fish for a living like his grandfather and father. Oh, he'd work with the sea all right, but he'd probably pursue his goal of studying ocean science. Spooner aspired to be an oceanographer just as much as many boys his age dreamed about becoming football players.

Dolphins! Hundreds of them arching out of the water in sleek, dark curves!

Spooner was so struck by the sight that he dropped the lobster trap that he was mending. He ran to the end of the wharf.

The dolphins were in the middle of the channel, moving toward Bald Point. Spooner strained his eyes, but the fog, edging nearer to shore, made it difficult to see the dolphins clearly.

Spooner scrambled down the worn, wooden steps to the pebbly beach. His shoes clattered on the smooth stones. The tide had already begun to go out. Pushing his family's rowboat to the water's edge, Spooner floated it and jumped in. He swung the small outboard motor into the water and yanked on the rope several times. This will be the day that the motor won't start, he thought. Finally the motor buzzed into life.

The fog was getting thicker. In a matter of moments, the dolphins would be swallowed up in the thick folds of the fog. Spooner headed the boat out into the narrow channel. He knew the waters of this rocky coast by heart. He knew that he could track down the dolphins.

Even so, Spooner nearly missed them in the fog. The narrow entrance to Bald Point Cove was only 50 feet wide, with low cliffs rising on both sides. Catching a movement in the water out of the corner of his eye, Spooner swung his boat toward land. Beaching the boat, he sprinted up the low cliff like a runner racing for the finish line.

The little cove was like a soup bowl 300 yards across. At high tide, the water in the cove was 20 feet at its deepest. At low tide, the cove was a stretch of mud.

Spooner stood looking down at the cove. Below he saw hundreds of dolphins swimming around the small pool. They darted this way and that, circling, confused. Something was very wrong.

Then Spooner remembered the story in the newspaper last year. More than 20 dolphins had died in shallow water off Cape Cod. Some scientists believed that the dolphins' ability to find their way by using echoes had failed for some reason. These dolphins must have lost their way and swum into the narrow channel by accident. Now they were trapped in the shallow water of the cove.

Spooner watched as the ebbing tide ran out of the cove like water out of a cracked bowl. The dolphins were swimming faster in crazier circles. He had to get help fast. He would head for home and get his sister Audrey. She wasn't very interested in the

sea, but she was a terrific organizer. She would help!

Only half an hour later, Spooner and Audrey watched Mr. Shell push back his sleeves and lean against his counter. "Look, kids, I'll be glad to help, but I can't leave the store just now. After six, when I close…"

"Then it will be too late!" cried Audrey.

Mr. Shell was the third person in the village that Audrey and Spooner had approached. They had gotten lots of sympathy but no help. Spooner had the feeling that no one really believed how much danger the dolphins were in. Spooner and Audrey ran out of the store and down toward the town wharf.

"Spooner! Audrey! What's up?" They turned to see Paul Sequeira coming up from the docks. He was 72 years old, but he still worked his lobster traps every day, as he had for more than 50 years.

"It's dolphins, Mr. Sequeira. Hundreds of them. They're trapped in Bald Point Cove, and the tide will be out soon!" Spooner quickly told Mr. Sequeira what he had seen.

"I heard on the radio that they were close to shore," said Mr. Sequeira. "Fog's so thick, everyone's coming in now. We'll round up some help. Come on."

It seemed only minutes later that Spooner, Audrey, Mr. Sequeira, and nine others hurried to the cove. More help was on the way. Mr. Sequeira had radioed the police, too.

Water was running out of the cove like sand from an hourglass. The water was only 3 feet deep and getting lower every minute. Spooner couldn't help looking back and forth from his watch to the widening stretch of mud in the cove.

Already a few dolphins were stuck in the mud. The others swam frantically in the shallow water. In less than an hour, all the water in the cove would be gone.

How could they get the animals out of danger? Suddenly Spooner remembered something that he had read. "Form a line! We'll move toward them and herd them into the channel!"

The rescuers moved into the water and did as Spooner said. They forced the dolphins toward the narrow channel leading to the sea. Audrey cheered as some of the dolphins slipped through the opening.

More people came. They herded more and more animals out to the sea. Unfortunately the dense fog

was making it difficult to see. The dolphins still in the cove darted about desperately. They were frantic and frightened.

"Audrey!" called Mr. Sequeira. "Get out to my boat and radio for some nets. Hurry!"

Audrey splashed through the shallow water, climbed the cliff, and slid down the other side. She rowed quickly but cautiously. The fog had almost totally hidden Mr. Sequeira's lobster boat anchored in the channel. When she was finally on board, she made contact with Port Hegen. The nets were on their way, but would they reach the cove in time? Audrey hurried back.

There were about 70 dolphins still in the cove when the water ran out completely. The rescuers couldn't bear to watch the stranded animals die in the mud. They used their heavy nets to drag and tug and slide the heavy animals into the channel.

The workers were able to save about half of the remaining dolphins. The rest had been stuck in the mud too long. Already they were dying.

Later on the wharf, Ralph Hemming put his arms around his son and daughter. "You did your best, kids. That's all you can ever do."

"Aye," said Mr. Sequeira. "If it hadn't been for you kids, hundreds of dolphins would have died. Think of the hundreds that we saved."

Spooner blinked away tears. "I know we saved most of them. Yet I can't help thinking that if we knew why they swam into the cove, we could have saved all of them."

In spite of the tragedy, Spooner's dad smiled to himself. He could see that his son planned to spend even more time in the library learning about the ocean. Perhaps some good would come out of the situation after all.

COMPREHENSION

Recalling details
1. Identify the main character in the story.

   Spooner Hemming is the main character.

Recalling details
2. Who is Paul Sequeira?

   Mr. Sequeira is the 72-year-old lobsterman who helps

   organize the dolphins' rescue.

Identifying cause and effect
3. Explain how the dolphins become trapped.

The dolphins swim into a shallow cove with a narrow

entrance. They can't find their way out when the tide ebbs.

Recalling details
4. List two methods that the rescuers use to save the dolphins.

The rescuers form a line to herd the dolphins toward

the sea. They later drag them in nets into the channel.

Identifying cause and effect
5. Explain why some of the dolphins die in spite of the rescue efforts.

The dolphins become stuck in the mud and die before

they can be dragged to the channel.

Identifying plot
6. What is the climax, or the most exciting event, of the story?

Answers will vary. The climax occurs when the rescuers

begin herding the dolphins toward the sea.

Using context clues
7. Draw a line to match each word with its meaning.

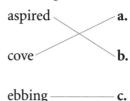

aspired   a. small, sheltered body of water

cove   b. dreamed of doing something

ebbing   c. flowing back, as the tide does toward the sea

CRITICAL THINKING

Understanding character
1. Circle three character traits that Spooner shows during the rescue.

selfishness   carelessness   (concern)

(determination)   (intelligence)   laziness

Inferring cause and effect
2. Describe the effect the sighting of dolphins has on the people of Port Hegen.

The townspeople are excited and concerned.

Making inferences
3. Discuss why some of the people in Port Hegen are willing to work so hard to save the dolphins.

Answers will vary. The people work so hard to save the dolphins because the dolphins are in trouble and

unable to help themselves. The people care about the helpless animals and do not want them to suffer.

Drawing conclusions
4. Why is Hemming proud of Spooner and Audrey at the end of the story?

He is proud because Spooner and Audrey are responsible for alerting the townspeople to the danger that the dolphins face.

They also work very hard to save the trapped dolphins.

Inferring theme
5. Circle the letter next to the statement that best states the theme of the story.

a. Living near the sea is dangerous.

b. Dolphins often get stranded in coves when the tide goes out.

c. People working together can overcome almost any problem.

d. Most people do not care about dolphins.

1. Several incidents in "The Dolphin Disaster" have outcomes that are uncertain at first. For example, as you read the story, you may have asked yourself the following questions.

   • Will Spooner be able to find the dolphins?

   • Will Spooner get enough help?

   • Will the nets arrive in time?

   • Will the rescuers save the dolphins before the water runs out of the cove?

   As a result of these uncertainties, what kind of mood, or atmosphere, has the author created?

   The author has created an atmosphere, or mood, of suspense.

2. In the list below, circle the letter next to the phrases and details that do *not* develop the story's mood.

   a. Skreek! A single sea gull wheeled across the low, gray sky.

   b. so struck by the sight that he dropped the lobster trap that he was mending

   c. only minutes later

   (d.) motor buzzed into life

   e. fast-ebbing tide

   f. Dolphins! Hundreds of them

   g. darted this way and that, circling, confused

   h. water was running out of the cove like sand from an hourglass

   (i.) Audrey was a terrific organizer.

   (j.) looking back and forth from his watch to the widening stretch of mud in the cove

   (k.) in the library learning about the ocean

3. Setting often contributes to a story's mood. In this story, a fog "was closing in on Port Hegen like a dirty cotton curtain" and "in a matter of moments, the dolphins would be swallowed up in the thick folds of the fog." What effect does the fog have on the mood of the story?

   The fog makes the mood even more suspenseful by increasing the uncertainty of whether Spooner can track the dolphins

   so that he and the other rescuers can save them.

Reading-Writing Connection

On a separate sheet of paper, write a paragraph describing a time when you worked on an important project with a team of family members, friends, or classmates. Create a mood in your paragraph.

Skill: Recognizing Propaganda

For lesson support, see page T80.

BACKGROUND INFORMATION

"Remember the *Maine*" tells about the 1898 sinking of the U.S. battleship *Maine* in Cuba, an event that led to the Spanish-American War. About 260 Americans died in the blast. At the time, Americans believed that the Spanish had sunk the ship. In 1976, Navy researchers again studied the incident. They concluded that heat from a coal fire might have caused ammunition aboard the ship to explode, sinking it. To this day, no one knows for sure exactly what happened.

SKILL FOCUS: Recognizing Propaganda

Propaganda is information that is designed to change or shape public opinion. It often twists or distorts the truth in order to convince people to believe or do something. Propaganda tells only one side of an issue. Only facts that support a group's point of view are given. To sway large numbers of people, these facts are often presented in an emotional way.

To recognize propaganda, follow these steps.

1. **Identify the facts.** Distinguish facts from opinions. Remember that a fact is a statement that can be proven or checked. An opinion is a judgment that cannot be proven.

2. **Identify errors of fact.** Look for ways that facts have been slanted to suit the writer's point of view.

3. **Analyze the emotional appeal.** Study the words used by the writer, and decide if they have been chosen to sway emotions.

4. **Reach conclusions.** Ask what the purpose of the propaganda is and whether this purpose has been achieved.

▶ The two headlines in the chart at the top of the next column appeared in different newspapers after a devastating forest fire at a national park. Read the headlines and put a check mark next to the one that uses propaganda. Then circle the words in the headline that helped you to decide that it is propaganda.

Headline	Uses Propaganda
Fire Claims 500 Acres of National Park	
(Careless) Campers (Destroy) our (National Heritage)	✔

CONTEXT CLUES: Footnotes

Sometimes unfamiliar names and words in a selection are explained in **footnotes**. Footnotes are numbered and appear at the bottom of a page. When you come across an unfamiliar word, check to see if there is a small, raised number after the word. Then find the same number at the bottom of the page. Following the number will be an explanation of the word's meaning.

Read the following sentence and footnote.

*At the same time, American **jingoists**[1] demanded that the United States show its strength by being more aggressive.*

[1] jingoists (JING goh ists): people who favor an aggressive foreign policy that might lead to war with other nations.

Notice the raised number 1, which is called a "superscript," after the term *jingoists.* This is a signal to look for a footnote. The footnote below it gives an explanation of the term.

▶ Read the sentence and the footnote below. Circle details in the footnote that tell you the meaning of the underlined phrase.

*These newspapers had a great influence on **public opinion**.[2]*

[2] public opinion: the expressed views of a group of people about issues of common interest or concern; views based not on what is certain but on what the people as a whole think to be true or likely.

As you read the selection, use footnote clues to find the meanings of the words *detention camps, man-of-war,* and *tenders.*

Strategy Tip

As you read "Remember the *Maine*," think about how propaganda was used to turn Americans against Spain.

Remember the *Maine*

ON FEBRUARY 15, 1898, the United States' battleship *Maine* sat in the harbor of Havana, Cuba. Suddenly the *Maine* blew apart in a huge explosion killing 260 American sailors.

To this day, no one is sure what caused the explosion. The ship's captain gave no cause for the disaster in his report. A Navy investigation failed to uncover any clear evidence. Yet most Americans believed that Spain blew up the ship. Americans repeated, "Remember the *Maine*." Emotions ran high. Soon the American people demanded war with Spain.

Why did Americans think that Spain had sunk the *Maine*? Why were they so eager to go to war? The story of the *Maine* is an important lesson in American history.

Dangers to Peace

In the beginning of 1898, the United States was at peace. The United States had not fought in a major war since the Civil War. A generation had grown up without knowing the horrors of war. The nation took peace for granted.

✘ However several events were occurring that were dangerous to peace. Some Americans wanted the United States to become a world power by controlling more land. They were called **imperialists** (im PIR ee ə lists), or empire builders. They dreamed of an American empire. At the same time, American jingoists[1] demanded that the United States show its strength by being more aggressive. Another danger to peace came from several of the leading U.S. newspapers. These newspapers tried to sway their readers' emotions to support a war. They paid little attention to facts in their news stories. These newspapers had a great influence on public opinion.[2] They played an important role in the story of the *Maine*.

Cuba

The island of Cuba is 90 miles (145 kilometers) off the southeastern coast of the United States. In the 1890s, it became a focus of American interest. Businesses had invested money in Cuba's sugar fields. Politicians recognized Cuba's geographic and military importance to the United States. Americans, in general, were concerned about the political situation in Cuba.

For years, Cuba had been under Spanish rule. Many Cubans wanted independence. In 1895, some Cubans attempted a revolt against Spain. The revolt failed. Spain sent a new governor, General Weyler, to the island. He treated the rebels cruelly. He set up detention camps[3] in which many Cuban prisoners became sick and died.

Americans were shocked by the news from Cuba. They wanted to know more. Two New York newspapers saw a chance to sell more copies. They made Cuba a hot news topic.

Yellow Journalism

The two New York newspapers were Joseph Pulitzer's *The World* and William Randolph Hearst's *Journal*. These newspapers competed with each other for stories about Cuba. They printed shocking stories with screaming headlines. In these stories, Spain was always the villain. A group of Cubans in New York was giving information to the papers. The information was slanted, or **biased** (BY əst), in favor of the rebels. It told only one side of the story.

The stories in *The World* and the *Journal* had little to do with the facts. Instead they tried to catch the readers' attention and sway their emotions. This kind of journalism became known as yellow journalism. Yellow journalism is a kind of propaganda.

---

[1] jingoists (JING goh ists): people who favor an aggressive foreign policy that might lead to war with other nations.
[2] public opinion: the expressed views of a group of people about issues of common interest or concern; views based not on what is certain but on what the people as a whole think to be true or likely.

[3] detention camps (di TEN shən KAMPS): places where people are held temporarily as prisoners. In an attempt to cut off supplies to Cuban rebels, General Weyler ordered peasants to gather in detention camps.

XX With great emotion, the newspapers reported about conditions in Cuba. One article read: "You would sicken at the sight of thousands of women and children starving to death in Cuba today… filthy skeletons dying on bare, foul boards." Another paper stated in an editorial: "If Spain will not put an end to murder in Cuba, the United States must."

✔ The two newspapers urged the United States to go to war with Spain. Hearst told one photographer who was going to Cuba, "You supply the pictures. I'll supply the war." The stories that the New York newspapers printed had a great effect. They were picked up by newspapers all over the country. Public opinion became set against Spain.

The Sinking of the *Maine*

Riots erupted in Havana, the capital of Cuba, in 1898. President McKinley ordered the battleship *Maine* into Havana Harbor. He wanted to protect American citizens in Cuba. Shortly after the *Maine* arrived in Havana, it exploded.

Captain Sigsbee was the officer in charge of the *Maine*. He immediately made the following report about the explosion.

Maine blown up in Havana Harbor at nine-forty tonight and destroyed. Many wounded and doubtless more killed or drowned. Wounded and others on board Spanish man-of-war[4] and Ward Line steamer. Send lighthouse tenders[5] from Key West for crew and the few pieces of equipment above water. No one has clothing other than that upon him. Public opinion should be suspended

---

[4] man-of-war: a fighting ship.

[5] tenders: ships that take care of other ships, supplying food, rescuing crew members, and so on.

The *Maine* explosion was reported on the front page of *The World*.

until further report.… Many Spanish officers, including representatives of General Blanco, now with me to express sympathy.

The newspapers reported the explosion to the American people in a very different way. On page 68 is a copy of the front page of *The World* from February 17, 1898, two days after the explosion.

War Fever

No one was ever able to prove that Spain had sunk the *Maine*. The explosion may have been an accident. Cuban rebels may have secretly caused it to draw the United States into war with Spain. Whatever the cause, American public opinion was against Spain.

President McKinley tried to keep war from breaking out. He offered a peace plan to Spain. The plan suggested that Cuba become independent. Spain turned down McKinley's plan.

War fever ran high in the United States. The newspapers continued printing stories against Spain. Finally President McKinley recognized Cuba as an independent country. As a result, Spain declared war on the United States. The next day, Congress declared war on Spain. The Spanish-American War had begun.

COMPREHENSION

Identifying cause and effect

1. Circle the letter next to the correct cause for the effect described in the sentence below.

   The New York newspapers reported shocking stories about Cuba because

   a. they cared about the Cuban people.

   (b.) they wanted to sell newspapers.

   c. they owned property in Cuba.

   d. the editors were Spanish.

Recalling details

2. Who gave the *Journal* and *The World* information about Cuba?

   A group of Cubans in New York gave the newspapers

   the information.

Identifying the main idea

3. Reread the paragraph with an ✗ next to it. Then underline the sentence that best states the paragraph's main idea.

Identifying the main idea and supporting details

4. Reread the paragraph with ✗ ✗ next to it. Underline the sentence that best states the paragraph's main idea. Then circle two details that support the main idea of the paragraph.

Using context clues

5. Complete each sentence by writing the correct word or phrase on the line.

   detention camps   man-of-war   tenders

   a. A ship that fights or is ready to fight is

      a _____man-of-war_____.

   b. Many Cubans died in ___detention camps___ set up by General Weyler.

   c. Survivors of the *Maine* were rescued

      by _____tenders_____.

CRITICAL THINKING

Inferring cause and effect

1. Match the words in the left column with their descriptions in the right column.

   _a_ imperialists   a. wanted the United States to control more land

   _c_ newspapers   b. wanted to use U.S. war power to show its strength

   _b_ jingoists   c. wanted to sell papers by printing war stories

   _d_ Americans   d. were convinced that Spain had sunk the *Maine*

Inferring comparisons and contrasts

2. In 1898, the Cuban people were fighting for independence from Spain. Compare this struggle to an event in American history.

Cuba's struggle for independence can be compared to the American Revolutionary War, in which the colonies fought for

their independence from England.

Distinguishing fact from opinion

3. Identify each of the following statements as a fact or an opinion. Circle the letter next to each statement that expresses an opinion.

(a.) "If Spain will not put an end to the murder in Cuba, the United States must."

b. The island of Cuba is 90 miles (145 kilometers) off the southeastern coast of the United States.

(c.) The United States should show its strength by being warlike toward other nations.

Inferring the unstated main idea

4. Reread the paragraph with a ✔ next to it. Write a sentence stating its main idea.

Answers will vary. Two New York newspapers helped turn public opinion in favor of war with Spain.

SKILL FOCUS: RECOGNIZING PROPAGANDA

Use Sigsbee's message and *The World*'s front page on pages 68–69 to answer the following questions.

1. Identify the facts and opinions.

a. List the facts in Captain Sigsbee's message.

Facts include: time of explosion (9:40 P.M.); many dead and wounded survivors aboard Spanish man-of-war and Ward

Line steamer; sailors need clothing; many Spanish officers came to express sympathy.

b. What opinion can you identify in his message?

He believes that public opinion should be suspended until further report.

c. List the facts in *The World* report.

The cause of the explosion not definitely known: *The World* has sent a tug with divers to investigate; Lee is asking for a

court of inquiry.

d. What information in *The World* report is based on opinions?

Information based on opinions include the headline "*Maine* Explosion Caused by Bomb or Torpedo," Captain Sigsbee's

reported opinion, and Pendleton's claim that there was a plot to blow up the ship.

2. Identify errors of fact.

a. What does Captain Sigsbee say in his message about the cause of the explosion?

He neither gives nor suggests a cause for the explosion.

b. What does *The World* report that Sigsbee thinks is the cause?

The newspaper reports that Sigsbee said the explosion was made possible by an enemy.

c. What does Sigsbee report about the actions of the Spanish after the explosion?

He says that the Spanish were helpful and sympathetic.

d. Does this information appear in *The World*?

No.

3. Analyze the emotional appeal.

a. Does Captain Sigsbee seem interested in turning public opinion against Spain?

No.

b. What effect might the drawing of the explosion in *The World* have on readers? Why?

Answers will vary. Because the picture looks as though the *Maine* has been blown up by an enemy in a war, Americans

might be angry and frightened and might want to get even.

c. The third headline in *The World* uses the word *enemy*. What emotional impact might this word have on readers?

It might give the impression that another country has attacked the United States and might inspire anger and fear in

readers.

4. Reach conclusions.

a. What overall message does *The World* report convey?

Answers will vary. The United States has been attacked by an enemy and should be ready to strike back.

b. What emotional effect does *The World* report have on a reader?

Answers will vary. Because the report suggests a foreign attack, the reader would probably be angry and want the

United States to strike back.

c. How might *The World*'s report have influenced the outbreak of the Spanish-American War?

Answers will vary. The report probably led Americans to believe that Spain was responsible for the explosion and was an

enemy. Public opinion against Spain was aroused, which influenced Congress to support military action in Cuba.

Reading-Writing Connection

Look through recent newspapers and find a photograph that catches your attention. On a separate sheet of paper, write a headline about what the photograph shows. Use emotional words to sway people's opinions.

LESSON 22

Skill: Cause and Effect

For lesson support, see page T81.

For ESL/ELL support, see highlighted words, page T81, and pages T28–T30.

BACKGROUND INFORMATION

In "The Amazing Sea Journeys," you will read about animals that migrate through the sea. Fish and other ocean animals migrate for several reasons. Some move in search of food. Others move to reproduce. Escaping colder waters in winter is another cause of migration.

SKILL FOCUS: Cause and Effect

A **cause** is an event that makes something happen. An **effect** is what happens as a result of a cause. In a cause-and-effect relationship, one event causes another event to occur. To find an effect, ask, "What happened?" To find a cause, ask, "Why did it happen?"

Sometimes two or more causes produce a single effect. Think about the causes and the effect explained in the following paragraph. Then study the Cause and Effect Chart that follows.

> Sadly, dams on many rivers prevent many salmon from reaching their spawning grounds. Water pollution and illegal fishing also kill many salmon on their way upstream. As a result, salmon populations are declining rapidly.

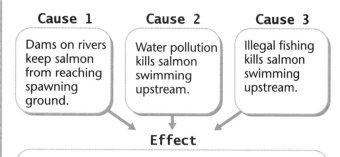

Cause 1
Dams on rivers keep salmon from reaching spawning ground.

Cause 2
Water pollution kills salmon swimming upstream.

Cause 3
Illegal fishing kills salmon swimming upstream.

Effect
Salmon populations are declining rapidly.

▶ Read the sentences below. Then fill in the Cause and Effect Chart in the next column.

> After spawning, the salmon are exhausted. They are susceptible to infection and are also liable to become easy prey for birds and bears. Therefore, many of them do not make it back to the sea.

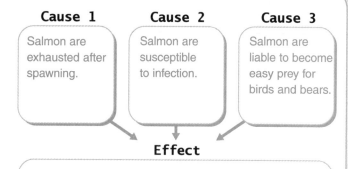

Cause 1
Salmon are exhausted after spawning.

Cause 2
Salmon are susceptible to infection.

Cause 3
Salmon are liable to become easy prey for birds and bears.

Effect
Many salmon do not make it back to the sea.

CONTEXT CLUES: Synonyms

Synonyms are words with similar meanings. You can use a synonym context clue to figure out the meaning of a new word.

Read the sentences below. Look for a synonym to help you understand the meaning of *metamorphose*.

> Before heading back to sea, however, the eels change their shape. They **metamorphose** into a more slender and streamlined form that is better suited for the long journey ahead.

If you don't know the meaning of *metamorphose*, the synonym *change* can help you. When animals metamorphose, they change their shape.

▶ Read the sentences below. Then circle the synonym that can help you figure out the meaning of the underlined word.

> Some scientists **speculate** that the whales find their way along the shore by trial and error. These scientists think that the whales simply swim close to shore and follow the outlines of the landscape.

As you read the selection, look for synonyms to help you understand the meanings of the underlined words *collectively*, *feat*, and *susceptible*.

> ### Strategy Tip
>
> As you read, look for causes and effects of animal migration in the ocean.

The Amazing Sea Journeys

HOW DO ANIMALS KNOW when and where to migrate? How do they manage to travel thousands of miles to the same locations every year? Scientists are only now beginning to find the answers to these intriguing questions.

The Mysterious Journey of the Eels

Eels are long, thin fish that look like snakes. Freshwater eels are found in rivers, streams, and ponds all over the world. For some reason, however, eels migrate thousands of miles out to sea to lay their eggs. Amazingly, they always end up in the same location in the vast Atlantic Ocean. Almost all eels are born in the Sargasso Sea, a large area of the Atlantic Ocean southeast of Bermuda.

At birth, the eels are less than .25 inch (0.6 centimeter) long. They drift helplessly with the tides. Later the young eels, called elvers, begin to swim back toward the freshwater streams from which their parents came. For some of them, it is a 3,500-mile (5,600-kilometer) trip that can take several years.

When the eels reach the mouth of a river, the males tend to stay in the tidal area there. The female eels, however, may mass together into giant balls or join together to form long eel ropes. Swimming collectively against the current in this way is easier than it would be for each eel to swim upstream by itself. Gradually the eels separate, breaking off to swim up smaller streams.

✔ Eels seem determined to find the waters from which their parents came. To do so, some eels have climbed over walls. Others have wriggled through wet grass like snakes. Observers have even seen eels travel over land on the backs of frogs. Eventually they arrive at the stream or pond where they will spend most of their lives.

When female eels are between 8 and 9 years old, the time arrives for their return migration to the sea. Little is known about the biological instinct that tells eels when and where to migrate. Before heading back to sea, however, the eels change their shape.

They metamorphose (met ə MÔR fohz) into a more slender and streamlined form that is better suited for the long journey ahead.

Swimming downstream, the female eels join some of the males, who have remained in the tidal waters. Together they make the long trip back to the Sargasso Sea, where each female lays millions of eggs. This egg-laying process is called spawning. In time, another generation of elvers will migrate to a freshwater river. For the adults, however, the journey is over. After spawning, the adult eels die in the Sargasso Sea.

The Return of the Salmon

Eels heading out to sea might encounter salmon, whose migration takes them in the opposite direction. Between the ages of 2 and 6 years old, most adult Atlantic salmon live far out in the ocean. There many of them grow to be more than 5 feet (1.5 meters) long.

When the time comes to spawn, schools of salmon make their way from the ocean to their freshwater spawning grounds. The timing of the migration varies according to the river each group of salmon is bound for. The fish somehow know how to time their trips so that they can breed in winter.

Salmon always return to the streams in which they were hatched. The explanation for this remarkable ability to return home lies in the salmon's sense of taste. Even after four years at sea, a salmon remembers the taste of the stream where it was born. It follows its taste buds home.

Many salmon must travel hundreds of miles upstream to reach their breeding grounds. During the migration, they can swim up to 70 miles (115 kilometers) per day. This is a remarkable feat, considering that they do not eat while in fresh water. Their achievement is also remarkable because they must often leap up waterfalls and overcome other obstacles to reach their destination.

Sadly, dams on many rivers prevent many salmon from reaching their spawning grounds.

SCIENCE

Water pollution and illegal fishing also kill many salmon on their way upstream. As a result, salmon populations are declining rapidly.

After laying and fertilizing their eggs in the river, the male and female adults drift slowly back to sea. After spawning, the salmon are exhausted. They are susceptible to infection and are also liable to become easy prey for birds and bears. Therefore, many of them do not make it back to the sea. Those that do survive spend the rest of the year in the sea. They return to the spawning ground the following winter.

After hatching, the young salmon gradually make their way downstream. They spend some time in the river **estuary** (ES chə wair ee), the tidal area where the river meets the sea. This gives them time to get used to a saltwater diet. Finally they enter the sea, where they usually stay for four years before starting the cycle all over again.

The Long Voyage of the Gray Whales

The great migrations of whales span the ocean, from the tropics to the poles. The gray whale has one of the longest migrations of all. It spends the summers in special feeding grounds in the polar seas above Alaska. Then in autumn, it migrates back to its winter breeding and calving grounds off the coast of Mexico. That is a journey of about 5,000 miles (8,000 kilometers). Like other animal travelers, gray whales return to the same locations each season.

This amazing journey, however, may not even be necessary. People once thought that gray whales needed warm water to raise their young but were unable to find enough food to survive there for long periods. However, scientists now know that many similar species of whales live in polar waters year-round. They are able to breed and raise their young in cold water. Gray whales could probably do this, too.

Why, then, do gray whales make their long migration? Some scientists think that ancient climate changes may account for the migration pattern. Thousands of years ago, food may have been much more plentiful in tropical seas than it is today. At that time, gray whales may have lived in tropical waters year-round. Over the centuries, therefore, they established a pattern of breeding and calving in warm water.

At some point long ago, changing ocean temperatures may have caused food supplies in tropical seas to decline. At the same time, the amount of food in polar regions could have been increasing. In search of nourishment, the gray whales may have gradually moved farther and farther into arctic waters. Over time, the gray whales could have established this annual pattern of visiting cold water for summer food and then returning to their traditional breeding areas in the tropics.

Different scientists have different theories to explain how gray whales find their way through the open sea. Some scientists speculate that the whales find their way along the shore by trial and error. These scientists think that the whales simply swim close to shore and follow the outlines of the landscape.

Another theory claims that whales are able to detect Earth's magnetic fields. Whales appear to move parallel to these magnetic fields. This behavior leads scientists to believe that the whales may have a "biological travel clock" that they can set to the magnetic fields of the regions they pass through. Small magnetic particles have been found in the brains of whales. These particles may detect and interpret the magnetic fields the whales swim through.

Magnetic fields may also explain why whales sometimes get stranded on beaches. Whales tend to get stranded in areas where magnetic-field lines cross an irregular coastline, rather than running parallel to shore.

Loggerhead Homecoming

Studies of loggerhead sea turtles support the theory that some ocean animals use magnetic fields during migration. Full-grown loggerhead turtles are 3 feet (90 centimeters) long and weigh about 350 pounds (160 kilograms). Their heavy heads give them their distinctive name. Between May and September each year, about 10,000 female loggerhead turtles migrate across the Atlantic Ocean from Europe to bury their eggs on the beaches of Florida, Georgia, and South Carolina.

Once the eggs hatch, the tiny turtle hatchlings scurry into the ocean. Ocean currents carry them out to sea. Scientists know that most of Florida's loggerheads wind up in the Mediterranean Sea off the coast of Spain.

At age 20, a female loggerhead is ready to lay eggs. After swimming thousands of miles across the Atlantic, she crawls ashore at the same beach where she hatched 20 years before. How is she able to find this exact spot after so many years at sea?

Scientists suspect that loggerheads may be **imprinted** at birth with an awareness of Earth's magnetic field at their home beach. Imprinting refers to a rapid learning process that occurs in some animals soon after birth that determines the animals' behavior for the rest of their lives.

To test this theory, scientists placed loggerheads in harnesses and suspended them in tanks of water. A system of magnetic coils around the tank let the researchers change the magnetic field the turtles encountered. By flipping the magnetic field 180 degrees, the scientists tricked the turtles into turning around and swimming in the opposite direction.

Scientists learned that the first light the turtles see determines their initial direction. If that first light comes from the east, for example, the turtles will immediately begin swimming toward magnetic east. They then follow Earth's magnetic fields to find their way back home.

As scientists develop new techniques and experiments for studying animal migration, they may make more discoveries about this fascinating aspect of animal behavior. However, some facts about these amazing animal journeys may forever remain a mystery.

Loggerhead turtle hatchlings are born on beaches and scurry to the ocean.

COMPREHENSION

Identifying the main idea
1. Find the paragraph with a ✔ next to it. Underline the sentence that tells its main idea.

Identifying cause and effect
2. Explain why eels metamorphose before migrating out to sea.

   They change into a more slender, streamlined shape

   that is better suited for a long journey in the ocean.

Identifying cause and effect
3. Describe how spawning salmon manage to return to the same stream in which they were born years earlier.

   They remember the taste of the water in the stream

   where they were born.

Recalling details
4. Identify where loggerhead turtles born in Florida spend most of their lives.

   They spend their lives in the Mediterranean Sea, off the

   coast of Spain.

Using context clues
5. Write the letter of each word's synonym on the line next to the word.

   __b__ collectively   **a.** liable

   __c__ feat   **b.** together

   __a__ susceptible   **c.** achievement

Comparing and contrasting

1. In some ways, the eel's migration to spawn is the opposite of that of the salmon. Explain.

    Eels live most of their lives in fresh water and then migrate to the sea to spawn. Salmon spend most of their lives in the sea

    but migrate to fresh water to spawn.

Making inferences

2. Describe how scientists might prove that gray whales or loggerhead turtles return to the same locations each time they migrate.

    Answers will vary. The scientists might tag or mark the animals in some way and then observe them.

Inferring cause and effect

3. Suppose gray whales *do not* use Earth's magnetic field to navigate through the sea. Give other possible reasons that might explain why the whales sometimes get stranded on beaches.

    Answers will vary. Darkness or fog might confuse the whales or prevent them from seeing the beaches. Currents might

    sweep them into shallow water and keep them from returning to sea.

SKILL FOCUS: CAUSE AND EFFECT

On the lines, write two causes for each effect the author presents in this selection. You may look back at the selection.

1. **Effect:** Female eels have little difficulty swimming upstream.

    a. **Cause:** The eels may mass together into balls.

    b. **Cause:** The eels may join together to form long ropes.

2. **Effect:** Thousands of years ago, gray whales began to roam farther and farther north.

    a. **Cause:** The ocean temperatures changed.

    b. **Cause:** Food supplies decreased in tropical seas but increased in polar seas.

3. **Effect:** Loggerhead turtles find their home beaches after 20 years at sea.

    a. **Cause:** Loggerheads are imprinted with the magnetic field of their home beaches at birth.

    b. **Cause:** Loggerheads use Earth's magnetic fields to find their way across the ocean to their home beaches.

Reading-Writing Connection

Use a library or the Internet to find out about another ocean animal that migrates. On a separate sheet of paper, write a paragraph that describes the animal's migration. Include two cause-and-effect relationships in your paragraph.

LESSON 23

For ESL/ELL support, see highlighted words, page T82, and pages T28–T30.

Skill: Word Problems

For lesson support, see page T82.

BACKGROUND INFORMATION

"Word Problems That Have Unnecessary Information" will help you solve math word problems. A word problem is any practical problem that you can use math to solve. Knowing how to solve a math word problem can make life a lot easier.

SKILL FOCUS: Word Problems

The sentences in a **word problem** include all the information you need to solve it.

Use the following five steps to solve word problems.

1. **Read the problem.** Think about the question that is being asked. Be sure that you know what the labels used with each number mean.

2. **Decide how to find the answer.** Decide how to find the answer—by adding, subtracting, multiplying, or dividing. Decide whether you will need to do one operation or two operations to get the answer. Then write the one or two mathematical sentences that will give you the answer. Sometimes a word problem includes facts that you do not need to solve it. Do not be fooled by this **unnecessary information**. Cross it out so that you do not get confused.

3. **Estimate the answer.** Make an educated guess about the answer, based on the information given. Use rounded numbers to make your estimate. If two operations are needed, estimate the answers to both.

4. **Carry out the plan.** Solve the first sentence you have written. Then solve the second one.

5. **Reread the problem.** Does your answer make sense? How close is it to your estimate?

▶ Read the following word problem. Then answer the questions in the next column.

Mei earned $240 this week working as a guide on a whale-watch ship. ~~That is $25 more than she earned last week.~~ This week, Mei put $50 of her money into her savings account. She spent half of what she had left getting her mountain bike fixed. How much did this week's repair cost?

Does the question ask about this week or last week?

this week

How much money did Mei earn this week? $240

What information in the problem is not needed to solve it? Mei earned $25 more this week than last week.

Now go back to the problem and cross out the unnecessary information.

WORD CLUES

As you read word problems, look for key words that will help you solve them. If two operations are needed to solve the problem, you must look for key words for both operations.

Key words such as *and*, *total*, *all together*, *times*, and *twice as much* usually tell you that the answer will be larger than the numbers in the problem. To find the answer, you will need to add or multiply.

Key words such as *how much more*, *left*, *divide*, and *each* usually tell you that your answer will be less than at least one of the numbers in the problem. You will need to subtract or divide.

▶ Underline the key words in this problem that show that you have to add and then divide.

On their fishing trip, the three Crosley brothers spent a <u>total</u> of $125 for a boat rental, $95 for fishing equipment, and $65 for other expenses. They agreed to <u>divide</u> the total cost of the trip <u>equally</u> among themselves. How much did <u>each</u> brother pay?

Strategy Tip

While reading each problem in "Word Problems That Have Unnecessary Information," decide which information is needed to solve the problem and which information is unnecessary.

Word Problems That Have Unnecessary Information

Many facts have been collected about the sea. These facts can be put together to solve word problems about the sea.

Use the following five steps in solving word problems.

1. Read the problem.
2. Decide how to find the answer.
3. Estimate the answer.
4. Carry out the plan.
5. Reread the problem.

Read the Problem

The Bathysphere dove to a depth of 914 meters in 1934. In 1948, the Benthoscope dove $1\frac{1}{2}$ times deeper. In 1960, the Trieste dove 8 times deeper than the Benthoscope. How many meters deep did the Trieste dive?

Read the problem again. Be sure that you know the label that is used with each number fact. Are there any words that you do not know? If so, look them up to find their meanings. What question does the problem ask? Often the question is asked in the last sentence of a word problem. *How many meters deep did the Trieste dive?*

Decide How to Find the Answer

The problem gives you many number facts. Written as sentences, the facts are the following.

1. The *Bathysphere* dove 914 meters.
2. The *Bathysphere* dove in 1934.
3. The *Benthoscope* dove $1\frac{1}{2}$ times deeper.
4. The *Benthoscope* dove in 1948.
5. The *Trieste* dove 8 times deeper than the *Benthoscope.*
6. The *Trieste* dove in 1960.

Enough facts are given in the problem to solve it. However, some of the facts given are not needed to solve the problem. When extra information is given, decide which facts are not needed and cross them out. In this problem, facts 2, 4, and 6 are not necessary to answer the question.

You will need to do two arithmetic operations to find the answer. First you need to figure out how deep the *Benthoscope* dove. When you know how deep the *Benthoscope* dove, you can then figure out how deep the *Trieste* dove. For the first operation, you must multiply. The key words are $1\frac{1}{2}$ *times deeper*. This is your mathematical sentence.

$$914 \times 1\frac{1}{2} = n$$

For the second operation, you must multiply again. The key words *8 times deeper* tell you to multiply. This is your mathematical sentence.

$$n \times 8 = m$$

In this mathematical sentence, the letter n stands for the answer to the first operation. The letter m stands for the number of meters the *Trieste* dove.

Estimate the Answer

Use rounded numbers to make an estimate. Round to the nearest 1 or 100.

First operation: $900 \times 2 = n$
$1,800 = n$

Second operation: $1,800 \times 8 = m$
$14,400 = m$

Your estimate is 14,400.

Carry Out the Plan

Do the arithmetic.

First operation: $914 \times 1\frac{1}{2} = n$
$1,371 = n$

Second operation: $1,371 \times 8 = m$
$10,968 = m$

Reread the Problem

After rereading the problem, write the complete answer. *The Trieste dove 10,968 meters. How close is* your answer to your estimate? If your answer is not close, you should start over.

Use the five steps to solve this problem.

Read: *In 1930, William Dow* extracted *90 micrograms of gold from 12,000 liters of sea water. In 1965, Dr. Bayer extracted 1.4 micrograms of gold from 100 liters of sea water. Who extracted more gold per liter of sea water?*

Decide: The problem lists four number facts.

1. Dow extracted gold in 1930.

2. Dow extracted 90 micrograms of gold from 12,000 liters of water.

3. Bayer extracted gold in 1965.

4. Bayer extracted 1.4 micrograms of gold from 100 liters of water.

The question can be answered using facts 2 and 4. Facts 1 and 3 are not necessary.

You will need to do two arithmetic operations to find the answer. First you need to figure out how much gold per liter Dow extracted and then how much gold per liter Bayer extracted. For both operations, you must divide. The key word for both operations is *per*. These are your mathematical sentences.

$$90 \div 12{,}000 = d$$
$$1.4 \div 100 = b$$

Estimate: Round each number.

$$100 \div 12{,}000 = d$$
$$.008 = d$$
$$1 \div 100 = b$$
$$.01 = b$$

Carry Out:
$$90 \div 12{,}000 = d$$
$$.0075 = d$$
$$1.4 \div 100 = b$$
$$.014 = b$$

Reread: *Dow extracted .0075 microgram of gold per liter. Bayer extracted .014 microgram of gold per liter. Bayer extracted more gold per liter of water than Dow did.*

COMPREHENSION

Recognizing sequence of events

1. In which step do you figure out which information is not needed?

   You figure this out in the second step, Decide.

Recalling details

2. Explain how you make an estimate.

   Round the numbers and solve the mathematical

   sentences.

Recalling details

3. What should you do if you have extra information in a problem?

   Do not use it. Cross it out.

Using word clues

4. Draw a line to match each operation to its key word.

   multiply   **a.** per

   divide   **b.** times

CRITICAL THINKING

Making inferences

1. Explain why a word problem might have extra information.

   Answers will vary. Extra information might be related to the necessary information, be interesting to know, or be a help in

   solving other problems.

Making inferences

2. Why are labels important in word problems?

   They let you know what the numbers mean.

Making inferences
3. In the second problem in the selection, tell why the letters *b* and *d* are used.

The letter *b* stands for Bayer, and the letter *d* stands for Dow.

Making inferences
4. In the first problem, why was the letter *n* used in both operations?

In the first problem, the answer to the first operation is needed to solve the second operation.

SKILL FOCUS: WORD PROBLEMS

To solve each word problem below, you will need to carry out two operations. Also, some problems contain unnecessary information. Cross out any facts that are not needed.

1. Read: In 1965, Americans used 310 billion gallons of water per day. By 1980, they were using 130 billion more gallons of water per day. Fifteen years later, however, Americans were using 38 billion gallons of water less per day. ~~Americans were using 500 gallons per day per person.~~ How much water per day were Americans using in 1995?

Decide: Add to figure out how much water was used per day in 1980. Subtract to figure out how much water was used

per day in 1995. $310 + 130 = n$; $n - 38 = w$

Estimate: $300 + 100 = 400$; $400 - 40 = 360$

Carry Out: $310 + 130 = 440$; $440 - 38 = 402$

Reread: Americans were using 402 billion gallons of water per day in 1995.

2. Read: A seaweed farm that covers 10 square kilometers produces 72,576 metric tons of seaweed. A dredging site that covers 21 square kilometers produces 272 metric tons of gold ~~for a profit of $150 million.~~ Is there more seaweed or more gold in a square kilometer of seawater?

Decide: Divide to find tons of seaweed per square kilometer of seawater. Divide to find tons of gold per square

kilometer of seawater. $72,576 \div 10 = s$; $272 \div 21 = g$

Estimate: $70,000 \div 10 = s$; $7,000 = s$; $300 \div 20 = g$; $15 = g$

Carry Out: $72,576 \div 10 = s$; $7,257.6 = s$; $272 \div 21 = g$; $12.95 = g$

Reread: There is more seaweed than gold in a square kilometer of seawater.

Reading-Writing Connection

On a separate sheet of paper, describe an everyday problem or situation that you could solve by using two mathematical operations. Write the word problem and solve it.

For ESL/ELL support, see page T83.

Skill: Syllables

For lesson support, see page T83.

RULE 5: Words With One Consonant Between Two Sounded Vowels

Many words have only one consonant between two sounded vowels. This rule will help you in dividing such words. Such words are divided differently depending on whether the first vowel is long or short.

Rule 5a A word that has one consonant between two sounded vowels with the first vowel long is usually divided into syllables before the consonant.

spider   spi der

A. Use Rule 5a to divide each word below into two syllables by writing each syllable separately on the line next to the word.

1.	pilot	pi lot	9.	bacon	ba con
2.	robot	ro bot	10.	odor	o dor
3.	music	mu sic	11.	flavor	fla vor
4.	private	pri vate	12.	major	ma jor
5.	even	e ven	13.	locate	lo cate
6.	human	hu man	14.	total	to tal
7.	spiral	spi ral	15.	moment	mo ment
8.	minus	mi nus	16.	student	stu dent

Rule 5b A word that has one consonant between two sounded vowels with the first vowel short is usually divided into syllables after the consonant.

rapid   rap id

B. Use Rule 5b to divide each word below into two syllables by writing each syllable separately on the line next to the word.

1.	shiver	shiv er	9.	pedal	ped al
2.	robin	rob in	10.	magic	mag ic
3.	closet	clos et	11.	seven	sev en
4.	dragon	drag on	12.	planet	plan et
5.	clever	clev er	13.	second	sec ond
6.	medal	med al	14.	melon	mel on
7.	travel	trav el	15.	legend	leg end
8.	river	riv er	16.	shovel	shov el

C. Say each of the words below to yourself. If the first vowel is long, use Rule 5a to divide the word into two syllables. If the first vowel is short, use Rule 5b.

1. cabin	cab in	7. model	mod el
2. paper	pa per	8. wagon	wag on
3. lilac	li lac	9. clover	clo ver
4. lemon	lem on	10. petal	pet al
5. silent	si lent	11. spinal	spi nal
6. lizard	liz ard	12. satin	sat in

RULE 6: Words With Blends

The word *zebra* has two consonants between two sounded vowels. Because the consonant blend *br* makes one sound, it is treated in the same way that a single consonant is treated. The word is divided in this way: *ze bra*.

In a word that has three consonants between two vowels, it is possible that two of the consonants are a blend or a digraph. You treat the blend or digraph as one consonant. For example, *congress* has a *gr* blend. You divide the word between the consonant and the consonant blend: *con gress*.

D. Circle the blend or digraph in each of the words below. Then divide the word into two syllables by writing each syllable separately on the line next to the word.

1. explore	ex plore	7. bushel	bush el
2. leather	leath er	8. surprise	sur prise
3. athlete	ath lete	9. gather	gath er
4. other	oth er	10. central	cen tral
5. pumpkin	pump kin	11. compress	com press
6. detract	de tract	12. imply	im ply

When a word ends in *-le*, the *-le* and the consonant before it make up a syllable, as in *bun dle*.

E. Divide the words below into two syllables by writing each syllable separately on the line next to the word.

1. cradle	cra dle	7. sample	sam ple
2. gentle	gen tle	8. stable	sta ble
3. bugle	bu gle	9. thimble	thim ble
4. handle	han dle	10. fable	fa ble
5. dimple	dim ple	11. title	ti tle
6. noble	no ble	12. maple	ma ple

Skill: Accented Syllables

For lesson support, see page T83.

When words contain two syllables, one of the syllables is stressed, or accented, more than the other. In dictionaries, the **accent mark** (') is placed at the end of the syllable that is said with more stress. For example, the first syllable in the word *picnic* is said with more stress than the second syllable.

pic'nic

Words that have three syllables usually are accented on one of the first two syllables. When you are trying to pronounce a word with three syllables, say the word with more stress on the first syllable. If the word does not sound right, say it again, giving the most stress to the second syllable.

com pu' ter

A. Say each of the following words to yourself. Write an accent mark after the syllable that should be stressed.

1. peo'ple
2. riv'er
3. con tain'
4. chem'i cal
5. pos'si ble
6. fig'ure
7. con'so nant

8. di rec'tion
9. hu'man
10. im por'tant
11. gar'den
12. de vel'op
13. or'gan ize
14. por'cu pine

15. car na'tion
16. mo tel'
17. buf'fa lo
18. ca noe'
19. wag'on
20. tor pe'do
21. for get'ting

Words of four or more syllables usually have two accented syllables. In the word *caterpillar*, the first syllable, *cat*, has the most stress. This syllable receives the **primary accent mark** ('). The third syllable, *pil*, has more stress than the remaining two syllables, but less stress than the first syllable. The **secondary accent mark** (') is placed after that syllable.

cat'er pil'lar

B. Say each of the following words to yourself. Write the primary accent mark (') after the syllable that has the most stress. Write the secondary accent mark (') after the syllable that has the second-most stress.

1. sec're tar'y
2. bron'to sau'rus
3. ar'ma dil'lo
4. hip'po pot'a mus
5. cem'e ter'y

6. e lec'tro mag'net
7. al'li ga'tor
8. mar'i o nette'
9. in'vi ta'tion
10. en cy'clo pe'di a

For ESL/ELL support, see page T84.

Skill: Schwa Sound

For lesson support, see page T84.

The vowels *a*, *e*, *i*, *o*, and *u* can all have the same sound. This sound is a soft sound like a short *u* pronounced lightly, as in *uh*.

Pronounce *around*. Did the *a* sound like a soft, short *u*? _____yes_____

Pronounce *agent*. Did the *e* sound like a soft, short *u*? _____yes_____

Pronounce *animal*. Did the *i* sound like a soft, short *u*? _____yes_____

Pronounce *collect*. Did the *o* sound like a soft, short *u*? _____yes_____

Pronounce *circus*. Did the *u* sound like a soft, short *u*? _____yes_____

This short, soft *u* sound is called the **schwa** sound. In dictionary respellings, the symbol ə stands for the schwa sound. If you look up the word *lament* in a dictionary, you will find it respelled this way.

lə ment′

A. Say each of the words below to yourself. Write an accent mark after the syllable that is stressed. Then circle the letter that stands for the schwa sound.

1. wag′(o)n
2. (a) ware′
3. gal′l(o)p
4. eas′(i)ly
5. (a)p ply′

6. gar′m(e)nt
7. pos′s(i) ble
8. s(u)p ply′
9. ze′br(a)
10. op′p(o) s(i)te

11. (a)p pear′
12. mov′(a) ble
13. ash′(e)n
14. (a)t tack′
15. se′r(u)m

16. stan′z(a)
17. choc′(o) late
18. sug′(a)r
19. mir′r(o)r
20. med′(i) cine

Look at the words in the list above. Does the schwa sound come in the accented or unaccented syllable? Write the correct word in the sentence below.

The schwa sound always falls in an _____unaccented_____ syllable of a word.

B. Read the passage below. Circle the letter or letters in each underlined word that stand for the schwa sound.

Animals in Africa

(Africa) has many large <u>animals</u>. One of the largest of all beasts is the <u>elephant</u>. It lives in a <u>family</u> herd of blood <u>relatives</u> and <u>travels</u> <u>around</u> eating grass and leaves. The <u>gorilla</u> is <u>another</u> fairly big <u>animal</u>. It is the <u>largest</u> of the apes. It looks fierce, but it is really a <u>peaceful animal</u>.

The <u>lion</u> and the <u>leopard</u> are <u>among</u> the <u>fiercest</u> of the land beasts. The <u>crocodile</u>, which lives in lakes, <u>rivers</u>, and <u>marshes</u>, is much feared. The <u>hyena</u> is disliked because of its <u>horrible</u> shrieks.

For ESL/ELL support, see page T84.

Skill: Main Idea and Supporting Details

For lesson support, see page T84.

When you read a paragraph that is packed with information, first find the **main idea**.
Second, find the **supporting details** that give more information about the main idea.

The following paragraph is about the American colonists. The main idea and supporting details are listed after the paragraph.

The American colonists were unhappy under the rule of England. In 1774, colonial leaders formed the First Continental Congress to decide on possible actions to take. They asked the King of England to abolish, or do away with, certain laws that the colonists thought were unfair. They also asked that British troops leave the colonies.

Main Idea:

The American colonists were unhappy under the rule of England.

Supporting Details:

a. They formed the First Continental Congress to decide on possible actions to take.
b. They asked the King of England to do away with laws that the colonists thought were unfair.
c. They asked that the British troops leave.

On the next page, write the sentence that states the main idea of each paragraph. Then write the supporting details in your own words.

1. The American Revolution began in 1775 in Massachusetts with confusing encounters between British troops and bands of American rebels. In April of that year, the rebels refused to let British troops march through Lexington. No one knows who fired first, but the untrained colonials soon managed to chase the British back to Boston. In June, the Americans occupied two hills outside Boston. The British eventually took both hills, but they lost nearly half their men in the process.

2. That same year, a new congress, the Second Continental Congress, decided to end British rule and govern the colonies itself. It formed an army to fight the British and made George Washington commander-in-chief. It issued and borrowed money. It set up a postal system and created a navy.

3. The idea of independence spread throughout the colonies. *Common Sense*, written by Thomas Paine, convinced the colonists that they must fight. The colonists in Massachusetts, New Jersey, and South Carolina rebelled against their British governors. A committee set to work on a statement telling the King of England why the colonies believed that they must break away from England. Thomas Jefferson, with suggestions from the committee, wrote this statement—the Declaration of Independence.

4. A young Frenchman named Lafayette offered to help the colonial army. Later France declared war on Great Britain. In 1780, France sent 6,000 soldiers to the colonies. The British kept them in Newport Harbor for eleven months. The following spring, the French sent a large squadron of ships and a lot of money. The French had come to the aid of the colonists.

5. In 1781, the colonists won the battle at Yorktown. The British General Cornwallis had marched his soldiers to Yorktown, Virginia. Knowing of Cornwallis's movements, the colonists put into action a plan that ended the Revolutionary War in their favor. Washington and his French allies pretended to move to New York, but marched to Yorktown instead. Meanwhile the French fleet took control of the waters off Yorktown so that Cornwallis could not get help from the British fleet. Surrounded by these forces, Cornwallis had no choice but to surrender.

Paragraph 1   **Main Idea:** The American Revolution began in 1775 in Massachusetts with confusing encounters between British troops and bands of American rebels.

Supporting Details:

a. In April, colonists in Lexington chased the British troops back to Boston.

b. In June, colonists occupied two hills outside Boston.

c. The British took both hills, but lost almost half of their men.

Paragraph 2   **Main Idea:** That same year, a new congress, the Second Continental Congress, decided to end British rule and govern the colonies itself.

Supporting Details:

a. It formed an army with Washington as commander.

b. It controlled money.

c. It set up a postal system and a navy.

Paragraph 3   **Main Idea:** The idea of independence spread throughout the colonies.

Supporting Details:

a. *Common Sense* convinced colonists to fight.

b. Three states rebelled against their British governors.

c. Thomas Jefferson wrote the Declaration of Independence.

Paragraph 4   **Main Idea:** The French had come to the aid of the colonists.

Supporting Details:

a. A Frenchman named Lafayette offered to help.

b. France declared war on Great Britain.

c. France sent 6,000 soldiers.

d. France sent a squadron of ships and a lot of money.

Paragraph 5   **Main Idea:** Knowing of Cornwallis's movements, the colonists put into action a plan that ended the Revolutionary War in their favor.

Supporting Details:

a. Cornwallis marched his soldiers to Yorktown.

b. Washington and the French marched to Yorktown.

c. The French controlled the waters off Yorktown.

d. Cornwallis had to surrender to Washington.

For ESL/ELL support, see page T85.

Skill: Making Inferences

For lesson support, see page T85.

> If you read carefully and think about what you read, you can **infer**, or figure out, information that is not stated directly in a selection.

Use the following steps to make inferences as you read.

1. Read carefully.
2. Think about what you have read. Be sure that you understand the information that is stated.
3. Read again and look for clues to information that is not stated.
4. Put together the information stated with information that you already know. Use clues to help you make inferences.

As you read the following selection about Phillis Wheatley, pay close attention to the facts. Use the facts to infer information that is not directly stated in the selection.

Phillis Wheatley

1. The year was 1761. Mrs. Wheatley walked out of her large house on an upper-class Boston street. The wife of a successful tailor, she was headed for a slave ship that had docked in Boston harbor. Although the Wheatleys had a few elderly slaves in their household, Mrs. Wheatley wanted a slave who would serve as her personal maid for years to come.

2. Mrs. Wheatley boarded the slave ship. She found hundreds of people cramped in small, dark, stuffy rooms. As she looked around, she was drawn to a thin, frightened-looking girl in a corner. The girl had been kidnapped from her home in West Africa to be sold in America. The long journey had been difficult for her. Mrs. Wheatley paid a small amount for this sickly girl. The ship's captain was pleased because he was afraid she was too sick to sell.

3. The sad life of the young girl was about to undergo a complete change. The girl reminded Mrs. Wheatley of a tiny tree in need of warmth, food, and care. Mrs. Wheatley named her Phillis, which means "a green branch of a tree." Although the girl spoke only the language of her West African group, Mrs. Wheatley explained to her the meaning of her new name. Phillis was pleased with it.

4. Phillis learned quickly. Although she was a servant in the Wheatley home, she was treated more like a member of the family. Instead of doing hard chores, Phillis learned to read English and Latin. She hungrily studied the Bible, mythology, ancient history, and eighteenth-century English poetry. Gradually Phillis became a well-read woman.

5. Phillis started to write poetry as a teenager. Her first poem, written in 1767, was about the death of George Whitefield, a famous English preacher. When it was published three years later, Phillis became the first African American woman and only the second woman of any race to publish in the colonies. Soon all of Boston knew of her. Her fame spread to England and the rest of Europe, as well.

6. Phillis became ill in the early 1770s, and the Wheatleys' family doctor recommended a change in climate. Phillis accompanied Mr. Wheatley on a business trip to England. She met the best of British society and was well received. With the help of her English friends, her book *Poems on Various Subjects, Religious and Moral* was published.

7. George Washington became commander-in-chief of the Revolutionary army in 1775. Phillis was

delighted that the colonists finally had a strong leader in the fight against England. To express how she felt, Phillis wrote a poem about Washington. She sent it to him with a letter. Much to Phillis's surprise, George Washington sent her a thank-you note praising her for her beautiful verses and inviting her to visit him. Phillis accepted his invitation.

8. After Mr. and Mrs. Wheatley died, Phillis was left alone. She married John Peters, a freed slave like herself. However he was never able to support the family. Phillis tried to raise money by publishing a second book. She put an advertisement in the newspaper seeking buyers for the book. Much to her disappointment, almost no one showed interest in her work. Shortly thereafter, at the age of 31, she died. Despite all of her hardships, Phillis Wheatley earned great fame as a poet in her time.

Put a ✔ next to the following statements that can be inferred from each paragraph. On the lines that follow, write the phrase or sentence from the paragraph that is a clue that helped you make the inference. Then explain how you inferred the information.

Paragraph 1 (check two):

a. ___✔___ The Wheatleys were wealthy.

b. _____ The Wheatleys had several children.

c. ___✔___ Mrs. Wheatley was looking for a young maid.

Clue: Mrs. Wheatley lived in a large house on an upper-class Boston street.

Explanation: People must be wealthy to own a large house on an upper-class street.

Clue: The Wheatleys had a few elderly slaves. She wanted someone who would serve for years to come.

Explanation: A young slave would be able to serve for years.

Paragraph 2 (check two):

a. _____ Many of the slaves died on the trip to America.

b. ___✔___ The slave ship carried its passengers as if they were cargo.

c. ___✔___ The healthy-looking slaves brought higher prices.

Clue: There were hundreds of people cramped in small, dark, stuffy rooms.

Explanation: These conditions were unsuitable for people.

Clue: Mrs. Wheatley paid a small amount for this sickly girl.

Explanation: People would pay more for a healthy slave who could work harder.

Paragraph 4 (check two):

a. _____ Phillis was not very good at doing household chores.

b. ___✔___ Phillis had an excellent mind and was eager to learn.

c. ___✔___ The Wheatleys allowed Phillis to read many books in their home.

Clue: She learned to read English and Latin.

Explanation: Someone who learns two languages is probably smart.

Clue: She hungrily studied the Bible, mythology, ancient history, and eighteenth-century English poetry.

Explanation: Someone studying these works would have to read many books. Phillis could not afford to buy books of her own.

Skill: Suffixes

For lesson support, see page T85.

> A **suffix** is a word part that is added to the end of a word to change its meaning. Study eight suffixes and their meanings in the chart below.

Suffix	Meaning	Suffix	Meaning
-ity	condition or quality	-ous	having or full of
-let	small, little	-ship	condition of or state of
-ly	like or every	-ure	act or result
-or	person or thing that	-ward	toward

A. Read each word below and the meaning that follows it. Write the correct suffix after each word.

1. month___ly___   happening every month

2. back___ward___   toward the back

3. acid___ity___   condition of being acidic

4. courage___ous___   having courage

5. direct___or___   person who directs

6. book___let___   little book

7. fail___ure___   act of failing

8. week___ly___   every week

9. friend___ship___   state of being friends

10. invent___or___   person who invents

11. west___ward___   toward the west

12. partner___ship___   state of being partners

B. Use one of the words from the chart above to complete each sentence below.

1. Karen looked ___backward___ to see if she had dropped anything.

2. Tabitha Babbit, the ___inventor___ of the circular saw, got the idea for it while watching her spinning wheel.

3. Because a ___booklet___ is little, it often has a paper cover.

4. The ___friendship___ between Joe and Ben started in second grade.

5. Jumping into the water to save a frightened child is a ___courageous___ act.

6. The author was discouraged by his ___failure___ to write a successful novel.

7. The drink's ___acidity___ made it taste sour.

8. Every Friday, Pete bought a ___weekly___ supply of groceries.

9. The ___director___ watched the play from backstage.

10. On the first day of the month, the employees had their ___monthly___ meeting.

11. Bill and Pat formed a ___partnership___ in order to buy a toy business.

12. The wind was blowing in a ___westward___ direction.

Skill: Using a Library Catalog

For lesson support, see page T86.

To locate a book in the library quickly and easily, use the **library catalog**. In most cases, the catalog will be a computer database. Although formats may vary, most library databases are set up to give the same basic information. You find information by choosing items from a **menu**, or list. The main menu often lists other resources as well as the library catalog. When you choose the catalog, a second menu will appear. You can then search for a book by its title, by the author's last name, or by its subject. If you do not have exact information about the book, you may be able to choose an item called **keywords**. The computer will search its database using one or two important words that you give it.

A library catalog gives more information than just the subject, author, and title of a book. Usually an entry for a book gives a summary of the book's contents, a description (size, number of pages, kind of illustrations), the publisher and date it was published, and a list of related subjects. It may tell how many copies of the book the library owns, which branches of the library have the book, and whether the book is currently available.

Subject Search

Suppose you want to read a true story about survival in the wilderness. First you select *Subject* from the catalog menu to do a **subject search**. Then enter a phrase such as *wilderness survival*. A list of subjects will appear. Choose one that is the same as, or close to, the phrase that you entered. A list of books about that topic will appear. Then choose a particular book to find out more about it.

Author Search

If you want to find out which books by a particular author are in the library, you can do an **author search**. Choose *Author* from the catalog menu,

and enter the author's name, last name first (for example: Miller, Dorcas). A list of the author's books will appear. You can then choose a particular book to find out more about it.

Title Search

If you already know what book you want, you can do a **title search**. Choose *Title* from the catalog menu, and enter the exact title. Information about the book will appear on the screen.

In each kind of search, the last step is to select a particular book. When you do, a screen similar to the screen in the left column appears.

Notice the **call number** at the top of the screen. This number appears on the spine, or narrow back edge, of the book. Every nonfiction book has its own call number, which tells where it is shelved in the library. Nonfiction books are kept in numerical order. This book would come before a book with the number 613.7 and after one numbered 612.06. The letters immediately following the number are the first two or three letters of the author's last name. Across from the call number is the word *status*. The information there tells you whether the book is on the shelf or is checked out.

```
Public Library              HOME   SEARCH
                                    AGAIN
Call Number  Nonfiction      Status:Checked Out
613.69 Mi
Author:      Miller, Dorcas (editor)
Title:       Rescue: Stories of Survival From Land
             and Sea
Publisher:   New York: Thunder's Mouth Press, ©2000
Description: 360 pages; ill.
Summary:     17 true stories and 2 fictional ones
             of people rescued from shipwrecks,
             avalanches, plane crashes, and other
             dangerous wilderness situations.
Subjects:    Wilderness Survival
             Survival
             Rescues
```

A. Use the screen on page 90 to do the following.

1. Circle the year that the book was published.

2. Is this book illustrated? Put two lines under the information that tells you.

3. If you wanted to find more books like this one, what subjects might you search under? Draw a box around each.

B. Circle the kind of search that you would do in order to answer each question.

1. Who wrote the book *Cowboy: An Album*?
   author search   (title search)   subject search

2. Which of Virginia Hamilton's books does the library have?
   (author search)   title search   subject search

3. Does the library have any new books about World War II?
   author search   title search   (subject search)

4. What is the call number for *The Forgotten Heroes: The Story of the Buffalo Soldiers*?
   author search   (title search)   subject search

5. Does the library have books on martial arts?
   author search   title search   (subject search)

6. Does the library have Laurence Yep's newest book?
   (author search)   title search   subject search

C. Use the information on the computer screen below to answer each question.

1. When was this book published?
   2000

2. The summary mentions survival in the desert. Under what subject could you look for more information on this topic?
   Desert survival—Handbooks, manuals, etc.

3. Would this book be shelved before or after one with call number 613.5 FAR?
   after

> **Public Library**   [HOME] [SEARCH AGAIN]
>
> Call Number Nonfiction   Status: In
> 613.69 St
> Author: Stilwell, ALexander
> Title: The Encyclopedia of Survival Techniques
> Publisher: New York: Lyon's Press, ©2000
> Description: 192 p; ill.
> Summary: Describes preparation, equipment,
>   and techniques for survival in the
>   desert, at sea, in the tropics, in
>   polar regions, and in the mountains.
> Subjects: Survival skills—Handbooks, manuals, etc.
>   Wilderness survival—Handbooks, manuals,
>   etc.
>   Desert survival—Handbooks, manuals, etc.

Skill: Outlining

> Sometimes you write a summary of a selection or of a chapter in a textbook to help you understand or study it. Another good way to understand and remember what you read is to make an **outline** of it. An outline can be written quickly and read easily. A good outline shows how the main ideas and supporting details in a selection are organized and related.

In a paragraph, the most important idea is the **main idea**. In an outline of a selection or chapter, the main idea of each paragraph is restated in a few words and written next to a Roman numeral: I, II, III, and so on.

The details that give important supporting information about the main idea are the **major details**. The major details are written next to capital letters: A, B, C, and so on. These letters are indented, or moved a little to the right, underneath the Roman numerals.

The details that give information about the major details are the **minor details**. The minor details are written next to numbers: 1, 2, 3, and so on. These numbers are indented underneath the capital letters.

Read the following paragraph. Then look at the outline next to it.

Cargo ships are classified into three groups according to the kinds of cargo they carry. Ships that carry packaged goods are called *general cargo ships*. Packaged goods include such items as chemicals, food, and furniture. *Tankers* carry liquid cargo. This might include petroleum—the thick, natural oil that fuel oil and gasoline are made from—or molasses. *Dry bulk carriers* haul products, such as iron ore and coal, that can be loaded loose on the vessels.

Cargo Ships

I. Classification of cargo ships
  A. General cargo ships
    1. Carry packaged items
    2. Examples—chemicals, food, furniture
  B. Tankers
    1. Carry liquid cargo
    2. Examples—petroleum, molasses
  C. Dry bulk carriers
    1. Carry loose items
    2. Examples—coal, iron ore

Notice that the main idea of the paragraph, *Classification of cargo ships*, is written next to Roman numeral I. *General cargo ships* is written next to capital letter A. This phrase is the first major detail about cargo ships. *Carry packaged items* is written next to number 1. This phrase is a minor detail about general cargo ships.

When you outline a selection, always include at least two main ideas. An outline of a selection can never have a *I* without a *II*. There should also be at least two major details under each main idea. Finally, there should always be at least two minor details under each major detail.

Each of the paragraphs on page 93 compares a type of cargo ship of the past with a type that is in use today. By completing the outline, you will organize information in a way that will help you understand and remember the main ideas and details.

In the early 1900s, most general cargo ships had three areas, called *islands*. The first island was called the forecastle. It held the crew's quarters. The bridge was the second island, located in the middle of the ship. The crew steered and navigated the ship from the bridge. The poop, which held the officers' cabins, formed the third island. Today freighters have one island for the bridge and the crew's quarters. This arrangement leaves extra room for hatches. With bigger hatches, it is easier to load and unload cargo.

The first oceangoing tanker, the *Gluckauf*, was launched in 1885. Built in Great Britain for a German oil company, it was 300 feet (91 meters) long and 37 feet (11 meters) wide. The *Gluckauf* carried 2,300 tons (2,090 metric tons) of oil. It could travel at a speed of 9 knots. Large tankers are often called supertankers today. The largest tankers carry about 555,000 deadweight tons. They can travel at a speed of about 15 knots (15 sea-miles per hour).

During the 1800s, the first dry bulk carriers hauled iron ore on the Great Lakes. Like tankers, they could carry only one kind of cargo. Unlike tankers, however, the ore carriers hauled solid cargo. For this reason, loading and unloading were more complicated than for tankers. Tankers needed only house connections and pumps for loading and unloading. Today oceangoing bulk carriers are much larger. Most of them are loaded with more than 100,000 short tons (91,000 metric tons) of cargo. These ships need motor-driven equipment on board to quickly remove enormous hatch covers so that the cargo can be reached easily.

II. General cargo ships

    A. Early 1900s—three islands

        1. First island—forecastle: crew's quarters

        2. Second island—bridge: navigation and steering

        3. Third island—poop: officers' cabins

    B. Today—one island

        1. Bridge and living quarters

        2. More room for bigger hatches—easier to load and unload

III. Tankers

    A. *Gluckauf* first oceangoing tanker—launched 1885

        1. Built in Great Britain for German oil company

        2. 300 feet long and 37 feet wide

        3. Carried 2,300 tons

        4. Traveled at 9 knots

    B. Modern supertankers

        1. Carry 555,000 tons

        2. Travel at 15 knots

IV. Dry bulk carriers

    A. First carriers hauled iron ore on Great Lakes in 1800s

        1. Carried only one kind of cargo

        2. Hauled solid cargo

        3. Complicated loading and unloading arrangements

    B. Modern oceangoing carriers are larger

        1. Carry more than 100,000 short tons

        2. Motor-driven equipment removes hatch covers for easy loading and unloading

For lesson support, see page T87.

Medicine can be helpful in curing an illness but dangerous if taken incorrectly. It is very important to read the **label** on the bottle or box *before* taking any medication. The label states the medical problems that the medication may help. It gives the **dosage**—how much medicine should be taken and how often. A label may also provide certain **warnings** to help prevent the wrong use of the medicine. Anyone using medication should read the label carefully to be familiar with the proper dosage and use.

Read the labels below from two different medications.

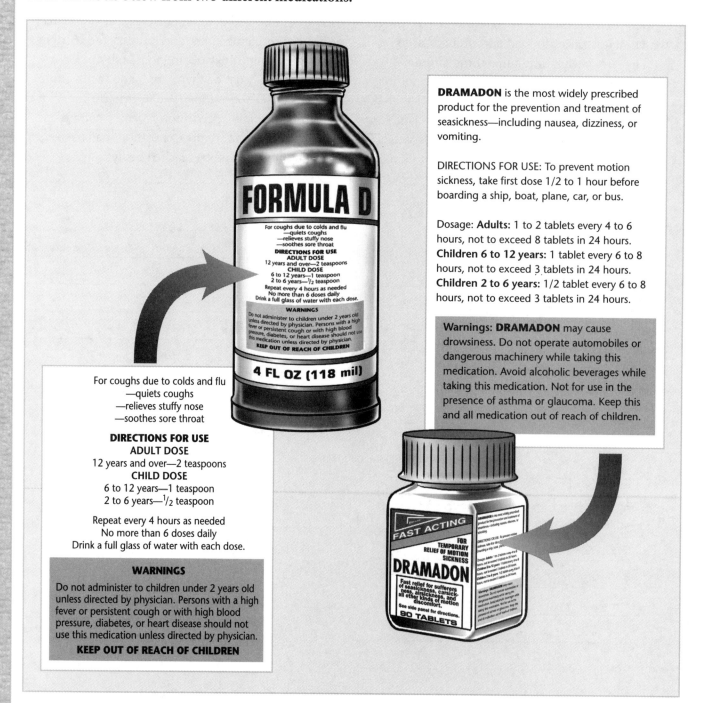

FORMULA D

For coughs due to colds and flu
—quiets coughs
—relieves stuffy nose
—soothes sore throat

DIRECTIONS FOR USE
ADULT DOSE
12 years and over—2 teaspoons
CHILD DOSE
6 to 12 years—1 teaspoon
2 to 6 years—½ teaspoon

Repeat every 4 hours as needed
No more than 6 doses daily
Drink a full glass of water with each dose.

WARNINGS
Do not administer to children under 2 years old unless directed by physician. Persons with a high fever or persistent cough or with high blood pressure, diabetes, or heart disease should not use this medication unless directed by physician.
KEEP OUT OF REACH OF CHILDREN

4 FL OZ (118 mil)

DRAMADON is the most widely prescribed product for the prevention and treatment of seasickness—including nausea, dizziness, or vomiting.

DIRECTIONS FOR USE: To prevent motion sickness, take first dose 1/2 to 1 hour before boarding a ship, boat, plane, car, or bus.

Dosage: **Adults:** 1 to 2 tablets every 4 to 6 hours, not to exceed 8 tablets in 24 hours.
Children 6 to 12 years: 1 tablet every 6 to 8 hours, not to exceed 3 tablets in 24 hours.
Children 2 to 6 years: 1/2 tablet every 6 to 8 hours, not to exceed 3 tablets in 24 hours.

Warnings: **DRAMADON** may cause drowsiness. Do not operate automobiles or dangerous machinery while taking this medication. Avoid alcoholic beverages while taking this medication. Not for use in the presence of asthma or glaucoma. Keep this and all medication out of reach of children.

DRAMADON

A. Use the information on the labels on to page 94 to complete each sentence.

1. The medication used to prevent seasickness is _____Dramadon_____.

2. The medication used to quiet coughs is _____Formula D_____.

3. You can tell that Formula D is not a tablet because the directions tell how many _____teaspoons_____ to take.

4. Each container of Dramadon contains _____90_____ tablets.

5. The symptoms—or signs—of seasickness are _____nausea, dizziness, or vomiting_____.

6. To prevent seasickness from occurring, you should take Dramadon _____$\frac{1}{2}$ to 1 hour before boarding_____.

7. The Dramadon label warns against driving an automobile while using the medication

    because the medication may cause _____drowsiness_____.

8. If an adult uses the maximum number of Dramadon tablets recommended for one day,

    then a container of Dramadon will last for _____$11 \frac{1}{4}$_____ days.

9. The medication that should be taken with a glass of water is _____Formula D_____.

10. If an 11-year-old takes the maximum number of recommended doses of Formula D in

    one day, then he or she will take _____6_____ teaspoonfuls of the medication. If a 4-year-old

    takes the maximum number of doses in a day, he or she will take _____3_____ teaspoonfuls.

11. A 1-year-old should not be given Formula D unless a _____physician_____ has recommended it.

12. "No more than 6 doses daily" means no more than 6 doses in _____one day_____.

B. Circle the letter next to one, two, or three answers to each question.

1. Which warning(s) is (are) given on both medications?
   - **a.** Keep out of reach of children.
   - **b.** Do not drive an automobile while using medication.
   - **c.** Do not use if you have glaucoma.

2. Both medications have different dosages for which age group(s)?
   - **a.** children 2 to 6 years old   **b.** children 6 to 12 years old   **c.** adults

3. How many teaspoonfuls of Formula D can an adult take every 4 hours?
   - **a.** 1   **b.** 8   **c.** 2

4. What is the most Formula D an adult should take in one day?
   - **a.** 2 teaspoonfuls   **b.** 12 teaspoonfuls   **c.** 8 teaspoonfuls

5. What are the benefits of Formula D cough syrup?
   - **a.** It helps to quiet a cough.   **b.** It relieves a stuffy nose.   **c.** It makes a sore throat feel better.

unit four

For ESL/ELL support, see highlighted words, page T38, and pages T28–T30.

Mountains to Climb

For theme support, see page T26.

LESSON 33

Skill: Setting

For lesson support, see page T88.

BACKGROUND INFORMATION

"Triumph and Tragedy" is the true story of a young man who, in 1865, became the first person to climb the Matterhorn, one of the highest mountains in Europe. Today mountaineers use high-tech equipment and benefit from experienced guides and teachers. In the mid-1800s, however, the sport of mountain climbing was new—and very dangerous.

SKILL FOCUS: Setting

Setting is the time and place in which story events occur. Sometimes you may have to figure out the setting from clues in the story.

To identify a setting and its effect on story characters, ask yourself the following questions as you read.

- Where and when do the story events occur?
- What details about setting does the author use?
- What difficulties does the setting create?
- How do the characters overcome the difficulties that arise because of the setting?
- What overall effect does the setting have on the characters?

▶ Think of a story you have read in which characters struggled against forces in the setting. On the chart below, describe the story's setting and its effect on the characters.

CONTEXT CLUES: Word Groupings

When you see an unfamiliar word, study the **word groupings** around it. They may name more familiar items that can serve as clues to the meaning of the new word.

Read the following sentence. Look for a word grouping that can help you figure out the meaning of the underlined word.

> *Young Edward Whymper grew up in England among hills and farmlands filled with crags and* <u>*moors*</u>.

If you don't know the meaning of *moors*, the words *hills* and *farmlands* can help you. *Moors* is grouped with other things in the same category, so you can figure out that moors are a type of landform.

▶ Read the following sentences. Circle the word groupings that are clues to the meaning of *besiege*.

> *His plan was "to return with a companion and* <u>*besiege*</u> *the mountain for so long that either it or we will be beaten." He wanted to* (attack and conquer) *the mountain, almost as if it were an* (enemy in battle.)

As you read the next selection, use word groupings to figure out the meanings of the underlined words *sheer*, *grappling*, and *catastrophe*.

Effects of Setting	
Title of story	Answers will vary on chart.
Time of setting	
Place of setting	
Difficulties caused by setting	
How characters overcame difficulties	

Strategy Tip

As you read "Triumph and Tragedy," look for details that describe the setting. Notice how the time and place of events cause difficulties for the characters.

Triumph and Tragedy

Young Edward Whymper grew up in England among hills and farmlands filled with crags and moors. He had never seen a mountain or even climbed a hill. That is, not until he came to the Alps at the age of 20. These famous mountains stretch through several European countries, including France, Italy, Switzerland, and Austria.

Whymper made illustrations for books. He had an assignment to make pictures of tall mountains. Since there are no large mountains in England, he came across the English Channel and journeyed over land to see the mountains for himself. These towering, snowcapped peaks were like nothing in England. Out of green valleys and clear lakes, the majestic mountains seemed to reach for the sky.

It was 1860, and mountaineering was just becoming a sport. A hundred years earlier, Horace Bénédict de Saussure, a scientist from Geneva, offered a reward to whomever could climb the highest peak of the Alps. This peak was Mont Blanc, at 15,771 feet (4,808 meters). More than 25 years later, Michel Gabriel Paccard and his guide, Jacques Balmat, succeeded. Before Mont Blanc was conquered, mountain climbing was almost unheard of. By the 1850s, however, at least a hundred large peaks in the Alps had been climbed for the first time.

The sheer peaks of the Alps attracted many climbers eager to conquer these steep, towering, challenging mountains. However, the surge of interest in climbing led one concerned climber to ask sadly in 1854, "Will our grandsons succeed in the future in conquering the last of all the alpine peaks?" The "Golden Age" of alpinism, the climbing of the Alps, had begun. So many English climbers came to explore the peaks of Europe that the Alps became known as the "Playground of Europe." By the 1870s, nearly all the important peaks had been conquered.

As difficult as it may be to believe today, the earliest alpine hikers didn't realize that climbing was dangerous. They had no experience that alerted them to the particular dangers of the sport. Attempts to climb the Matterhorn finally helped people understand the dangers of mountaineering. That is where Edward Whymper returns to the story.

Located on the Swiss-Italian border, the Matterhorn looks like a sharp, pointed pyramid. Its steep face challenges even the most experienced climbers today.

After journeying in the Alps for almost a year, Whymper first saw the Matterhorn in the summer of 1861. Though he had never climbed a hill before coming to the Alps, he decided to climb the Matterhorn. His first attempt failed. Whymper was inexperienced, and the equipment he had was not good enough for climbing such a steep mountain. Even the best mountaineers said that the Matterhorn was impossible to climb. That did not stop Whymper. He resolved to succeed in his climb someday. His plan was "to return with a companion and besiege the mountain for so long that either it or we will be beaten." He wanted to attack and conquer the mountain, almost as if it were an enemy in battle.

Climbing the Matterhorn is a challenge to even the most experienced mountain climbers.

Whymper thought he had found his companion in Giovanni Antonio Carrel. Carrel grew up in Italy, at the foot of the Matterhorn. It had been his dream since he was a young boy to be the first person to climb it. Back in 1857, he had tried to climb it with his brother and another mountaineer, but the mountain proved overwhelming. Still Carrel was determined to climb the Matterhorn, and he knew in his heart that he would succeed.

The two determined men could surely make it together. Whymper went back to England, where he devoted his time to planning for the trip. He created a mountaineer's tent that could be carried. By using it, the climbers could bivouac (BIV ə wak)—make a camp—with some protection from the wind, snow, ice, and cold. A bivouac allows climbers to spend nights on steep rock faces when getting to a flat space would take more than one day. Whymper built new kinds of equipment, such as a grappling iron that could help the climbers grab onto the impossibly steep rock faces. He also built two ladders that could be folded up, which the climbers could carry with them.

In 1863, Whymper was ready. He and Carrel had decided that their best route up would be the Italian ridge. However, they had to wait for conditions that were suitable for climbing. There is snow on these high peaks year-round, but summer offers the best chance for success. Finally in the summer of 1865, all signs indicated that it was time. When Whymper arrived in Italy, he spoke with Carrel. He found out that his would-be companion had decided to go up with some Italian climbers instead. What had been a partnership had turned into a rivalry.

Whymper was disappointed but not beaten. He had come this far. There was no way he would turn back now. He found other companions and used his special equipment to climb the mountain. As it turned out, Whymper and his party reached the top first. Whymper is considered the first person ever to climb the Matterhorn. Finally he had realized his dream! The young man who, until five years earlier, had never rested his eyes on a mountain peak had climbed a mountain most people said was impossible to climb.

According to one account by Whymper, his cries of triumph were heard by Carrel and his party on the Italian side of the peak. Whymper said that he and another climber sent rocks sliding down the mountain to be sure that the Italians knew of their victory.

It didn't take long for Whymper's great joy to turn to grave catastrophe. On the way down the mountain, disaster struck. One of the men in his party slipped. Three of his companions who were attached to the same rope were pulled off the mountain with him. When the rope snapped and the four men fell from the mountain, Whymper could only watch in horror. Afterward, he described the tragic accident: "For a few seconds we watched our unfortunate companions tumble down the slope, fighting with outstretched hands for some kind of finger-hold. They were still unhurt as one by one they disappeared from view and crashed from cliff to cliff down a drop of almost 4,000 feet."

No one knows whether the rope broke in midair or whether it was cut as it slid against a rock. Some people have even suggested that a member of the

In spite of the dangers of mountaineering, most of the important peaks of Europe had been conquered by the 1870s.

party cut the rope or gave the climbers who fell a weaker rope. Historians do not believe these stories. They point out that until this time, climbers weren't really aware of just how dangerous the sport could be.

Although there had been other deaths and accidents, this disaster quickly changed what people thought about mountain climbing. People all over the world heard about the accident. Climbers and nonclimbers began to realize how truly dangerous the pursuit of mountain peaks could be.

The more people climbed mountains, the more accidents happened. People died from slipping off footholds or from pieces of mountain breaking off the main rock face. They were killed by exposure to the wind and cold and by equipment failures. Accidents in which people were injured but not killed made the trip much more dangerous for those in the party who had to carry the injured person. Climbing down a sheer rock wall was already a life-risking course of action. Trying to do it while carrying a badly hurt climber was even more dangerous.

In 1896, near Vienna, Austria, three climbers were buried by an avalanche. After this tragedy, the first mountain-rescue service was founded. The service responds to climbers all over the world, and its members have been called "The Angels of the Mountains."

Today's climbers wear up-to-date safety equipment. They train and practice before attempting to climb great peaks. Lightweight but warm clothes, shoes with spikes, and belts that help hold hikers to the mountain are just some of the modern inventions that now help climbers. In addition, climbing clubs and schools around the world teach people proper safety techniques. In the United States, there are even indoor climbing clubs, where people can practice climbing with the safety of soft mats to cushion their falls.

Of course, climbing remains dangerous. Avalanches, snowstorms, equipment failures, and carelessness still cause injuries and deaths. However, the sport has come a long way since Whymper's climb of triumph and tragedy.

COMPREHENSION

Recalling details
1. Who was Edward Whymper?

He was a young illustrator from England. He later

became the first person to climb the Matterhorn.

Recalling details
2. Who was Whymper's rival from Italy?

Giovanni Antonio Carrel was his rival.

Identifying cause and effect
3. Explain why Whymper's first attempt to climb the Matterhorn was unsuccessful.

He was inexperienced, and the equipment he had was

not good enough for climbing such a steep mountain.

Identifying cause and effect
4. Why did Whymper need years of preparation before he was ready to return to the Matterhorn?

He needed time to build new equipment.

Recalling details
5. Describe the kind of equipment that Whymper built to help him in his climb.

He built a tent that could be carried, ladders that would

fold up, and a grappling iron.

Recognizing sequence of events
6. Tell what Whymper and his party did when they reached the top of the Matterhorn.

They gave cries of triumph, and they sent some rocks

sliding down the mountain.

Identifying mood
7. Circle the word that best describes the mood or atmosphere in this story.

(adventurous)   humorous   peaceful

8. Answer each question by writing *yes* or *no* on the line provided.

    a. Should a beginning skier learn to ski on a mountain's <u>sheer</u> slopes? _____no_____

b. Could a sailor use a <u>grappling</u> tool to anchor his boat to another boat? _____yes_____

c. Would a wonderful birthday party be a <u>catastrophe</u>? _____no_____

CRITICAL THINKING

Making inferences

1. Explain why you think Whymper thought that Carrel was his rival.

Whymper had planned his whole trip hoping that Carrel would come along. Then he found out that

Carrel went with several Italian climbers instead. Both men wanted to be the first to climb the Matterhorn.

Making inferences

2. Tell why mountain climbers might tie ropes around themselves that attach them to one another.

If one begins to fall, the others who are hooked more securely to the mountain can keep him or her

from falling too far.

Making inferences

3. Describe how you think Whymper felt when he returned from climbing the Matterhorn.

Answers will vary. He may have been proud at his achievement, but sad that four of his fellow climbers

had fallen to their deaths.

Drawing conclusions

4. Whymper had resolved "to return with a companion and besiege the mountain for so long that either it or we will be beaten." Describe which happened.

Answers will vary. Whymper beat the mountain because he reached the top. *or* The mountain beat Whymper

and his party because four men died.

Understanding character

5. Circle three character traits demonstrated by Edward Whymper in his climb of the Matterhorn.

    (determination)   laziness   shyness

    (inventiveness)   (resolve)   fearfulness

Making inferences

6. a. Using the illustration on page 98, describe in one sentence the clothing climbers wore and the tools they carried in the mid-1800s.

They wore tall boots, hats, and jackets, and they carried ropes and walking sticks.

    b. Using details from the story, how do you think modern climbers would be dressed?

They would be wearing lightweight and warm clothing, shoes with spikes, and belts that would help

them latch onto the mountain.

7. Do you think that Edward Whymper would have wanted to climb the Matterhorn again? Explain your answer.

Answers will vary. No. Once he had succeeded, the mountain had lost its challenge for him and returning would have

brought back a tragic memory. *or* Yes. He wanted to help others go up the mountain safely.

SKILL FOCUS: SETTING

Use information in the story, the photograph on page 97, and the illustration on page 98 to answer the following questions.

1. Identify where and when Edward Whymper's climb took place.

It took place on the Matterhorn in the summer of 1865.

2. a. Using details from the story, describe the setting in one sentence.

The Matterhorn is steep and dangerous, with snow, ice, and wind.

b. Using details from the photograph, describe the setting in one sentence.

The Matterhorn is sharp, pointed, and snow-covered.

3. What difficulties did the setting create for Whymper and his party?

The steep, snow-covered slopes made climbing difficult. When the four men fell, rock might have broken their rope.

4. Explain how Whymper prepared for the setting.

He constructed new equipment that would make climbing easier.

5. Describe the effect the setting had on Whymper and his party.

They struggled to get up the mountain, and in the end, four men died.

Reading-Writing Connection

Think of a sport that can be dangerous. On a separate sheet of paper, write a paragraph describing some of the safety equipment recommended for this sport.

LESSON 34

For ESL/ELL support, see highlighted words, page T89, and pages T28–T30.

Skill: Reading a Map

For lesson support, see page T89.

BACKGROUND INFORMATION

"The Great Mountain Ranges of the World" describes eight of Earth's major mountain ranges. To be a mountain, a landform must rise at least 2,000 feet (600 meters) above sea level. Usually mountains rise together in groups called ranges. Life in high mountains is hard. For one thing, the air is thinner than at sea level, making breathing more difficult. In addition, many high mountains are snow-covered year-round and support little plant life.

SKILL FOCUS: Reading a Map

There are many types of maps. You may be familiar with road maps, bus or train maps, or even maps of a mall. Social studies textbooks have many types of maps. Some are political maps, showing the cities and states of a country. Others show population, rainfall, or the products of a region.

A **relief map** is another type of map. It shows the differences in height of various parts of the earth's surface. Some landforms, such as mountains, rise high into the air. Other landforms, such as valleys and plains, are low. A relief map shows these differences.

The height of a landform is called its **elevation**. Elevation is measured in feet or meters above sea level. The elevation at sea level is zero feet or meters. Relief maps use different colors to show different elevations. Each relief map has a **key** that shows these colors. The key indicates the range of elevations that each color on the map stands for.

An **elevation illustration** is another way to compare the heights of landforms. This type of illustration makes it possible to compare landforms that are not close together geographically. An elevation illustration has a **vertical elevation scale**. At the bottom of the scale is sea level. Landforms, such as mountains, are drawn to their proper heights according to the scale.

▶ Look at the map of the United States on this page. What type of map is it? How do you know?

It is a relief map. The key shows a range of elevations;

different areas of the map are shown in different colors, depending on elevation.

CONTEXT CLUES: Details

Details in surrounding sentences often serve as clues that can help you figure out the meanings of new words. In the sentences below, look for details that show the meaning of the underlined word.

The Rockies were formed millions of years ago when there was a great __upheaval__ in the earth's crust. Hot, liquid rock inside the earth pushed the crust upward thousands of feet above sea level, forming the Rockies.

The meaning of *upheaval* in the first sentence is explained by details in the sentence that follows it.

▶ Circle the details below that help show the meaning of *obstacle*.

The Rockies were an __obstacle__ for settlers in the East who wanted to move to the West. The (difficulty) of crossing this (huge wall of mountains) (discouraged) the settlers.

As you read the selection, use details to figure out the meanings of the underlined words *avalanche*, *moderate*, and *eke*.

> ## Strategy Tip
>
> As you read "The Great Mountain Ranges of the World," study the elevation illustration and the relief map. Using them along with the text will help you to compare the elevations of various landforms.

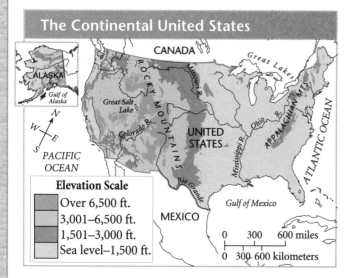

The Continental United States

ALASKA
Gulf of Alaska

CANADA

Great Lakes

ROCKY MOUNTAINS
Missouri R.
Great Salt Lake
Colorado R.

UNITED STATES

Ohio R.
Mississippi R.
APPALACHIAN MTS.

ATLANTIC OCEAN

PACIFIC OCEAN

Rio Grande

MEXICO

Gulf of Mexico

Elevation Scale
- Over 6,500 ft.
- 3,001–6,500 ft.
- 1,501–3,000 ft.
- Sea level–1,500 ft.

0   300   600 miles

0   300 600 kilometers

The Great Mountain Ranges of the World

DURING THE LONG HISTORY OF THE EARTH, the mighty forces of nature have been tirelessly at work. These natural forces have shaped the landscape of our world. Among nature's greatest works of art are mountains. Eight major mountain ranges crown the continents of Earth. To the people who live among them, these mountains are things of both beauty and danger.

The Rocky Mountains

The largest mountain range in North America is the Rocky Mountains. This range stretches for more than 3,000 miles (4,800 kilometers) from Canada's Yukon Territory to New Mexico. In places, the Rockies are 350 miles (560 kilometers) wide. The highest peak is Mount Elbert in Colorado. It rises 14,433 feet (4,399 meters) above sea level. (See elevation illustration below.)

The Rockies were formed millions of years ago when there was a great upheaval in the earth's crust. Hot, liquid rock inside the earth pushed the crust upward thousands of feet above sea level, forming the Rockies. Glaciers, wind, and rain have, over time, carved them into a variety of shapes and sizes. The Rockies form a huge, high wall. For this reason, they are called the **Continental Divide**. On one side of the Divide, rivers flow east toward the Gulf of Mexico and the Atlantic Ocean. On the other side, rivers flow west toward the Pacific.

The Rockies were an obstacle for settlers in the East who wanted to move to the West. The difficulty of crossing this huge wall of mountains discouraged the settlers. When the South Pass was discovered, however, wagons could cross the mountains more easily, opening the West to settlement.

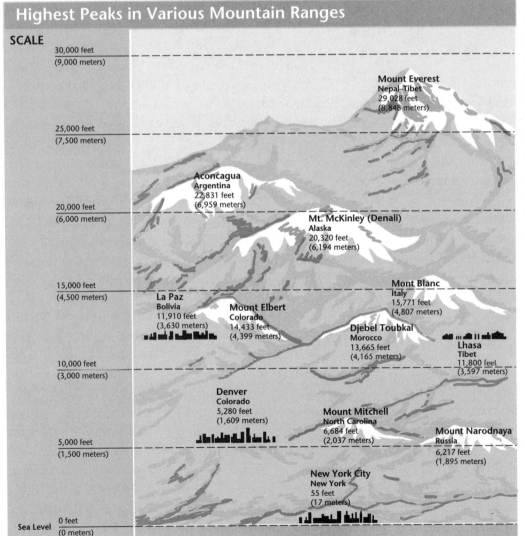

Highest Peaks in Various Mountain Ranges

SCALE

30,000 feet (9,000 meters)

Mount Everest
Nepal–Tibet
29,028 feet
(8,848 meters)

25,000 feet (7,500 meters)

Aconcagua
Argentina
22,831 feet
(6,959 meters)

20,000 feet (6,000 meters)

Mt. McKinley (Denali)
Alaska
20,320 feet
(6,194 meters)

15,000 feet (4,500 meters)

La Paz
Bolivia
11,910 feet
(3,630 meters)

Mount Elbert
Colorado
14,433 feet
(4,399 meters)

Mont Blanc
Italy
15,771 feet
(4,807 meters)

Djebel Toubkal
Morocco
13,665 feet
(4,165 meters)

Lhasa
Tibet
11,800 feet
(3,597 meters)

10,000 feet (3,000 meters)

Denver
Colorado
5,280 feet
(1,609 meters)

Mount Mitchell
North Carolina
6,684 feet
(2,037 meters)

Mount Narodnaya
Russia
6,217 feet
(1,895 meters)

5,000 feet (1,500 meters)

New York City
New York
55 feet
(17 meters)

Sea Level
0 feet
(0 meters)

The highest mountain in the world, Mount Everest, towers over the peaks of other ranges.

SOCIAL STUDIES

The Appalachian Mountains

The Appalachian (AP ə LAY chee ən) Mountains stretch through eastern North America from Quebec in the north to Alabama in the south. This mountain range is more than 1,500 miles (2,400 kilometers) long. The Appalachians are a relatively low range. Their highest point is Mount Mitchell in North Carolina, 6,684 feet (2,037 meters) above sea level. (See elevation illustration.)

The Appalachians also stood as a barrier to early pioneers as they tried to settle the continent. In the late 1700s, Daniel Boone led a group of settlers through the Cumberland Gap in Kentucky to open up for settlement the land west of the Appalachians.

Today hikers can walk 2,000 miles (3,200 kilometers) through the range on the Appalachian Trail. This trail is a marked footpath that stretches from Maine to Georgia, running mostly along the crest of the mountains.

The Alaskan Mountains

The Alaskan range includes the highest peak in North America, Mount McKinley, also called Denali (də NAHL ee). McKinley reaches a height of 20,320 feet (6,194 meters) above sea level. The Alaskan Mountains are truly Arctic mountains. Huge rivers of ice, called **glaciers** (GLAY shərz), move down their slopes and fill the valleys with great ice fields. The climate of the range is so threatening that some areas remain unmapped. The Alaskan mountains contain some of the most beautiful scenery in the world. Mount McKinley National Park is in the northern part of the range.

The Andes Mountains

The Andes form the longest mountain chain in the world. It stretches 4,500 miles (7,200 kilometers) from the northern tip to the southern tip of South America along its west coast. The highest peak is Aconcagua (ah kawn KAH gwah), which stands 22,831 feet (6,959 meters) above sea level. (See elevation illustration.)

The Andes were formed millions of years ago by a great uplift of the earth's crust. Many active volcanoes in the Andes can still spread disaster when they explode with fire and liquid rock.

The native people of South America live in many of the high regions of the Andes. Because of the altitude, the air is very thin. These native South Americans have adapted to their environment over the centuries. They have larger-than-average lungs to take in more air. They also have 20 percent more blood than a lowlander, which allows them to carry more oxygen to their body cells.

The Atlas Mountains

The Atlas range in northwest Africa is rich in legend and history. Ancient Greeks believed that the mountains were the home of a giant, or Titan, named Atlas. Atlas was thought to hold up the heavens on his mighty shoulders. For many centuries, the Atlas Mountains were a mystery because they were impossible to cross.

The people living in the Atlas range have always been proud and independent. The Berber people from the Atlas region swept across North Africa and Spain in the twelfth century. They created an empire that lasted a century. The French gained control of much of northern Africa in the late 1800s. The mountain people, however, resisted French control until the 1930s.

From the north, the Atlas range is especially beautiful. The mountains begin as foothills and then climb higher and higher on the horizon. The highest peak, Djebel Toubkal in Morocco, reaches 13,665 feet (4,165 meters). (See elevation illustration.)

The Alps

The Alps are the largest mountain range in Europe, extending from France across Switzerland, the Balken regions, Austria, and northern Italy. The highest peak is Mont Blanc, 15,771 feet (4,807 meters) above sea level. The beautiful peaks of the Alps are separated by deep valleys dotted with clear lakes.

Today alpine villages nestle under the towering mountains in scenes out of picture postcards. The beauty of the mountains can suddenly turn to terror, however. In winter and spring, an avalanche is a common occurrence. During an avalanche, tons of snow and ice suddenly break off the mountains and slide into the valleys below. The force of the snow can destroy everything in its path. To protect

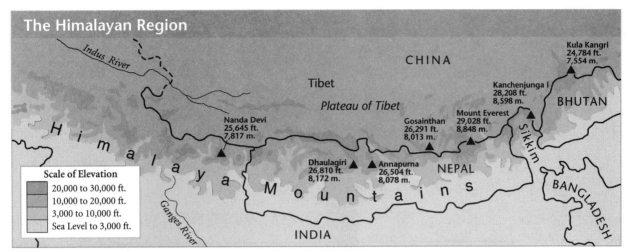

The Himalayan Region

Kula Kangri
24,784 ft.
7,554 m.

CHINA

Tibet

Plateau of Tibet

Kanchenjunga I
28,208 ft.
8,598 m.

BHUTAN

Indus River

Nanda Devi
25,645 ft.
7,817 m.

Gosainthan
26,291 ft.
8,013 m.

Mount Everest
29,028 ft.
8,848 m.

Sikkim

Himalaya Mountains

Scale of Elevation
20,000 to 30,000 ft.
10,000 to 20,000 ft.
3,000 to 10,000 ft.
Sea Level to 3,000 ft.

Dhaulagiri
26,810 ft.
8,172 m.

Annapurna
26,504 ft.
8,078 m.

NEPAL

BANGLADESH

Ganges River

INDIA

The Himalayas rise sharply from the plains of India and the Plateau of Tibet.

themselves, villagers plant trees and erect snow fences around their homes. Mountain roads are sheltered by snow sheds. Still, avalanches claim many lives every year in the Alps.

The Ural Mountains

The Ural Mountains stretch for about 1,500 miles (2,400 kilometers) through Russia and Kazakhstan. The Urals form a north-to-south line that is often considered the dividing point between Europe and Asia. Because the Urals are very old mountains that have been worn down by time, they are of only <u>moderate</u> height. Their rounded hills are generally low and rolling, with steeper slopes on the eastern side. In the north, they average 3,300 to 3,600 feet (1,000 to 1,100 meters) high. The highest point is Mount Narodnaya at 6,217 feet (1,895 meters) above sea level. (See elevation illustration.)

Much of the Ural range is covered by thick forests. Within the mountains are rich mineral deposits. As early as the 1500s, miners found salt, silver, and gold in the Urals. In the 1800s, the mountains became a famous source of gemstones. Takovaya emeralds are especially prized. During World War II, the Urals supplied the Soviet Union with such valuable resources as iron, copper, asbestos, and potash. Today the Ural range is a leading industrial region.

The Himalaya Mountains

The Himalayas are truly the giants of Earth. They form the highest mountain range in the world. Located in Asia, the Himalayas stretch across parts of Pakistan, Kashmir, India, Tibet, Nepal, Sikkim, and Bhutan. The Himalayas are also the world's youngest mountain range. They are still being pushed higher by earthquakes and other forces.

The Himalayas are a complex and beautiful group of mountains. There are many famous peaks in the range, but the most famous of all is Everest. Mount Everest is the highest mountain in the world. It reaches an altitude of 29,028 feet (8,848 meters). (See elevation illustration.)

The name *Himalaya* comes from the Sanskrit language and means "house of snow." For several different groups of people, the Himalayas are home. In some areas of the mountains, holy men of the Hindu and Buddhist religions live in mountain monasteries. In the Tibetan Himalayas, **nomadic** (noh MAD ik), or wandering, groups live as herders of yaks. Yaks provide them with wool, leather, milk, cheese, meat, and transportation. On the lower slopes of the Himalayas in Nepal, native Sherpas <u>eke</u> out a living as herders and farmers. They have a difficult time raising crops. The farmers cut terraces, like huge steps in the mountainside, to make room for the crops. Rice, wheat, corn, and lentils are the chief terrace crops. They also grow barley, jute, pepper, and tobacco. Sherpas are often among the climbers on Mount Everest.

All the great mountains of the world have now been conquered by mountaineers. Even Everest, the roof of the world, has been scaled many times.

Recognizing sequence of events
1. Describe what happened after a pass was discovered in the Rocky Mountains.

   Pioneers were then able to settle the land west of the

   Rockies.

Identifying main idea
2. Reread the paragraph with an ✗ next to it. Underline the sentence that states its main idea.

Comparing and contrasting
3. List one similarity between the Rocky Mountains and the Appalachian Mountains.

   Answers will vary. They are both in North America. They

   both slowed migration west.

Comparing and contrasting
4. List one similarity and one difference between the Berbers group and the Sherpa herders.

   Answers will vary. The Berbers and the Sherpas are

   both mountain people. The Berbers live in the Atlas

   Mountains, while the Sherpas live in the Himalayas.

Recalling details
5. Match each peak in the left column with its mountain range in the right column. Write the letter of the range on the line next to the mountain.

c	Aconcagua	a. Alps
d	Everest	b. Alaskan Mountains
a	Blanc	c. Andes
e	Elbert	d. Himalayas
b	McKinley	e. Rockies

Using context clues
6. Complete each sentence with the correct word below.

   avalanche   moderate   eke

   a. Actors without acting jobs often ___eke___ out livings as waiters.

   b. A(n) ___moderate___ amount of rainfall is neither very great nor very small.

   c. The mountain was closed to skiers because of a(n) ___avalanche___.

Inferring details
1. a. Which of the eight great mountain ranges is farthest north? The Alaskan Mountains are farthest north.

   b. How does its location affect its climate?

   It is an Arctic mountain range with glaciers and ice fields.

Making inferences
2. Explain why mountains no longer prevent travel as they used to do.

   Airplanes can cross over mountains easily. Also mountain roads and railroads have been built.

Inferring cause and effect
3. Many peoples living on mountains have lived the same way for hundreds of years. Give a reason why their lives might not have changed as much as those of other people.

   Answers will vary. The mountains are barriers that isolate them from the rest of civilization.

Inferring unstated main idea
4. Reread the paragraph with a ✔. Write a sentence stating its main idea.

   Answers will vary. Avalanches are a great danger to people living in the villages of the Alps.

A. Study the relief map of the Himalayas on page 105. Read the map key. Then answer the questions that follow.

1. How many elevation ranges are shown on this map? _____4_____

2. **a.** What is the highest elevation range shown? The highest elevation range is 20,000 to 30,000 feet.

   b. What is the lowest elevation range shown? The lowest elevation range is to 3,000 feet.

3. In which elevation range is Mount Everest? It is in the highest range (20,000 feet to 30,000 feet).

4. Which area has the higher elevation, the Tibetan plateau to the north of the Himalayas or the Indian plain to the south of the Himalayas? The Tibetan plateau has the higher elevation.

5. How many peaks shown are higher than 25,000 feet? _____6_____

B. Turn to the elevation illustration on page 103. Study the elevation scale and the mountain peaks. Then answer the questions that follow.

1. Which mountain shown has the lowest elevation? What is its elevation?

   Mount Narodnaya 6,217 feet (1,895 meters)

2. Which mountain has an approximate elevation of 20,000 feet (6,000 meters)?

   Mount McKinley

3. Which two mountains are close in elevation to Mount Elbert?

   Djebel Toubkal and Mont Blanc

4. What is the approximate difference of elevation between Mount Everest and Aconcagua?

   About 6,000 feet (1,800 meters)

5. Which city shown in the illustration is closest to sea level?

   New York City

6. Which city shown in the illustration has the highest elevation?

   La Paz

Reading-Writing Connection

Research facts about mountain ranges in or near your own state. On a separate sheet of paper, write a paragraph describing the highest peaks in the range, and explain how the mountains affect the climate and economy of surrounding areas.

Skill: Cause and Effect

For lesson support, see page. T90.

For ESL/ELL support, see highlighted words, page T90, and pages T28–T30.

BACKGROUND INFORMATION

"The Theory of Plate Tectonics" describes a scientific theory that explains why the continents and oceans have their present shapes. Scientists believe that the oceans and continents lie on giant slabs of rock called tectonic plates. These plates, scientists say, move between 1 and 5 centimeters (0.39 and 1.97 inches) each year. This movement causes earthquakes and volcanoes.

SKILL FOCUS: Cause and Effect

A **cause** is an event that makes something happen. An **effect** is what happens as a result of a cause. To find an effect, ask, "What happened?" To find a cause, ask, "Why did it happen?" The words *because*, *since*, *due to*, and *as a result* often signal cause-and-effect relationships.

Often a single cause has more than one effect.

Cause

Hot liquid rock erupts out of underwater volcanic mountains.

Effect 1

The eruption pushes the earth's plates apart.

Effect 2

The liquid rock cools and hardens into new crust.

Sometimes an effect can be the result of more than one cause.

Cause 1

Scientists observed that continents look as if they could fit together like a jigsaw puzzle.

Cause 2

Scientists observed similar rocks and fossils on continents that are now far apart.

Effect

Scientists created a theory that all the continents had once been joined together as one landmass.

▶ Read the following sentences. Circle the two effects. Underline the one cause.

When two tectonic plates pull apart, an earthquake can result. This movement can also cause volcanic eruptions.

CONTEXT CLUES: Antonyms

Antonyms are words with opposite meanings. As you read, you can sometimes find a nearby antonym to help you figure out the meaning of a new word.

In the following sentence, look for an antonym that can help you figure out the meaning of *debatable*.

*Although scientists are certain of the boundaries of the plates, the question of how the plates move is still **debatable**.*

If you do not know the meaning of *debatable*, the word *certain* can help you figure it out. *Debatable* and *certain* are antonyms. *Debatable* means "open to debate" or "not certain."

▶ Read the following sentences. Circle the antonym that helps you figure out the meaning of *segmented*.

*It begins with the idea that the crust of the earth is not continuous, but **segmented**. According to the theory, the earth is made up of seven major plates, or sections, and several smaller plates.*

In the selection, use antonyms to figure out the meanings of the underlined words *rifts*, *advocated*, and *gradually*.

Strategy Tip

As you read "The Theory of Plate Tectonics," look for cause-and-effect relationships. The maps and diagrams in the selection, along with the text, will help you recognize causes and effects.

The Theory of Plate Tectonics

A THEORY IS AN EXPLANATION of observed facts. Scientists base their theories on facts that have been observed or examined. Theories are always subject to change if new evidence is found that contradicts them. The most recent theory about the movement of the earth's crust is the theory of **plate tectonics** (tek TAHN iks). It begins with the idea that the crust of the earth is not continuous but segmented. According to the theory, the earth is made up of seven major plates, or sections, and several smaller plates. These plates make up the topmost, solid part of the earth. The topmost part of the earth is called the **lithosphere** (LITH ə sfir). It covers the floor of the oceans and all the continents.

The seven major lithospheric plates are the Pacific, the North American, the South American,

the Eurasian, the African, the Antarctic, and the Australian. The boundaries of the continents are not necessarily the same as the boundaries of the plates. For example, the eastern edge of North America and the western edge of Europe are not the boundaries of plates. The plates that these continents rest on extend into the Atlantic Ocean. These plates include part of the ocean floor. (See Figure 1.)

Two of the smaller plates are the Caribbean and the Arabian. The Arabian plate includes the Arabian Peninsula, the Red Sea, and the Persian Gulf. The Caribbean plate lies between North America and South America.

Although scientists are certain of the boundaries of the plates, the question of how the plates move is still debatable. Many scientists believe that the lithospheric plates float like rafts on the

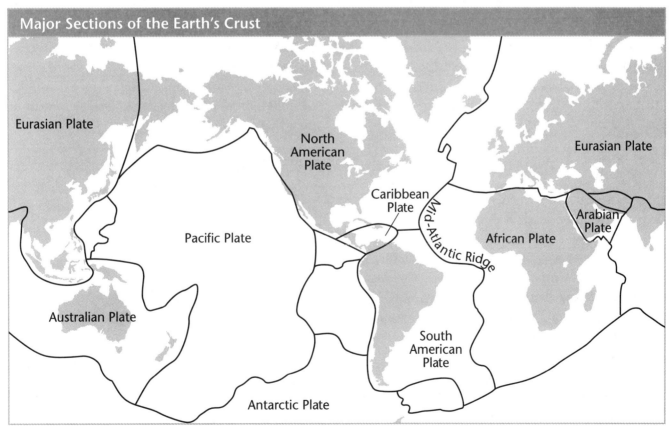

Major Sections of the Earth's Crust

Eurasian Plate

North American Plate

Eurasian Plate

Caribbean Plate

Pacific Plate

Mid-Atlantic Ridge

African Plate

Arabian Plate

Australian Plate

South American Plate

Antarctic Plate

FIGURE 1. **This map shows the seven major lithospheric plates and two smaller plates. The Mid-Atlantic Ridge is one of the midocean ridges.**

asthenosphere (as THEN ə sfir), the layer of the earth beneath them. The asthenosphere is made up of hot, liquid rock. The hot liquid and gases flow outward from the inner part of the asthenosphere. This flow of hot, liquid rock below the lithosphere causes the plates to move.

Ocean-Floor Spreading

Midocean ridges are large systems of underwater volcanic mountains. They are found in all the oceans. Deep <u>rifts</u> run through the center of these otherwise solid ridges. When hot, liquid rock flows up from the asthenosphere, it erupts, or explodes upward out of the rifts. This action pushes the plates apart. When the liquid rock, or lava, cools and hardens, new crust is formed. The eruption of lava from between plates can cause the opposite edges of the plates to be pushed down into the asthenosphere. (See Figure 2.) This process is called **ocean-floor spreading**. The theory of plate tectonics resulted in part from scientists' discovery of ocean-floor spreading.

In the 1950s, scientists discovered that rocks directly next to the midocean ridges on either side are younger than rocks farther away. The youngest rocks are in the center of the ridges. These differences in age convinced scientists that new ocean floor is being formed along the ridges. The creation of new ocean floor causes ocean-floor spreading.

Continental Drift

Ocean-floor spreading supports an earlier theory about the movement of the earth's crust. The theory of **continental drift** was first suggested in the early 1900s by a German scientist named Alfred Wegener. Wegener <u>advocated</u> this theory, although most other scientists of the time opposed it. Wegener believed that all the continents were once part of a single landmass. He named the landmass **Pangaea** (pan JEE ə). (See Figure 3.) The landmass broke into separate continents that <u>gradually</u> drifted apart. This did not happen suddenly, but over a long period of time. As a result, there are now seven continents. Most scientists today accept the theory of continental drift. Many scientists believe that the continents are still drifting.

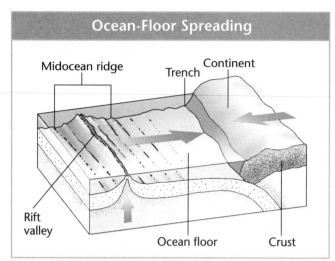

FIGURE 2. This diagram shows the process of ocean-floor spreading. This discovery, in part, brought about the theory of plate tectonics.

The theory of plate tectonics is of great interest to scientists today because it helps explain many natural events. For example, earthquakes can be caused by crustal plates sliding past each other, moving apart, or colliding. Volcanic activity and mountain building are also related to such movements. When the plates move apart, hot, liquid rock can erupt from the asthenosphere. As the rock cools and hardens, mountains or volcanoes can be formed.

The theory of plate tectonics also combines the ideas of continental drift and ocean-floor spreading.

The Theory of Continental Drift

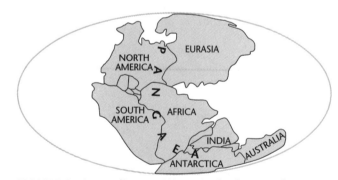

FIGURE 3. According to Wegener's theory, the continents of the Earth were once part of one large landmass, called Pangaea. This map shows how the continents may have been connected.

Recalling details
1. What is a theory?

A theory is an explanation of observed facts.

Recalling details
2. Define the term *lithosphere.*

It is the topmost, solid part of the earth.

Recalling details
3. How many major plates make up Earth's crust?

There are seven major plates.

Recalling details
4. Tell what the asthenosphere is made up of.

It is made of hot, liquid rock and gases.

Recalling details
5. What are midocean ridges?

They are large systems of underwater volcanic mountains.

Identifying cause and effect
6. What natural events can be explained by the movement of crustal plates?

Earthquakes, volcanic activity, and mountain building

can all be explained by the movement of plates.

Using context clues
7. Decide if each statement is true or false. Write *T* or *F* on the line.

___T___ a. Lightning hitting a wooded area could result in <u>rifts</u> in trees.

___F___ b. If you <u>advocated</u> building a new library, you would be against it.

___T___ c. A patient who <u>gradually</u> recovered from sickness is now healthy.

Making inferences
1. The fact that some of the continents look as if they could fit together like a jigsaw puzzle supports the idea that
   a. the continents were once of equal size.
   b. the continents can float on water.
   (c.) the continents were once joined together.
   d. the continents were once hit by meteors.

Making inferences
2. The hot, liquid rock and gases in the asthenosphere flow
   (a.) from a hot area to a cooler area.
   b. from a cold area to a warmer area.
   c. from a high area to a lower area.
   d. from a low-pressure area to a high-pressure area.

Making inferences
3. The volcanic mountains that make up the midocean ridges
   a. are made up of shells and coral.
   b. are made up of the skeletons of deep-sea fish.
   c. are made of dinosaur bones.
   (d.) are made up of lava from the asthenosphere.

Making inferences
4. Ocean-floor spreading does not cause the crustal plates to become larger because
   a. parts of them evaporate.
   (b.) parts of them are pushed down into the asthenosphere.
   c. parts of them burn up.
   d. parts of them become mountains.

1. Explain what process in the asthenosphere causes the movement of lithospheric plates.

   The flow of hot, liquid rock and gases outward from the inner part of the asthenosphere causes the

   movement of the lithospheric plates.

2. What causes the lithospheric plates to be pushed apart?

   The eruption of lava between plates causes the lithospheric plates to be pushed apart.

3. List one effect of scientists' discovery of ocean-floor spreading.

   Discovery of ocean-floor spreading led to the development of the theory of plate tectonics.

4. What was the effect of the breakup of Pangaea?

   The breakup of Pangaea caused the formation of seven continents.

5. Identify the three movements of crustal plates that can cause earthquakes.

   The three movements of crustal plates that can cause earthquakes are sliding past each other,

   moving apart, or colliding.

6. What effect can occur when crustal plates move apart?

   When the crustal plates move apart, they can cause the formation of mountains or volcanoes.

7. Underline two effects of ocean-floor spreading.

   a. heats up the asthenosphere
   b. pushes apart crustal plates
   c. pushes opposite edge of plates into asthenosphere
   d. causes movement of icebergs
   e. makes oceans deeper

Reading-Writing Connection

Research a particular geographic feature in your state. On a separate sheet of paper, write a paragraph explaining what caused the geographic feature and what effect it has on the land around it.

For ESL/ELL support, see highlighted words, page T91, and pages T28–T30.

Skill: Reading Percents

For lesson support, see page T91.

BACKGROUND INFORMATION

In "How to Read Percents," you will learn about percents, a very useful mathematical tool. You make use of percents all the time. When a store announces a 40 percent off sale, you might go shopping. When there is an 80 percent chance of rain, you might grab an umbrella. When unemployment rises to 8 percent, you know that jobs are getting harder to find. Knowing about percents helps you understand many different kinds of information.

SKILL FOCUS: Reading Percents

The symbol % stands for **percent**. The word *percent* refers to a certain number compared to 100. For example, 83% means 83 parts out of 100.

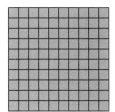

100%

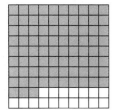

83%

Percents are very useful for comparing amounts. For example, you might read that 3 of every 7 mountains in the world are taller than 8,000 meters. You might also read that 5 of every 9 mountains are snow-covered during the summer. Comparing these two amounts is difficult, however. Which is more: 3 out of 7 or 5 out of 9?

Using percents makes the comparison easier. Another way to write 3 out of 7 is 43%. Another way to write 5 out of 9 is 56%. Comparing these percentages lets you see at a glance that the

number of snow-covered mountains is greater than the number of peaks over 8,000 meters.

▶ Each grid below has 100 squares. Fill in the first grid to represent 43%. Fill in the second grid to represent 56%.

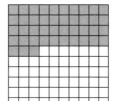

Shade in 43 squares.

Percentage of mountains over 8,000 meters

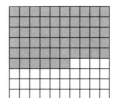

Shade in 56 squares.

Percentage of mountains snow-covered in summer

WORD CLUES

The word *percent* comes from two Latin words, *per centum*, meaning "per one hundred" or "for each hundred." Knowing the origin of *percent* will help you understand how to use percents.

When reading the selection, also look for the important words *fraction*, *decimal*, and *change*.

Strategy Tip

Note that "How to Read Percents" has four headings. The information under each heading will teach you how to carry out an important mathematical operation. Be sure that you understand how to do each operation before going on to the next section.

How to Read Percents

The word *percent* refers to a certain number compared to a hundred. Many facts about the mountain ranges of Earth can be stated using percentages. One is below.

Mountains cover about 20 percent of Earth's surface.

The statement above means that if the earth's surface were divided into 100 equal sections, mountains would cover about 20 of them.

The symbol % stands for percent. Twenty percent can be written as 20%. You can think of the percent symbol as two zeros separated by a one. These are the same digits that make up 100.

$$\% = 100$$

Because 20% means 20 out of 100, you can write the same value as the **fraction** $\frac{20}{100}$. Therefore, 20% and $\frac{20}{100}$ are the same. You can also write the fraction $\frac{20}{100}$ as a **decimal**. Because $\frac{20}{100}$ means 20 one-hundredths, you can write the same value as 0.20. Therefore, 20%, $\frac{20}{100}$, and 0.20 all express the same value.

What are three ways to explains the following percentage value?

North America makes up about 16 percent of the earth's land surface.

16 percent can be written as 16%.

$$16 \text{ out of } 100 = \frac{16}{100}$$

$\frac{16}{100}$ written as a decimal is 0.16.

$$16\% = \frac{16}{100} = 0.16$$

The number in the next example can also be stated as a percent, a fraction, or a decimal.

Approximately 75 percent of all active volcanoes lie in one area of the world.

$$75\% = \frac{75}{100} = 0.75$$

Changing a Percent to a Decimal

To **change** a percent to a decimal, move the decimal point *two places to the left*. Then remove the % sign.

$$92.6\% = 92.6\% = 0.926$$

Sometimes you have to put in one or more zeros.

$$3.7\% = 03.7\% = .037$$

Often a decimal point is not shown in the percent. You then have to put a decimal point at the end of the number and then move it two places to the left to make it a decimal.

$$27\% = 27.\% = 0.27$$
$$9\% = 09.\% = 0.09$$

Changing a Decimal to a Percent

To change a decimal to a percent, move the decimal point *two places to the right*. Then add the % sign.

$$.132 = .132 = 13.2\%$$

Sometimes you have to put in one or more zeros.

$$.7 = .70 = 70\%$$

Sometimes a decimal point is not shown.

$$3 = 3. = 3.00 = 300\%$$
$$17 = 17. = 17.00 = 1,700\%$$

Changing a Percent to a Fraction

To change a percent to a fraction, remove the percent sign to form the numerator, and add the denominator 100.

$$93\% = \frac{93}{100}$$

The numerator of the above fraction is 93. The denominator of all percent fractions is 100.

$$8\% = \frac{8}{100}$$
$$137\% = \frac{137}{100}$$
$$16\% = \frac{16}{100}$$

Changing a Fraction to a Percent

Two different types of fractions may be changed to a percent. If the denominator of the fraction is 100, just remove the denominator and add a percent sign.

$$\frac{29}{100} = 29\%$$
$$\frac{7}{100} = 7\%$$

If the denominator is not 100, it must first be changed to 100. You need to multiply the numerator and denominator by a number that will change the denominator to 100. For example, to change $\frac{3}{4}$ to a percent, multiply both the numerator and the denominator by 25 to change the fraction to $\frac{75}{100}$.

$$\frac{3}{4} \times \frac{25}{25} = \frac{75}{100} = 75\%$$

To change $\frac{1}{5}$ to a percent, do the following.

$$\frac{1}{5} \times \frac{20}{20} = \frac{20}{100} = 20\%$$

Study these four rules.

1. To change a percent to a decimal, move the decimal point two places to the *left*. Remove the % sign. Add a decimal point and zeros when they are needed.

2. To change a decimal to a percent, move the decimal point two places to the *right*. Add a percent sign and zeros when they are needed.

3. To change a percent to a fraction, first remove the percent sign. Then write the number over the denominator 100.

4. To change a fraction to a percent, remove the denominator if it is 100, and add a percent sign. If the denominator is not 100, multiply both the numerator and the denominator by a number that will change the denominator to 100. Then add a percent sign to the numerator.

COMPREHENSION

Recalling details
1. Define the word *percent*.

The word *percent* refers to a certain number

compared to 100.

Recalling details
2. Explain how to change a percent to a decimal.

To change a percent to a decimal, move the decimal

point two places to the left. Remove the % sign. Add a

decimal point and zeros when needed.

Recalling details
3. Explain how to change a percent to a fraction.

To change a percent to a fraction, remove the percent

sign. Write the number over the denominator 100.

Recalling details
4. Explain how to change a fraction to a percent.

If the denominator is 100, remove it and add a percent

sign. If the denominator is not 100, multiply the numerator

and the denominator by the same number so that the

denominator is 100. The numerator then becomes the

percent.

CRITICAL THINKING

Making inferences
1. Explain why moving the decimal point two places changes a percent to a decimal and a decimal to a percent.

Moving it two places multiplies or divides by 100.

Making inferences
2. Give two or three examples to show how percents might be used in ads.

Answers will vary. They are often used to show discounts, price reductions, or interest rates on loans and credit cards.

Making inferences
3. Explain why percents are used to score tests.

They compare scores to a perfect score of 100.

Making inferences
4. What part of something is 100% of it?

One hundred percent (100%) refers to all of something.

A. Fill in the blanks. The first one is done for you.

1. 15% = $\frac{15}{100}$ = .15

2. 13% = $\frac{13}{100}$ = .13

3. 137% = $\frac{137}{100}$ = 1.37

4. 36% = $\frac{36}{100}$ = .36

5. 8% = $\frac{8}{100}$ = .08

6. 34.7% = $\frac{34.7}{100}$ = .347

7. 1.1% = $\frac{1.1}{100}$ = .011

8. 3% = $\frac{3}{100}$ = .03

9. 75% = $\frac{75}{100}$ = .75

10. 50% = $\frac{50}{100}$ = .50 or .5

B. Change the percents to decimals and the decimals to percents.

1. 14% = .14

2. 73% = .73

3. 5% = .05

4. 100% = 1.00

5. 83.9% = .839

6. .16 = 16%

7. .84 = 84%

8. .03 = 3%

9. 1.04 = 104%

10. .752 = 75.2%

C. Change the fractions to percents and the percents to fractions.

1. $\frac{79}{100}$ = 79%

2. $\frac{7}{100}$ = 7%

3. $\frac{3.7}{100}$ = 3.7%

4. $\frac{1}{4}$ = 25%

5. $\frac{3}{5}$ = 60%

6. 67% = $\frac{67}{100}$

7. 29% = $\frac{29}{100}$

8. 2% = $\frac{2}{100}$

9. 125% = $\frac{125}{100}$

10. 43% = $\frac{43}{100}$

D. Write the percent, fraction, and decimal for the following amounts.

1. twenty-five and nine tenths percent $25.9\% = \frac{25.9}{100} = .259$

2. eight twenty-fifths $\frac{8}{25} = \frac{32}{100} = 32\% = .32$

3. twelve tenths $\frac{12}{10} = \frac{120}{100} = 120\% = 1.2$

4. forty-two hundredths $\frac{42}{100} = 42\% = .42$

Reading-Writing Connection

Where do you read percents in your daily life? On a separate sheet of paper, describe three places where you have seen numbers written as percents recently.

Skill: Evaluating Opinions

For lesson support, see page T92.

What is the difference between a fact and an opinion? A **fact** is a statement that can be checked and proven. An **opinion** is a statement that tells how someone feels or what someone thinks about something. Some opinions may be more valid, or reliable, than others because they have one or more facts to back them up. When you find an opinion in your reading, decide how valid it is.

Read the following selection.

The Sierra Nevada

The Sierra Nevada is a huge mountain range in eastern California. *Sierra Nevada* means "snowy, saw-toothed mountain" in Spanish. The Sierra Nevada is the site of three national parks—Yosemite, Sequoia, and Kings Canyon—and beautiful Lake Tahoe. Donner Memorial State Park, a historic landmark, is also in this mountain range.

The Sierra Nevada is like a granite wall extending north and south for 430 miles (692 kilometers) through California. It is about 70 miles (110 kilometers) wide. At one time, the earth's crust lifted and tilted to the west to make a long, gentle slope on the mountain's western side and a steep slope on its eastern side. The highest point of the Sierra Nevada is Mount Whitney. Its elevation, or height, is 14,494 feet (4,418 meters). In fact, Mount Whitney is the second-highest point in the United States. Several other peaks of the Sierra Nevada are almost as high as Mount Whitney.

Many rivers, such as the Feather, American, and San Joaquin, flow in the Sierra Nevada. Rushing mountain waters have cut deep canyons in the long western slope of the mountain range. Yosemite Valley is the most outstanding of these canyons. Yosemite was originally cut by streams. Later, glaciers moved down the valley, eroding it further. The glaciers created the Sierra Nevada's granite cliffs and impressive landscapes. On the shorter, steeper eastern slope, many creeks descend and join the Owens, Walker, Carson, and Truckee rivers. The cliffs, meadows, evergreen forests, lakes, and waterfalls make the Sierra Nevada a beautiful mountain range.

In the Sierra Nevada, rainfall increases as elevation increases. This is true up to about 4,500 feet (1,350 meters). From there to the top, the rain decreases. In a typical winter, 30 to 40 feet (9 to 12 meters) of snow accumulates at Lake Tahoe and Donner Pass, but as much as 60 feet (18 meters) of snow can fall in some years. It is no wonder that skiers are attracted to this region.

A variety of vegetation grows on the Sierra Nevada at different elevations. Shrubs and grasses grow near the Sacramento and San Joaquin valleys at the western base of the Sierra Nevada. From 3,000 to 4,000 feet (900 to 1,200 meters) are forests of yellow pine, sugar pine, cedar, and fir. These trees are a valuable source of timber. Within the forest are sequoia trees, the largest plants on Earth. At 6,000 to 7,000 feet (1,800 to 2,150 meters), lodgepole pine, Jeffrey pine, and red fir grow. Above the timberline is rocky land that is barren except for scattered evergreens. The rivers of the western slope of the mountain range supply water for irrigation. The farms in the Sacramento and San Joaquin valleys and the Tulare Basin receive this water. The largest cities in California receive their water supply from these rivers, too. Hydroelectric plants on the rivers generate the power for farmlands and cities.

The Sierra Nevada forms a barrier to east-west travel. However, cars, trucks, and buses can cross the mountains through several passes. Major highways use six passes, each at a different elevation. A road at 9,625 feet (2,935 meters) over Tioga Pass connects Yosemite Valley and Mono Lake. Unfortunately this road is usually closed nine months of the year because of snow. Railroads also travel over the Sierra Nevada. Hikers and pack trains, or groups of mules, use the various trails to cross the mountain range.

The gold rush of 1849 began when gold was discovered in the Sierra Nevada. This attracted many people to the foothill region in the mid-1800s.

Mining of gold and other metals is no longer important, however. Now tourism is the area's chief industry. All kinds of camping and recreational facilities are located throughout the Sierra Nevada for people who enjoy summer or winter sports. Other industries in the region are fruit-growing, lumbering, and grazing.

Read the opinions about the Sierra Nevada in the left column. Then select none, one, or two of the facts in the right column that support each opinion. Write the letter of each supporting fact on the line. Write *none* if the opinion has no supporting facts.

Opinions

1. _d, f_ The Sierra Nevada is a huge mountain range.

2. _none_ Lake Tahoe is one of the most beautiful lakes in the world.

3. _h_ Yosemite Valley is the most outstanding canyon in the United States.

4. _b, l_ The Sierra Nevada is a beautiful mountain range.

5. _a, g_ The best skiing in the West is in the Sierra Nevada.

6. _c, k_ No forests can offer as large a selection of timber as those of the Sierra Nevada.

7. _none_ Visitors to California should spend their time seeing the Sierra Nevada rather than Disneyland.

8. _none_ Some of the best fruit in the United States is grown in the Sierra Nevada.

9. _e, j_ If not for the rivers of the Sierra Nevada, California would be without water.

10. _i_ Mount Whitney seems very high.

Facts

a. Each year, the Sierra Nevada receives 30 to 40 feet (9 to 12 meters) of snow.

b. The range has meadows, cliffs, and forests.

c. At 4,000 feet (1,200 meters) is yellow pine, sugar pine, cedar, and fir.

d. The Sierra Nevada is over 400 miles (640 kilometers) long.

e. Rivers on the western slope supply California's largest cities with water.

f. The Sierra Nevada is about 70 miles (110 kilometers) wide.

g. Some winters, 60 feet (18 meters) of snow falls.

h. Glaciers moved down the Yosemite Valley and created cliffs and impressive landscapes.

i. The peak of Mount Whitney is 14,494 feet (4,418 meters) high.

j. Rivers on the western slope irrigate farmlands.

k. At 7,000 feet (2,150 meters) is lodgepole pine, Jeffrey pine, and red fir.

l. The range has waterfalls, such as those in Yosemite Valley.

Skill: Improving Reading Rate

For lesson support, see page T92.

People have so much to read today that the ability to read quickly has become important. The typical reader of a century ago had fewer books, newspapers, and magazines to read. For this reason, you may read more in a week than your great-grandparents did. Having a rapid **reading rate** helps you to read more in a short period of time. However, it is always important to keep in mind that to read material without understanding it is a waste of time, no matter what the speed.

A rapid rate of reading has no particular value in itself. A good reader is able to read at several speeds, depending on the type of material being read. When reading materials are difficult or unfamiliar, a good reader reads more slowly. For example, social studies, science, and mathematics may be more difficult to read than literature. Therefore, these materials are read more slowly. Even literature can be difficult. Sometimes a reader needs to slow down when words or sentences are difficult or unfamiliar, or reread a paragraph to understand a complex idea. A good reader also stops to read diagrams and maps. This requires increased attention, making a slower reading rate necessary.

The best way to increase your reading rate is to get rid of bad reading habits. If you have any of the habits below, practice these suggestions for overcoming them.

Lip moving	Hold your finger over your lips, or hold a piece of paper between your lips.
Finger pointing	Hold your book with both hands, one on each side of the book.
Head moving	Rest your chin in the palm of one hand and hold it still.
Reading one word at a time	Work hard at trying to take in several words at each glance.

The following paragraph is marked off into word groups. See if you can read it by taking in each group of words in one glance.

Bertela lives / on an island / that belongs / to Denmark. / There are / beech trees / in the woods / near her home. / Every fall / she gathers beech nuts / in these woods. / The squirrels gather / the nuts, too. / The nuts are so plentiful / that there are / enough of them / for both Bertela / and the squirrels.

On the next page is a selection that can be used in checking your reading rate. Use a watch or a clock with a second hand to time yourself. Start right on a minute, such as four minutes past ten o'clock. Write your starting time at the beginning of the selection. Then read the selection. Write your ending time at the end of the selection.

At the top of the hill, the three riders reined their horses to a stop. They wore blue coats, tan trousers, high boots, and three-cornered hats. The tallest of the riders lifted a pair of field glasses to his eyes and looked out over the fields and woods.

"Tell us, General Washington, what do you see? British soldiers? Campfires?" asked one of the riders.

Washington smiled. "Remember, Lafayette, it will take the British a few days to reach this area from the Delaware River."

Lafayette looked disappointed. Then General Greene, the third rider, spoke. "General Washington, we have ridden all over this land today, and we still have not found a good place for battle against the British."

"True enough," Washington sighed.

Greene looked up at the darkening sky. "Look, sir, it's going to storm."

The three riders started toward a field below them. Black clouds raced across the sky. It began to thunder.

"There's a house ahead!" shouted Lafayette. "Let's stop there."

"Yes, hurry!" Washington led the dash to the farmhouse.

Just as the riders reached the barn near the house, the rain came pouring down. They got off their horses and looked around. A farmer was staring at them. "Why, it's General George Washington. Here on my farm! General, sir, welcome. Come into my house and have some food. My son, Tom, will look after your horses. Our name is Small."

Washington smiled and went into the house with the farmer. Lafayette followed the general. Greene stayed with the horses. He was worried. Suppose these were friends of the British. The boy might hide their horses, and they would be trapped. Finally, however, he decided to follow the others.

Inside the warm house, Washington sat at the table, talking with the farmer. Lafayette was pacing from window to window. Washington looked out the window and said, "Mr. Small, I see this storm will last for hours. I wonder if you would let us stay the night?"

Both Lafayette and Greene looked worried. Greene whispered to the general, "Sir, we can't stay. We don't know if these people are friends or enemies. We might be in British hands by morning!"

Washington said coldly, "We will stay."

Dinner was good, and even Greene enjoyed it. For a while, he felt at ease and almost forgot his fears. Lafayette also seemed to relax and was talking happily. When they went upstairs, however, all of Greene's fears returned. Without undressing, he lay on top of the bed with his eyes open. He jumped up with each new sound.

Just before sunrise, Greene heard a horse whinny and a dog bark. Silently he went downstairs and out to the barn. The horses seemed safe. He put his hand on his gray horse.

"Don't do it, sir." A low voice cut the darkness.

"Who's there?" Greene whirled around.

"Me! Tom Small! Don't run away. The general needs you."

"Run away? What do you mean?" asked Greene.

Tom looked at his feet. "I've been standing watch because I was afraid you were going to slip away with your horse."

"Fool!" shouted Greene. "You think me a traitor?"

Tom looked uneasy. "Well, you acted so strange, sir. I just thought....There have been lots of deserters—traitors, too."

Suddenly Greene laughed. "Tom, we're a pair! We both were worried about the same thing. I came down here because I heard some noise and thought the British had trapped us."

Two hours later, at breakfast, Washington looked at Greene and said, "You look like you didn't sleep all night. What's wrong?"

Greene winked at Tom. "Nothing, sir. Tom and I just stood watch all night."

Washington looked from one to the other but said nothing. Later, after they had left the Smalls', they stopped to rest. Washington broke the silence. "You know, you were right. I did take a risk last night. I was quite wrong."

Greene could only nod. But Lafayette held out his hand to Washington. "Ah, my general, only a great man will say, 'I was wrong.'"

Ending time: _____

To find the total time that it took to read the selection, do the following:

1. Subtract your beginning time from your ending time.

2. Divide the number of words in the selection by your reading time expressed in seconds. For example, if it took you 3 minutes and 5 seconds (3 × 60 + 5 = 185 seconds) to read the selection, you would have read 3.7 words per second (692 ÷ 185 = 3.7).

3. To find the number of words per minute (WPM), multiply your rate per second (WPS) by 60. Your answer would be 222 WPM.

Words in selection: 692

	Hr.	Min.	Sec.
Ending time:	_____	_____	_____
Starting time:	_____	_____	_____
Total time:	_____	_____	_____

No. seconds (min. × 60 + sec.): _____

Rate (sec.): 692 ÷ _____ sec. = _____ WPS

Rate (min.): _____ WPS × 60 = _____ WPM

Circle the letter next to the correct answer to each question.

1. Where do the three riders stop the first time?
   a. at a farmhouse
   b. under a tree
   (c.) at the top of a hill
   d. on a battlefield

2. Who looks through the field glasses?
   a. General Greene
   (b.) General Washington
   c. Lafayette
   d. Tom Small

3. How do you know that Greene does not sleep very much at the Smalls'?
   a. He doesn't undress.
   b. He sits on the bed.
   (c.) He keeps his eyes open.
   d. He hears a dog bark.

4. Who looks after the riders' horses?
   a. General Greene
   b. General Washington
   c. the farmer
   (d.) Tom Small

5. Why is Lafayette pacing from window to window?
   a. He is hungry.
   b. He is afraid of thunder.
   (c.) He is worried about the British.
   d. He wants to go home.

6. What does Tom mean when he says, "There have been lots of deserters"?
   a. Many American soldiers stole horses.
   b. Many farmers hid American soldiers.
   (c.) Many American soldiers ran away.
   d. Many American soldiers were spies.

LESSON 39

Skill: Taking Notes

For ESL/ELL support, see page T93.

For lesson support, see page T93.

When reading new information that you need to remember, it is a good idea to take notes. **Taking notes** will help you remember the information as you read it. Taking notes is especially helpful in recording the information from several references before writing a report.

It is not necessary to remember every minor detail you read. When taking notes, write down only the important information, especially main ideas and major supporting details. Following are some suggestions to help you take notes.

1. Find the main idea of each paragraph, and include it in your notes.

2. Look for major details that answer such questions as *who, what, where, when, why,* and *how.* Write these details under the main ideas. Leave out minor details, or information that is not needed.

3. Arrange your notes in the same order in which the information appears in the selection. Group each main idea and its supporting details together.

4. Label your notes by writing the subject at the top of the page. Write your notes in your own words. Do not copy entire sentences, but do write down key words and phrases. Be brief so that you can read your notes quickly.

The following selection is written in chronological order, the order in which the events take place. Using the space provided on page 123, take notes as you read the selection. Make sure your notes show the correct sequence of the visits of the Spanish explorers to the New World.

Explorations to the New World

Columbus's voyages to the New World led the way to further exploration of North and South America. By the Treaty of Tordesillas, Spain claimed the right to most of the New World. Early Spanish explorers heard stories of wealthy kingdoms in the Americas. Such reports encouraged new expeditions. Until 1519, Spanish control of the New World was limited to small settlements in the West Indies. With the many Spanish expeditions that followed Columbus's, Spain gradually gained control of most of South and Central America and parts of North America.

Hernando Cortés

In 1519, Hernando Cortés, a clever fighter and skillful leader, landed on the coast of Mexico in search of gold. He soon heard about the powerful Aztec Empire that demanded huge payments from the people it conquered. Cortés sought out the support of the many native groups who hated their Aztec rulers. He marched his small army of about 400 soldiers and 16 horses into the crowded Aztec capital of Tenochtitlán, where he confronted the Aztec ruler, Montezuma.

After months of negotiations, Montezuma agreed to become a subject of the Spanish king. In 1520, the Aztecs revolted against the Spanish. Cortés and his army barely escaped with their lives. However, with the help of his allies, Cortés surrounded Tenochtitlán. In 1521, he attacked and destroyed the Aztec capital. Within a few years, the Aztec Empire crumbled.

Francisco Pizarro

Nine years later, in 1530, Francisco Pizarro, another Spanish explorer, received permission to explore the Inca Empire, located in what is now Peru. With 180 metal-clad soldiers—less than half of Cortés's force—Pizarro marched into the Inca kingdom. Luck was with him. When he arrived, the Incas were caught up in a civil war.

Pizarro launched a surprise attack, imprisoned the Inca leader, Atahualpa, and killed most of his attendants. The attack stunned the Incas, weakening their resistance to the Spanish. By 1535, Pizarro had captured Cuzco, the Inca capital, and crushed nearly all opposition.

Francisco Coronado

In 1540, Francisco Coronado led an expedition in search of the "seven cities of gold" reportedly nestled in the hills of what is now New Mexico. For about two years, Coronado, along with many Spanish soldiers, searched in vain for these cities of gold, which did not really exist. In the process, he explored much of what would become the southwestern United States. One of his lieutenants was the first European to see the Grand Canyon.

Hernando de Soto

While Coronado was looking for gold in the West, Hernando de Soto led another gold-hunting expedition into what would become the southeastern United States. From 1539 to 1542, his army wandered as far north as the Carolinas and as far west as present-day Oklahoma. When de Soto died, the expedition returned without having found any large supplies of gold. Even before de Soto's death, the Spanish had begun to concentrate on settling the area to the south, in what is now Mexico, the Caribbean, and South America.

Answers will vary.   Notes on Early Exploration

_____
_____
_____
_____
_____
_____
_____
_____

Taking notes can help you remember and review what you have read. Use the information from your notes to complete the chart. The name of the first explorer has been provided.

Explorer	Areas Explored	Dates	Importance
Cortés	Mexico	1519–1521	He defeated the Aztecs.
Pizarro	Peru	1530–1535	He defeated the Incas.
Coronado	southwestern United States	1540–1542	He explored much of what is now the southwestern United States.
de Soto	southeastern United States	1539–1542	He explored what is now the southeastern United States, from the Carolinas to Oklahoma.

For ESL/ELL support, see page T93.

Skill: Reading a Road Map

For lesson support, see page T93.

It is a good idea to have a **road map** in your car at all times. A road map shows how to get from one place to another by car and how far it is between places. It also shows the location of points of interest.

Look at the road map below. It shows the Great Smoky Mountains National Park and some of the surrounding areas.

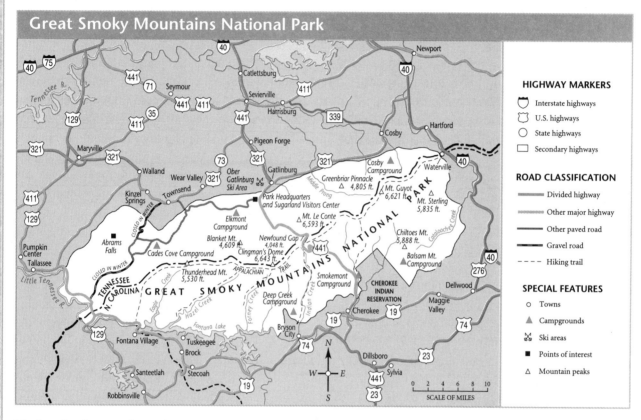

Great Smoky Mountains National Park

Notice the **key** to the right of the map. A key explains the symbols used on a map. The **scale of miles** in the lower-right corner of the map helps you figure out the distance from one place to another. The **road classification** symbols identify different kinds of roads. **Special symbols** also mark such features as towns, campgrounds, ski areas, and other points of interest. Maps usually include a direction symbol known as a **compass rose**. The compass rose indicates north, south, east, and west with the abbreviations N, S, E, and W. Notice the compass rose at the bottom of this map.

A. Read the definitions in the left column. Then read the words in the right column. On the line next to each definition, write the correct word.

1. _____key_____ explains map symbols   **a.** scale of miles

2. _____compass rose_____ indicates directions   **b.** road classification

3. _____scale of miles_____ shows distance from one place to another   **c.** key

4. _____road classification_____ identifies different kinds of roads   **d.** special symbols

5. _____special symbols_____ show campgrounds, ski areas, mountain peaks   **e.** compass rose

B. Decide if each of the following questions can be answered using the map on the opposite page. Write *yes* if you can find the answer on the map. Write *no* if the map cannot provide the answer to the question.

____yes____ 1. Are there hiking trails in Great Smoky Mountains National Park?

____yes____ 2. What towns are south of the park?

____no____ 3. How long does it take to drive through the park?

____yes____ 4. Are there campgrounds inside the park itself?

____no____ 5. Are there hotels and motels near the park?

____no____ 6. Which roads are closed in the winter?

____yes____ 7. Which rivers run through the park?

____yes____ 8. How high is Newfound Gap?

____no____ 9. How many miles is it from the park to New York City?

____yes____ 10. How can you get from Gatlinburg to the Cherokee Indian Reservation?

C. Circle the letter next to the phrase that correctly completes each sentence.

1. The Great Smoky Mountains National Park is in the states of
   a. North Carolina and South Carolina.
   b. Tennessee and North Carolina.
   c. Tennessee and Kentucky.
   d. Kentucky and North Carolina.

2. If you travel south through the park from Gatlinburg, you will first reach
   a. Park Headquarters and Sugarland Visitors Center.
   b. Newfound Gap.
   c. Smokemont Campground.
   d. Pigeon Forge.

3. To get from Gatlinburg to Cosby, you can travel on
   a. US 441.   b. Route 339.   c. Route 73.   **d.** US 321.

4. The interstate highway that is closest to the park is
   a. Interstate 82.   b. Interstate 75.   **c.** Interstate 40.   d. Interstate 80.

5. The highest point in Great Smoky Mountains Park is
   a. Newfound Gap.   **b.** Clingman's Dome.
   c. Mt. Le Conte.   d. Thunderhead Mountain.

6. A large body of water on the southern border of the park is called
   a. Rainbow Falls.   **b.** Fontana Lake.   c. Forney Creek.   d. Eagle Creek.

unit five

For ESL/ELL support, see highlighted words, page T94, and pages T28–T30.

The Struggle to Win

LESSON 41

Skill: Conflict and Resolution

For lesson support, see page T94.

BACKGROUND INFORMATION

"The Campaign for Kate" is a play about a young woman who must decide whether or not to devote herself totally to swimming in order to make the U.S. Olympic team. Training for the Olympics takes time, energy, and total commitment. Many young competitors begin training as early as age five. They practice their sport many hours daily and often give up other activities they enjoy to achieve their dreams.

SKILL FOCUS: Conflict and Resolution

The main character of a story usually has a goal or faces a problem. The struggle to achieve this goal or to solve this problem is called **conflict**.

Story characters face three main types of conflict.

1. A character may have a **conflict with self**. Such a character struggles with feelings within himself or herself. This struggle is called an **internal conflict**. An example is a person overcoming a fear of water after nearly drowning.

2. A character may have a **conflict with another character**. For example, two story characters may have an argument or compete against each other in a race. This type of struggle is called an **external conflict**.

3. In some stories, there is a **conflict with an outside force**. A character may struggle against nature or society. An example is a firefighter trying to save people inside a burning house. This type of struggle is also called an **external conflict**.

By the end of a story, the main character succeeds or fails at solving the problem or achieving the goal that is causing the conflict. The way a conflict is settled is called the story's **resolution**.

▶ Read each conflict on the chart at the top of the next column. Write which of the three types of conflict each character faces.

Character's Problem	Type of Conflict
Tai's mother wants her to go to college, but Tai wants to get a job instead.	conflict with another character
Carlo wants to ask Anita to the prom, but he feels too shy.	conflict with self
The apple trees in Hannah's orchard are dying from a strange new disease.	conflict with an outside force

CONTEXT CLUES: Using a Dictionary

Sometimes there are no clues to help you figure out a new word's meaning. To understand some new words, look them up in a dictionary.

Think about the underlined word in this sentence.

*Besides, my eyes are always red from the **chlorine** in the pool.*

You can tell from the context that *chlorine* is something in the pool. However, there are not enough clues to help you figure out exactly what chlorine is.

▶ Read the following sentence. Look up the underlined word in a dictionary, and write its definition on the lines.

*And for what—so I can someday say I'm a great swimmer in the **butterfly** event?*

a swimming stroke done with the face down; the arms are stretched out and then brought forward and down in a circular motion

In the play, use a dictionary to find the meanings of the underlined words *clamber*, *priority*, and *fatigue*.

> ### Strategy Tip
> As you read "The Campaign for Kate," think about the conflict the main character faces as she tries to achieve her goals.

The Campaign for Kate

Cast

Kate Fenton, member of a swim team
Maria Cortez, member of a swim team
Mr. Meacham, coach of the swim team

Scene 1

Late in the afternoon at the Hillside High School pool. Mr. Meacham stands at the edge of the pool, stopwatch in hand. When Mr. Meacham speaks, the team stops doing laps. Everyone leaves the pool but Kate and Maria, who hang on to the edge and talk.

Mr. Meacham *(loudly)*: All right, team, that's enough for today. I'll see you all tomorrow, bright and early. Remember, be here no later than 6:30 A.M.

Kate *(to Maria)*: He'll see me, but I won't see him. I'll be swimming, but I'll probably nap through my first four laps! I don't know if I can keep this up.

Maria: Mr. Meacham says it's important to work out every day for several hours, especially with the all-county meet coming up on Saturday.

Kate: Well, I'm beginning to get tired of this stuff. Besides, my eyes are always red from the chlorine in the pool. It doesn't do my hair any good, either. Furthermore, practicing five hours a day doesn't leave me time or energy for anything else. All this so I can someday say I'm a great swimmer in the butterfly event?

Maria: I know. I'm tired, too, but now I take Mr. Meacham's advice and go to bed an hour earlier. Maybe you should try that.

Kate: Agh! I go to bed early as it is. I need some time to myself, to do other things. If I go to bed any earlier, I'll sleep away my whole life. You know, I used to love swimming. I had dreams *(pause)* … dreams of becoming an Olympic champion. Now it's more like a nightmare than a dream.

Maria: I heard Mr. Meacham say you have the talent to make the Olympic team someday.

Kate: He did—but I keep wondering if I can throw myself into swimming and train the way he wants me to. I don't know if I'm ready to give up everything just to try for it.

Maria: Here comes Mr. Meacham. We'd better talk about this later.

Mr. Meacham *(very enthusiastic)*: Good workout, Maria. Your time is improving. *(turns toward Kate, showing concern)* Kate, you've just got to think about your kick as you finish each lap. It's cutting down your speed. You could lose a race that way. Tomorrow morning we'll work on it. I think you're either daydreaming or not getting enough sleep.

Kate: I'll be all right, Mr. Meacham.

Mr. Meacham: Well, you'd better hit the showers and then go home to hit the books. I want my team to get decent grades, too!

Kate and Maria clamber out of the pool and head for the showers.

Kate *(takes off her swimming cap):* By the way, some of the kids want me to run for the student senate. What do you think?

Maria *(throws a towel over her shoulders):* It sounds great, but do you have the time? Mr. Meacham says swimming has top priority.

Kate: I'll just have to make the time. Anyway, Maria, you take Mr. Meacham too seriously. Just because you want to be a swim coach someday.

Maria: I have to work harder than you, Kate! *(getting angry)* You have a natural talent that I could never match. I'll be glad if I can be a coach someday.... You can set your sights even higher. I get angry when you won't!

Kate: Okay! Okay! Sorry. Friends?

Maria *(pause):* Friends.

Scene 2

Saturday. Kate and Maria sit on a bench in the locker room before the swim meet begins.

Maria *(concerned):* You look tired, Kate.

Kate *(fatigue shows in her voice):* I'm beat. I was at a campaign meeting until 11:00 last night. We were painting posters and writing slogans. How does this one sound? "Get in the swim—vote for Kate!"

Maria: Sounds great! Now let's get in the swim ourselves. Let's go out there so you can beat me and everyone else without even trying, as usual!

Kate and Maria rise and walk toward the locker room doors.

Scene 3

Maria and Kate cling to the edge of the pool after the race.

Kate *(despite her disappointment):* Congratulations, Maria! First place, and your best time ever! You even beat my best time!

Maria *(happy and relieved):* I can hardly believe it myself, beating you and everyone else in the pool! I've never done that before!

Kate: You deserve it. You work hard, Maria.

Mr. Meacham *(walks toward Maria and Kate):* Maria! That was great! Congratulations! *(turns to Kate and becomes very serious)* Now, Kate, I want to talk to you. You've got to work on your kick as you make the turn.

Kate *(raises her voice; becomes angry):* Mr. Meacham, can't you leave me alone? I hate my kick! I hate this pool! I'm not meant for this. I'll never be an Olympic athlete! I can't even win a high school race! *(gets out of the pool and walks over to the starter's table)*

Mr. Meacham *(follows Kate):* You certainly won't make the Olympic team with that attitude.

Kate: Well, you saw today that I haven't got what it takes.

Mr. Meacham *(very calmly):* All I saw today was a swimmer who wasn't concentrating. Kate, you have a natural talent. It's far greater than that of any other member of the team. Maria knows it. Today was a lucky break for her. It may not come again. Maria knows her best shot is to study to be a coach. However, you could be a star if you work to develop your talent.

Kate: I don't know if I can work that hard at swimming. You said it was important to be well-rounded. Some kids want me to run for a place as representative in the student government. On a day like today, that sounds like a good idea. Why shouldn't I do it?

Mr. Meacham (*very patiently*): For most kids, it would be a great idea. However, your talent is special, Kate. You shouldn't give up your chance at an Olympic medal someday by trying to do too many other things at the same time. (*pause*) I have an idea. You continue to come to practice, but don't compete for the next three weeks. Run for the student senate. However, you must make up your mind by the end of the three weeks. If you decide to swim in the meet on the fourteenth, you've committed yourself to swimming. If you don't race on the fourteenth, you're off the team.

Kate: Okay. (*walks slowly toward the locker room*) I can accept that.

Scene 4

The following week. Kate and Maria chat in the pool.

Maria: Did you hear, Kate? I won again yesterday! Our whole team won.

Kate: I heard! I heard! Mr. Meacham must be pleased.

Maria: Oh, sure, but he misses you. I even miss swimming four strokes behind you!

Kate: Maria, you put yourself down too much. You work hard. You deserve to win.

Maria: Speaking of winning, how is your campaign coming?

Kate: I have until the fourteenth to officially begin my campaign.

Maria: That's the day of the next race!

Kate: I know. I know.

Kate and Maria swim to the end of the pool to start their laps.

Scene 5

The fourteenth. Hillside High School pool, less than 20 minutes before the swim meet. Kate is nowhere in sight.

Mr. Meacham: Maria, have you seen Kate? Is she coming?

Maria (*sits on the bench near the locker room door*): I don't know. Last night on the phone she said something about showing us her new campaign posters.

Mr. Meacham (*his disappointment is obvious*): Then she's decided.

Kate (*bursts into the pool area*): I thought you'd like to take a look at these. Here's one for you, coach. (*Mr. Meacham slowly takes the poster from Kate*) Here's one for you, Maria.

Maria (*eagerly reads*): "Get in the swim with Kate— and vote for someone else!"

Mr. Meacham: Great, Kate! Let's get ready for the Olympics!

Curtain

COMPREHENSION

Comparing and contrasting

1. Explain how Kate's goal is different from Maria's.

   Kate wants more in her life than swimming. Maria wants

   to concentrate on swimming to become a swimming

   coach.

Comparing and contrasting

2. Discuss why Maria feels that she is not as good a swimmer as Kate.

   Maria feels that Kate has a natural swimming talent that

   she does not have.

Identifying cause and effect

3. Tell why Kate is so tired the day of the first swim meet.

   Kate is tired because she was at a campaign meeting

   late the night before.

Identifying cause and effect

4. What does Mr. Meacham say was the cause of Kate's loss at the swim meet?

   He says that her loss was due to her kick on the turn.

   He also says that she was not concentrating.

5. Explain why Kate says that Maria deserves to win first place.

    Maria works hard. All of her practicing helped her beat

    Kate's best time.

6. Circle the word that correctly completes each sentence.

    a. Very young children _____ on a jungle gym.

        swim   (clamber)   somersault

b. Something considered more important than other things is a _____.

    lap   campaign   (priority)

c. Someone who is extremely tired is suffering from a feeling of _____.

    (fatigue)   disgust   failure

CRITICAL THINKING

1. How are Maria and Kate different?

    Answers will vary. Maria is not a naturally gifted athlete but is committed to swimming. She does all that her coach tells her

    to do. Although Kate is a more gifted swimmer than Maria, she is not as dedicated to the sport and has other interests.

2. Tell why Kate and Maria argue if they are friends.

    Answers will vary. Kate and Maria are concerned about what is good for each other. They are also competitors on the swim

    team.

3. Explain why training as a swimmer is so demanding.

    Answers will vary. Training takes a lot of time every day. It's tiring and hard on the body.

4. Describe how you think Kate feels when she hears about Maria's second victory.

    Answers will vary. Kate is probably pleased for Maria but probably also regrets not having competed herself.

5. From the stage directions in Mr. Meacham's dialogue, describe what kind of person you think Mr. Meacham is.

    Answers will vary. Mr. Meacham is concerned about the swimmers on his team. He is patient with his swimmers' conflicts, but

    he wants them to perform as well as they can. He demands that his swimmers work hard, concentrate, and make sacrifices.

6. What is the message of this play?

    Answers will vary. A person's goals and dreams often demand hard work, sacrifices, and hard choices.

1. Of the three kinds of conflict described on page 126, which kind of conflict does Kate face? Kate faces
   conflict with herself.

2. Discuss Kate's conflict with swim training. The demands and pressures of swim training clash with Kate's other
   interests.

3. Explain how Mr. Meacham, the coach, helps Kate with her problem. Mr. Meacham gives Kate a deadline by
   which she has to decide if she really wants to dedicate herself to swimming. Having a deadline forces Kate to make a
   choice, something she was unable to do on her own.

4. Describe how the conflict is finally resolved. Kate finally realizes that she wants to compete in swimming, even if it
   means sacrificing other activities.

5. Is Kate's conflict internal or external? Explain. Kate's conflict is an internal conflict. Kate has to struggle with her own
   inner feelings of anger and confusion.

6. There is also a minor conflict in the story. It is an external conflict. Circle the letter of
   the statement that identifies this minor conflict. Then tell how it is resolved on the
   lines below.

   a. Maria has to deal with being second best.
   b. Maria gets angry with Kate over her unwillingness to work hard.
   c. Maria does not get along with her coach.
   d. Maria is jealous of Kate's swimming ability.

   Maria's anger disappears when Kate returns to the swim team, ready to work hard.

7. Maria also has a conflict with herself about her love of swimming and her knowledge that
   she is not a first-class swimmer. Explain how she resolves this conflict.

   She works hard at her swimming and plans to be a swimming coach.

Reading-Writing Connection

On a separate sheet of paper, write a paragraph describing a recent conflict in your life or
in the life of someone you know. Explain how the conflict was resolved.

For ESL/ELL support, see highlighted words, page T95, and pages T28–T30.

Skill: Reading a Timeline

For lesson support, see page T95.

BACKGROUND INFORMATION

"Swifter, Higher, Stronger" is a brief history of the Olympic Games. The history of the Olympics is divided into two parts. The original games were held in ancient Greece and went on for 1,200 years. They finally ended in A.D. 394. The modern Olympics did not begin until 1896. Now in their second century, the modern Olympics promote peace and understanding among nations.

SKILL FOCUS: Reading a Timeline

A **timeline** is a chart that lists events in chronological order—the time order in which they occurred. Some timelines show major historical events over a long period of time. Others show events that occur during just a few hours or days.

Each section on a timeline stands for a specific period of time. It could be one year, ten years, a century, or some other length of time. When you read a timeline, look at how much time each section stands for. Then look for the dates and times of specific events.

A timeline shows a sequence of events in a brief, clear form. It helps you understand when an event happened in relation to other events. A timeline can also give you a quick overview of the history of a topic, region, or period.

▶ Use the following timeline to answer the questions at the top of the next column.

Notable Early Events in the Modern Olympics

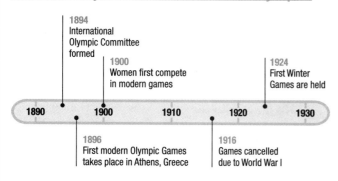

How much time does each section of the timeline stand for?

ten years

When did women first compete in the Olympic Games?

1900

CONTEXT CLUES: Appositive Phrases

Sometimes the meaning of a new word follows the word and is set off by commas or dashes. This type of context clue is called an **appositive** if it is one word. If it is more than one word, it is called an **appositive phrase**.

Read the sentences below. Find the appositive that explains the meaning of the underlined word.

The Olympics started in ancient Greece. They began so long ago that their <u>origin</u>, or beginning, is not recorded in history.

If you do not know the meaning of *origin*, the appositive *or beginning* can help you. *Origin* means "beginning."

▶ In the sentence below, circle the appositive phrase that helps you figure out the meaning of the underlined word.

Other events, including <u>chariot-racing</u>—races between horse-drawn, two-wheeled cars—came later.

As you read the selection, use appositives and appositive phrases to help you understand the meanings of the underlined words *sound, pentathlon,* and *decathlon.*

Strategy Tip

As you read "Swifter, Higher, Stronger," pay attention to the timeline on pages 133–134. It will help you understand the sequence of events that the text describes.

SWIFTER, HIGHER, STRONGER

GIFTED ATHLETES from around the world gather to compete against each other as individuals. They are also **representatives** (REP ri ZENT ə tivz) of their countries. These men and women are Olympic athletes.

The Olympic Games have a history reaching back to ancient Greece. Many people think that the modern Olympics are the most exciting of sports events. Athletes the world over devote their lives to training for the games. Like the early Greeks, these athletes have as their goal the motto *Citius, altius, fortius,* meaning "swifter, higher, stronger."

The oldest event in the Olympic Games is track and field. It was, and still is, the heart of the games. Even the Olympic motto is directed to the track-and-field athlete. The Latin words encourage the athlete to run faster, jump higher, and throw harder.

The Beginning of the Olympics

The Olympics started in ancient Greece. They began so long ago that their origin, or beginning, is not recorded in history. The ancient Greeks believed in excellence in every area of life. A Greek citizen was expected to be sound, or healthy, in both mind and body. The Olympics were a celebration of the human body and what it could achieve.

The first Olympics recorded in history took place in 776 B.C. The Greeks have left us a picture of what the event was like. The games took place in the beautiful valley of Olympia. This was a sacred place where the Greeks came to worship their gods.

The grassy slopes of the valley served as a stadium for the games. In 776 B.C., more than 45,000 Greeks watched and cheered the athletes in the games. The first person ever to have his name put in an Olympic record was Coroebus (kə REE bəs). Coroebus was a cook from the city of Elis (EE lis). He was the winner of a footrace of about 200 yards (180 meters).

An Olympic winner became a great hero in ancient Greece. He was crowned with an olive wreath. The people of his city welcomed him home with parades. Poems were written about him, and statues were built in his honor.

The Greeks admired physical strength and skill because they were often at war. Warfare at the time meant hand-to-hand battle, and young Greek men might be called upon at any time to defend their country.

The Modern Olympic Games

Winter Olympics				1924	1928	1932	1936	1940	1944
Host Nation				France	Switzerland	U.S.A.	Germany	Canceled-World War II	Canceled-World War II
Number of Participating Nations				16	25	17	28	–	–

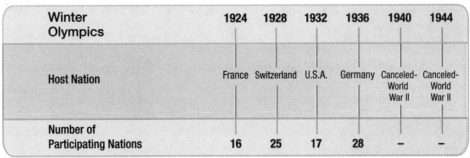

Summer Olympics	1896	1900	1904	1908	1912	1916	1920	1924	1928	1932	1936	1940	1944
Host Nation	Greece	France	U.S.A.	England	Sweden	Canceled-World War I	Belgium	France	Netherlands	U.S.A.	Germany	Canceled-World War II	Canceled-World War II
Number of Participating Nations	13	22	12	23	28	–	29	44	46	37	49	–	–

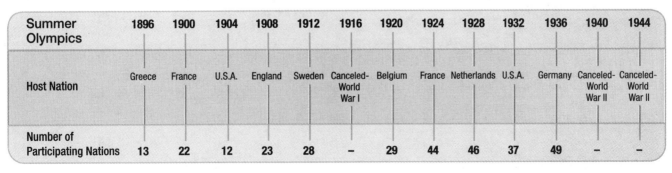

SOCIAL STUDIES

The Early Games

✓ In the first Olympic Games, there were only footraces. The <u>pentathlon</u> (pen TATH lon)—a contest consisting of five events—was later added to the games. The pentathlon tested an athlete in the long jump, javelin throw, footrace, discus throw, and wrestling. Wrestling soon became a favorite event in the games. Other events, including chariot racing—races between horse-drawn, two-wheeled cars—came later.

One of the stories of outstanding Greek athletes is about the famed Milo (MY loh) of Croton (KROHT ən). He won the wrestling crown in six Olympic Games. He developed his great strength, it is said, by lifting a baby calf on his shoulder every day until it was a huge bull.

The Olympics began when the Greek empire was at the height of its power. When Greece declined as a world power, the games lost their noble spirit. The last of the early games was held about A.D. 390. Then in A.D. 393, they were outlawed by the Christian Emperor Theodosius I. After about 1,200 years, the Olympics ended. During that long time, they had not been interrupted once, not even by war. Though the games were no longer played, their memory and spirit lived on.

The Modern Olympic Games

In 1896, the Olympics were reborn. For the first time in 1,506 years, an Olympic winner was crowned with an olive wreath. Once again, athletes met to find out who was swifter, higher, and stronger.

The credit for the **revival** of the Olympics belongs to one person, Baron Pierre de Coubertin of France. Coubertin believed that the Olympic Games could serve the modern world as they had ancient Greece. The games would encourage physical fitness in young people. They would also promote world understanding and peace.

Alone, Coubertin began a campaign to revive, or bring back, the Olympics. Finally in 1894, he gained support for his idea. Two years later, the first modern Olympic Games were held. Fittingly, the first modern Olympics took place in Athens, Greece. The games created excitement and enthusiasm throughout the world. At first, the United States did not support the Olympics. After the 1896 games, however, the country caught Olympic fever. A major reason for the sudden interest was the success of American athletes. They competed in the track-and-field events in 1896 and won nine out of the twelve events.

The Modern Olympic Games

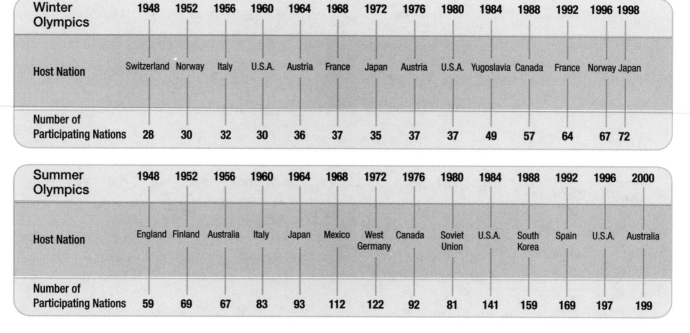

Winter Olympics	1948	1952	1956	1960	1964	1968	1972	1976	1980	1984	1988	1992	1996	1998
Host Nation	Switzerland	Norway	Italy	U.S.A.	Austria	France	Japan	Austria	U.S.A.	Yugoslavia	Canada	France	Norway	Japan
Number of Participating Nations	28	30	32	30	36	37	35	37	37	49	57	64	67	72

Summer Olympics	1948	1952	1956	1960	1964	1968	1972	1976	1980	1984	1988	1992	1996	2000
Host Nation	England	Finland	Australia	Italy	Japan	Mexico	West Germany	Canada	Soviet Union	U.S.A.	South Korea	Spain	U.S.A.	Australia
Number of Participating Nations	59	69	67	83	93	112	122	92	81	141	159	169	197	199

Many new games were included in the Olympics in 1896. These included gymnastics, shooting, swimming, fencing, and weight lifting.

In 1912, the challenging <u>decathlon</u>—a track-and-field contest of ten events—was added to the Olympics. Athletes compete in this contest for two days. There are five events the first day. These include the 100-meter dash, long jump, shot put, high jump, and 400-meter run. Five more events follow on the second day. They are the 110-meter hurdles, discus throw, pole vault, javelin throw, and 1,500-meter run.

In 1908, ice skating was first included in the Summer Games in London. Many people wanted Winter Games to be organized. However, Coubertin believed that winter sports were snobbish activities enjoyed only by the rich. The first Winter Games were finally held in 1924. They included figure skating, speed skating, skiing, and a bobsled race.

The Winter Games were an immediate success and have remained so ever since. From 1924 to 1992, both the Summer Games and the Winter Games were held every four years in the same years. Since 1994, however, the Summer and Winter Games have alternated every two years.

Over the years, the number of participants and the number of events in the Summer Games and Winter Games have grown. Women as well as men compete in today's Olympics. At their best, the Olympics reach the goal that the Baron de Coubertin had in mind when he revived them. In 1896, Coubertin wrote these words about the games: "The important thing in the Olympic Games is not to win, but to take part, just as the important thing in life is not the triumph but the struggle. The essential thing is not to have conquered but to have fought well."

COMPREHENSION

Recognizing sequence of events
1. Number the following events in the order in which they happened.

    <u> 5 </u> **a.** The first Winter Games were held.

    <u> 1 </u> **b.** Coroebus set an Olympic footracing record.

    <u> 4 </u> **c.** The first modern Olympic Games were held in Athens, Greece.

    <u> 3 </u> **d.** Theodosius outlawed the Olympics.

    <u> 2 </u> **e.** Wrestling was added to the games.

Identifying cause and effect
2. Tell what effect the decline of the Greek empire had on the early Olympic Games.

They lost their noble spirit.

Recalling details
3. Identify where the early Olympics and the first modern Olympics were both held.

They were both held in Greece.

Recalling details
4. List the new events that were added to the Olympics in 1896.

Gymnastics, shooting, swimming, fencing, and weight

lifting were added.

Recalling details
5. Explain why Baron de Coubertin revived the Olympics.

The Baron de Coubertin believed that the Olympic Games

would encourage physical fitness in young people and

would promote world understanding and peace.

Identifying the main idea and supporting details
6. Reread the paragraph in the selection marked with an ✘. Underline its main idea. Then circle two or more details that support the main idea.

Using context clues
7. Draw a line to match each word with its meaning.

sound   a contest of five events

decathlon   healthy

pentathlon   a contest of ten events

Inferring cause and effect
1. Write the cause for the effect described below.

    Cause: Greece fought many wars, so young Greek

    men had to be fit to fight.

    Effect: Many of the early Olympic events tested physical skills needed by Greek soldiers.

Inferring comparison and contrast
2. The ancient Greeks believed in both a sound body and a sound mind. Compare their beliefs with the feelings of Americans today.

    Answers will vary. Many people today are physically fit

    and agree with the need for a sound body and a

    sound mind *or* Many Americans spend too much time

    watching TV and do not develop either their bodies or

    their minds.

Inferring details
3. During what large time period were the Olympic Games *not* held?

    The Olympics were not held from A.D. 390 to 1896.

Inferring the unstated main idea
4. Explain why the events in the Olympics changed over the years.

    New sports developed and grew popular over the years.

Inferring cause and effect
5. Reread the paragraph in the selection that has a ✔ next to it. Write a sentence that expresses its main idea.

    Answers will vary. The number of events in the early

    Olympic Games increased over the years.

Drawing conclusions
6. Do you think Baron de Coubertin's statement about the Olympics on page 135 is still true about the Olympics today? Explain.

    Answers will vary.

Distinguishing fact from opinion
7. **a.** Is Baron de Coubertin's statement a fact or an opinion?

    opinion

    b. In two sentences, tell why you agree or disagree with the statement.

    Answers will vary.

Drawing conclusions
8. Do you think the Olympic motto "Swifter, higher, stronger" is still fitting for today's Olympic Games? Explain.

    Answers will vary. Yes. The motto is still fitting because

    athletes must still run fast, jump high, and throw with

    strength.

Drawing conclusions
9. Explain how the Olympic Games have always been democratic in spirit.

    Both ancient and modern games allow the best

    athletes to compete and win regardless of race,

    religion, or income.

Drawing conclusions
10. Tell why the decathlon might be considered the most challenging Olympic event.

    Answers will vary. It is a two-day, ten-event competition.

    It is the fullest test of an athlete's strength, speed, and

    skill.

Use the timeline on pages 133 and 134 to answer the following questions.

1. How frequently were the Olympic Games held until 1992? _____ every four years _____

2. In what year did the greatest number of nations participate in the games? _____ 2000 _____

3. **a.** In what three years were the Olympic Games canceled? _____ 1916, 1940, and 1944. _____

   b. Why were the games canceled?

   These were the years when World War I and World War II were being fought. The aim of the games is to promote world

   peace and understanding; athletes from around the world meet in peaceful competition. This is not possible when nations

   are fighting against each other in a world war.

4. Where were the Summer and Winter Olympics held in the first games after World War II?

   The Summer Games were held in England, and the Winter Games were held in Switzerland.

5. Where and when were the first Winter Olympic Games held? They were held in France in 1924.

6. In what year were both the Summer and the Winter games held in Germany? _____ 1936 _____

7. As of 2000, how many games, Summer and Winter, had been held in the United States? _____ 7 _____

8. In which two countries have the most Olympic Games been held? _____ France, United States _____

9. Look at the number of nations participating in the Summer Olympics.

   What trend do you see from 1896 to 2000?

   Except for the years 1976 and 1980, the number of participating nations has been on the rise since 1896.

10. Have the Winter Olympics ever been held in Greece? Explain why this might be so.

    No, Greece is not cold enough for outdoor winter sports.

Reading-Writing Connection

On a separate sheet of paper, write a paragraph describing your favorite sport in the Summer or Winter Olympics. Explain why it is your favorite.

For ESL/ELL support, see highlighted words, page T96, and pages T28–T30.

Skill: Following Directions

For lesson support, see page T96.

BACKGROUND INFORMATION

"Work and Machines" describes two simple machines, the lever and the pulley, and explains how these machines make work easier for people. In all, there are six simple machines: the lever, the pulley, the inclined plane, the wedge, the screw, and the wheel and axle. Complex machines are made up of different combinations of these simple machines.

SKILL FOCUS: Following Directions

Following directions is an important skill in science. To perform any science experiment, you must follow the steps of the directions exactly. The directions for many experiments are divided into five parts.

1. **Problem** The problem is often a question that you should be able to answer at the end of the experiment.

2. **Aim** The aim is a description of what will be done during the experiment.

3. **Materials** Materials are the objects and equipment needed to perform the experiment.

4. **Procedure** The procedure lists the steps you must carry out in order to do the experiment.

5. **Observations or Conclusions** At the end of the experiment, you should make observations or draw conclusions based on its outcome.

Use the following four steps to help you read a selection with directions for an experiment.

1. Read the paragraphs that explain the ideas on which the experiment is based.

2. Read the five parts of the directions carefully.

3. Study any pictures or diagrams.

4. Reread and be sure that you understand the Problem, Aim, Materials, Procedure, and Observations or Conclusions.

▶ Think about a science experiment you completed in school recently. On the lines, write the problem and the aim of the experiment.

Problem: _____ Answers will vary. _____

Aim: _____ Answers will vary. _____

CONTEXT CLUES: Diagrams

A **diagram** is a drawing that helps explain a thing by showing all the parts, how it is put together, and how it works. A diagram shows in pictures what a text is describing in words. Be sure to read the title, the caption, and the labels on the diagram to help you interpret what you see.

The diagram below shows a man using a simple machine called a lever to lift a weight. What does the diagram show you about the meaning of the term *resistance force*?

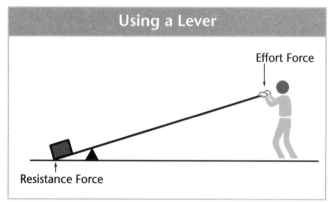

Using a Lever

Effort Force

Resistance Force

A lever helps to lift a weight.

By looking at the diagram, you can figure out that the resistance force is the force or weight that the lever must lift.

▶ Look at the diagram and write a sentence that tells what *effort force* means.

The effort force is the force applied by the user of the lever.

As you read the selection, use the diagram on page 139 to help you understand the meanings of the words *fulcrum*, *effort arm*, and *resistance arm*.

Strategy Tip

After you read "Work and Machines," study the directions for the experiment on page 140. Use the steps described in the Skill Focus on this page to help you understand the experiment.

Work and Machines

PEOPLE USE MACHINES EVERY DAY. Some machines are complicated and have many moving parts. Others are so simple that most people don't think of them as machines. A **machine** is any invention that makes work easier or faster.

What Is Work?

To a scientist, *work* has a special meaning. *Work* means "the use of force to move an object through a distance." The object is moved in the direction of the force. This meaning for work can be expressed in an equation.

$$\text{Work} = \text{Force} \times \text{Distance}$$

To move an object, a machine must overcome the force that resists the movement of the object. This force is the **resistance**. The distance through which the machine moves the object is called the **resistance distance**.

How Do Machines Make Work Easier?

When a machine is used, some work goes into making the machine function. The force applied by the user to a machine is called the **effort**. The distance through which the user applies the effort is called the **effort distance**. Some machines make work easier by increasing the amount of force that is applied to them and using it against the resistance force. The amount by which a machine increases a force is called the **mechanical advantage** of the machine.

$$\text{Mechanical Advantage} = \text{Resistance} \div \text{Effort}$$

A lever is a simple machine made up of a rigid arm that pivots on a point called a fulcrum.

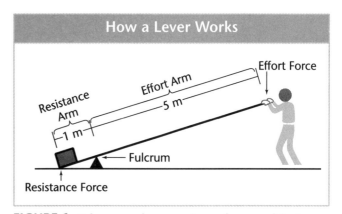

How a Lever Works

Resistance Arm — 1 m
Effort Arm — 5 m
Effort Force
Fulcrum
Resistance Force

FIGURE 1. **A lever makes moving a heavy object easier by applying force through a greater distance.**

Levers

A **lever** is a simple machine that can multiply a small effort force to overcome a large resistance force. A lever is like a seesaw. It has a rigid arm that rocks back and forth on a fixed point called the fulcrum. The woman in the photograph is using a simple lever. What is the resistance? How is the effort being applied?

The rigid arm of every lever has two parts. The effort arm is the distance between the fulcrum and the effort force. The resistance arm is the distance between the fulcrum and the resistance force. You can figure out the mechanical advantage of a lever by dividing the length of the effort arm by the length of the resistance arm.

$$\text{Mechanical Advantage of Lever} = \text{Effort Arm} \div \text{Resistance Arm}$$

In Figure 2, the resistance arm is 1 meter, and the effort arm is 5 meters. The mechanical advantage of this lever, then, is 5. On a seesaw, the effort arm and the resistance arm are equal. Therefore, the mechanical advantage of a seesaw is 1.

You can figure out how much effort is needed to move an object if you know the mechanical advantage of a machine. To do this, you divide the resistance by the mechanical advantage.

$$\text{Effort} = \text{Resistance} \div \text{Mechanical Advantage}$$

SCIENCE

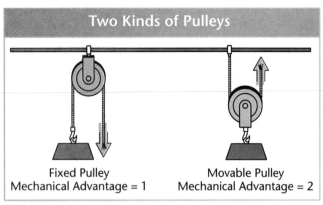

Two Kinds of Pulleys

Fixed Pulley
Mechanical Advantage = 1

Movable Pulley
Mechanical Advantage = 2

FIGURE 2. A fixed pulley is held in place by a support beam. A movable pulley moves freely.

Pulleys

A **pulley**, another highly useful simple machine, is a form of a lever. A pulley makes work easier by changing the direction of a force. (See Figure 3.) A pulley is a grooved wheel over which runs a cord. To lift an object with a pulley, you pull on the cord. Your pull is the effort. The object that is pulled is the resistance. A pulley attached to a wall, a beam, or any other support frame is called a **fixed pulley**. Window shades and flagpoles often have fixed pulleys. Fixed pulleys do not multiply the effort force put into them. They only change the direction of the force. Often it is easier to pull against a resistance than to lift it.

A greater advantage is gained through using a movable pulley. A **movable pulley** is hung on a rope attached to a support frame. The rope runs through the pulley. The pulley itself moves up the rope as the rope is pulled. A movable pulley makes it easier to lift a heavy weight. You can figure out the mechanical advantage of a pulley by dividing the resistance distance by the effort distance.

Mechanical Advantage of Pulley =
Resistance Distance ÷ Effort Distance

EXPERIMENT

The following experiment will show the advantage of a fixed pulley.

PROBLEM
What mechanical advantage can you obtain by using a fixed pulley?

AIM
In this experiment, you will measure the mechanical advantage of a fixed pulley.

MATERIALS
You will need a support frame, a single lightweight pulley, a length of cord, a 2-kilogram weight, a spring balance, and a meter stick.

PROCEDURE
1. Attach the weight to the spring balance. What is the weight of the load, or the resistance?

2. Remove the weight from the spring balance. Tie the weight to one end of the cord. String the free end of the cord over the pulley. Hang the pulley on the support frame and attach the top of the spring balance to the free end of the cord. Pull slowly on the spring balance. Read the spring balance to determine the value of this effort. How does the effort compare to the resistance? Was it easier to lift the weight by hand or to lift it with the use of the pulley? Why?

3. Use the meter stick to see how far you must pull down the cord to lift the weight 1 meter. Then compare the two distances. What is the mechanical advantage of a fixed pulley?

OBSERVATIONS OR CONCLUSIONS
The mechanical advantage of a fixed pulley is 1. Think about what this means. Why is a fixed pulley useful?

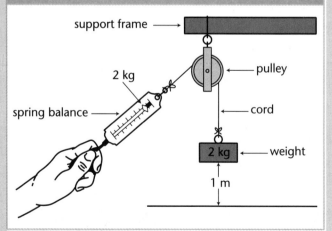

Measuring the Mechanical Advantage of a Fixed Pulley

Compare the effort force and effort distance to the resistance force and resistance distance.

Recalling details
1. Define *machine*. A machine is an invention that
makes work easier or faster.

Recalling details
2. Describe the mechanical advantage of a
machine. It is the amount by which a machine
increases a force.

Reading text with diagrams
3. In Figure 1, what object is the fulcrum?
The fulcrum is the small brick.

Using context clues
4. Draw a line to match each term with its explanation.

fulcrum   a. distance between the fulcrum and the effort force

effort arm   b. distance between the fulcrum and the resistance force

resistance arm   c. fixed point over which a lever rocks

Making inferences
1. If a lever has an effort arm of 4 meters and a resistance arm of 2 meters, what is the mechanical advantage of the machine?
The mechanical advantage is 2.

Making inferences
2. Tell which tool is not a lever: a pair of scissors, a nutcracker, a crowbar, an axe.
An axe is not a lever.

Making inferences
3. A pair of scissors is a kind of lever. Explain where the fulcrum is on a pair of scissors.
The screw joining the blades is the fulcrum.

Making inferences
4. a. On a pair of scissors, where is the effort applied? The effort is applied on the handles.

    b. What provides the resistance? The object being cut provides the resistance.

Making inferences
5. How far must you raise the cord of a movable pulley in order to lift a load 2 meters?
You must raise the cord 4 meters.

Making inferences
6. Explain how you could make a seesaw work better as a lever. A seesaw's arms are equal. Making its resistance
arm shorter or its effort arm longer would give it a greater mechanical advantage. In other words, a seesaw works better if
the heavier person moves closer to the fulcrum, while the lighter person sits at the very end.

This experiment should show how much force it would take to lift an object of a certain weight with two different levers. Complete the directions, using the experiment on page 140 as a model. Use a ruler or a meter stick for the arm, a block of wood for the fulcrum, a weight for the resistance, other weights to measure the effort needed to lift the resistance, and a spring balance. Number the steps in the Procedure part. In the box, draw and label a diagram to show this experiment. The Problem and Aim have been completed.

Wording of steps will vary.

EXPERIMENT

PROBLEM

Compare the effort needed to lift an object of a certain weight with two different levers.

AIM

In this experiment, you will compare the effort force needed to lift a resistance of a certain weight with two different levers. The effort arm of one lever should be twice the length of the resistance arm. The effort arm of the other lever should be four times the length of the resistance arm.

MATERIALS

You will need a ruler or meter stick, a block of wood,

weights, and a spring balance.

PROCEDURE

1. Construct Lever A by placing a meter stick across a

block of wood. The effort arm should be twice the length of

the resistance arm.

2. Weigh the resistance weight on a spring balance. Then

place it at one end of the lever.

3. Add weights to the effort arm until the resistance is

lifted. Weigh the effort weights.

4. Construct Lever B as in Step 1, except this time the

effort arm should be four times the length of the resistance

arm.

5. Place the resistance weight on the end of the lever.

6. Repeat Step 3. Compare the results.

OBSERVATIONS AND CONCLUSIONS

The effort needed to lift an object grows less as the effort

arm gets longer.

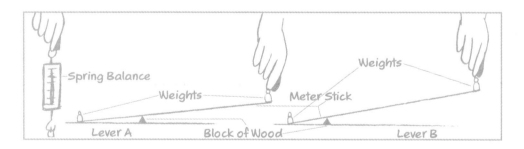

Reading-Writing Connection

On a separate sheet of paper, write a paragraph describing a kind of pulley or lever that you use daily. Include an explanation of how the pulley or lever works.

Skill: Reading a Graph

For ESL/ELL support, see highlighted words, page T97, and pages T28–T30.

For lesson support, see page T97.

BACKGROUND INFORMATION

"Costs of World War II" provides information about the long struggle to win World War II (1939–1945). The war killed more people, cost more money, and damaged more property than any other war in history. During the war, the Allies—led by the United States, the Soviet Union, Great Britain, and France—struggled against the Axis nations. The Axis nations included Germany, Japan, and Italy. As a result of the war, there were far-reaching changes in Asia, Europe, and the United States.

SKILL FOCUS: Reading a Graph

A **graph** shows numerical information visually. You can find information in a graph more quickly than you can in a paragraph of text. Graphs also make it easier to compare information. Newspapers, magazines, and textbooks often present information in the form of graphs.

Different types of graphs are used for different purposes. **Circle graphs** are used to show parts of a whole. For that reason, circle graphs usually show percents. For example, a circle graph might show the results of a public-opinion poll. By looking at a graph, you can see at a glance the percentage of people who approve, disapprove, or have no opinion on an issue.

To use a circle graph, first read its **title**. The title tells what kind of information is shown on the graph. Also pay attention to the **labels** on each section of the circle. The labels will help you find the information you need. Be sure to compare the sizes of the sections on a circle graph to see what part of the whole each section represents.

Reading the paragraphs that come before and after a circle graph is important, too. These paragraphs might explain the purpose of the graph. They might also include background information that will help you understand and use the facts shown on the graph.

▶ Look at the circle graph below. Then answer the questions.

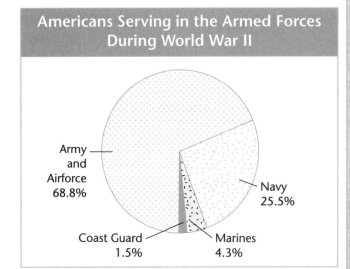

Americans Serving in the Armed Forces During World War II

Army and Airforce 68.8%

Navy 25.5%

Coast Guard 1.5%

Marines 4.3%

What is the title of the circle graph?

Americans Serving in the Armed Forces During World War II

In World War II, what percentage of the U.S. armed forces were in the Marines?

4.3 percent

WORD CLUES

Look for the important words *sectors*, *label*, and *data* in "Costs of World War II." Knowing these words will help you understand circle graphs.

Strategy Tip

In "Costs of World War II," read the title of each graph before studying the graph itself. Also take time to understand what the labels mean. Understanding the title and the labels will help you interpret the information the graph presents.

COSTS OF WORLD WAR II

According to one estimate, World War II cost $1,154,000,000,000 to fight. That is more than one trillion dollars. Dozens of nations took part in the war and paid part of the cost. Circle Graph 1 shows the percentage of the total cost paid by some of the largest nations.

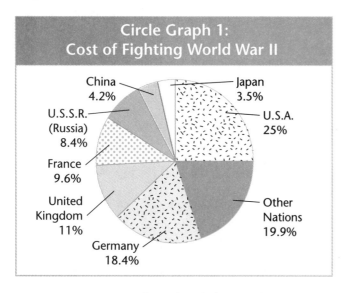

**Circle Graph 1:
Cost of Fighting World War II**

As you can see, the title of the graph is *Cost of Fighting World War II, by Country*. Also notice that the graph is divided into eight sections, or **sectors**. Each sector has a **label**. The labels tell you what each sector stands for. The labels also identify the **data**, or numerical information, represented by each sector. On Circle Graph 1, each label names a country. It also tells the percentage of the total cost paid by that country.

You can use the sectors in Circle Graph 1 to compare how much of the total cost different nations paid. You can see, for example, that the United States paid about 25 percent, or $\frac{1}{4}$, of the total cost of the war. Germany was the second-largest spender. France and the United Kingdom each spent about 10 percent of the total. Notice that one of the sectors has the label *Other Nations*. This sector shows the total percentage of the cost that dozens of smaller nations paid.

At the peak of World War II, more than 70 million people were in uniform. They fought for more than 50 countries. Circle Graph 2 lets you compare the sizes of the armed forces of different nations during the war. The labels tell the names of major countries that fought. They also tell the percentage of the total number of soldiers that each country supplied.

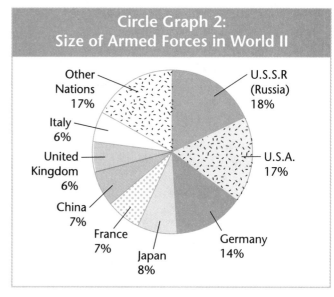

**Circle Graph 2:
Size of Armed Forces in World II**

The graph shows that the U.S.S.R., now Russia, supplied 18 percent of all the armed forces in World War II. The United States supplied almost as many, 17 percent. You can also see from the graph that China and France, for example, each supplied about 7 percent.

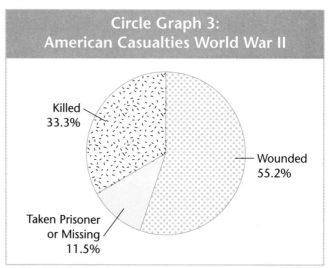

**Circle Graph 3:
American Casualties World War II**

During World War II, the United States suffered many casualties. In all, about 1,216,000 soldiers were killed, wounded, taken prisoner, or declared missing. Circle Graph 3 shows the percentage of the total casualties represented by each of these groups.

Circle Graph 3 shows that about one-third, or 33.3%, of the American casualties were killed. It does not, however, show the actual number of soldiers who were killed. If you know the total number of American casualties, however, you can figure out how many Americans were killed. Use the following numerical sentence.

$$33.3\% \text{ of } t = k \text{ or } \frac{1}{3} \times t = k$$

The symbol t stands for the total number of casualties. The symbol k stands for the number of Americans who were killed.

Since the paragraph at the top of this column mentions that there were 1,216,000 casualties in all, you can solve the sentence:

$$\frac{1}{3} \times 1,216,000 = k$$

$$\frac{1,216,000}{3} = k$$

$$405,333.3 = k$$

The figure of 405,333.3 is not an exact number because percents on circle graphs are usually rounded. Rounding your answer, you can say that about 405,333 Americans were killed during World War II.

If the labels on a circle graph do not include percents, you can still compare the size of the sectors just by looking at them. You can see which sector represents the largest percentage. You can see which one represents the smallest percentage. You can also see which sectors represent about the same amount.

You can also estimate the amounts represented by each sector by using fractions. If a sector takes up about a quarter of the circle, for example, it represents about $\frac{1}{4}$, or 25%, of the total amount.

When the labels include percents, you can figure out how much larger one sector is than another. Also, if you know the total amount represented by the whole circle, you can figure out the amount represented by each sector. Just multiply the total amount by the fraction or decimal represented by each sector.

COMPREHENSION

Reading graphs
1. Look at Circle Graph 1. What percentage of the total cost of the war was paid by the United States, the United Kingdom, and France together?

About 45.6 percent

Reading graphs
2. Look at Circle Graph 2. What percentage of the armed forces in the war were supplied by Germany?

14 percent

Recalling details
3. How can you figure out the amount represented by each sector if you know the total amount represented by the circle?

When the total amount is given, you can multiply the

total by the fraction represented by each sector to figure

out the amount represented by each sector.

CRITICAL THINKING

Making inferences
1. Tell what determines the size of a sector in a circle graph.

The percentage of the total amount that the sector represents determines its size in the graph.

Inferring cause and effect
2. State what would happen to the other sectors if the size of one sector of a circle graph were increased.

One or more of the other sectors would be decreased so that the total of all the sectors would still equal 100 percent.

3. Put a ✔ next to the idea that could best be shown in a circle graph.

_____ **a.** the reasons that World War II began

✔_____ **b.** how many Americans were in favor of, opposed to, or had no opinion about entering World War II in 1940

_____ **c.** political changes that occurred in Europe after World War II

_____ **d.** annual increases in U.S. government spending for the years 1939–1945

SKILL FOCUS: READING A GRAPH

Use the following paragraph and circle graph to answer the questions.

The four major air powers in World War II were the United States, Germany, Japan, and the United Kingdom. In all, these four nations lost about 240,000 military airplanes during the war. The circle graph on this page shows what percent each lost.

Losses of Military Aircraft of Major Air Powers in World War II

Germany 40%
United States 25%
United Kingdom 15%
Japan 20%

1. What is the title of this circle graph?

   Losses of Military Aircraft of Major Air Powers in World War II

2. How many sectors are shown on the graph?

   Four sectors are shown on the graph.

3. What are the labels of the sectors?

   Germany, United States, Japan, United Kingdom

4. What is the sum of the percents given in the labels?

   100 percent

5. Which country shown on the graph lost the fewest airplanes?

   The United Kingdom lost the fewest airplanes.

6. What percentage of the airplanes shown on the graph was lost by the United States?

   25 percent

7. How many of the 240,000 airplanes did the United States lose?

   The United States lost 60,000 airplanes. ($\frac{25}{100}$ × 240,000 = 60,000)

Reading-Writing Connection

Take a poll of your classmates to find out their opinions on a current issue. On a separate sheet of paper, make a circle graph to show the results of your poll.

For ESL/ELL support, see page T98.

Skill: Multiple-Meaning Words

For lesson support, see page T98.

> A word may have a different meaning in literature, social studies, science, mathematics, or music. Study the following words with **multiple meanings**.

band	change	crop	legend	pupil
cell	cone	yard	power	plot

Read the two definitions for each word below. Choose a word from the list above that fits those two definitions. Write the word on the line above the definitions.

1. _____ yard _____

   Mathematics: a measure, 36 inches in length

   Social Studies: an open place used for a business or special purpose

2. _____ band _____

   Music: a group of musicians playing instruments together

   Social Studies: a group of people joined to do something

3. _____ cell _____

   Social Studies: a small room in a prison or jail

   Science: the basic unit of living matter, usually very small

4. _____ cone _____

   Mathematics: a solid object that narrows evenly from a flat circle at one end to a point at the other

   Science: the part of evergreen trees that bears seeds

5. _____ change _____

   Mathematics: money returned when one has paid more than the amount owed

   Social Studies: places or conditions that become different as time passes

6. _____ plot _____

   Literature: the action, or series of events, in a story

   Social Studies: a secret plan, in politics or during a war, to gain power or harm an enemy by misleading people, usually by dishonest methods

7. _____ power _____

   Science: energy or force that has the ability to do work

   Social Studies: a person or group that has authority, right, or control over others

8. _____ pupil _____

   Science: the dark opening in the center of the eye

   Social Studies: a person being taught by a teacher

9. _____ crop _____

   Social Studies: the full amount of produce grown by a farmer in one season

   Science: a pouch in a bird's gullet where food is softened for digestion

10. _____ legend _____

    Literature: a story handed down through the years and connected with some real events, but probably not true in itself

    Social Studies: a key or brief explanation accompanying a chart or map

Skill: Using an Index

For lesson support, see page T98.

A quick way to find information in a textbook or reference book is to use the **index** at the back of the book. An index lists all the important subjects included in the book.

On the following page is part of an index from a science textbook. The **topics** are arranged in alphabetical order. Find the topic *Oil*. Below it, three subtopics are listed alphabetically: *pollution from*, *source*, and *use*. **Subtopics** list the specific kinds of information given in the book about the topic. Notice that some subtopics have such words as *in* and *of* before them. These short words do not affect the alphabetical order of the subtopics.

The numbers after each topic or subtopic are the page numbers on which information is found. Numbers separated by dashes indicate that information begins on the page before the dash and ends on the page after the dash. Numbers separated by commas show that information appears on only the pages for which numbers are given.

Study the index on page 149. Then answer the following questions.

1. On what page(s) would you find information about mud? _____165_____

2. How many subtopics are listed under the topic *Moon*? _____12_____

3. On what page(s) would you find information about craters on the moon? _____79, 104–105_____

4. How many pages does the book have on nuclear energy? _____3_____

5. On what page(s) would you find information about the moons of Pluto? _____78_____

6. How many pages does the book have on the Milky Way? _____10_____

7. On what page(s) would you find information about nitrogen in the soil? _____324, 469_____

8. What two planets' moons are discussed on the same page? _____Neptune, Uranus_____

9. If you wanted information on life in the oceans, which page would you *not* read between pages 250 and 256? _____255_____

10. On what page(s) would you find information about nickel in the earth's core? _____192–193_____

11. What five subtopics about the moon are discussed on page 105?

    _____craters on, marias, orbit of, phases, revolution of_____

12. What topic comes between nickel and nuclear energy? _____nitrogen_____

13. If the book had information about mold, after which topic would it be listed? _____Mohs scale_____

14. If the book had information about fish farms in the oceans, before which subtopic would it be listed? _____gases in_____

Methane, 475
  in atmosphere, 262
  in outer planets, 75, 77
Milky Way, 25–28, 38–41, 47, 57
Minerals:
  chemical weathering of, 320–324
  conservation of, 473–474
  crystals, 138–140, 161–162
  deposits, 171–172
  gems, 143–145
  identification of, 138, 145–153
  in lithosphere, 29
  in rocks, 158, 161, 168, 323
  soil and, 324–327, 330
  sources of, 141–142, 470–472, 489
Mining, 471–474
Moho, 187, 188
Mohs scale, 148–149
Molecules, behavior of, 122–124, 125
Moon:
  age of, 103, 444–446
  atmosphere of, 104
  axis, rotation of, 102–103
  craters on, 79, 104–105
  eclipses, 108–109
  gravity of, 102
  marias, 103–104, 105
  orbit of, 105
  phases, 105–107, 108
  revolution of, 105
  size, 102
  tides and, 109–111
Moons:
  of Jupiter, 75
  of Mars, 74
  of Neptune, 77
  of Pluto, 78
  of Saturn, 76
  of Uranus, 77
Moraines, 345–346
Mountains, 200–202, 452, 454
  belts, 202
  earth's mantle and, 367–368
  erosion and, 30, 201
  faults and, 372
  folds and, 375, 376
  magma and, 377
  oceanic, 240, 248–250, 404–406
  ores in, 333
  ranges, 201–202, 402–403, 411, 453, 456
  soils, 332–333
  system of, 202
  weathering and, 30
Mud, 165

N

Nebulae, 40
Nekton, 251, 252, 253
Neon:
  in atmosphere, 94
  in meteoroids, 81
Nickel:
  in the earth's core, 192–193
  in meteoroids, 81
Nitrogen:
  in atmosphere, 30, 94, 263–265, 275
  from carbon, 14, 443
  living things and, 264–265, 481–482
  in oceans, 242
  in soil, 324, 469
Nuclear energy, 492–494
Nucleus, 127

O

Oceans:
  basins, topography of, 244–250, 255, 257
  continental margins, 245–246
  depths, 238, 241, 243, 245–246, 250, 251, 252, 253–254
  gases in, 242
  life in, 250–254, 256, 426
  minerals in, 490
  oceanography, 13, 239, 241, 254–257
  salinity, 239–242, 251, 256
  spreading of floor, 404–407, 454
  temperatures and, 241, 242–243, 256, 309
  trenches, 249, 406–407
Oil:
  pollution from, 482–483
  source, 474, 475
  use, 324, 476
Orbit, 24, 69
  of planets, 68–69, 70–76
  of satellites, 87–89
Orbital velocity, 87–89
Ores, 141–142, 143, 333, 470–471
  mining, 471–472
  refining, 472–473
Oxidation, 320–321

Skill: Comparing Travel Packages

For lesson support, see page T99.

In planning a vacation, people need to decide where they will go, how long they will stay, where they will stay, what they want to see, and how much money they will need to spend. **Travel packages** are arrangements made by a travel agent or travel company to cover vacation plans. These arrangements may include air travel, hotels, meals, and extras such as sightseeing. Before making a decision on travel plans, many people look into several travel packages to compare what they offer.

Read and compare the following travel packages.

---

*Experience Relaxation
while exploring the historic past.*

GALVESTON: *A 19th-Century Island City*

The historic Gulf Inn Resort combines gracious charm with comfort. Overlooking the Gulf of Mexico, the resort is within walking distance of the city's finest shops and historic homes. Dimly-lit dining is provided in the Gulf Room Restaurant. In addition, a pool, an indoor gym, and tennis courts offer relaxing recreation for our guests.

$80 per person per night, double occupancy

PACKAGE INCLUDES:

- Deluxe Room with balcony
- Half-day bus tour of city
- Full breakfast
- Half-day walking tour of historic homes
- Relaxing massages
- Free use of recreation facilities
- Free "Historic Galveston Travel Guide"
- Free parking

PHONE your travel agent
or call the Gulf Inn Resort at
713-555-8686

Enjoy FAMILY FUN in historic
WILLIAMSBURG!
THREE-NIGHT SPECIAL
(includes, hotel, breakfast, sightseeing)
$120 per adult, double occupancy
Mon.-Thurs., excluding holiday periods

Stay
at the Colonial Motel
- Up to two children under 15 stay free
- Free breakfast
- Free parking
- Free swimming pool and game room

Visit
the Historic Past
- Free full-day guided tour of Williamsburg
- Sights include the capital building, Bruton Parish Church, Governor's Palace, and restored homes on Duke of Glouchester Street

Dine
in Historic Williamsburg
- Midweek Special includes one dinner for two at any of three fine restaurants. (Up to $20.00 per person)

Enjoy
Other Family Attractions
- For just $20 a day, you can rent a car with unlimited mileage to visit nearby family attractions and amusement parks.

MAKE YOUR RESERVATIONS *NOW!*
PHONE "Sunstar Travel Group" TOLL FREE
800-555-3742

A. Circle the letter next to the phrase that correctly completes each sentence.

1. The Galveston package stresses
   a. family fun.   **b.** sightseeing.   **c.** relaxation.   **d.** bargain prices.

2. The Williamsburg package stresses
   a. family fun.   **b.** sightseeing.   **c.** relaxation.   **d.** bargain prices.

3. The rates for both packages are based on "double occupancy." This means that
   a. the charge is the same for two people in the room as it is for one person.
   b. the actual price is half the quoted rate.
   c. the room rate changes with each additional person in the room.
   d. the per-person charge is based on two people in a room, so the price of the room is actually twice the quoted rate.

4. If a family wants to save money, it may prefer the Williamsburg package because
   a. up to two children can stay free in the motel in Williamsburg.
   b. Williamsburg offers a holiday discount.
   c. the Galveston package does not offer a free breakfast.
   d. the Galveston package does not include free tours.

5. For three nights, the Galveston package costs
   a. $240.00 per person.   **b.** $240.00 per room.   **c.** $80.00 per person.   **d.** $480.00 per person.

6. Both the Galveston and Williamsburg packages include
   a. a special three-day rate for rooms.
   b. a room rate based upon double occupancy.
   c. a car rental.
   d. special holiday discounts.

B. Compare the two travel packages by completing the chart below. If no information is given for a particular item, write *no information*. Then answer the questions below the chart.

Travel Package Information	Galveston	Williamsburg
price per night per adult	$80.00	$40.00
number of people per room	2	2 adults + 2 children
days available	every day	Mon.–Thurs.; no holidays
children's rates	no information	up to two under 15 free
meals included	breakfast	breakfast, one dinner for two
free recreation facilities	pool, gym, tennis, sightseeing	pool, game room, sightseeing
number of tours	two half-day tours	one full-day tour
car rental	no information	$20.00/day, unlimited mileage
how to reserve	call travel agent or resort	call travel group toll-free

1. Which package is less expensive per night? _____ Williamsburg _____

2. Which package includes more free recreation facilities? _____ Galveston _____

3. Which package has a special children's rate? _____ Williamsburg _____

4. Which package is available on weekends? _____ Galveston _____

unit six

For ESL/ELL support, see highlighted words, page T100, and pages T28–T30.

The Computer Age

LESSON 48

Skill: Point of View

For lesson support, see page T100.

BACKGROUND INFORMATION

"The Principal Problem" is a story told through a student's journal entries. Carmen's life changes dramatically when a computer arrives at her school. As computers have become more common, people have criticized them for different reasons. Workers fear they will lose their jobs to the machines. People complain about computer errors and how hard they are to correct. Whatever their drawbacks, however, computers are here to stay.

SKILL FOCUS: Point of View

Point of view is the eye through which a story is written. Some stories are told from the first-person point of view. Others are told from the third-person point of view.

In the **first-person point of view**, a character in the story tells the story. This character uses the first-person pronouns *I*, *me*, and *we* to tell the story. A **first-person narrator** tells his or her own experiences and thoughts. This type of narrator cannot enter the minds of other characters or describe events that he or she has not seen.

In the **third-person point of view**, the narrator is outside the story. The narrator uses the third-person pronouns *he*, *she*, and *they* to tell what the characters think and do. A **third-person narrator** can tell what different characters are thinking and doing.

▶ Read the following sentences. On the lines below, write the narrator's point of view and how you determined it.

Walking home, I heard someone running toward me. I was frightened. A tall man ran by me. He raced to an emergency police phone.

You can tell it's first-person point of view because the narrator

participates in the story and uses first-person pronouns.

CONTEXT CLUES: Using a Dictionary

When you read a new word, context clues might give you a general idea of the word's meaning. If you want a detailed definition of the word, however, you need to look it up in a dictionary.

Read the following sentence, and think about the meaning of the underlined word.

__Technicians__ have been trying to put together the six computer pieces so that our new principal can start functioning properly.

The context clues suggest that technicians work on computers. A dictionary might say that a technician is an expert on a technical subject.

▶ Think about the meaning of *policy* below.

Mr. Alioto must have announced six different big changes in school __policy__ over the public-address system today. Twice he changed a policy that had been set only yesterday.

What do you think a policy is?

a rule

Now look up *policy* in a dictionary. Write its definition on the lines.

A policy is a plan of action adopted as the best way to

manage affairs to achieve some purpose.

As you read, use a dictionary to define *coincidence*, *aerobics*, and *malfunctioned*.

Strategy Tip

As you read "The Principal Problem," think about who is telling the story. Is the information you learn limited to the narrator's own thoughts, feelings, and observations?

THE PRINCIPAL PROBLEM

September 10 It had to happen, of course. Summer vacation has come to an end. Today, I, Carmen Soares, began my last year at Gloria Willis Junior High. I wish it were my last week, though I'm relieved to have Miss James for my homeroom teacher. She's got potential; she just has to be trained right. Seat assignments were handed out, and I'm right in front of Harry Seely. How's that for luck? He asked to borrow a pencil, and I very coolly said, "Keep it, Harry; I've got zillions of them." Definitely a good start!

September 11 A weird thing happened at our first assembly of the year. Mr. Alioto, the assistant principal, announced that Mrs. Uxley would not be returning as principal. I guess she's retiring or something. When one of the kids asked about Mrs. Uxley's replacement, Mr. Alioto didn't say anything for a moment. Then he answered, "Her replacement will be delivered next week."

September 14 I've done nothing for the last three days but wonder about our new principal. How do you "deliver" a principal?

September 19 Well, I got my answer today—you deliver a principal in boxes. Our principal was delivered in six boxes, to be exact. It's a computer—talk about new ideas! It's a good thing that I'm heading for high school after this year. Yet Luis Garcia says that won't make a bit of difference. He told me that once they get a bad idea in one school, they usually take it around to all the others.

September 23 Technicians have been trying to put together the six computer pieces so that our new principal can start functioning properly. They've been running in and out of the principal's office. Rumors are racing around the school, but no one really knows what's happening. Harry Seely borrowed another pencil. That makes three. What does he do with them?

September 24 Two items of interest! First they put a suggestion box in each classroom. Then they gave everyone, even teachers, a form to complete. In the top part, you had to write your hobbies, your favorite television shows, even the kinds of food that you like best. Also they wanted you to suggest how life at Gloria Willis could be improved. They also handed out this funny note.

GLORIA WILLIS JR. HIGH

OFFICE OF THE PRINCIPAL

HELLO,

MY NAME IS T12H2679DELTA. CALL ME DELLIE. I AM YOUR NEW PRINCIPAL. ALL NEW DELTA COMPUTERS ARE PRO-GRAMMED FOR TOP PERFORMANCE IN A SPECIFIC TYPE OF JOB, AND I AM NO EXCEPTION. A SUGGESTION BOX HAS BEEN PLACED IN YOUR CLASSROOM. PLEASE USE IT OFTEN SO THAT YOU CAN HELP ME IN MY JOB. I THINK WE CAN HAVE FUN TOGETHER, DON'T YOU?

September 26 As if things weren't bad enough, I just saw a magazine article about my new principal. It said that there were two Delta computers now in use: ours and one that's working as a town manager out in some small Midwestern town. The article talked about how the other Delta has to be a diplomat, which means it has to consider everybody's opinion before it makes any decisions. Our Delta principal, on the other hand, is supposed to act like a dictator. It makes decisions without considering anyone's opinion. I think we're in big, big trouble at Gloria Willis—really gigantic trouble!

September 27 I detest Harry Seely—he's been borrowing Rita Korngold's pencils, too.

September 28 All's well that ends well. Rita Korngold was shipped off to the other side of the room. I don't think it had anything to do with my suggestion, although it was really a very funny coincidence. I dropped another suggestion into the box just to be sure.

September 29 That'll teach me. I thought I was safe telling Milos Kelly, the track star, about the suggestion box, but that just shows how smart I really am! When Miss James said gym was being replaced by <u>aerobics,</u> I knew whose suggestion that was. I just hope she keeps her promise not to tell anyone else.

October 2 Now I know what Milos Kelly's promises are worth! When I walked into class this morning, there was a long line of kids waiting to drop suggestions into the box. To make things worse, when I went to my seat, I found out that Harry Seely was no longer sitting in back of me. He'd been moved to the other side of the room, to a seat next to—guess who? They put Ronnie Franks behind me in Harry Seely's place. What a trade that was! Now I'll have to stop wearing my hair in a braid. Ronnie Franks is that kind of neighbor. After I finish writing this, I'm going to spend at least two hours writing suggestions.

October 3 Things are getting weird, to say the least. There's a ten-minute wait at just about every suggestion box in school—at any time of day! Mr. Alioto must have announced six different big changes in school policy over the public-address system today. Twice he changed a policy that had

been set only yesterday. I wonder who suggested that we be allowed to bring our pets to school.

October 5 War was declared in school today, and it's our class against 9C. They started it. Just after we sat down in the auditorium, Mr. Alioto said, "It's been suggested that some of the classes change places at assembly." He said, "some of the classes," but he changed only two. Guess which two? What hurt was the way the kids in 9C laughed as we walked to the rear of the auditorium.

October 6 Every kid in class suggested that we change assembly places again. Later, during hide and seek, Mr. Alioto announced that there wouldn't be homework anymore. Everybody shouted and clapped, but I felt kind of sad. I wonder what's wrong with me.

October 7 I told my mother that I wanted to move to a new school. When she asked me why, I didn't know what to say. How could I explain that I was tired of seeing movies and playing games all day? She'd take me to a doctor; I'm sure she would.

October 8 I spent most of the day in the nurse's office. Cindy Marshall's snake bit me. Looking over the magazines that they have at the nurse's office now, I happened to see a story about that Delta computer that's running a town out in the Midwest. It seems the people in that town are having a lot of trouble with their computer. It makes them stand in lines according to their height and punishes them when they are late. In a way, I wish that our principal was more like the town manager.

October 13 A quiet day: our clown phoned in sick, and the movie projector exploded. I dropped six suggestions into the box, suggesting that we be allowed to do plain old schoolwork again. No one can ever know about those suggestions! We still didn't get our old seats back in assembly.

October 14 Miss James told us there would be an election in school next month. When we asked her what the election was for, she became very upset. Ronnie Franks tapped me on the shoulder and threatened, "You better vote for me next month, or you'll be sorry!" When I asked him what he was running for, he answered, "Homeroom teacher."

October 16 9C was sent down to the basement for a fire drill. They were the only class to go, so you can guess whose idea the whole thing was. They didn't come back until the afternoon relay races. I think I know why we never got our assembly seats back, and why we still haven't been given plain old schoolwork, as I suggested. It's simple mathematics. There are 32 kids in 9C, and 31 kids in our class. We were outnumbered and outsuggested!

October 19 What a day! First our water balloon fight was called off. Then at eleven o'clock, people from the board of education broke down the front door and took over the school. At first they thought that our computer principal had <u>malfunctioned</u>, but, as it turns out, we were sent the wrong computer. We should have gotten the one that went out to the Midwest, and they should have gotten ours. *We* got the diplomat, and *they* got the dictator! Nobody would have discovered the mistake if our principal hadn't ordered ten tons of popcorn for the hot-lunch program.

November 14 The last three weeks have been great! I love doing math, history, and English again. I feel as if the first month of school was all a bad dream. I'd better save this journal, or else no one will ever believe what happened. Of course, I can always show people the scar where Cindy's snake bit me.

November 16 Something's wrong again. I saw Miss James crying, and she wouldn't tell me why.

November 18 I found out why.

___GLORIA WILLIS JR. HIGH___
OFFICE OF THE PRINCIPAL

IN A SURPRISE MOVE, THE NEW PRINCIPAL OF THE GLORIA WILLIS JUNIOR HIGH SCHOOL FIRED ALL OF THE SCHOOL'S TEACHERS. WHEN ASKED WHY THE TEACHERS WERE FIRED, T12H2679-DELTA ANSWERED, "I HAD TO. ALL THEY DID FOR THE PAST MONTH WAS PLAY GAMES, WATCH MOVIES, EAT COTTON CANDY, AND CAMPAIGN FOR THEIR JOBS." WHEN ASKED IF REPLACEMENTS COULD BE FOUND QUICKLY, T12H2679-DELTA ANSWERED, "WITHOUT A DOUBT! MANY OF THEIR REPLACEMENTS HAVE ALREADY BEEN DELIVERED."

COMPREHENSION

Identifying setting
1. Describe the setting of the story.

   The setting of the story is September to November, at

   Gloria Willis Junior High School, sometime in the future.

Identifying cause and effect
2. Explain why Gloria Willis Junior High School was getting a new principal.

   Mrs. Uxley, the present principal, left, probably to retire.

Recalling details
3. Tell how the new principal arrives.

   The new principal is delivered in six boxes.

Recalling details
4. Where and how is the second Delta computer being used?

   It is working as a town manager in a small Midwestern

   town.

Comparing and contrasting
5. Are the two Delta computers alike or different? Explain your answer.

   The computers are different: The computer working as a

   town manager in a small Midwestern town is strict. The

   computer working as a principal lets the students make

   all of the decisions.

Using context clues
6. Draw a line to match each word with its meaning.

   coincidence   **a.** failed to work as programmed

   aerobics   **b.** events happening at about the same time that seem to be connected but really are not

   malfunctioned   **c.** physical exercises that improve the circulation of the blood

Making inferences

1. Explain why Carmen is sorry after she tells Milos about the suggestion box.

    Milos tells others that suggestions put in the box are carried out.

    _____

Inferring comparisons and contrasts

2. Describe the ways that life at Gloria Willis Junior High School changes with the
    delivery of the new principal.

    After the new principal arrives, there is a suggestion box for improvements, all of which are carried out. Gym is replaced by

    aerobics classes, seats are changed in classrooms and at assemblies, major policy changes are made daily, and so on.

Distinguishing facts from opinions

3. Identify the following statements as facts or opinions. Write *F* or *O* on the lines
    provided.

    __O__ a. Luis Garcia says that once they get a bad idea in one school, they usually take it
             around to all the others.

    __F__ b. Miss James told us there would be an election in school next month.

    __O__ c. I think we're in big, big trouble at Gloria Willis—really gigantic trouble.

    __O__ d. The last three weeks have been great! I love doing math, history, and English
             again.

Understanding character

4. a. Describe how Carmen feels about Dellie when it first arrives.

       Carmen is not very enthusiastic about having a computer principal.

       _____

    b. Describe how Carmen feels about Dellie a few weeks later.

       Carmen misses the old ways so much that on October 7, she tells her mother that she wants to move to a new

       school—a school without a computer principal.

    c. How does Carmen feel after the board of education discovers that the wrong
       computer was delivered to the school?

       Carmen is happy doing math, history, and English again. She feels as though the first month of school was a bad dream.

       _____

Making inferences

5. Explain why Miss James is fired.

    Miss James, like the other teachers, is fired because for the past month she has not taught her students. Instead, under

    Dellie's orders, she has allowed them to play games and watch movies.

Drawing conclusions

6. Do you think a computer could be a good assistant to a principal? Give
    reasons.

    Answers will vary. Students should consider tasks that a computer could do more efficiently than a person, as well as tasks

    that involve judgment.

1. Who is the narrator of the story?

   Carmen Soares, a student at Gloria Willis Junior High School, is the narrator.

2. Is the narrator a participant in the story's events or an outsider? Explain.

   Carmen is a participant. She is a student at the school where the principal is a computer.

3. Why is the first person a good point of view from which to tell this story?

   Answers will vary. It allows the reader to share Carmen's thoughts, feelings, and confusion as she figures out, little by little,

   what is really going on at her school—and why.

4. In her journal entries, the narrator reveals thoughts and feelings about what is going on at Gloria Willis. List two or three of the narrator's thoughts about having a computer principal.

   Answers will vary. "It's a good thing I'm heading for high school after this year." "I think we're in big, big trouble at Gloria

   Willis—really gigantic trouble." "Things are getting weird, to say the least."

5. Why does the reader not know how the other students feel, or what they think, about the computer?

   Because the story is written from the first-person point of view, the narrator cannot enter the minds of the other characters.

   Carmen, the narrator, can reveal only what she sees others doing.

6. Why is it not possible for Carmen to tell in her journal entry how Miss James felt?

   A first-person narrator can only tell what he or she personally thinks or feels or what other people say about their thoughts

   and feelings.

Reading-Writing Connection

On a separate sheet of paper, write two paragraphs describing how you would feel if the teachers in your school were replaced by computers. Use the first-person point of view.

Skill: Making Generalizations

For lesson support, see page T101.

BACKGROUND INFORMATION

"From the Abacus to the Personal Computer" traces the historical development of the computer. Only in the last 60 years have amazing developments in electronics made the idea of computers a reality. The computer is only the latest development in people's centuries-old quest to find more efficient ways to calculate. An ancient Chinese calculator called the abacus, for example, is more than 2,500 years old!

SKILL FOCUS: Making Generalizations

A **generalization** is a broad statement that applies to many examples or events. You can make a generalization by thinking about related facts and what they have in common.

Read the following group of related facts.

- At school, Tasha does research on a computer.
- Ryan's favorite pastime is playing computer games.
- Mrs. Curtis pays her bills on the Internet.
- At his after-school job, Ramón uses a computer to design and print posters.

Based on these facts, you could make the following generalization. *Computers play an important role in many areas of everyday life.*

Certain words can signal generalizations. They include *all, most, many, few, always, everyone, overall,* and *generally.* These signal words show that the generalization is a broad statement that is supported by many examples.

▶ In the chart below, write a generalization based on the three facts.

CONTEXT CLUES: Using a Glossary

Many social studies and science selections include specialized vocabulary words. Often these words are organized in a glossary at the end of a chapter or book. A **glossary** is an alphabetized list of words and their meanings.

Suppose you read the following sentence in a selection that includes a glossary.

In 1833, he tried to build the first __digital__ computer.

If you do not know the meaning of the word *digital,* and there are no context clues to help you figure it out, look up the word's meaning in the glossary. *Digital* means having data in number form.

▶ Read the sentence below. Then use the glossary on page 162 to find the meaning of the underlined word. Write the meaning on the line.

They could work so fast that their operation was measured in __nanoseconds.__

one-billionth of a second

As you read the selection, use the glossary on pages 161–162 to find the meanings of the underlined words *computer, data, binary,* and *CD-ROM.*

Strategy Tip

As you read "From the Abacus to the Personal Computer," try to make generalizations about the development of the modern computer.

Fact 1	Fact 2	Fact 3
The first British computer was called Colossus because it was so big.	In 1946, the first American computer, called ENIAC, filled a huge room.	All the computers used by NASA to send astronauts to the moon in 1969 had about as much power together as one of today's personal computers.

Generalization

Answers will vary. Early computers were much larger and much less powerful than today's computers.

FROM THE ABACUS TO THE PERSONAL COMPUTER

THE COMPUTER REVOLUTION (REV ə LOO shən) has been underway for some time. It has brought about more changes than the **Industrial Revolution** did. What makes this revolution so amazing is that the computer did not exist 60 years ago.

In that sense, the computer is a modern invention. However, many of the ideas used in computer design date back several hundred years. There has always been a need for efficient and accurate counting. In the beginning, people used their fingers for counting. As their needs became more complex, however, they needed help from machines.

The Abacus

At least 2,500 years ago, the Chinese invented an efficient way of counting. Their invention, the abacus, is still in use. This early mechanical calculator consists of a hand-held rectangular frame. In the frame are many fixed rods strung with movable beads. Numbers are recorded by moving the beads. A skilled abacus operator can easily keep pace with a person using a modern calculator.

The abacus has been in use since ancient times.

Machine Arithmétique

In 1642, the French mathematician Blaise Pascal invented the world's first calculating machine that could add and subtract. He called his device *Machine Arithmétique.* Pascal's machine used gear-driven counterwheels to record amounts. It worked something like the speedometer in a car. Over the next 300 years, many types of mechanical calculators used a similar technique.

Pascal's *Machine Arithmétique* (1642) was the world's first calculating machine.

The Analytical Engine

Charles Babbage was an English mathematician born in 1791. He was the first person who tried to make a calculator that could do more than just add and subtract. In 1833, he tried to build the first digital computer. He called this machine the Analytical Engine. It had all the features of a modern computer, including memory, control, and input/output abilities. In one minute, it could do 60 additions or subtractions. More important, the Analytical Engine could actually be **programmed** to carry out different kinds of processes.

Unfortunately Babbage could not get the support he needed to continue his project. He died in 1871, frustrated and unhappy. However, his ideas would make him famous long after his death.

Punched Cards and the Tabulating Machine

The needs of the U.S. Census Bureau led to the development of punched cards and the **tabulating** (TAB yoo layt ing) machines that read them. In 1880, the Census Bureau did its survey of the American population, as it does every ten years. By 1885, however, the Bureau was still struggling to count the results. It became clear that this job might actually take longer than the ten-year span between censuses. A faster way of doing the job was needed.

Herman Hollerith, a worker at the Census Bureau, figured out a way of recording the census data on strips of paper. His method was quite

SOCIAL STUDIES

simple. Information was coded on strips of paper by means of a series of punched holes in a planned pattern. Each hole had a specific meaning.

This coding system proved to be an efficient way of recording information. The paper strips were soon replaced by three-by-five-inch cards. Each card contained punches that coded the entire record of an individual or a family. To process these coded cards, Hollerith made a tabulating machine that could read the codes of about 65 cards per minute.

The use of the punched card and tabulating machine saved the government a great deal of time and money. It was so successful that Hollerith decided to make similar machines that businesses could use. To manufacture his invention, he formed the Tabulating Machine Company. This successful company would eventually merge with other companies. It became the giant company we know today as the International Business Machines Corporation, or IBM.

Hollerith's punched card tabulating machine was first used for a U.S. census.

The First Computers

In 1944, a scientist named Howard H. Aiken worked with IBM to make a new computing device. It performed arithmetic on data input on punched cards. This machine, MARK I, was an early form of today's digital computer.

✔ By 1947, the University of Pennsylvania had built the Electronic Numerical Integrator and Computer, ENIAC. ENIAC filled a space as large as a two-car garage. It gobbled up 140,000 watts of electricity, and it contained 18,000 vacuum tubes. These tubes were large and costly and produced a lot of heat. While ENIAC worked 1,000 times faster than MARK I, it had one major weakness. To perform different operations, it had to be rewired by hand. This task could take several days.

A scientist named John Von Neumann suggested feeding data into the computer through a keyboard. The first computer to have this input device was UNIVAC I, the Universal Automatic Computer. In 1951, UNIVAC I became the first mass-produced, commercially available computer.

✗ The most important contributions to the development of computers were made by John Von Neumann. His work resulted in improvements in areas from the computer's design to its electronic circuits. With others, he developed the ideas of the stored program and the binary number system. These concepts are still used in most modern computers.

Modern Computer Generations

In recent years, computer developments have been far-reaching and numerous. Because of this rapid progress, computers have been categorized by **generations**. Each generation of computers features an important advance over the previous generation.

First Generation (1942–1959)

These computers used vacuum tubes for the storage of data. Vacuum tubes were bulky and caused major overheating problems. They were also unreliable. These "maxi," or mainframe, computers were large and expensive.

Second Generation (1959–1965)

These computers replaced vacuum tubes with **transistors** (tran ZIS tərz). A transistor is a small electronic device made up of crystals that control the flow of electric currents. Second-generation computers were smaller and worked faster. They could perform a single operation in one-tenth the time it took computers that used vacuum tubes. With the second generation of computers, manufacturers began producing business computers with more efficient storage and faster input/output abilities. These mini-computers were smaller, more reliable, and cost less than earlier models.

Computers have advanced quickly from the large mainframe computers that took up entire rooms to small desk-sized, laptop, and handheld computers to multimedia systems.

Third Generation (1965–1970)

These computers had tiny integrated circuits on a chip, or plate, as small as a dime and as thin as paper. The parts on the chip were so small that they were hardly visible to the naked eye. In addition, new input/output devices could communicate with computers over great distances, using telephone lines. They could display pictures on a screen and accept voice input. These computers also had tremendous memory capacities. They could work so fast that their operation was measured in nanoseconds.

Fourth Generation (1970–present)

These computers brought the microprocessor into use. A microprocessor uses a chip that contains the integrated circuits and the whole central processing unit (CPU) of a simple computer.

The Future Is Now

Sixty years ago, there were just a few slow, garage-sized computers available only to scientists. Today there are millions of small, lightning-fast personal computers available to everyone. Thanks to <u>CD-ROM</u> drives and modems, a tremendous amount of information is now available to us at the click of a mouse. The Internet and e-mail connect us instantly to friends, libraries, and businesses around the world. It is a world that most of us take for granted. It is also a world that would not have been possible without the efforts of countless forward-looking scientists, engineers, and technicians of the twentieth century.

Glossary

binary   having a two-number system consisting of the digits 0 and 1

calculator   machine that rapidly adds, subtracts, multiplies, and divides, often by electronic means

CD-ROM   (Compact Disc Read-Only Memory) an optical disk containing text and multimedia data that can be retrieved by a laser beam

central processing unit   (CPU) control center for an entire computer system

computer   electronic device used to calculate, store, and select data

data   information or instructions that a computer can interpret

digital   having data in number form

e-mail   electronic mail transmitted from one computer to another

input   data inserted or fed into a computer

integrated circuit   a tiny unit that combines many electronic parts and the connections between them in one small slice of material

Glossary

Internet a worldwide computer network with millions of subscribers

mainframe computer largest and most powerful of the early computers

microprocessor a chip having the capabilities of a simple computer

modem a device for sending data, usually over telephone lines, between computers

nanosecond one-billionth of a second

output information that has been processed through a computer

stored program series of commands that directs what the computer does

---

COMPREHENSION

Recognizing sequence of events

1. Number the following events in the order in which they occurred.

  <u>3</u> **a.** construction of Babbage's Analytical Engine

  <u>1</u> **b.** invention of the abacus

  <u>5</u> **c.** creation of ENIAC

  <u>2</u> **d.** invention of Pascal's *Machine Arithmétique*

  <u>6</u> **e.** production of UNIVAC I

  <u>4</u> **f.** development of Hollerith's punched cards

Recalling details

2. How have the stages in the development of computer technology been labeled?

They have been labeled as "generations."

Identifying the main idea and supporting details

3. Reread the paragraph marked with an ✗. Underline its main idea. Then circle two details that support the main idea.

Using context clues

4. Write three sentences, each using one or more vocabulary words listed below.

computer	data	binary	CD-ROM

Answers will vary.

  a. A CD-ROM encyclopedia can hold more information than all the volumes in a standard encyclopedia.

  b. The digital computer uses the binary number system.

  c. My computer can process a huge amount of data in just a nanosecond.

CRITICAL THINKING

Inferring comparisons and contrasts

1. The ancient Chinese had a need for efficient and accurate counting. Their need resulted in the invention of the abacus. Compare their need with present-day needs.

Answers will vary. Because of the huge quantity of information available today, people have a much greater need for faster, more efficient, and more accurate counting.

2. Reread the paragraph with a ✔ next to it. Then circle the letter of the statement that best states the main idea of the paragraph.

   a. ENIAC worked faster than the earlier MARK I.

   b. The first fully electronic digital computer worked much faster than earlier types, but it was large and difficult to program.

   c. The early electronic computers contained thousands of vacuum tubes.

   d. The 18,000 vacuum tubes in ENIAC produced a lot of heat.

SKILL FOCUS: MAKING GENERALIZATIONS

Following the box below are three groups of facts. Study each group of facts. Then choose the statement in the box that is the best generalization for each group. Write the letter of the statement on the line.

> a. Computers have gradually become smaller, more efficient, and more available.
>
> b. The computer's influence is evident in business, medicine, and education.
>
> c. Many features of today's computers are the result of discoveries made many years ago.

1. **Facts:** • Computers are used to store employee payroll data, such as weekly salary, taxes, and benefits contributions.
   • Computers are used to diagnose medical problems and to monitor patients' progress.
   • Computer-assisted instruction is found in most schools.

   Generalization: ____b____

2. **Facts:** • The abacus was the first mechanical calculator.
   • Babbage's Analytical Engine could be programmed to carry out different functions.
   • Hollerith's punched cards and tabulating machine were used to compile information for the 1880 census.

   Generalization: ____c____

3. **Facts:** • Transistors reduced the size of the computer and increased its working speed.
   • Integrated circuits and the microchip made communication possible over great distances, using telephone lines.
   • The microprocessor led to the development of small home computers.

   Generalization: ____a____

Reading-Writing Connection

On a separate sheet of paper, write a paragraph that explains how a computer can make learning more interesting for you.

For ESL/ELL support, see highlighted words, page T102, and pages T28–T30.

Skill: Making Inferences

For lesson support, see page T102.

BACKGROUND INFORMATION

"What Is a Computer?" explains what computers can do and how they work. We are all living in "the computer age." At home, computers help run our appliances and our cars. In schools and libraries, students use computers to research, write, and learn about many subjects. To make the most of these amazing machines, we should learn more about them.

SKILL FOCUS: Making Inferences

Writers don't always tell you everything in a text. Sometimes you have to make **inferences**, or figure out information that is not stated. To make an inference, you need to combine the details in a selection with what you already know.

Read the following conversation. Think of an inference you can make about where Dr. Dao lives.

> "I'd like to have a math conference with Dr. Dao at 9:00 A.M. tomorrow," Vance told Alicia. "Can you be on-line at his Web site then?"
>
> "9:00 A.M.!" Alicia replied. "Dr. Dao doesn't live here in New Jersey. It's three hours earlier where he lives."
>
> "Oh, I forgot about that," said Vance. "Okay, I'll e-mail him and see if he can do it at 9:00 A.M. his time."

The conversation tells you that Vance and Alicia live in New Jersey. It also tells you that Dr. Dao lives somewhere where the time is three hours earlier. You may already know that the time on the West Coast of the United States is three hours earlier than the time in New Jersey. So you can infer that Dr. Dao lives somewhere on the West Coast.

▶ Use the details in the conversation to make an inference about who Dr. Dao is. Write your inference on the line.

Answers will vary. Dr. Dao is a math expert, perhaps a professor.

CONTEXT CLUES: Diagrams

Sometimes new science terms are explained in a paragraph and are also shown in a **diagram.** A diagram is a drawing or chart that helps explain a thing by showing all its parts and how it works.

You can use the text and the diagram below to figure out the meaning of the term *Internet Service Provider*.

> Your **Internet Service Provider** is your link to the Internet. Once you have logged on to it through your computer, it will send an electronic greeting through a telephone or cable network to the **server** where information about the Web site you are looking for is stored.

▶ Use the sample paragraph about the Internet, and the diagram to write the meaning of *server*.

A server is a large computer that holds information for

Web sites.

As you read the next selection, use context clues and the diagram on page 166 to help you understand the meanings of *arithmetic unit, input equipment,* and *output equipment*.

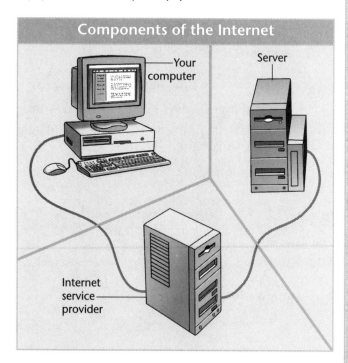

Components of the Internet

Your computer

Server

Internet service provider

Strategy Tip

Before you read "What Is a Computer?" preview the boldfaced words and labels in Figure 1 on page 166.

What Is a Computer?

1. A COMPUTER IS AN ELECTRONIC machine that can store and handle information and solve problems. You could think of a computer as a file cabinet, information organizer, and problem-solver all rolled into one.

2. Computers are sometimes called electronic brains because of the kinds of work they do. A computer can do many of the things that the human brain can do. However, a computer cannot truly understand ideas. It cannot create, or make things up. Unlike human beings, a computer has no imagination. The information that goes into a computer comes from people or from machines controlled by people. The problems computers work out also come from people. Even the methods for working out the problems come from people. Computers can do only what people program them to do.

3. A computer has certain advantages over the human brain. In some ways, a computer is much faster and more efficient than the human brain. A fast computer can solve millions of problems in a few seconds. Also computers do not make many mistakes. They can handle one dull problem after another without getting tired or bored. They are not distracted by noise or other interruptions.

4. The first computers could do only one kind of job. They could **compute**, or mathematically work out, number problems. Today's computers can do much, much more. They can store company records and create company payrolls. They can be used as teaching aids. They can help pilots fly. They can help weather forecasters predict weather. They can ring up a bill at the supermarket. They can help the grocer keep track of stock. They can deal with words as well as numbers. If a number or word problem can be worked out in a series of fixed steps, a computer can do it.

TYPES OF COMPUTERS

5. Not all computers are the same. They do not all work in the same way. They are not all used for the same purposes.

Digital Computers

6. The most common computers are **digital** computers. The word *digital* comes from the word *digit*, which means "number." Before information goes into the computer, it is changed into a code, in which groups of digits stand for letters, symbols, and numbers. The coded information goes into the machine as electronic signals. The computer works by reading, or counting, these signals. Most digital computers are general-purpose machines. They can do many kinds of work. For instance, a computer might store information about the people in a company. It might also process paychecks.

Analog Computers

7. **Analog** computers work by measuring physical happenings. For example, they might measure the flow of gas and air in an engine. They might measure the speed and direction of an airplane. They change these measurements into electronic signals for the computer to process. Most analog computers are special-purpose machines. They are built to do one kind of job.

Hybrid Computers

8. Some computers both measure and count. They combine the features of digital and analog computers. These computers are called **hybrid** computers.

COMPONENTS OF COMPUTERS

9. Each digital computer has three basic components, or parts. The basic components are made up of many smaller, complex parts. These basic mechanical parts of a computer are called its **hardware**.

Central Processing Unit (CPU)

10. The main component of any computer is its **central processing unit**, or **CPU**. It is in the CPU that information and instructions are stored and processed. The CPU has a memory, or storage, unit. This unit stores information and instructions. It holds information and instructions until they are needed. In some computers, the memory is a group of magnetic cores, or doughnut-shaped rings. In others, it is a magnetic tape, disk, or drum. Information appears on tapes and disks as magnetic spots. In the smallest computers, the memory, or even the whole CPU, may be on a tiny piece of equipment called a **chip**.

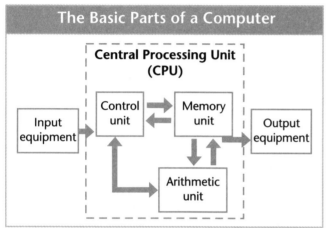

The Basic Parts of a Computer

FIGURE 1. **The three basic components of a digital computer are the CPU, the input equipment, and the output equipment.**

11. The CPU also has an arithmetic unit. This is the working part of the computer. It sorts information and computes—adds, subtracts, and so on.

12. The control unit of the CPU controls the work of the computer. It is the "captain" of the computer. First it gets instructions from the memory. Then it tells the memory what information to send to the arithmetic unit. Finally it tells the arithmetic unit how to process the information.

Input Equipment

13. **Input** means information that is fed into a computer. Before a computer can do any work, information and instructions must be put into it. Such information and instructions for a computer are called **software**. The input equipment takes information and instruction from the outside world. Then it puts it into code for the computer to use. Special keyboards serve as input equipment on most home computers.

Output Equipment

14. **Output** means information delivered from a computer according to coded instruction.

Information can come out of a computer in many forms. It can show up on a display screen, or it can be presented on paper by a printer.

15. Often input equipment and output equipment are attached to the CPU. However, input and output equipment can also be far away from the CPU. Then they are connected by cables, wires, or remote-control equipment. Remote control is the ability to control the operation of a machine by means of radio waves.

16. The mechanical components of a computer are called hardware. The instructions and information that go into or come out of a computer are called software.

COMPUTER CODES

17. Information and instructions enter the computer in the form of electronic signals. The computer knows only two signals. In many computers, these two signals are *on* and *off*. Therefore, all information going into the machine must be put into an "on/off" code.

18. In one computer code, the digit 0 stands for *off*, and the digit 1 stands for *on*. Each letter, symbol, and number that goes into the computer has its own code of eight digits—a pattern of 0s and 1s. Figure 2 shows that 00000010 is the code for the number 2. This passes into the computer as *off, off, off, off, off, off, on, off*. All the *on*'s show up in the memory as magnetic spots. All the *off*'s show up as blank spaces.

19. Each digit in the computer code is called a **bit**. A group of eight bits is called a **byte**. You can tell if a computer has a large or small memory by the number of bytes it can hold. A kilobyte is 1,000 bytes. A typical personal computer today might have from 15 to 30 gigabytes. A **gigabyte** is a billion bytes.

1 = 00000001	A = 01000001
2 = 00000010	B = 01000010
3 = 00000011	C = 01000011
4 = 00000100	(−) = 00101101
5 = 00000101	(+) = 00101011

FIGURE 2. **These are examples of an eight-bit computer code.**

Recalling details

1. Define the term *computer*.

A computer is an electronic machine that can store

and handle information and solve problems.

Recalling details

2. Circle the letter next to each task that a computer can do.

a. organize   **c.** create

b. solve problems   **d.** understand

Recalling details

3. Name three kinds of computers.

Three kinds of computers are digital, analog, and

hybrid.

Recalling details

4. Name the three main components of a computer.

The three main components are the central processing

unit (CPU), input equipment, and output equipment.

Recalling details

5. Define *hardware* and *software*.

Hardware is the computer's mechanical parts. Software is

information and instructions that are put into the computer.

Recalling details

6. Explain what each component of a computer does.

The CPU stores and processes information and

instructions. Input equipment takes in information and

instructions. Output equipment delivers information on

a screen or through a printer.

Recalling details

7. Define the term *byte*.

A byte is a part of a computer's code—a group of

eight bits that represents a letter, symbol, or number.

Using context clues

8. Draw a line to match each term with its explanation.

arithmetic unit   **a.** computer component that receives information and instructions

input equipment   **b.** computer component that delivers information

output equipment   **c.** computer component that sorts information and solves problems

CRITICAL THINKING

Making inferences

1. Name the kind of computer that would be used to keep track of air temperature and humidity.

An analog computer would be used to keep track of air temperature and humidity.

For items 2 and 3, circle the letter next to the correct answer.

Making inferences

2. In the future, computers will probably be

a. larger and able to do more.

b. the same size and able to do less.

c. larger and able to do less.

d. smaller and able to do more.

Making inferences

3. In the future, computers will probably replace workers who

a. do large projects keeping track of things.

b. solve problems that require inventing mathematical theories.

c. create new ideas for designing things.

d. try to understand how to prevent war.

Read each of the paragraphs. Put a ✔ next to each statement that can be inferred. Then write the details from the paragraph and what you already know that helped you make the inference.

Paragraph 2 (check two):

_____ **a.** A computer cannot store as much information as the human brain.

✔ **b.** A computer is like the human brain in some ways but not in others.

✔ **c.** The human brain can think, understand, create, and process information.

Details From Paragraph: A computer can do many of the things that the human brain can do. However, a computer cannot truly understand ideas. It cannot create.

What I Know: A computer cannot think, understand, or create. The human brain can. A computer can, however, work out problems given to it by people.

Paragraph 3 (check two):

_____ **a.** Some human beings never make mistakes.

✔ **b.** Human beings get tired and bored from handling dull problems.

✔ **c.** Human beings sometimes make mistakes when they handle dull problems.

Details From Paragraph: Computers do not make many mistakes. They can handle one dull problem after another without getting tired or bored.

What I Know: A computer does not get tired or bored like a human brain does, and it does not make many mistakes. Therefore, it must be that human beings do get tired and bored and will make mistakes in the same situation.

Paragraphs 17 and 18 (check one):

_____ **a.** Computer codes are all the same.

_____ **b.** Computer codes can be read by anyone.

✔ **c.** Computer codes stand for different things depending on the spacing of the *offs*.

Details From Paragraph: 0 stands for *off*; 1 stands for *on*. Each letter, symbol, and number that goes into the computer has its own code of eight digits—a pattern of 0s and 1s. All the *offs* show up as blank spaces.

What I Know: The spacing of the *offs* changes the pattern of the codes.

Reading-Writing Connection

On a separate sheet of paper, write a brief explanation of what happens inside a computer from the time you type in information on the keyboard until the information comes out of the printer.

Skill: Understanding Computer Language

For ESL/ELL support, see highlighted words, page T103, and pages T28–T30.

For lesson support, see page T103.

BACKGROUND INFORMATION

In "Computer Language," you will learn about computer language. Before a computer can perform a task, it must be programmed. To do that, computer programmers type certain commands into the computer. A computer language is a large collection of these commands. In this next selection, you will practice using a few commands from a computer language called BASIC.

SKILL FOCUS: Understanding Computer Language

Programming a computer is a little like "talking" to it. This talking, or instruction, is done through the computer's input devices. Computer programmers must use a **language** that the computer understands. Usually they ask the computer to solve a certain type of problem. The programmers include a list of steps for the computer to follow to solve the problem. The computer then presents the solution to the problem through its output devices.

There are many types of computers and many types of **computer languages**. All computers, however, process information by using binary numbers. The word *binary* means "a number system that has 2 as its base." This number system uses only two digits, 0 and 1. The binary number system is used as the basis for computing because the digits 0 and 1 can be represented by an electric current. The current is turned on to show the number 1. It is turned off to show the number 0.

▶ Fill in the blanks in the sentences below with the correct words.

A _____programmer_____ types in a problem for the computer to solve, using the computer's

_____input_____ devices. The computer then processes this information by using

_____binary_____ numbers. When the problem is solved, the computer presents the answer

through its _____output_____ devices.

WORD CLUES

When reading the selection, look for the important words *input devices, output devices, BASIC, RUN, PRINT, LET, END, GOTO, loop,* and *compiler.* They will help you to understand more about computers and computer language.

Strategy Tip

As you read "Computer Language," remember that the words of a computer language have a specialized meaning. Although some of these words may have familiar, everyday meanings, you need to learn their meanings as they apply to computers.

Computer Language

Computers can solve problems much more quickly than people can. A computer gets its instructions from various **input devices**, such as a **keyboard**, a **mouse**, a **light scanner**, and a **light pen**. The instructions present a problem to the computer. The computer presents the solution on a monitor. The solution can also be delivered by a printer or a modem. These viewing mechanisms are called output devices. The instructions are carried out in the central processing unit, or CPU.

Computer Programmers

A programmer is a person who communicates with computers. To communicate with a computer, a programmer needs to use a language that the computer understands. Some computer languages, such as COBOL, FORTRAN, C, and C++, are used for business. The simplest computer language to learn and use is called BASIC (Beginners All-purpose Symbolic Instruction Code).

Learning BASIC

Learning BASIC is like learning a foreign language. Commands in BASIC have very precise meanings. The computer understands commands only if they are written in a certain way.

Each line of a program has a number. The lines are read by the computer in the order in which they are numbered. After the program has been put in, the programmer types RUN. Then the program is interpreted by the CPU, and the output is shown.

For example, PRINT tells the computer to write whatever follows. The programmer might input this statement in BASIC.

10 PRINT "I AM A COMPUTER"

The output would be I AM A COMPUTER.

The programmer might input these lines.
10 LET X = 32
20 PRINT X

30 END
The output would be *32*.

Line 10 puts the number 32 into the memory of the computer. The memory labels that number as X. Line 20 tells the computer to output whatever is in memory X.

The last line of a program is always *END*. It tells the CPU that the program is over.

The programmer could input this program.

10 PRINT "I AM A"
20 PRINT "COMPUTER"
30 GOTO 20
40 END

The command GOTO tells the computer to go back to line 20. The computer would read line 10, line 20, and line 30 and then go back to line 20, on to line 30, back to line 20, on to line 30, and so on. This is called a loop because the computer makes a circle as it reads the lines. The program would never end unless the programmer stopped it by pressing a key on the keyboard. The output would look like the following.

I AM A
COMPUTER
COMPUTER
COMPUTER (and so on)

Machine Language

When a program is put into the computer, the instructions are translated into a language that the machine understands. This is called a machine language. The **compiler** inside the computer translates the numbers and letters of machine language into **binary numbers**. The number 0 can be represented as a broken circuit—an electric current that is turned off. The number 1 can be represented as a completed circuit—an electric current that is turned on. All the numbers and letters of a language can be changed into current turned off and current turned on.

Recalling details
1. Name four input devices. <u>Four input devices are</u>
   <u>the keyboard, mouse, light scanner, and light pen.</u>

Recalling details
2. Explain the following commands.

   a. PRINT <u>PRINT tells the computer to print something</u>
   <u>or to display it on a monitor.</u>

b. END <u>END tells the computer the input is finished.</u>
   <u> </u>

c. GOTO <u>GOTO tells the computer to go to a certain</u>
   <u>line.</u>

CRITICAL THINKING

Inferring cause and effect
1. Explain what the quotation marks do in the following line. 10 PRINT "HOW ARE YOU?"
   <u>They tell the computer where to start and stop printing.</u>

Drawing conclusions
2. What would the computer print if you gave the command PRINT X? PRINT "X"?
   <u>It would print the value of X. It would print the letter X.</u>

SKILL FOCUS: UNDERSTANDING COMPUTER LANGUAGE

Write the letter of the output on the line next to the input.

Input	Output
<u>c</u> **1.** 10 PRINT "HELLO" 20 PRINT "GOODBYE" 30 END	**a.** HELLO 5 GOODBYE
<u>b</u> **2.** 10 LET X = 7 20 LET Y = 2 30 PRINT X + Y 40 END	**b.** 9
<u>d</u> **3.** 10 LET X = 9 20 PRINT "THE ANSWER IS"; X 30 END	**c.** HELLO GOODBYE
<u>a</u> **4.** 10 PRINT "HELLO" 20 LET X = 5 30 PRINT X 40 PRINT "GOODBYE" 50 END	**d.** THE ANSWER IS 9

Reading-Writing Connection

On a separate sheet of paper, write your own four-line computer program, using commands of your choice.

MATHEMATICS

Skill: Using Reference Books

For lesson support, see page T104.

You use **reference books** to find all kinds of information about a subject that you are studying or want to know more about. You need to know the kind of information contained in different types of reference books so that you can select the one you need. By using the right reference books, you can locate the kind of information you need.

Dictionary

Suppose that some friends of yours are discussing a gibbon and you do not know what a gibbon is. You can find the word *gibbon* in a **dictionary**. You already know that a dictionary defines words. It also shows how words are spelled, pronounced, and divided into syllables and what parts of speech they are. Because many people do not know what a gibbon looks like, some dictionaries include an illustration with the entry.

Below is a sample dictionary entry for the word *gibbon*.

gib·bon (gibʹən) *n.* a small ape of southeastern Asia, with very long arms.

to 65 cm (26 in.) long, head and body

Encyclopedia

After you learn what the word *gibbon* means, you may want to find out more about the animal. You may become curious about exactly what part of southeastern Asia it is from or if it can be found at a zoo. The next reference book that you would use is an **encyclopedia** because it contains articles on many different subjects. An encyclopedia would provide an explanation of a gibbon that is more detailed than a dictionary definition.

Here is an encyclopedia article about the gibbon.

Gibbon is the smallest of the apes. It also ranges over a wider area than the other members of the ape family—the bonobo chimpanzee, gorilla, and orangutan. The gibbon lives in the forests of the Indian state of Assam, and in Myanmar, Thailand, Malaysia, Indonesia, and elsewhere in Southeast Asia. There are several species of gibbons. All have long arms and legs, but no tail. A gibbon weighs about 15 pounds (7 kilograms) and stands about 3 feet (91 centimeters) high. It ranges from black to pale brown.

Gibbons live in the tops of trees and rarely come to the ground. They eat fruits and leaves. Gibbons use their arms to swing from branch to branch. They also walk on top of tree branches using only their legs. This way of walking is similar to the way human beings walk on the ground. Gibbons live in family groups that usually consist of a male, a female, and one or two of their young. A gibbon family claims an area called a *territory* and uses loud calls and songs to warn other families to stay away.

From the *World Book Encyclopedia*. © 2002 World Book, Inc. By permission of the publisher.

Atlas

After you have read the encyclopedia article for *gibbon*, you may become curious about Assam, one of the places where the gibbon lives. You may want to look at a map to see the location of Assam in India. The best reference book to check is an atlas. An **atlas** contains different kinds of maps.

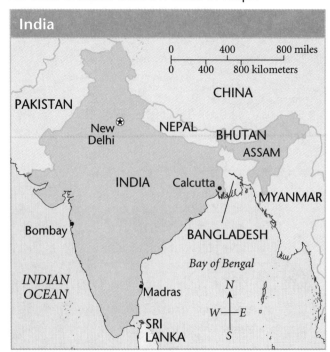

India

Almanac

Once you learn where Assam is, you may want some specific information about India, including its size and population. To locate this kind of information, you would use an almanac. An **almanac** is a book with the most up-to-date information on many different subjects. The information in an almanac is more current than information found in other references because it is published every year. An almanac contains weather reports, statistics, facts about the United States and other countries, current events, sports facts, and world records.

Area and Population by Country
Mid-2000 Estimates

Country	Area[1]	Population	Country	Area[1]	Population
Afghanistan	250,000	25,888,797	Hungary	35,920	10,138,844
Albania	11,100	3,490,435	Iceland	39,770	276,365
Algeria	919,590	31,193,917	India	1,269,340	1,014,003,817
Angola	481,350	10,145,267	Indonesia	741,100	224,784,210
Antigua and Barbuda	170	66,422	Iran	636,290	65,619,636,
Argentina	1,068,300	36,955,182	Iraq	167,920	22,675,617

[1] Square miles

From *TIME Almanac 2001.* © 2000 by Family Education Company.

Complete each sentence by underlining the name of the correct reference book. More than one answer may be correct.

1. If you want to know how to spell the word *cantaloupe*, you should use the _____.
   atlas   <u>dictionary</u>   almanac

2. If you want to find out about the mountains of South America,
   you should use the _____ or the _____.
   dictionary   <u>atlas</u>   <u>encyclopedia</u>

3. If you want to know how many people were married in the United States
   in 2001, you should use the _____.
   atlas   encyclopedia   <u>almanac</u>

4. If you want to find out how to pronounce the word *kayak*, you should
   encyclopedia   almanac   dictio

5. If you want to learn which types of birds live in cold c
   dictionary   <u>encyclopedia</u>

6. If you want to find out how many miles or kilometers it is
   Massachusetts, to Newport, Rhode Island, you should use the
   <u>atlas</u>   dictionary   encyclope

7. If you want to see how to divide the word *molecule* into syllables,
   atlas   <u>dictionary</u>   almanac

LESSON

Skill: Reading a Job Application

For lesson support, see page T104.

When you apply for a job, an employer may ask you to fill out a job application.
A **job application** is a written form that asks for information about your work
experience, your education, and your interests.

Study the sample job application below.

CAL COMPUTER COMPANY

APPLICATION FOR EMPLOYMENT

(type or print in ink)

PERSONAL

Name	Last	First	Middle/Maiden	Telephone
	LORENZ	SARAH	ANN	555-7431

Address	Number	Street	City	State	Zip	Social Security No.
	1154	23rd Street	SANTA MONICA	CA	90404	209-68-8429

EDUCATION

	Name and Location	Dates Attended From	To	Diploma Received
High School	SCOTTSDALE HIGH SCHOOL SCOTTSDALE, AZ	9/93	6/96	HIGH SCHOOL DIPLOMA
College	ROLLINS COLLEGE SCOTTSDALE, AZ	9/96	6/00	B.S.
Other	COMPUTER TRAINING INSTITUTE SANTA MONICA, CA	9/01	1/02	COMPUTER CERTIFICATE

Hobbies and Interests   SWIMMING, PLAYING THE PIANO, SPEAKING SPANISH

EMPLOYMENT RECORD (Start with last job)

Name and Location of Employer	Dates From	To	Job Title	Name of Supervisor
LINDSEY AND STERLING ACCOUNTANTS SANTA MONICA, CA	1/02	7/02	BOOKKEEPER	BERT GOLDBERG
DAILY NEWS SCOTTSDALE, AZ	7/00	8/01	WORD PROCESSOR	ROSA ALVAREZ

REFERENCES (Not former employers)

	Name	Address	Telephone
1.	MS. DIANE BARTON	80 WILSHIRE BLVD. LOS ANGELES, CA	555-4418
2.	DR. LOUIS GRAYSON	880 W. CALMELBACK SCOTTSDALE, AZ	602-555-3099

EMPLOYMENT DESIRED

Position COMPUTER PROGRAMMER   Date you can start 8/17/02   (Check one) Full-time ✔ Part Time ____

Today's Date 8/10/02   Signature Sarah A. Lorenz

Most job applications begin with a section for personal information. The first space is for your last, first, and middle names. Sometimes a married woman writes her maiden name, or her last name before she was married, in the space for the middle name. Spaces are provided for your address, telephone number, and Social Security number.

Most applications have sections for your education or training. Certain jobs require a certain amount of education or training.

Most applications have a section for information about jobs you have held in the past. This section may be labeled "Work Experience" or "Employment Record." Start with your most recent job and work backward in time. You will usually be asked to list your employer (the company for which you worked), the dates you worked for the employer, your job title (what you did for the company), and the name of your supervisor (the person who gave and monitored your work).

Applications often require you to provide references. References are people who know you well enough to give information about you and how you might perform on a job. Family members and friends should not be listed as references.

Reading a Job Application

Possible references might include a teacher; a family doctor; or a pastor, priest, or rabbi. You should ask these people if you can use them as references before you do so.

Applications may ask for your interests and hobbies, such as playing tennis or speaking French.

A section labeled "Employment Desired" may provide a space for the name of the job that you want and the date that you can begin. You usually sign your name at the end of the application.

Print in ink or type your answers on the application. A neat application with complete answers will make a good impression on an employer. Correct grammar and spelling and clear expression will also make a good impression.

A. Circle the letter next to the phrase that correctly completes each sentence.

1. An employer is a
   a. person hired by another person or company.
   b. person or company that hires people.
   c. person who can give information about your education.
   d. person applying for a job.

2. A supervisor is a
   a. person who oversees your work.
   b. place where you have a job.
   c. family member who can give information about you.
   d. person applying for a job.

3. An example of a good reference to use on a job application might be
   a. an employer you did not get along with.
   b. your best friend.
   c. your English teacher.
   d. your mother.

4. An application may ask for the name of your supervisor at a previous job so that this person
   a. will be informed if you get another job.
   b. may be offered the job that you applied for.
   c. may recommend other applicants for the job.
   d. may be called to confirm information about you.

B. Use the information on the application on page 174 to answer each question.

1. Who filled out the application? _Sarah Ann Lorenz_

2. What job is she applying for? _computer programmer_

3. What was her last job? _bookkeeper_

4. How long did she work at her last job? _6 months_

5. How soon can she begin a new job? _8/17/02_

CONTEXT CLUE WORDS

The following words are treated as context clue words in the lessons indicated. Each lesson provides instruction in a particular context clue type and includes an activity that requires you to use context clues to find word meanings. Context clue words appear in the literature, social studies, and science selections and are underlined or footnoted.

CONCEPT WORDS

In lessons that feature social studies, science, or mathematics selections, words that are unique to the content and whose meanings are important in the selection are treated as concept words. These words appear in boldface type and are often followed by a phonetic respelling and a definition.